Reading the Archival Revolution

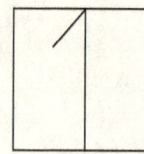 **SQUARE ONE**
First Order Questions in the Humanities

Series Editor: **PAUL A. KOTTMAN**

READING THE ARCHIVAL REVOLUTION

Declassified Stories and Their Challenges

Cristina Vatulescu

STANFORD UNIVERSITY PRESS
Stanford, California

Stanford University Press
Stanford, California

© 2024 by Cristina Vatulescu. All rights reserved.
Foreword © 2024 by the Board of Trustees of the Leland Stanford Junior University. All rights reserved.

No part of this book may be reproduced or transmitted in any form or by any means, electronic or mechanical, including photocopying and recording, or in any information storage or retrieval system, without the prior written permission of Stanford University Press.

Printed in the United States of America on acid-free, archival-quality paper

Library of Congress Cataloging-in-Publication Data
Names: Vatulescu, Cristina, 1976– author. | Krakus, Anna, contributor.
Title: Reading the archival revolution : declassified stories and their challenges / Cristina Vatulescu.
Other titles: Square one (Series)
Description: Stanford, California : Stanford University Press, 2024. | Series: Square one : first-order questions in the humanities | Includes bibliographical references and index.
Identifiers: LCCN 2024028145 (print) | LCCN 2024028146 (ebook) | ISBN 9781503640276 (cloth) | ISBN 9781503641020 (paperback) | ISBN 9781503641037 (ebook)
Subjects: LCSH: Intelligence service—Europe, Eastern—Archival resources. | Intelligence service—Former communist countries—Archival resources. | Official secrets—Europe, Eastern—Archival resources. | Official secrets—Former communist countries—Archival resources. | Europe, Eastern—History—1945–1989—Archival resources. | Former communist countries—History—Archival resources.
Classification: LCC DJK50 .V38 2024 (print) | LCC DJK50 (ebook) | DDC 327.127300947—dc23/eng/20240802
LC record available at https://lccn.loc.gov/2024028145
LC ebook record available at https://lccn.loc.gov/2024028146

Cover design: Gabriele Wilson, based on an image from *Reconstruction* (2001), directed by Irene Lusztig

*For my mother,
Rodica Vățulescu,
and for my daughters,
Veronica and Teodora Vățulescu-Eleches,
with all my love*

Contents

Foreword by Paul A. Kottman ... ix

Acknowledgments ... xiii

Introduction
Challenges of Reading the Archival Revolution ... 1

1 **Silences:** Foucault in Poland ... 32
(co-authored with Anna Krakus)

2 **Intermedia:** The Files, Film, and Photo Albums of a Socialist Bank Heist ... 63

3 **Fictions:** Literary Guides to Reading in the Secret Police Archives ... 107

4 **Silences (Take Two):** Gendered Archival Lacunae ... 134

5 **Data:** The Iron Curtain's Origins and Translations ... 155

Postscript
Toward a Polyphonic Reading Practice, II ... 190

Notes ... 209

Works Cited ... 261

Index ... 281

Foreword

Paul A. Kottman, Series Editor

Like most of us who teach literature for a living, Cristina Vatulescu is keenly aware that we seem to be living through the end of an era—an era that could be described as "peak literacy." The historical period that extended from the time of Gutenberg until the advent of television, or perhaps the internet, saw an unprecedented rise in reading. In that historical period, the sheer number of readers and of things to be read increased exponentially.

Nowadays, as Vatulescu notes, the culture of new media makes reading—at least, of that historically formed sort—an increasingly rare way to spend one's time. This might simply be a way of saying, not that reading no longer occurs, but that we now largely ask machines to do the reading for us. "Reading is a key tool in Big Brother's repertoire," as Vatulescu puts it. At any rate, without question the sheer quantity of things to be read now far exceeds any person's—or, for that matter, any culture's—capacity to "keep up" with the sheer historical-archival accumulation. As Vatulescu notes, we are living through what is often called an "archival revolution" or an "archival turn."

Faced with these facts, many readers nowadays find that "keeping up" with reading means keeping track of what is circulating in the obdurate present: newspapers, social media feeds, whatever the current "conversation" seems to be. In other words, reading now appears parasitic on, or reflective of, the current moment in time. As with other forms of criticism (or "hot takes") that deal with whatever has just dropped into view—movie or book reviews, journalism, polemics, breathless gossip, posts by trendsetting influencers—readers and publishers increasingly organize their activity around whatever the turning of the seasons brings. If so, then reading no longer functions to safeguard historical tradition, but only as another mode of "monitoring" (as the philosopher Stanley Cavell once described television-watching) whatever is going on in the present.

All this stands in tension, of course, with the age-old traditions of literary criticism that continue to shape practices of reading. Even before modern literature departments existed, the work of interpretation and the development of hermeneutic methods focused readers' attention on the meanings that lay hidden in, say, the Holy Bible. In this tradition, the assumption is (or was) that meanings lie dormant in texts that come down from the past, and that these meanings are somehow important enough to need uncovering in the present—compelling literary critics to constantly ask *what* texts from the past mean and *how* they mean. The textual transmission of meaning and new modes of interpretation go together to form "literary criticism" in its highest vocation.

A great virtue of *Reading the Archival Revolution* is that it faces up, unflinchingly, to this collision of literary criticism with the archival revolution. Throughout Vatulescu draws on traditional tools of literary critics as well as recent works of scholars for whom archives—especially archives that evidence massive forms of historical domination of one group of people by another—pose the paradigmatic ethical challenge to contemporary reading practices. Moreover, she raises the stakes by taking as her case study "the most dramatic archival revolution of the twentieth century": the opening of miles of classified archives following the fall of the Berlin Wall.

Her first-order question is: what can reading do when faced with these documents?

Vatulescu's scholarship and fluency make her approach to this archive worthy of attention, and her book is an important contribution to the efforts of historians and literary scholars to untangle what happened and is still happening in Russia, Eastern Europe, and Eurasia. But she also offers a more general set of reflections on what reading itself is called to do in the face of the archival turn. Vatulescu sees the declassification of Stasi and Eastern Bloc archives as an impetus to rethink literary criticism itself.

The declassification of secret police archives blasts a hole in our stubborn attention to the present. These archives insistently press the demands of the past upon readers in ways unanticipated by historical traditions of textual transmission but which, nevertheless, Vatulescu claims, do not leave us "helpless." If the aims of traditional literary criticism have been to uncover meaning, then the demands of archives now echo as a plea for justice. At issue is whether we as readers are up to the task of responding humanely to Big Brother's voracious appetite for things to read about us.

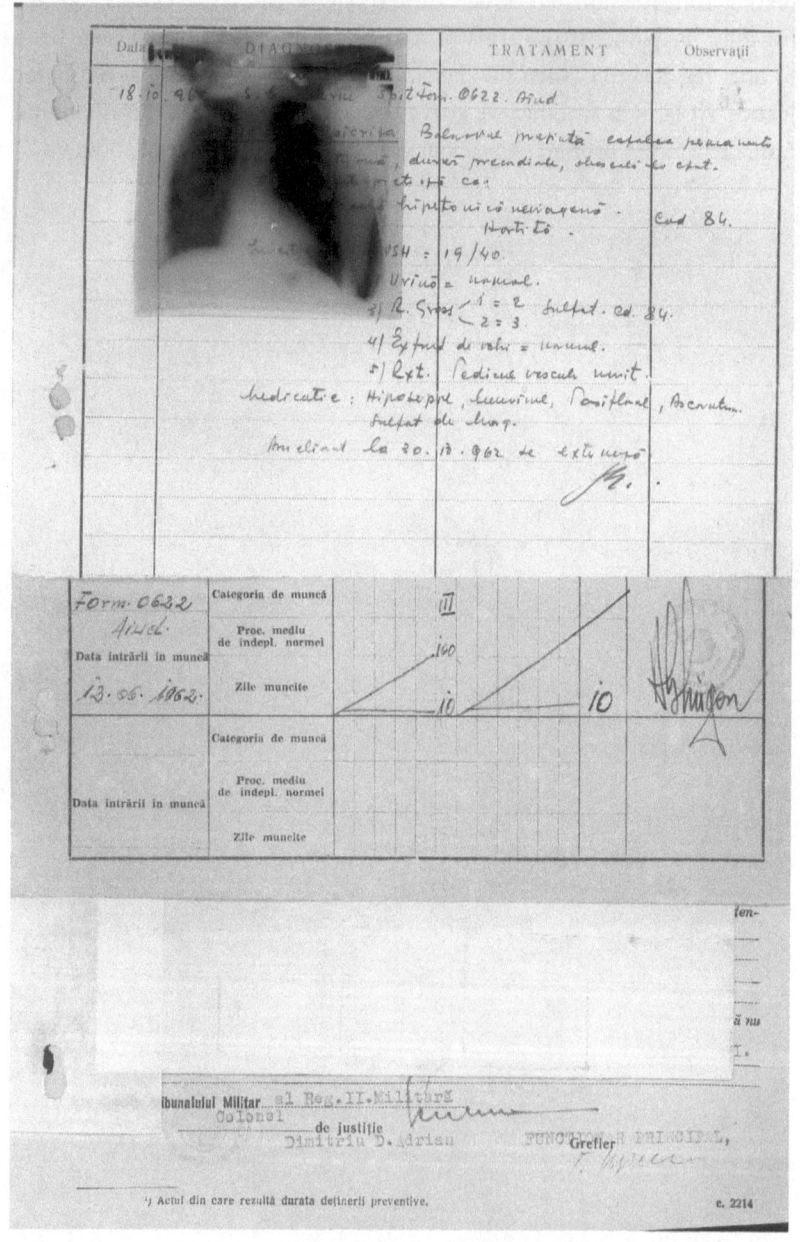

FIGURE 1. X-ray image and collage effect produced by its archived superimposition over a medical form, hospital release form, forced labor camp work log, empty page fragment, and tribunal sentence. P 336, Fond Penal, 4:54, ACNSAS.

Acknowledgments

This book may have stemmed from the x-ray reproduced on the facing page. I first encountered the x-ray in the archival reading room, clipped inside a labor camp prisoner's file. I had already dedicated years to reading Soviet-era secret police files, yet I was none the wiser when faced with this image, which was, de facto, illegible to me. Was it proof that the prisoner was healthy or in critical condition? Was it proof of maltreatment, maybe torture, or of the prison medical staff's care for their patient? Before I could read the image, it did a lot to me. I felt goosebumps. My pulse, previously slowed by the perusal of the file's standardized forms, quickened. Since their discovery, x-rays have baffled and fascinated people. The X in their name was given by the scientist who discovered them, W. C. Röntgen, "to underline the fact that their nature was unknown."[1] Even contemporary scientific explanation turns figurative when defining them: an x-ray "represents the 'shadows' formed by the objects inside of a body" when penetrated by "electromagnetic radiation, similar to visible light."[2] This peculiar light had traveled inside the prisoner's body and then helped imprint on state-sponsored film that body's deepest secrets. The "shadows" formed by the prisoner's lungs on film made me viscerally aware of his past bodily presence and present bodily absence. The x-ray embodied some of the reading challenges that kept me coming back to the archives.

Prison literature and academic work on "illness and inhumanity in the Gulag" had primed me to expect that this was a significant document, through what it conveyed and what it covered up.[3] But what exactly did it signify? My reaction was also primed by previous encounters with body imaging, whether x-rays or ultrasounds. The anxiety-filled moments before a doctor starts reading you the image that holds information about the diagnosis for a loved one. Sometimes your own body, made legible to a stranger on a screen that you are staring at without a clue. And sometimes, as in fetal ultrasounds, the image epitomized my limits in reading the literally vital signs of my closest kin and of my own self, together with the illegible boundary between us. In withholding its meaning, the prisoner's x-ray reminded me of my limits as a reader as well as of my affectability. While in the meantime I've learned to think of affectability as "the capacity to be affected," and as a good starting point for reading in these archives, the actual experience at the time was feeling at a loss.[4] I was painfully moved to understand the image but frustrated by my lack of expert knowledge in reading the x-ray. So I reached out for help. My radiologist friend, Oana Panțel Nebunescu, was able to both interpret the x-ray and decipher the Romanian medical jargon scribbled by a prison doctor in 1962; yet many questions remained.[5] Archival challenges kept pushing me to reach for help. And here I come to what is by far the most pleasant task in writing this book—acknowledging that help.

From the point of view of the Soviet-era secret police, acknowledgments would be the most precious section of a book. For this is where the author traces their debts, professional and personal, to institutions as well as individuals—mentors, colleagues, friends, and family. The key task of establishing a "subject's network" often took innumerable surveillance hours, plodding through school transcripts and personnel forms, even trips to the suspect's birthplace to track down family and friends. Since acknowledgments in books were not common at the time, the secret police had to content themselves with other front matter: dedication pages, for example, were routinely ripped out of books and appended to files. Once researched and mapped, such networks were mined for potential informers and compromising relationships. Across the Soviet space, the secret police prioritized first mapping and then undermining such networks by sowing suspicion and eroding trust. Imagine their delight at having their research done for them by the author in the acknowledgments. Imagine my delight at being in a position to express my debt and gratitude openly.

It may well be in response to getting a front-row view of this deliberate fraying (sometimes, full-on ripping) of the social fabric that scholars of these declassified archives are often a model of working together across languages and disciplines. I am grateful to this deeply sustaining and spirited academic community. Golfo Alexoupolos, David Brandenberger, Igor Cașu, Michael David-Fox, Saygun Gokariksel, Emanuela Grama, Agnes Hesz, James Kapaló, Gail Kligman, Irina Livezeanu, Alice Lovejoy, Kinga Povedak, Molly Pucci, Andrea Ritivoi, Oksana Sarkisova, Anca Sincan, Lavinia Stan, Ioana Macrea-Toma, Tatiana Vagramenko, and Katherine Verdery come together in a far-from-complete list of inspiring interlocutors. I would also like to thank Consiliul Național pentru Studierea Arhivelor Securității, in particular Alina Ilinca, Csendes Ladislau, Ancuța and Valeriu Median, and Silviu Moldovan, for granting and facilitating my access to materials from the former Securitate archives. Irene Lusztig shared the secret police files and film concerning her grandmother, Monica Sevianu, and generously provided high-resolution screen shots from her *Reconstruction*. I thank Iosif Király for enlightening conversations and generous permission to reproduce his work. Laurence Le Bras and Ariana Sforzini gave precious help with Fonds Michel Foucault at Bibliothèque Nationale de France, Archives et manuscrits, and Philippe Artières advised on the Archives Centre Michel Foucault/IMEC. Many thanks to Renata Szulc and to Michał Rosenberg for their help navigating the Instytut pamięci narodowej (IPN) archives in Warsaw and Krakow. At the Open Society Archives, Budapest, I thank Anna Kovecsi and Csaba Szilági. Andriy Kohut, the director of the State Archive of Security Service of Ukraine, has been a model of openness and responsiveness.

Chapter 1 revises and expands a previously published co-authored article. I thank my co-author, Anna Krakus, and Johns Hopkins University Press, for kind permission to publish the current version as a book chapter. To Anna I am also grateful for precious intellectual companionship and sustaining friendship. An earlier and much shorter section of chapter 5 has been published in *Perspectives on Europe*. I acknowledge the permission to revisit some parts of that article here granted by the Center for European Studies hosted at Columbia University by the European and Harriman Institutes.

At New York University, the departments of Comparative Literature and Russian and Slavic Studies, the Jordan Center for Russian Studies, and the Center for European and Mediterranean Studies have formed a stimulating academic home. A semester-long sabbatical leave and a Faculty Fellowship at the NYU Center for the Humanities in 2021–22 enabled me to complete a full draft of the manuscript. For illuminating conversations, support, and advice on the manuscript, I thank Uli Baer, Gabriela Basterra, Eliot Borenstein, Carol Brandt, Diane Brown, Jane Burbank, Brigid Cohen, Martin Daughtry, Toral Gajarawala, Yanni Kotsonis, Ilya Kliger, Anne Lounsbery, Alla Roylance, Nancy Ruttenburg, Mark Sanders, Bryan Waterman, and Larry Wolff. Eric Berlin, Sylvia Gorelick, Emma Hamilton, Anastassia Koustrioukova, Alexandra Lazau-Ratz, Nicoleta Marinescu, Simon Nagles, Mihaela Păcurar, and Oksana Popova, provided precious research and editorial assistance. Putting together the 2016 symposium *Re-mediating the Archive* and the 2023 symposium *Archival Turns, Twists, and New Directions* and a related *Comparative Literature Studies* special issue has occasioned many illuminating conversations on archive-related topics. I am in particular grateful to Paula Amad, Nergis Erturk, Tinashe Mushakavanhu, Sven Spieker, Ann Stoler, Diana Taylor, and Zeb Tortorici. Students in my "Documents and Archives" courses continue to teach me and make it all worthwhile, long after taking the class and becoming treasured colleagues and friends: Nicolas Cadena, Vero Chai, Tanya Efremova, Emma Hamilton, Chad Hegelmeyer, Natalia Klimova Plagmann, Anneke Rautenbach, Michael Simon, Rebekah Smith, Aniko Szucs, Agata Tumilowicz, and many others.

At Stanford University Press, I thank Erica Wetter, who first welcomed my project and then, together with Caroline McKusick, guided it through all the stages of peer-review and up to publication. Their model professionalism, receptivity, and intellectual engagement made our collaboration one of the most vital and treasured components of working on this book. I am grateful to Paul Kottman for thought-provoking questions about the manuscript and for welcoming me into the Square One series he directs. Many thanks to Chris Peterson, Michele Wetherbee, and Gabriele Wilson for their work on the book's production and design, and to Lys Weiss of Post Hoc Academic Publishing Services for copyediting. I am also indebted to both readers for getting involved with my project and offering invaluable advice for its revision. Reader A's manifest erudition about Eastern European culture and thoughtful engagement with the theoretical and methodological questions that center my manuscript broadened my field of references and helped clarify key theoretical arguments. Through its depth and generosity, this was a truly sustaining reading.

My mentors—Patricia Bloom, Svetlana Boym, Julie Buckler, Gemma Farrell, Barbara Johnson, Fred Nădăban, Mary Reilly Nichols, Monica Onojescu, and William Mills Todd—have continued to inspire me, in person and in spirit. I remain deeply grateful to them.

My friends and family give me boundless joy and the best perspective of my work: Jenny Barber; Tuți Băncilă; Paul, Laura, Simina, and Vlad Bodea; Peter Brown; Frank Buffone; Ionuț Cioană (Mircea Nicolae); Alan Dee; Sarah Demeuse; Lia and Rica Elecheș-Lipsitz; Janet Irons; Sidney Kwiram; Keena Lipsitz; Dave and Michelle Merrill; Hajer Mubarak Madhi; Bia Pandrea; Grigo, Renate, and Grigore Pop- Elecheș; Cathy Popkin; Amy Powell; Susan Protheroe; Shi Shi Tembo; Owen Wozniak; and Tara Zahra. The memories of my father and my grandparents—Dan, Ana, and Pantelie Vățulescu, Maria and Toader Marian—brighten every day. My husband, Kiki Pop- Elecheș, remains the first person I turn to. For anything: help, advice, training plans, Excel graphs, love, laughter—you name it. (Even when I don't name it, he's got it.) This time, the dedication goes to my mother, Rodica Vățulescu, and to my daughters, Veronica and Teodora Vățulescu-Elecheș. A small part of the rationale for this pairing will become evident in the introduction. The main reason is my gratitude for their miraculous day-to-day love, which holds me in their midst.

INTRODUCTION

Challenges of Reading the Archival Revolution

The historic opening of miles of classified archives following the fall of the Berlin Wall was the most dramatic archival revolution of the twentieth century. Long defined by bureaucracy and secrecy, the Eastern Bloc spectacularly spilled its gargantuan paper guts. Introduced to audiences worldwide through video footage of German protesters storming the Stasi archives in January 1990, this archival revolution is still unfolding throughout the region, gradually or in fits and starts. This book brings together some of the most compelling stories I have encountered over the past decades of working in the declassified archives. Michel Foucault honey-trapped by the Polish secret police with the help of his lover. A Romanian secret police reenactment movie of a bank heist, with the Jewish intellectuals accused of the crime acting their own parts before police cameras. The contentious secret police files of a recent Nobel Prize–winning author, Herta Müller, complete with the literal and figurative origins of her writing. The story of the Cold War's defining metaphor—the Iron Curtain—from its origins as Churchill's brainchild, through Stalin's own tendentious translation into

Russian, to a veritable war of words and translations that reaches all the way to today's war in Ukraine.

These stories are captivating in their own right, yet I chose them primarily as case studies that illuminate the enormous challenges posed by the declassified archives. Indeed, after the initial rush of excitement caused by archival access, we have gradually discovered that these archives pose myriad reading challenges, to the point of threatening illegibility. My book identifies and takes on these key reading challenges: their troubling silences and fictions, their overwhelming volume, and their cacophony of languages, mediums, and technologies. I show how attending to these challenges offers alternatives to dominant textual, monolingual, and disembodied models of reading expertise, even to the point of redefining what reading can mean and do. Indeed, this book asks not only: What have we learned from reading these declassified archives for the past three decades? It also asks: What have we learned about reading from all the reading we have done in these archives? I traded reading beloved novels and poems for secret police documents for a good part of my career as a literary scholar because I wanted to put my belief in reading to the hardest test I knew. What can reading do when faced with these documents?

Reading the Archival Revolution is ultimately about the limits and potential of reading documents, fictions, and each other. I posit that reading unfolds over a continuum: across documents and fictions, people and their filed representations. We read words and images and faces and silences in ways that deeply intermingle and inform each other.[1] For instance, the ways in which secret archives circumscribed the reading of personal files had an impact on how people viewed each other in the past. They continue to have an impact on how we read these people, and maybe people in general, in the present. Important scholarly and public debates have addressed the complicity between reading and power, while grappling with records designed to control, misrepresent, silence, or disappear their subjects. Seismic shifts in individual and societal reading practices brought on by digitization and artificial intelligence render these debates all the more urgent.[2] On one extreme, we have the sinister image of reading as a key tool in Big Brother's repertoire. On the other, we have the nostalgia-tinged image of cultured reading that is breathing its last under the attack of new media and technologies. My book offers alternatives to both critiques of reading, as either outmoded cultural practice or sinisterly powerful political weapon.

These are difficult challenges, but we are far from helpless. In fact, there is a lot of help both in contemporary work around archives and in the long history of reading practices honed in literary studies and neighboring disciplines. There are also inspiring alternatives to reading secret police archives even inside these very archives: wiretapped conversations on cultural topics, confiscated autobiographies, and even fiction. As we will see in chapters 3 and 4, sometimes these multilingual writings were translated and analyzed at length not just by expert informers but also by the writers themselves or members of their literary circles. People whose life depended on what was written about them in these archives thought deeply about them: thus, some of my most helpful guides to reading in the archives are their very subjects. More recently, the work of rethinking our reading practices has been most urgently conducted by scholars attending to "hostile archives" and their long-suppressed records and subjects, most notably in the postcolonial context.[3] My book puts the insights of this influential scholarship in dialogue with the less well-known yet dynamic scholarship and artistic practices emerging around Eastern European archives. Produced over a century and across the vast territories under Soviet influence, the masses of documents declassified during the Eastern European archival revolution have so far been largely left out of the theoretical conversations occasioned by the archival turn in Western academia. Rather than simply viewing Eastern European materials through existing theoretical lenses, I test the fit of these lenses to the challenges of this massive archival revolution. In the process I adjust, rework, and supplement these methodologies in ways that expand the contemporary search for new modes of reading.

My choice of the term "archival revolution" deliberately echoes critical terms such as "archival turn" and "archival impulse," yet it speaks most directly to the specificity of the phenomenon under our consideration: the declassification of the Eastern European archives after the collapse of the Iron Curtain.[4] "Archival revolution" was introduced by historians of the Soviet Bloc to describe the "quantum leap" in access to archives of the party, government, and secret police in the 1990s.[5] In the meantime, we have come to understand that the archival revolution was rooted more deeply in the Perestroika changes of the 1980s, and continues to this day despite the uneven and sometimes regressive measures affecting different, but especially Russian, archives under the Putin regime. While access to secret police archives in Russia has become progressively more challenging, the secret police archives from the former Soviet republics and satellites opened refreshingly decentered vistas onto the archival revolution. In his exhaustive review of the topic, Michael David-Fox argues that the opening of such repositories in Ukraine in 2015 can be seen as the latest "phase of the 'archival revolution' begun in the 1990s . . . in Moscow and the Russian Soviet Federative Socialist Republic (RSFSR) but has now shifted to former union republics that became independent states."[6] He adds that "from today's perspective, we can perceive that the first, post-1991, archival historiographical 'opening' in the study of the Soviet secret police was not only partial in its focus but largely domestic or national in its preoccupations, as opposed to international, comparative, or transnational."[7] This book—based on archival materials emerging after 2000 in Romania, Poland, and in lesser measure the former Soviet Union—attempts to join recent research in offering a comparative perspective deliberately rooted in the periphery. The ongoing war in Ukraine has made salient the need to understand peripheral perspectives in a region whose study has long privileged Russia. Since March 2022, the call to question that privilege and decolonize our scholarship has emerged with unprecedented urgency.[8] *Reading the Archival Revolution* is my answer to that call.

A standard term in the field of Eastern European, Russian, and Eurasian studies, "archival revolution" sounds oxymoronic outside of its context, especially if we think—as we have long done—that archives are either stuffy or sinister institutions that preserve the writing of power. From this point of view, what can be less revolutionary than archives, as power and past ossified? And if some archives may not fully deserve this bad rap, the Eastern European secret police archives surely do provide myriad illustrations for this critique, often with the clarity of caricature. Indeed, these archives did not merely record the workings of the secret police over a century—they were instrumental to those workings. The secret police archives kept the writing of power away from public scrutiny; they also framed these documents as objects of fascination, intimidation, and fear, routinely wielding them as weapons. It is indeed a proof of these archives' heightened imbrication with power that even the start of archival declassification required watershed political change—Perestroika and the downfall of the Iron Curtain. The history of the incomplete and uneven declassification over the last three decades proves once again that archival access is not just illustrative of political change but also at the heart of such change. Besides the quantity of declassified documents, it is these archives' significant role in transitional justice—their turn from an illegible instrument of terror into a publicly accessible collection of documents that can count as evidence against that terror, and potentially lead to knowledge, rehabilitation, remembrance and reparation—that further justifies the choice of the term "archival revolution."

Declassification is, however, more complicated than a simple dichotomy of secret/illegible versus public/legible would lead us to believe. The declassification of the archives has brought some incontestable accomplishments, such as the rehabilitation of former political prisoners and the belated removal of old criminal records, which had continued to legally, materially, and psychologically affect the victims long after the collapse of the Iron Curtain.[9] Yet access to these sensitive, unreliable, and often toxic documents has also triggered countless sensationalist, manipulative, profiteering, abusive, ignorant, tactless, and self-righteous readings. Indeed, it often seemed that the more problematic these readings were, the more public attention they garnered.[10] At the same time, quietly, slowly, a loose yet active community—survivors, scholars, artists, lawyers, investigative journalists—has been producing alternative readings of these archives. Three decades into this process, it has become clear that the archival revolution cannot be judged just by the mass, however great, of declassified documents lying in the archives, but must also be judged by the ways in which we read them.[11] This book attempts to identify and tackle the key challenges that I—and other readers—have repeatedly encountered in the reading of this archival revolution. In this book, then, "archival revolution" expresses both the amplitude of the phenomena at stake as well as my attention to the entangled ethical, political, and aesthetic valences of archival reading.

A reading challenge is, at some level, just another way of saying a reading problem. Yet a challenge is also not just any problem—it is a hard problem that interpolates you; according to *OED Online,* it is "a calling into question, a disputing, the state of being called into question"; it is "a defiance," "a difficult or demanding task, one seen as a test of one's abilities or character." In sticking with the most challenging case studies that I encountered in the archives, I was inspired by Jane Hirshfield's insight that "the recalcitrant case interests most," as its "challenges to preconception," to expectation, and to previous knowledge are the greatest.[12] For this reason, recalcitrant case studies are also likely to yield the most insight, not just into the subjects depicted in the writing but also into the reader and the process of reading. And unlike the object of reading, readers and their reading habits have the potential to change in response to these challenges. It is fitting that the word "change" is already contained in the word "challenge," its half-hidden promise. Unlike a well-behaved case study that answers the research question we bring to it, the recalcitrant case study resists both our questions and our methodologies. It can trigger a search for new methodologies, throwing into the foreground the usually invisible tools, labors, and ruses of sense-making and interpretation.[13] All of this book's recalcitrant case studies occupied me for inordinate amounts of time. A reviewer of an earlier version of chapter 2, "Silences: Foucault in Poland," called it "a ten-year-long archival research project that reads like a thriller." The thrill was not in the results of the search—precious little—but in the vertiginous exposure and dismantling of one scholarly expectation after another, and in the new perspectives allowed by letting go of previous frameworks.

Difficulty can, however, also set traps for the reader. In military parlance, a challenge can also be, again according to *OED Online,* "a particular calling to account, *esp.* the act of a sentry in demanding the countersign." In this sense, the *OED* instructs that the verb "to challenge" can be said of a sentinel, and that in "derived figurative uses," a challenge asks, "Who goes there?"[14] In the process of facing the challenges that these archives pose to our reading, we can learn not only about the archives but also about our own reading's answer to the question of who goes there. This challenge further sets us up to search for the countersign—the secret answer to the sentinel's question, the answer that the sentinel already knows and expects. Indeed, the most obvious reason why these archives present such a difficult reading challenge is that we lack the original countersign—we are not the intended readers. This gigantic archival world of signs, countersigns, watchwords, and passwords was meant for internal circulation, and while the sentinel at the door of these archives may have changed, and may even be willing to grant us access, our reading is continually challenged by the documents themselves. At the most basic level they challenge our reading with their encryptions, pseudonyms, and euphemisms, and with the spectacle of secrecy and declassification, the red "strictly secret" stamps hastily struck through with the blue ink of declassification.

This is a misleading challenge, I believe, and one that if followed reveals the kinship of challenge with provocation and its deeply buried etymological cousin, calumny.[15] This is a challenge that traps reading into becoming a sort of deciphering: learning the language and countersigns of the police in order to find what this spectacle of secrecy frames as these documents' authoritative meaning. As I concluded after trying out this kind of reading in my first book, *Police Aesthetics*, the results are usually a letdown: reading as deciphering often confirms Hannah Arendt's theory that in totalitarian society the spectacle of secrecy was necessary to camouflage the absence of a real secret.[16] In the best-case scenarios, when there is something to be discovered at the end of this deciphering, it is information that the police always already had before us, contemporary readers. There is certainly important information that we have uncovered in this way, and it is probably impossible to read at all in these archives without practicing some reading as deciphering. However, by itself, this is a limited, often misleading reading, better complemented with other approaches.[17] If we need to learn the countersign to get past the sentinel, we can also get past reading as countersign, for to answer the sentinels' challenge in the way that they expect lures us into giving them the answer—the countersign—that they already know, thereby confirming their knowledge and authority.

My case studies showcase the variety and shiftiness of secret police practices (including archiving practices) over time and space: these institutions were defined by their longevity as well as by their internal purges and resulting changes. Furthermore, no single timeline of these changes holds across the vast expanses of space lumped together under the term "Soviet Bloc," even when it comes to watershed moments like de-Stalinization. The chronotopes (or time/space configurations) of these institutions are radically discontinuous.[18] Juxtaposition of even just the first two case studies— Foucault in Poland and the bank heist in Romania—offers a stark warning against convenient generalizations about Eastern European secret services; instead, it demonstrates the extraordinary range in the degree of power held by the Polish and the Romanian secret police in 1959.[19] The surprising shortage of basic surveillance technology and manpower evident from the Foucault case study paints a vivid picture of the extent to which the Polish secret police was decimated by drastic internal purges. In contrast, the sinisterly powerful Romanian institution had not undergone de-Stalinization: its agents could, for instance, casually appropriate the know-how of the country's leading filmmakers and the latest visual technology of the newly established National Documentary Film Studio in the service of their own filmmaking needs. When I started work on my first book, *Police Aesthetics*, I felt the need to orient the reader (and, to be honest, myself) by charting the anatomy of the secret police file and tracing its development across the twentieth century. Twenty years later, thanks to the prolific multidisciplinary and multilingual scholarly community studying the secret police files, we are now ready for the more granular, locally and temporally differentiated knowledge allowed by case studies.

These case studies facilitate engagement with key, often contentious, questions about the secret police and its archives—their timelines and discontinuous chronotopes, the degree of their power during the Soviet period, and their continuing influence in post-Soviet societies. The case studies also bring our attention to understudied aspects of the archives, such as their uses and abuses of media, art, and technology, as well as their treatment of sexuality and gender. Thus, chapter 1 opens a window onto the secret police treatment of homosexuality, and chapters 3 and 4 reveal how women were targeted, interrogated, detained, and archived in gendered ways. The same chapters offer a new perspective on "fiction in the archives," through considering the actual literary fiction that abounds in these archives alongside disinformation, testimony, and autobiographical writing. These case studies also enable us to reconsider the relationship between the personal file and other types of powerful but less-studied files, such as the problem file, the institution file, and the group file. Such an approach allows us not only to train our attention on exceptional individuals but also to better understand the secret police's defining preoccupation with networks of people. Furthermore, while research so far has mostly turned its spotlights on victims, informers, and—to a certain extent—agents, my case studies bring to light how the archives were also populated and shaped by a network of more ambiguous figures—the host of the informant house, the passer-by caught in the crossfire of surveillance, the extra in the secret police film, the cameraman drawn overnight into the making of a secret police film. In my previous book, I tried to bring the archivist out of the shadows; this book pays attention to another *éminence grise* of the archives—the secret police translator.

READING AS EVENTFUL ENCOUNTER

I've learned firsthand how easy it is to fall into the trap set by the secrecy of the archives and sometimes abetted by the drama of declassification. Decades ago, in the beginning of my work in the CNSAS (Consiliul Național pentru Studierea Arhivelor Securității), the institution that holds the declassified archives of the Romanian Securitate, I was interviewing one of the council members when an employee entered with a peculiar dossier. It was made of fragments from the file of a legendary Romanian poet, Nina Cassian, that the CNSAS was considering blacking out for the public as abusive of her privacy. The parts of the documents soon to be blacked out were not just visible—they were singled out so as to ease my interlocutor's task. He had been asked to approve the redactions, "quickly, if possible," because a researcher was waiting for photocopies of the files, which could not be made before the redactions were approved. My interlocutor turned to me, saying, "there, right up your alley, a poet," and handed me the file of redactions. Before I knew it, I was reading and partaking in the extreme abuses of privacy that the police had initiated decades ago. The police often took a strong interest in their subjects' personal lives and sexuality with a view of blackmailing or discrediting them, and Cassian had been targeted in this way. I closed the file a few minutes later, a few minutes too late. Through the years, I've made a concerted effort to forget what I saw, but some writing, not always the best, is sticky.

To be clear, it's not that these clippings were more disturbing than those in other files I have read over the years. One of the projects that I have been most consistently engaged with, and whose results you will see in chapter 2, is to identify traces and—where possible—proof of torture in the files. Like most CNSAS researchers, including the one who had already read Cassian's file and was requesting photocopies, I have reading access to unredacted files; it is typically just when a researcher asks for photocopies and permission to make them public that redactions are made. Looking back, I think what made this dossier of redactions so disturbing to me was the lack of context and thus of warning about its abuses. The only thing that held the redactions together in the file was their abusive nature and their secrecy: there was no other narrative, no other raison d'être for this file. I succumbed to the temptation to read, a temptation whetted by the hypersecrecy of the redactions, without the benefit of the many-layered contexts and reading strategies that usually help me to avoid getting stuck on such intrusive passages. Not that I am always aware of my own process—indeed, it was only when I skipped that process, in the hurried reading of this material chosen exclusively for its heightened secrecy, that I became aware of how much work goes into preparing for such passages and how helpful the layered contexts that we bring to the files can be. Even the immediate context of such passages—the file itself, as controlled as it was by the secret police—can offer some help. Once you have some experience with a file, you usually know when such passages are coming—often in the reports of particularly indiscreet informers or in transcripts of wiretapping sessions recorded in private spaces such as bedrooms. Usually I skip large parts of such passages. If I think I have a good reason to read, I constantly keep in mind, while reading, the parts of the file that remind me of the subject's dignity, their other stories and silences, which can also often be found in informer and wiretapping reports. I tend to go into the archive having spent time with writing by or about the maligned subject. Alongside such readings, I bring to the archives my lifetime's collection of literature, scholarship, prayers, and memories, reshuffled on any given day. For a while I imagined these as a kind of shield that I could use to steel myself against such demoralizing content. (I had always loved the story of Achilles' shield, the artful representation of the world, designed to protect the vulnerable body.) But what was amazing about my previous readings was that, while at times they did steel me against whatever pettiness or horror lay before me, they just as often softened me to other parts of the files.

These former readings banded together in chorus with other, less-textual memories—voices, songs, shades of light and darkness, bodily sensations—to form the accompaniment to my seemingly silent reading in the archives. This internal chorus accompanied the files with dirges, nocturnes, requiems, curses, bard song irony, and Soviet-era black humor, but occasionally also included one of the lullabies I was singing at that time to my children each night.[20] A mind-blowing, and sometimes mind-saving, chorus, even when what it came up with was no music at all but noise and static. These sometimes did a better job of creating the needed distance between me and the most intrusive parts of a wiretapping report than the ubiquitous interference technology that made radio static into a phonic signature of those times. The metaphor of the mental chorus, however, only goes so far—partly because so much of what I brought to the files were memories of former readings alongside bodily sensations. I am a painfully unmusical person, which is why I choose this metaphor—to make sure it is understood that I did not compose the songs, nor did I even arrange their timing. At times I searched for them, and at times I welcomed them when they found me; mostly I just made space for them, and carried them within me in and out of the archives.

This is where the notion of polyphonic reading (which I will elaborate on later with the help of Mikhail Bakhtin and Tina Campt) emerged. A reading that attends to the call and response among the many voices, silences, and "low frequencies" haunting the archives and the many voices, silences, noises, and their in-betweens that we carry within us.[21] Polyphonic reading is rooted in the encounter among all these multitudes, an encounter that took place in these archives not only through my mind but also through my body, in an inextricable way perhaps best described in the cognitive science refutation of Cartesian dualism—"the mind is embodied and the body is mindful."[22] As I am writing this paragraph, I am recoiling. In some ways, the last thing that I want to bring to the attention of my reader is my own mind; even less, my body; and even less, their interconnection. It is an act of self-exposure, and I experience an intense desire to stop writing, or to switch genres, back to a more familiar academic style. An academic style that first shields the reader behind the writer, then shields them both in its reasonable conventions, and finally pulls that magic trick—the one my young daughters already know is the ultimate—invisibility. This readerly invisibility, another facet of what Denise Ferreira da Silva calls the transparency of the privileged subject of power, is safer.[23] From its safety, I could then read about the abuse of privacy against Cassian, a very different kind of subject, an "affectable" subject. That is precisely how these files were meant to be read, by a supervising agent who had more power than both the subject of the files and even its writers. The files were written by the "subaltern," for the reading eyes of the "superior." Incidentally, the words "subaltern" and "superior" are in Romanian; I did not translate them. They are the actual military-derived jargon used by the secret police.

Silva's critique of the transparent subject sensitized me to the power dimensions of the relationship between the invisible reader and the affectable subject of the secret police archives. I try to oppose this powerful fiction of the reading dynamic by an understanding of reading as an eventful encounter in which all parties, including the readers, are affectable. In this, I am inspired by Brian Massumi's understanding of Spinoza's affect—"the capacity to affect and be affected"—as being "directly relational, because it places affect in the space of relation: between an affecting and a being affected. It focuses on the middle, directly on what happens 'between.' More than that, it forbids the separating of passivity from activity. The definition considers 'to be affected' *a capacity*."[24] Here Massumi gives the illuminating example of the blow, usually conceived as a relationship of active force and passive reception, showing that in fact the blow is "the product of an impinging force *meeting* a force of resistance," which can "absorb, deflect, dodge, or even, as in martial arts, turn its force toward its author."[25] I think it is useful to perform the same operation on our understanding of reading as Massumi performs for our understanding of the blow, by conceiving both as dynamic encounters. This means going beyond the traditional understanding of reading as a passive activity, and fathoming, but not settling into, the opposite conception of a reading endowed with the active force of the blow. This force could be largely invisible, yet powerful, as in the reading of secret police "superiors." My aim is to destabilize both of these polar understandings of reading—as powerless passivity or as sinister force—and instead to tap reading's potential as an eventful and dynamic encounter. This understanding of reading as an event taps into the event's "reservoir of political potential."[26] According to Massumi,

> even in the most controlled political situation, there is a surplus of unacted-out potential that is collectively felt . . . You can return to that reservoir of real but unexpressed potential, and re-cue it. This would be a politics of microperception: a micropolitics . . . Micropolitics, affective politics, seeks the degree of openness of any situation, in hopes of priming an alter-accomplishment. Just modulating a situation in a way that amplifies a previously unfelt potential to the point of perceptibility is an alter-accomplishment.[27]

To do this, I think it is necessary to fully gauge the secret police reading's often invisible power of shaping the files and their subsequent readings, but also to step out of the protective cone of reader invisibility and "learn [and relearn] to be affected."[28]

It is easy to slip into the powerful readerly position that these texts have long created, or that, maybe more accurately, created these texts. As a countermove, it is also tempting—and I imagine not just for someone who came of age under the last decades of an extreme police state—to jump sides, in well-intentioned identification with the affected subject of the file. The positions are so clearly staked out, so starkly arresting in the spotlight of history, that the audience, the reader of the files, often becomes invisible; we easily forget ourselves while reading. It is easier. Yet I think it is worth trying to displace the reader from their painstakingly, indeed often violently, constructed invisibility and to recognize the awkward and vulnerable affectability of the reader's position as its fraught potential toward "reading other-wise."[29] Approaching reading as an event starts us on the path of practicing reading as a way of attending to others and to the otherness within oneself, to one's own affectability. While most of this book follows the conventions of current academic style, it seemed at first honest, then necessary, to at times acknowledge the embodied nature of the act of reading. The good news is that bringing attention to our reading process is less about navel-gazing than about orchestrating dialogues among what is currently in front of our eyes and the readings that have long been stored in our embodied minds. So while the embodied reader is the point through which this encounter passes, this reader is an open portal of communication between such readings, unlike the navel of navel-gazing, which is a sealed portal testifying to a past point of contact.

While I will periodically return to this embodied readerly experience throughout the book, for now I am more than ready to move on to the partial resolution of the Cassian redaction file dilemma. What ultimately helped me move past the distorting mirrors of the redacted passages, was reading, years later, Herta Müller's novel *The Appointment*. Reading *The Appointment* reframed Cassian's redactions file in my mind as evidence to be added to Müller's testimony that the secret police pursued women differently, actively framing women intellectuals as sexually promiscuous and delinquent. In other words, reading these two texts alongside each other reframed the redactions—originally written as incriminating evidence of Cassian's "promiscuous character"—as evidence of secret police abusive practices against Cassian; conversely, this parallel reading also added more evidence supporting the testimony set forth in Müller's fiction. This imaginary encounter between the novel and the redactions file drew my attention early on to one of the key, if long-overlooked, questions this book came to address: the gendered differences in the secret police's treatment of its subjects, from surveillance and harassment to recording and archiving.

ILLEGIBILITY AND THE HUBRIS OF READING

While I appreciate how the experience of reading Cassian's file retrained my attention to the gendered dimensions of these archives, I remain uneasy about that initial trespass. If I had been hoping to justify my original trespassing through my reading, it never quite worked.[30] However, the trying—and the failing—helped disabuse me of the hubris of reading that I think was always hiding somewhere at the foundation of my project. The hubris that I would eventually produce a reading so against the grain of how the police wrote their subjects, albeit years later, that it would amount to my own version of poetic justice—readerly justice—turning the weapon of the secret police, their writing, against them. Before you start reading this book, I should warn you, there will be only so many happy or even just endings conferred through reading alone. This is not for lack of trying—indeed, you will see me try again and again, in an attempt that I believe is necessary even if we are likely to fall short.

As Cassian's redactions file demonstrates, one of the real dangers of this hubris of archival reading is reenacting the violence and trespassing that define much of the writing about the archived subjects. Placing the ethics of archival reading at the forefront of her work, Anca Șincan shares an instructive case study from her research in the Romanian secret police files on the Calendarist community, a religious minority outlawed until 1989.[31] In an impressive initiative that attempts to share research findings with the affected community, Șincan contacted this community's representatives, who she expected would be interested in both the information and the researcher's aim to recover objects and materials that the secret police had confiscated (according to European law, the archives' subjects can strike from the archive materials that regard them personally).[32] One would expect the community's interest to only increase when Șincan's findings "took an interesting turn that imbued the contact with the community with an even greater significance. Along with the usual books, icons, religious texts, and paraphernalia, the secret police had also confiscated a body—that of the Bishop Evloghie Oța, whom the secret police disinterred and reburied" in an unknown location. The community members were indeed interested in the fate, and potential return, of their bishop's body. However, "unfortunately, the file, which contained five volumes' worth of surveillance on Bishop Oța . . . offered few clues as to his body's whereabouts."[33] While such withholding of the answer to the most pressing question that readers bring to a file never fails to surprise and disappoint, it is actually a common experience, to be explored in chapters 1 and 4. This is partly what makes secret police files such recalcitrant case studies—they tease and resist contemporary questions and expectations. Instead, in a bait-and-switch gesture that is also common, this file surprised the researchers with its collections of written religious confessions, an unorthodox genre of religious text (confessions are traditionally spoken face to face), intercepted along with other "correspondence to and from the monastery."[34] For a historian of religions, the written confessions represent a fascinating "hybrid" genre, testifying to the creativity of religious practice under repression.[35] For the secret police, the confessions represented a treasure trove of compromising information on the church members: "fornication, adultery, homosexual acts, stealing, gossip, fights within the community."[36] For the surviving members of the Calendarist community, these confiscated confessions and the researcher's offer to facilitate the community's access to the files represented not just the history of multiple violations but also a still very present danger of violating the sanctity of the intercepted confessions, and thus committed a major sin. So when Șincan pulled up the scanned files on her laptop to share them, the monks abruptly turned their backs to her screen.[37]

Șincan's story reminds us that despite the researcher's best intentions, individuals and communities who have long tried to make themselves invisible, inaudible, and illegible to the secret police may not want to be made legible now.[38] While I have long drawn inspiration from archival research that is animated by ethical and political attempts to listen to and honor those unwillingly written about in these hostile archives, the Calendarist community's refusal to read and to be read gave me pause. Their striking body language, in particular—the turn of the back toward the files—gave me pause, and not because I had not encountered it before; on the contrary, I recognized it as the tip of the iceberg of a phenomenon of (self-)obfuscation that is as widespread and defining of the files as it is difficult to perceive. Archival subjects often attempted to make themselves invisible and, when that was impossible, to make themselves illegible. When even that was impossible, they resisted employing on themselves or others the reading and deciphering strategies devised by the state. These attempts "to make oneself (and members of one's community) obscure" were violently countered by the state and, in particular, by what I will argue were the intertwined secret police master narratives of identification, forced visibility, and legibility.[39] Kligman and Verdery see the secret police files, alongside employment registers and penal files, as "*new devices of legibility* [that] created means for identifying and tracking individuals."[40] As I will show at length, the power of these archives rested not just in their classified files but more insidiously in a carefully orchestrated visual and textual pedagogy that aimed to impose particular ways of reading documents as well as people. There are precious moments when the variegated resistances to being made visible and legible within the master narrative of these archives are made graphically evident—the Calendarists' turning of their backs to the files recalls for me the leitmotif of turned backs and covered faces that I identified in secret police films.[41]

Tatiana Vagramenko and Gabriela Nicolescu similarly document moving attempts made by subjects in files from the Ukrainian branch of the KGB to turn their faces away from mug shots: when the agent's hand forcefully held their faces before the camera, their determination to close their eyes, grimace, or sing amounted to a desperate attempt to "move" the picture toward illegibility.[42] These examples are precious because they are the rarely visible remains of a remarkable, yet largely invisible, phenomenon that defined these archives—their subjects' attempts to make themselves obscure. The archives are strongly, if usually imperceptibly, shaped by this resistance to visibility and, further, legibility. Most often the very act of turning the back to the police is itself obfuscated—under inane information, under the pretense of not understanding, a missed appointment at the headquarters, and very likely under disguises and subterfuges that worked so well we still can't see through them, or even see them at all.[43]

The goal of my book is then not to make the archives legible, against all challenges, but to sketch and at times stretch the limits of their legibility, while recognizing that much illegibility will remain. *Reading the Archival Revolution* draws attention to this illegibility precisely as a question, without an easy answer. At times this remaining illegibility is a temporary failure of reading that can be eventually corrected through other readings. But at times, this illegibility is reading's carefully assumed limit. Attending to the challenges of reading in the archives is sometimes about making these archives more legible, but it is also often about acknowledging what cannot be read. If reading can be reparative, it first needs to drop the pretense or arrogance of being a panacea. Just because we lack the correct reading glasses to see the hurt, it does not mean that the hurt never happened. The history of medicine provides a ready illustration of the dangers of hubris. It is so much easier to attend to the cases you have treatments for, and ignore or deny the cases that the medical community has not yet made legible. Yet there are always suffering patients before the disease gets a name, be it AIDS, Lyme, or COVID-19, and their hurt is magnified by the lack of recognition and even by denial. The hubris of reading is especially pernicious when its assumption that everything is or can or should be made legible denies the existence or relevance of what it cannot fix, comprehend, or fully perceive.

Treating archival reading as a challenge can too easily incite the hubris of reading, its drive to make everything legible, despite the arduous work of its subjects to make themselves illegible. I believe that recognizing and resisting this temptation is a necessary precondition of any reparative, or at least responsible, reading; thus my choice to foreground the hubris of reading here. Yet I don't think that refraining from reading or not attending to the illegible parts of the archives makes the problems vanish. The illegibility of these archives is not a clearly demarcated margin that can be avoided while making sense of the more legible parts; it is instead the teeming negative space that, when heeded, can open alternative meanings in the salient writing of power. Only by paying attention to this space of illegibility can we produce readings that go beyond privileging and relaying the too legible writing of power. Only when attuned to these challenges of illegibility can we learn to read "other-wise," which at times may mean not reading in any traditional sense but being aware of our reading's limits. Thus the vital importance of learning to recognize those negative spaces that resist our reading, sensitized by a deep regard for those subjects written against their will.

BACKSTORY OF AN ARCHIVAL ENCOUNTER: THE (RE)PRODUCTION OF THE READER

With the hubris of reading kept in check by many repeated attempts and failures at responsible reading, the aim of this book has shifted over time. My interest in the secret police archives started long ago, when as a teenager I witnessed the Romanian Revolution of 1989. Over the following days, months, and then years, the half-whispered fragments of stories I had heard from family or by eavesdropping on Radio Free Europe were replaced by a deluge of information about the past. Much of it came over television.⁴⁴ For me, however, the most formative was the reading of a book, Nicolae Steinhardt's *Happiness Journal*, which hooked me through its use of literary experimentation and erudition to represent the author's experience of incarceration.⁴⁵ My avid interest in the past, I've come to realize, has long been framed by my entrance into the topic through the gate of *Happiness Journal*: I was, without being fully aware, trying to learn ways to respond to what Steinhardt presented as the Soviet-era limit situation par excellence, the encounter with the secret police, in his case in a dramatic arrest and interrogation. This strange identification with the journal's author speaks of my youth and vulnerability to a history long repressed and suddenly brought excessively close through often melodramatic black-and-white TV images and words that were more captivating than the gray and complicated reality of everyday life during the post-Soviet transition.

When I first entered the secret police archives in 2000, part of me was still trying to find my own solution to Steinhardt's challenge: how do you respond ethically to the limit situation of Soviet time, the encounter with the secret police? Of course, that first encounter had happened long before my entrance into the archives or into Steinhardt's dramatic account of the interrogation. For many of us, that encounter started even before our birth; indeed, I am not alone in owing my existence in part to my mother's encounter with the secret police. Like many of the children born after the 1966 decree banning abortion in Romania, I was a *decrețică*, a "child of decree 770."⁴⁶ My mother told me when I was still a child that she had intended to abort me, as she had a medical condition that made it dangerous for her to have more children. Luckily for her, this was one of the rare medical conditions that could have exempted her from Ceaușescu's draconian ban. She was painfully aware of the Kafkaesque process of securing a legal abortion, and came to dread so much the presence and questioning of the secret police agent at the gynecological examination needed for approval of the procedure that, when it came to me, she finally decided to risk her health and keep the pregnancy. In my black comedy moments, I think of that secret police agent, whose presence at the gynecological exam my mother feared so much, as a peculiarly late socialist avatar of a Fate ushering me into the world. Indeed, my very existence is to some degree owed to my mother's fear of encountering him, and to her decision to avoid that meeting, while I was still a fetus. I am living proof that power in socialist Romania was not just, as Foucault argued, productive but also reproductive. Roxana Cazan convincingly argued that the womb was a place of dissent in communist Romania.[47] If so, then my gestation and birth were a quelling of that dissent: I emerged from the womb as the regime's little accomplice against my mother's desired resistance to the state's appropriation of her body through the most aggressive pronatalist policy in the world.[48]

My story is in no way unique. The year after the abortion ban, the number of infants born in Romania doubled. In other words, half of the children born to Romanian mothers in 1967 were unwanted, and would most likely have been aborted had there been no fear of the police state.[49] If I were to choose from the many repressive practices that the Securitate oversaw in late communist Romania the one that most deeply affected not just me but the largest number of people, it would be the pronatalist policy.[50] It stands to reason that my early history—my mother's encounters and missed encounters with the secret police—shaped my entrance into the secret police archives, even though you would be hard-pressed to find any sign of it in my first book on the topic. Indeed, I think it was precisely because of that complicated history and because of my position as a teenager and young woman during Ceaușescu's grim last years and the troubled transition period that I did not work on this issue—which I now see as my elephant in the archive reading room. Instead, when I entered the secret police archives in 2000, I still conceived of the heroic narrative of arrest and interrogation of mostly male intellectuals like Steinhardt or Foucault as the ultimate limit experience of living in a police state, an experience that I was drawn to in part as a way of preparing for such a powerfully feared—even if strangely anachronistic—encounter. My original research topic, "cultural figures and the secret police," was probably more manageable than writing about the more widespread limit situations in late Romanian communism that were closer to a teenage girl's universe—becoming pregnant, securing contraception or an abortion.

Having spent years studying records of interrogations, I did learn some valuable archival lessons: that my leading question going into the archive could be a screen for more difficult questions I was not yet able to articulate; that what is missing in the archives (such as the record of my mother's missed encounter with the secret police that resulted in my birth) could be more relevant than whatever is found in the archive, and could shape the quality, focus, and blind spots of my reading; and that my questions going into the archive were often wrongly formulated, in need of revision in the face of the material. For instance, in time I recognized that interrogation records are not the place to look for lessons in dissent or humanity, even if these were interrogations of some of the artists and human beings I most admired. Indeed, the kind of interrogation practiced by the secret police should be considered a test of the humanity *not* of the interogatee, whom I've long stopped judging, but of the interrogator, and even further, of the whole structure for which the interrogator was the most visible representative. I've also come to recognize the obvious fact, long made strangely invisible to me by the mechanisms of readerly identification, that I am the reader rather than the hero. A much less glamorous and less difficult role, but a role that, once assumed, proved difficult and relevant enough for me. For if, as I believe, the secret police documents do not just record human actions but also foster and teach particular ways of perceiving and interpreting them, if the visual documents in the secret police archive were not just images but the visual aids for a whole visual pedagogy whereby the police taught people to look not with or at but through each other, then finding ways of reading and watching and listening that do not follow the *mode d'emploi* contained in these documents is worthwhile.

I may make my meaning clearer by considering the split within a newer sense of the word "challenge"—its medical use. The dangers and hubris of challenge can be seen in its most recent uses in medicine, where according to *OED Online* a challenge is "the action or process of administering an immunogenic agent to an animal or person in order to study the resulting immune response, or of exposing an animal or person to an infectious agent, esp[ecially] to measure the efficacy of a vaccine." Part of what I was trying to do when I first started reading the secret police archives, I think, was to immunize myself against their power. I thought that reading the files would act as a sort of vaccine, whereby I would take in a controlled amount of information (a virus is often defined not as a stand-alone organism but as information), so that I would then become immune in case of an actual attack. It may have been easier than dealing with the fact that the virus itself was changing, that the litmus tests were changing, and that they had always been in the plural: before, during, and after the Soviet period. I now believe that if reading in these archives can act as a sort of vaccine, a vaccine that has to be continuously tinkered with and improved, then what we need most urgently at this time is a reader's vaccine. By reading in these hostile archives we can potentially inoculate ourselves against the contagion of hostile readings. Accepting this challenge does not come without dangers. Yet my hope is that we can learn how to resist the many ways in which these archives write experience and the lives of others that invite, coax, rehearse, or even coerce hostile readings, in an attempt to open up more possibilities for reparative readings.

TRANSLATION, EMBODIMENT, AND ARCHIVAL HYBRIDITY

I hope this introduction has by now given some sense of the scholarly, ethical, political, and aesthetic aspects of the reading challenges posed by the secret police archives.[51] Given the sheer mass of documents in declassified Eastern Bloc archives, as well as the Babel of languages in which they were written, an exhaustive or even synthetic approach to these challenges risks oversimplification. Since my purpose is not to overwhelm the reader but rather to identify and tackle the key reading challenges I have met in the last couple of decades of studying in the secret police archives, the book follows a practical organization: each chapter is clearly structured around one main reading challenge. The first, paradoxical for such enormous collections, concerns what is missing from these archives. The book thus starts where many research projects end: with the "no hit," the silences that meet and expose our expectations during many a search. It ends with the challenge of archival excess facing us in the mountains of declassified data. In between these framing chapters on silence and excess, the body of the book takes on the challenges posed by the mixtures of languages, mediums, and fictions that characterize these documents.

The "reading map" at the end of this introduction gives concrete descriptions of each challenge and its chapter: silences, mediums, fictions, silences (take two), and data. The recurrence of "silences" in the title of chapter 4 intentionally underscores their centrality to the book; it is also meant to signal, from the very beginning, that none of these challenges is ultimately solved within a single chapter, and that different case studies can throw different—whether complementary or nuancing—light on each challenge. Indeed, focusing each chapter on one main reading challenge is a heuristic device meant to lend clarity to the structure of the book. However, when we read in the archives, these challenges rarely keep neatly separate. Each chapter is thus attentive to the ways its main challenge is complicated by others.

Even the two seemingly opposite bookends, absence and excess, are shown to be intricately connected. For a start, the sheer mass of documents masks the charged silences, erasures, and gaps in the files. There were three reading challenges that defied any effort to contain them within a single chapter. The first is multilingualism and the attendant problems of translation. The archival materials considered in this book contain originals in Romanian, German, Polish, French, and Russian, while Eastern Bloc archives at large draw on dozens of other languages. Furthermore, translation shaped the archives long before any readers arrived. One of the book's contributions is to bring to light the figure of the secret police translator, long left in the shadows, from the nitty-gritty of translator recruitment and pay rates to the ways in which their translations inculpated or exculpated the originals and their writers. Each chapter attends to the ways in which translation threads through both the production and reception of these archives, taking stock of its powerful, if often overlooked, influence.

The second overarching challenge concerns the body. These archives teem with bodily traces that trip up our reading habits. Photos and films preserve the indexical imprints of bodies and light. Then there are fingerprints, signatures, and handwriting. Even type, unmistakably shaded by the different weight that a particular hand assigns to each letter, was used by the police to identify subversive writers. There is a long history of overlooking the body in the archive, yet archives handle bodies in myriad ways—ceremoniously embalming, sublimating, disciplining, or silencing them. *Reading the Archival Revolution* builds on Vivian Sobchack's distinction between body and embodiment in current literature: "The focus here is on what it is to *live* in one's body, not merely to look at bodies." Embodiment foregrounds "the lived body as, at once, both an objective subject and as a subjective object: a sentient, sensual, and sensible ensemble of materialized capacities and agency that literally and figuratively makes sense of, and to, both ourselves and others."[52] The book is attentive to what the digitization of archives often leaves behind: the materiality of the archives and their objects—chief among them, the human body. The book shows that one way out of this challenge is attending to the embodied experience of reading, moving through and being moved by the archives, including their digital avatars. Once we pay attention to the encounter between differently embodied and mediated archival subjects, ourselves included, we can start to remedy our historic and newly acquired blind spots.

The third challenge that threads through the book is archival hybridity. The declassified archives never ceased to surprise me with the hybridity of their holdings. In this I am not alone. Other researchers, such as Katherine Verdery and Sonja Luerhmann, have commented on the "inevitable polyphony and multiple authorship" of these records.[53] The most immediately noticeable type of hybridity is that of mediums, the topic of chapter 2. The case file analyzed there contains everything from surveillance photographs and maps to police sketches and baby photos, filmed reenactments and production stills, endless inventories of seized goods, informer reports, letters, and wiretapped kitchen conversations. Furthermore, there is extreme hybridity even within each medium. For example, texts run the gamut from forms and statistics to confiscated diaries, fiction, poetry, published literature, manuscripts destined for the drawer, and intercepted love letters.

Scholars working in various archives around the world easily relate to this encounter with archival hybridity. For example, many archives are predicated upon the possibility of different mediums coexisting, and maybe even interacting within a single collection, and as such they are fundamentally—rather than incidentally—intermedia hybrids. This is why I believe that the term could be relevant outside of its immediate context. Yet the secret police archives are a particular type of intermedia. They are intermedia on steroids because in these archives, the standard preservation requirements (i.e., that photographs and other visual material be kept separately from print to ensure their survival through time) were overridden by the forensic need to have words and images in one place, in one case file. Additionally, the lack of recognized boundaries as to what constitutes a collection or a file, and the police manuals' insistence that every word, whether published, drafted, whispered, overheard, or violently extracted, and that any object (recall the Calendarist case cited above), whether prayer books, photographs, icons, or clothes, was fair game for inclusion in the investigation further heightened the hybridity of these archives.

I used to think that the striking hybridity of the police archives must have been for its agents a professional nuisance, something they would have rather done without, but that these misgivings—in the absence of a better solution—were quickly quelled within univocal reports. After all, isn't hybridity a hyped term of cultural discourse, one that has migrated from postcolonial studies, where it celebrated multiplicity of voices, points of view, and contexts, to, more recently, media studies, where it describes (sometimes inflated to the term "super-hybridity") the mind-boggling diversity of mediums and contexts available to the contemporary artist?[54] It turns out that there are hybridities and hybridities. In my research, I discovered that in the secret police archives medium hybridity is often a carefully choreographed source of archival authority. In a situation where the event—what actually happened—is by definition in question (for otherwise there would be no investigation), one of the main narrative devices is to verify words and images against themselves and each other. Think of the police sketch, based on the spoken portraits (*portraits parlés*) composed by witnesses, or the mug shot, largely useless without its caption, the proper name. Sometimes these verifications raise questions, poke holes in a definite version of a story. Usually, however, by reinforcing words with other words and images the police aim to bolster their representation of the event. In the absence of the elusive event itself, I found that the medium hybridity of the secret police archives often buttresses a single master narrative. In the process, the material is stripped of its ambiguities, questions marks, and silences. The secret police archives made meaning, and wielded power, not within one medium, and not even in neatly separated multimedia, but rather through intermedia, in the crafted collusion of different mediums. By exposing and further unhinging this collusion between words and images, and further among textual genres and other types of archival hybridity that the secret police hijacked, we can allow different configurations of these materials to emerge. This is no easy task because we often come up against the secret police modus operandi that created and preserved these archives.[55]

TOWARD A POLYPHONIC READING PRACTICE, I

This book mines a variety of archival practices and theories to provide inspiration for the reclaiming of archival hybridity. The extreme hybridity of these collections soon shows the limits of any single reading lens, so I built upon diverse and even opposing methodologies. To start with, the book never strays too far from close readings but concludes by interweaving them with graphs and "distant readings" of digitized archives.[56] Sometimes, the same document, such as an informer report, yields stereophonically to both the paranoid and the reparative readings that Eve Kosofsky Sedgwick identified in stark opposition.[57] Similarly, I share Ann Stoler's practice of reading "along the archival grain" in the belief that these archives can yield volumes about the values, fantasies, and anxieties of the institutions that created them.[58] At the same time, these archives were co-written, from various positions of power and abjection, by many kinds of subjects, some made and some unmade in the process of these writings. So the book also mines the rich traditions of reading against the grain and between the lines, developed in Eastern Europe in response to censorship, bureaucratese, surveillance, and the threat of annihilation epitomized by these files.[59] My book also brings the productive lenses of phenomenology, affect theory, gender studies, and neurocognitive poetics to the archives. Building onto this multidisciplinary scholarship on embodiment and embodied cognition, I work toward developing embodied archival reading practices and investigate the mechanisms at work in erecting and preserving the division between affectable archival subjects and transparent archival readers.

Reading the Archival Revolution orchestrates a dialogue among this wide variety of reading methodologies and ultimately aims at what I call, in a tribute to Mikhail Bakhtin and Tina Campt, an embodied and polyphonic reading practice.[60] By "polyphonic reading," I mean reading that is aware of the limitations of its proper domain, and aware of the urgent need to go beyond itself and attend to what has been left out, such as silenced voices or even the lower, less audible frequencies of archived subjects, their imprints and afterimages.[61] For unlike Luehrmann, I believe that polyphony, in the utopian sense it acquired in literary studies through Bakhtin's work, is anything but "inevitable" in the archives. On the contrary, I think that given the defining secret police modus operandi that created and preserved these archives, authoritative discourse carried the day. I do think, however, that these archives have a long-repressed polyphonic potential that can at times be activated through our reading.

So, how do we engage in a polyphonic reading practice? Prescriptions are bound to fail, proving too rigid for the rich and tortuous terrain of these archives. Fortunately, though, there is plentiful guidance in the archival (reading) practices of others, coming before us, as well as in the very texts buried in the archives. As Saidiya Hartman observes, "the promiscuity of the archive begets a wide array of reading."[62] I was inspired by scholars, like Hartman herself, who have pushed to further widen this array (and disarray) with new methodologies, while remaining alert to the limits and potentially violent overreach of archival reading. For Hartman's sentence, referring to the murdered slave girl whose archival story she tells in "Venus in Two Acts," ends thus: "the promiscuity of the archive begets a wide array of reading, none that are capable of resuscitating that girl."[63] Even in the best intentioned drive to listen to the archive's many buried voices, there is always a danger: the danger of hearing voices, of ventriloquizing, of taking our own words for those irretrievably absent. This is a danger and lure deeply inscribed in the dominant subject position of the archival reader, as famously inaugurated by Jules Michelet, who saw his nineteenth-century archival research on French history as "breathing life" into "the souls who have suffered so long ago and who were smothered now in the past."[64] Much recent work, often rooted in (post)colonial archives, has taught us the risks and violence inherent in such a dominant readerly position.[65] Yet as Hartman argues, "the necessity of trying to represent what we cannot, rather than leading to pessimism or despair, must be embraced as the impossibility that conditions our knowledge of the past and animates our desire for a liberated future."[66] The claim of resuscitating or saving past lives from their archival burial grounds often exposes little more than archival hubris. Yet spending time in the company of their traces and learning to listen may save *us* from reenacting the violence that attempted to replace their polyphony with the sham monologue of authoritative discourse. I say "sham" because learning to discern polyphony in these archives eventually empowers us to also see through the pretense of the coherence and unity of power.[67] Practicing polyphonic reading can further save us from ourselves, from our own tendencies to impose our own monologic perceptions on the past. In the process, we come to realize *our* limits in resuscitating the past, as well as *its* power in teaching us how to read and protect its polyphony along with that of the present, future, and, last but not least, the polyphony of our own voices.

While it relies and builds on a wide array of theoretical and methodological works, polyphonic reading is not a theory or set of rules but rather a practice that has emerged from my attempt to respond to the many challenges of these archives as manifested in my case studies. Readers interested mostly in the theoretical and methodological aspects may want to turn to the postscript, "Toward a Polyphonic Reading Practice, II," where I reflect on the theoretical inspiration and the urgent political and ethical stakes of this practice in light of my experience researching and writing this book. However, I would invite readers to join me in reckoning with at least one of the five recalcitrant case studies before jumping to the theoretical conclusion, as a way to better ground our reading.

THE READING MAP

Let me briefly trace the book's temporal and spatial coordinates. The timeline stretches from the beginnings of Soviet domination in Eastern Europe in the wake of World War II up to the present moment. The framing chapters each span the whole time period, as well as the whole geographical expanse—from Poland to Russia. To achieve added depth and nuance, the middle three chapters sharpen their focus on Romanian secret police archives, and advance chronologically from the 1950s to the end of the socialist regime. Thus historically and spatially grounded, the book also develops its comparative lens throughout its chapters. Eastern Europe during this period was defined by its double marginality to the Soviet Union and to the West. Developing a comprehensive comparative lens is necessary for updating our understanding of these defining relationships to the competing centers of power, while also attending to the long-ignored "periphery-periphery" relations that preoccupy recent scholarship. At the time when access to Russian archives for international scholars has reached a new historic low, peripheral views of Soviet and Russian history from the perspectives of Eastern European, Baltic, or Central Asian archives are being contemplated by many researchers as a heuristic solution. My book's main grounding in declassified Eastern Europe archives shows that a transnational peripheral perspective yields not just access, but also new insights and alternatives to the Russocentrism that has long dominated scholarship on the region.

1. Silences: Foucault in Poland

Michel Foucault relished telling a Cold War story: in 1959, the Polish secret police "trapped him by using a young translator" and then "demanded his departure" from Poland, where he had arrived less than a year before as director of the French Cultural Center. Foucault, the father of Western archive theory, believed himself fatefully inscribed in the archives of the Eastern Bloc. This chapter, co-authored with Anna Krakus, investigates the archival traces surrounding this "honey trap" story and Foucault's engagement with Poland until his death in the 1980s, paying particular attention to the baffling and instructive archival silences. Our research in French and Polish archives, with an emphasis on the latter secret police archives, tracks the vertiginous relationships between documents, events, nonevents, rumors, and ellipses. The story of Foucault in Poland serves as a window onto the intersection of Western and Eastern surveillance as well as archive theories and practices. It also allows us a privileged angle into the understudied question of secret police treatment of homosexuality. Ultimately, the narrative of this search, with particular attention paid to archival silences, leads to a reevaluation of Foucault's archival theory as well as of our understanding of Soviet-era secret police archives and surveillance practices.

I open the book in an unorthodox manner with a co-authored chapter to foreground my collaboration with Anna Krakus, as one possible way of working across language barriers (in this case, Polish and French) and also to turn the spotlight on the array of formative, if often unexamined, expectations and methodologies that researchers bring to an archival problem. Beyond participating in the dynamic, multidisciplinary, and multilingual study of secret police archives through workshops and edited volumes, co-authorship has powerfully mitigated the burden of working on such difficult topics, as well as the pressure for relevance that beleaguers individual researchers in small fields with generalizations and partisanship.

2. Intermedia: The Files, Film, and Photo Albums of a Socialist Bank Heist

The early decades of the Eastern European archival revolution were textually dominated, as scholars attempted to access and then process vast amounts of documents and information. We are now confronted with the visual wave of this archival revolution, as images (still and moving) are emerging en masse. To tackle these problems, in chapter 2 I examine the case of a 1959 Romanian bank heist that hinges on the intersection of texts, drawings, maps, photographs, and films. The chapter shows how these archives make meaning and wield power, not within one medium, and not even in neatly separated multimedia, but through intermedia, in the crafted collusion of various mediums. This poses a real challenge to our specialized—often discipline- and medium-specific—methodologies. In its attempt to develop methodologies for this intermedia challenge, the chapter takes cues from existent archival theory and the work of Eastern European visual artists and filmmakers who engage with the visual component of these archives and with their legacy.

3. Fictions: Literary Guides to Reading in the Secret Police Archives

In the Eastern European context, one inescapable association of "fiction" in the archives links to the infamous disinformation departments of the secret police, the precursors of fake news.[68] The archives of the Eastern Bloc burst at the seams with fictions of all kinds. Alongside the fictions spun by their disinformation departments, the secret police archives also teem with literary manuscripts, some displaced within investigation files and some neatly catalogued in secret libraries. This chapter tracks the unequal struggle between the Securitate's fictitious creation of an informer doppelgänger meant to compromise Herta Müller, on the one hand, and her literary fiction, which she started writing as a survival weapon, on the other. Both the fiction of disinformation and Müller's early literary fiction challenge any hurried readings of these archives. Yet unlike the fictions of disinformation, Müller's early fictions—dismembered, mistranslated, and ruthlessly incriminated inside her file—also haunt the archive and unsettle its master narratives. My book turns these arrested literary fictions against their captors. I argue that when carefully attended to, the literary fictions in these archives can transform from reading challenges into reading guides.

4. Silences (Take Two): Gendered Archival Lacunae

This chapter revisits the first challenge—silence—considering its differently gendered underpinnings in the lacunae of Herta Müller's personal file. Long before she became a Nobel Prize laureate, Herta Müller was a young writer associated with a subversive literary group of German-language writers in Romania. In her Nobel Prize lecture, Müller traced the beginnings of her writing to the experience of being harassed and threatened with death for refusing to become a Securitate informer. Müller further claimed that this fateful harassment, as well as many of her future interactions with the Securitate, were purged from her Securitate file. This chapter investigates this redaction charge alongside Müller's three-volume Securitate file. It also considers separate files of her literary associates and the forty-six-volume file concerning the German minority in Romania. In the course of this lengthy investigation, I found that the missing beginning may well have been the result of the Securitate's blind spots and biases when it came to female suspects. The search for the missing beginning of the file also led me to other fundamental lacunae: the systematic silencing through omissions, euphemisms, and standardized narratives. This verbose silencing of the file's subject is as easy to miss as the missing documents themselves; yet together they constitute the often-invisible cornerstones of these archives.

5. Data: The Iron Curtain's Origins and Translations

While, during the first years of the Eastern Bloc archival revolution, the challenge was access to missing or classified documents, nowadays we are more often challenged by the overabundance of documents. Chapter 5 takes on this challenge of reading archival excess, by focusing on the double-edged sword of digital access, which can both magnify the problem and help tackle it. In the last few years, the enormous archives of all Russian and Soviet press from the 1917 revolution to the present have been made accessible through the EastView databases. But how do we read in these massive digital archives? What is the use of our existent archival methodologies, such as close reading against or "along the archival grain," in these new digital collections? Chapter 5 attempts to gauge the challenge and mine the potential of these new digital archives through an archaeology of what was arguably the strongest, and strangest, political metaphor of the twentieth century—the Iron Curtain. EastView allows us to view every single mention of the phrase in the Soviet press since its 1946 coinage by Winston Churchill to the present day. The graphs that I created based on these data points allow us an unprecedented view into the origin and development of this trope, which we see morphing from a literal term for a fire protection feature in theaters to a chameleonic political metaphor. Its translations and recontextualizations range from the original meaning as a curtain of secrecy raised by the Soviets to its opposite—a smoke screen created by the West to hide its belligerence. Its translations in the Romanian press, the country that topped the infamous list whereby Stalin and Churchill divided Europe, cast it as a circus curtain drawn over a cage. This chapter tracks the term to the present day, through its fateful transformations during and after the Russian annexation of Crimea, meddling in US elections, and invasion of Ukraine. The chapter combines data analysis with close readings of this rhetorical war of words and translations, demonstrating the necessity of drawing upon diverse methodologies and developing new ones to tackle the challenge of archival data excess.

The postscript, "Toward a Polyphonic Reading Practice, II," attempts to move us further in the direction first broached in an earlier section of this introduction. The postscript revisits the origins, revisions, and new directions in understanding polyphony's migration from a musical term to a literary one, starting with Bakhtin and extending to the present. It also attempts to clarify the meaning and stakes of polyphony by comparing it to two kindred, if significantly different, terms—*counterpoint* and *heteroglossia*. I close the book with a call for a polyphonic reading practice that leaves behind the pernicious fantasy of the transparent archival reader and the affectable archival subject, and instead assumes reading as an eventful encounter among embodied and affectable subjects.

ONE

Co-authored with Anna Krakus

Silences
Foucault in Poland

A FAMOUS ANECDOTE AND ITS ARCHIVAL SILENCES

Michel Foucault's biographies repeat more or less *ad litteram* the story of his 1958–59 stay in Warsaw and his abrupt departure due to a honey trap set by the Polish secret police (Służba Bezpieczeństwa [SB]) through his lover. "[Foucault's] writings and thick manuscripts on imprisonment, along with the company he keeps, worry Gomułka's police, who trap him using a young interpreter and demand his departure [from Poland]."[1] The "writings" mentioned here were most likely linked to Foucault's dissertation, "The History of Madness," which he completed in Poland. Foucault arrived in Warsaw in October 1958 to serve as founder and director of the French Cultural Center, and gradually came to "play the role of cultural advisor to [French ambassador Étienne] Burin des Roziers."[2] These positions entailed close "company" with the diplomatic and cultural elite, both French and Polish, and thus "worried" the SB. Much of this information is confirmed in Roziers's warm recollections of Foucault's time in Warsaw, except for the details regarding the abrupt departure. Roziers diplomatically skipped over the episode, merely stating, "Foucault had to leave suddenly due to unforeseen circumstances."[3]

The little that was known about Foucault's scandalous exit can be traced to his own testimony, passed on to friends and to his long-term partner, Daniel Defert.[4] Following that thread, Anna Krakus, this chapter's co-author, interviewed Defert in 2009, at the beginning of our project.[5] Defert confirmed that Foucault was the source of the story, and added a few other details, among them the nickname of the lover, "Jurek."[6] Defert also shared with Anna the story of Jurek's visiting Foucault in Paris in the early 1960s. Early in the visit, while driving past the building of the French Communist Party, Jurek broke down and confessed to Foucault that he worked as an informer and was allowed to travel to Paris contingent on his promise to inform on his lover. Foucault responded by offering to write an informer report on himself, which Jurek would then translate into Polish. This story not only supported our initial hunch concerning the existence of a Foucault file in the SB archives, it also gave us intriguing hints as to its contents: besides regular informer reports by Jurek, we could also expect such a report on Foucault by Foucault!

Our project started with these clues. The Foucault in (and especially out of) Poland story promised a window onto the intersection of Western and Eastern surveillance and archive theories and practices. The most influential Western theorist of surveillance believed that his writing and sexuality made him the target of Eastern Bloc surveillance. The groundbreaking theorist and lover of archives suspected himself inscribed in Eastern Bloc secret police archives. The anecdote pointed to far-reaching ramifications, especially given the history of Foucault's relationship to Eastern Europe in general and Poland in particular. Scholars of Eastern Europe and Russia have fiercely debated Foucault's engagement with the region and the applicability of his work to their fields.[7] The resulting literature is often at its best when it turns back on Foucault, showing how, as liminal cases par excellence, Russia and Eastern Europe disrupt some of the most powerful universalizing claims of his work—such as the chronological progression from punishment and discipline,[8] or the under-historicized East–West dichotomy of a fundamentally Eurocentric thinker.[9]

In a magisterial article, Laura Engelstein demonstrated the ways in which the chronological vector of Foucault's universalizing thinking about legality, discipline, and punishment is challenged to the breaking point by the complexities of Russian legal history.[10] In his exhaustively researched "Foucault's Gulag," Jan Plamper has carefully documented Foucault's theoretical, journalistic, and activist engagements with the Gulag. Starting with a mention in 1971, Foucault's attempt to subsume Soviet penal practices in his punishment and discipline narrative traced a real "zig-zag course" of contradictory positions.[11] The recurring sense of paradox that Foucault expresses with respect to the Gulag is to Plamper an indication that "Foucault understood not having understood the Russian-Soviet case." Plamper traces the methodological and epistemological causes of this limit to Foucault's understanding, chief among them being Foucault's pervasive Eurocentrism and his under-historicized East/West dichotomy. Plamper convincingly argues that "as a liminal case, Russia casts problems associated with the seemingly universal claims and applicability of Foucault's work in even sharper relief than wholly 'Other' regions of the so-called Third World, from where, in the context of post-colonial discourse, most decentering challenges to Foucault have so far emanated."[12] Like Laura Engelstein before him, Plamper cautions against hasty or even "dangerous" applications of Foucault to Russia, convincingly arguing that "pulling Foucault's tools out of one's toolbox involves a selection process. The criteria for this selection should be founded on a careful study of the logic of the field [to which] one is contributing."[13] Plamper argues that Foucault's leveling of sources, as well as his aversion toward thinking about traditional historical questions like causes and agency, obstructs his judgment of "phenomena like the Gulag and the Great Purges [and lends] the question of causes and perpetrators a special poignancy, since the answers put forward are immediately relevant not only to traumatized individuals but also to collective identities, as well as to legal-financial issues of compensation and restitution."[14]

As this chapter will explore in depth, we found inspiration for the challenges of reading Eastern European secret police archives in Foucault's rethinking of archives and archival silence, the key challenge to be addressed in this chapter. However, our research also reveals Foucault's blind spots and his distortions of the Eastern European context in his writings, particularly his anecdotes and testimonies about his time in Poland. So rather than applying Foucault's theories to the Eastern European archives, we first examined Foucault's earliest and longest engagement with the region: his relationship to Poland. Poland was important in his biography as well as in his intellectual, political, and ethical formation. He spent a critical year there in 1958–59, and he returned repeatedly, most notably in 1982 as part of a humanitarian mission in support of Solidarność. His denunciation of France's neutrality toward the declaration of martial law in Poland made headlines and was the focus of televised interviews that resonated in public opinion as well as in the highest echelons of power.[15] Foucault felt apprehensive enough about the 1982 trip that he wrote his will beforehand.[16] His stance on Poland led him to break with the French socialist government.[17]

As recounted by Defert, Foucault's story fit well with the prevailing views on the secret police in Eastern Europe, both then and now. By the time of Foucault's first visit in 1958, the notion that "every Soviet citizen had a file" had received the imprimatur of Hannah Arendt in her *Origins of Totalitarianism*.[18] The belief survived the collapse of the Iron Curtain and was widespread in both East and West. Reviewing the recent literature on SB archiving practices, surveillance of intellectuals and foreigners, and its position on homosexuality, we found further support for our expectations for a Foucault dossier. In the 1950s, any foreigner from a capitalist nation, particularly one in a diplomatic position, would have been a prime candidate for being suspected as a spy. At the end of the decade, Poland was just emerging from the "spy mania" that had characterized the first decade of Soviet influence.[19] The host country still regarded Western cultural institutions with suspicion, as either agents of Western cultural imperialism or covers for espionage. Into this milieu entered an openly homosexual French intellectual riding to his job at the French embassy in a flashy white sports car. From the vantage point of the Polish authorities, such an individual was at the very least controversial and at worst a member of counterintelligence.[20]

Recent research confirms that, like "any other communist political police, the SB kept detailed records of its activities, and compiled files on both its victims and informers."[21] While there is disagreement regarding most aspects of the secret police files in Poland, including their numbers, three things appear uncontestable. First, the quantity of files was great.[22] Second, the SB tracked oppositional activities "obsessive[ly]" when they set their eyes on a target.[23] And third, many of these files are no longer available, due to either removal amid routine archival upkeep or deliberate destruction, or, in the case of existing documents, the withholding of access to their contents. Thus, after the 1955 thaw a vast amount of documents were removed from the archives, such that their numbers plummeted from 5.2 million in 1953 to a mere 1.6 million two years later.[24] As regards the illegal destruction of documents, it is known that SB agents started expunging files as early as 1989.[25] The extent of this destruction was enormous: in 1996, "five officers were found guilty of destroying from 30–50 percent of the military intelligence of the secret archive."[26] This prevalent image of the Polish secret police accorded with Foucault's story: it seemed likely that his writing, sexuality, and social and professional networks would be perceived as inimical to the regime and thus warrant surveillance in 1958. The same would also be true in 1982, which saw the height of police repression amid martial law, a time when both Foucault and his anti-Soviet stance were well known.

With this in mind, we headed over to the Institute of National Remembrance (Instytut pamięci narodowej [IPN]), the present-day repository of the archives of the Polish secret police, expecting a thick dossier on Foucault. To our surprise, the first search for Foucault in the IPN database came up empty.[27] Despite the mountains of files in the archives of former Eastern European secret police services, this "no hit" is a rather typical experience. Hundreds of researchers have received similar no-hit responses. Most move on, just as we did many times, for instance, after getting zero hits in our searches for files on Paul Celan and Roland Barthes in the archives of the Romanian secret police archives. These no-hits are a common shared experience among researchers in these archives. Sometimes, after years of stubborn searches, we finally unearth miscatalogued, misshelved, or long-classified files.[28] We decided to persist with our Foucault study for many reasons, which we detail later. For now, suffice it to say that we continued partly in the hope of the documents emerging with time. We also thought the no-hit phenomenon was widespread and symptomatic enough to deserve analysis in itself. So we turned the no-hit into a departure point rather than a dead end. Rather than the anticipated one file we had envisioned consulting, we read almost ninety files and returned to the IPN annually as the project spread over eight years. Instead of one archive, we consulted eight.[29]

In what follows, we will reveal our finds in the archives of the said, but also, more importantly, in the archives of the sayable, the unsayable, and the unsaid, terms that follow Foucault's own revolutionary rethinking of archives. Foucault shifted our thinking on archives when he proposed going beyond their definition as a collection of physical documents or buildings housing those documents, regarding the archive instead as *"the general system of the formation and transformation of statements."*[30] In simpler terms, he explained in an interview, "What can we talk about? The 'sayable' rather than 'the said.'"[31] In this chapter, we will consider the archival traces that Foucault left behind him in France, where different sections of his archives are housed, and in the archive of the French Cultural Center he founded in Warsaw; we will then focus at length on the holdings of the Polish IPN archive. In examining these materials, we try to uncover the literal archive of the said, while also engaging in the more arduous and, we believe, more instructive task of reconstructing "the archive of the sayable," the ensemble of statements that could have been made about Foucault in the context of his visits to Poland in 1958–59 and 1982. This project of reconstruction required us to investigate the policies, expectations, anxieties, and fantasies that the secret police harbored toward French intellectuals and diplomats in 1958–59. In order to paint a more complete picture of Foucault's experience in Poland, we also set out to research the SB's stance on homosexuality, as well as the extent of surveillance, blackmailing, and information gathering and storage at this time.

Foucault warned that it is never possible to speak outside of one's archive. Yet, as he cautiously encouraged, bringing that archive into contact with previous archives can help us see our own limits as well as those of the past, thereby "depriv[ing] us of our continuities," of our false knowledge of the past and the present. This falsity is best exposed in our unmet expectations.[32] Our project of reconstruction entailed a rigorous study of the context of the case alongside careful attention to unmet expectations and resulting misrepresentations. Keeping in mind the past and present archives of the said and the sayable, and putting them into dialogue, may, we hope, engender illuminations of the kind Foucault pointed to. In addition, our project was inspired by Foucault's vow, made at the time of his first Polish sojourn, to write not just the "history of [the] language" of power, but, rather, "the archaeology of . . . silence."[33] We argue that it takes constant fine-tuning of our archival methodologies to perceive these silences; our narrative below performs our quest for such a new archival methodology and ethics.

FOUCAULT'S FRENCH ARCHIVES ON POLAND

Do you know that *Ubu Roi* is set in Poland, in other words nowhere.
Tu sais qu'Ubu se passe en Pologne, c'est-à-dire nulle part.
—MICHEL FOUCAULT, "Letter to a friend," November 1958[34]

The scene takes place in Poland, that is to say everywhere.
La scène se passe en Pologne, ça veut dire partout.
—MICHEL FOUCAULT, "Un si cruel savoir," 1962[35]

We soon learned why stacks of books on Foucault reproduce the same, few shreds of information pertaining to his first stay in Poland: there are very few archival documents corresponding to this period. Responding to our query for materials, the Centre des Archives Diplomatiques in Nantes, charged with overseeing the archives of the French embassy and cultural agencies in Poland, stated, "There are no documents pertaining to the Center for French Civilization" from the years 1951 to 1964.[36] Even after this period, all the way until the 1980s, the archives of the Nantes agency remain defined by their dearth—"*très lacunaires.*"[37]

The Foucault archives of IMEC (Institut mémoires de l'édition contemporaine) tantalizingly contain a folder titled "Pologne 1958."[38] However, upon close examination of its contents, we discovered that the name of the folder is an archival error. In fact, all documents in the folder relate to Foucault's planning of a short trip to Warsaw in 1963. The response of the Bibliothèque Nationale de France's (BNF) Foucault archives to our inquiry about its holdings started with "*malhereusement*": "unfortunately—according to the finding aids, the archives of Michel Foucault do not contain documents on his stays in Poland ... [except] for a few pages surrounding a conference in Gdańsk."[39] In the meager remnants of the Foucault holdings of the French Cultural Center at Warsaw University, we had already uncovered similar documents concerning Foucault's lecture on Guillaume Apollinaire at the Gdańsk conference and previously in Warsaw, together with a review article describing the reception following the lecture.[40] Yet, upon our visit to the BNF archives, it turned out that they have the whole text of the "Gdańsk Conference on Apollinaire, 1958," long believed by specialists to have been lost.[41] Apparently, Foucault used Apollinaire's Polish parentage to attract his Polish audience to the lecture, but he quickly discarded the topic, along with any biographical approach. After starting the lecture with shocking details regarding Apollinaire's death, he moved briefly through a section titled "Apollinaire and Poland."[42] In a way that echoes our own question about Foucault in Poland, he asked what remained of Apollinaire's ties to Poland. His answer was a laconic "little" (*peu*). Then, he swiftly abandoned the question and turned to the theoretical issues preoccupying him at the time, such as "the edge of silence" (*bord de la silence*), where French poetry had been taken by Mallarmé and Rimbaud, and the ways in which Apollinaire had managed to move past this aporia, "by a detour, to find the absolutely new."[43]

Other documents written around the time of his 1958–59 stay in Poland, such as his thesis defense for "History of Madness," preserved in manuscript form at the BNF, are also prefaced by this leitmotif of silence, or, more precisely, what has been silenced or not yet expressed. "This text is simultaneously project and dust of a text which has not been written. The book of an absent book" (*Livre d'un livre absent*).[44] The archival note accompanying the document deems it necessary to warn the reader of "numerous erasures" (*numereuses ratures*). In the very personal opening to the "Lives of Infamous Men," Foucault refers to the "resonance" that motivated his work: "[the resonance] I still experience today when I happen to encounter these lowly lives reduced to ashes in the few sentences that struck them down. The dream would have been to restore their intensity in an analysis."[45] Yet, Foucault confesses, both in the case of the *History of Madness* and in "The Lives of Infamous Men," "the first intensities" that had motivated him remained outside the book itself, and his "inadequacy," "his [lack of] the necessary talent," "pledged him to the frugal lyricism of citation."[46] Foucault pauses at length on the echoes between the "erasures" and the "frugality" of his own writing, and the "dryness" of these "lives of a few lines."[47]

In the BNF folder that precedes "Gdańsk Conference on Apollinaire, 1958," we find another oblique reference to Poland, on the verso of pages titled "Seminal Text," dedicated to Georges Bataille. This reference appears in the story of Pauliska, the Polish heroine of Révéroni de Saint Cyr's *Pauliska ou la perversité moderne* (1798).[48] When in 1962 Foucault published his reading of *Pauliska* as "Un si cruel savoir," he began with the striking phrase "The scene takes place in Poland, that is to say everywhere."[49] This sentence recalls almost word for word the famous opening of Alfred Jarry's 1896 *Ubu Roi*: "You know that Ubu happens in Poland, that is nowhere." In fact, Foucault was not only familiar with the quote, he used it to begin his account of his Polish experience in a November 1958 letter to a friend in France.⁵⁰ In Foucault's writing, then, Poland is suspended between being everywhere and nowhere. Poland was literally, legally, a no-place in 1896 when Jarry wrote his absurdist play about a buffoonish, murderous king: the country no longer existed on any map, having been partitioned among three superpowers and nullified. While the quotes about Poland being nowhere and everywhere may offhandedly appear to discard its particularities, such as its history, in "Un si cruel savoir," Foucault actually refers to the 1795 partition, as a "millenary," rather than private, conflagration that pushes Pauliska to flee her country.⁵¹ In his archival reading notes on Ruthière's *Anarchie de Pologne*, Foucault also documents Russian cruelties against the Poles.⁵² Foucault's quote from Jarry about Poland being nowhere could thus be a comment on the Polish loss of autonomy as it now operated under foreign (Soviet) influence; much like Père Ubu, the Polish Socialist Party had announced itself as leader, and now everyone quietly had to play along. On a personal level, Poland also appears as a cultural no-place for Foucault. Here he was, tasked with staging plays and cultural events in a state controlled by buffoonish and ubiquitous Ubus.

Regardless of Foucault's intention, his biography makes the joke strangely literal: he was in Poland, but Poland might as well have been nowhere, given the paucity of concrete traces of the country in Foucault's archives or work. His friend Bernard Kouchner was shocked to learn while en route to Poland in 1982 that Foucault had been there before, as Foucault had kept the story quiet. However, in an interview, Defert told Anna Krakus that even though not stated explicitly, there was a strong link between Poland and Foucault's work: "Tunisia and Poland are always there in Foucault's texts, even when they are not explicitly mentioned."⁵³ This gave us a first hint for our project: that Foucault may also be in the Polish secret police archives even when not overtly mentioned. Our project started as an attempt to make Foucault's time in Poland no longer a no-place in his biography.

FOUCAULT IN THE FBI, CIA, AND SB ARCHIVES

Before Anna left for Poland, we consulted archives on our side of the ocean. In response to our Freedom of Information Act request for Michel Foucault's FBI file, we received a notice that "eleven pages of this file had been deleted" and photocopies of just seven pages of a passport file covering "checks for all information (subversive and non-subversive) in view of travel permissions between 1972–1976.[54] (Foucault had been a member of the Communist Party). The FBI's own checks for information come out empty every time.[55] The subversive philosopher who traveled frequently between Paris, San Francisco, and New York, and repeatedly experienced visa problems, did not leave other declassified marks filed under his name in the FBI's archives.[56] The explanation may be found in the declassified CIA document, which starts and ends its long in-depth report on the French intellectual milieu with Michel Foucault.[57] Featuring a photo of Foucault on the first page, the report sees him as "France's most profound and influential thinker," who gave "kudos" to the new intellectual right for their critique of the Enlightenment.[58] This appraisal of Foucault as well as the dearth of archival documents in the FBI and CIA archives could lead the reader to reasonably infer a potential wealth of documents in the archives of Eastern European security services. In the opposing logic of the Cold War, the FBI's lack of interest in following his actions in the United States, and the CIA's assessment of Foucault as such a significant anti–Soviet Bloc intellectual, could be inferred to mean opposite actions on the other side of the Iron Curtain, where Foucault's anti-Soviet stance would be perceived as inimical and would warrant surveillance.

In June 2009, we visited the main IPN office in Warsaw, ready to tackle Foucault's dossier and the SB investigation of the theorist of surveillance. We confidently entered "Foucault" into the clunky search engine and were taken aback when it returned no hits at all. Every scholar of Eastern Europe among the many we consulted shared our initial belief that there would be a Foucault file, given his testimony about the honey trap. Similarly, the overseers of the IPN archives, including its director, Łukasz Kaminski, were of this belief.[59] The discovery of a file on the honey trap could have confirmed our expectations about the SB and added some details to Foucault's testimony. The absence of this find challenges deep-seated assumptions concerning these archives, assumptions held by contemporary scholars as well as by Foucault himself. Complemented by the narrative of our archival search and our alternative finds, this surprising archival silence turned out to be more instructive than any confirmation. In the twists and turns of our search, we lost many clichés; instead, we found previously missing pieces of the SB puzzle. Learning about its treatment of cultural figures, diplomats, and homosexuals in Foucault's circles, we gained new insight into the agency's ambitions, fears, and limitations. Foucault's honey-trap story and the search for his file formed the Ariadne's thread that guided us through this archival labyrinth. Ultimately, the narrative of this search and its silences would lead us back to a reevaluation of Foucault's archival theory, as we discuss later in this chapter.

When we encountered that first no-hit, we reminded each other that files are not always perfectly organized. A secret police dossier has gone through many hands and has stood on many shelves. Each file tends to have three or four sets of page numbers that testify to purges and reorganizations; the same case could potentially be of interest to multiple units in multiple cities at multiple times. A foreign visitor, for example, might originally have only a file with the passport and visa department, but these materials would eventually change hands to one of the bureaus dedicated to foreigners, diplomats, or tourists.

In some instances, a case might turn cold and the file be sent off to "Biuro C," where it would sit inactive and collect dust unless it was decided that the materials lacked any importance, in which event they might be removed. Another common occurrence was that a file would be placed with someone else's materials when it became used in conjunction with another investigation; in this way, dossiers and documents might move from one unit to another, not always leaving a trace. Adding a further layer of confusion, files at IPN are now organized according to a new logic, its own system. In 2009, the archivists at IPN might not even have gotten as far as beginning to reorganize files pertaining to Foucault. Thus, we turned our attention from the search for a personal file to a search for Foucault's traces in other files.

Pursuing Foucault through his diplomatic acquaintances appeared to be the surest route to locating his file. This presumption was bolstered by the way SB prioritized foreign diplomatic posts for its surveillance even when the secret police had limited technical capabilities. Room bugging was used very infrequently; even the most important divisions had barely twenty such devices in place between 1949 and 1954.[60] The rare instances of phone and room bugging were planted in diplomatic, consular, and trade missions.[61] Of all Foucault's connections, his host ambassador, Étienne Burin des Roziers, was the most prominent target for the secret police; as luck would have it, he did have a file in the archive.[62] It arrived on our desk a few weeks after that initial visit to the IPN. To our surprise, a meager forty-five pages were devoted to the ambassador, who in 1958 was one of the most important diplomats from a capitalist state in Poland. Perhaps even more surprising, these pages contain very little information on the life and whereabouts of the ambassador; many are simply indexes and forms requesting that the information in the file be sent to other units in the agency working similar cases. A marginal note in a biography page from October 1958 reveals that Roziers was of special interest because he was suspected of attempting "to examine in Warsaw possibilities to act against the Germans, both the Federal Republic of Germany and the German Democratic Republic."[63] Throughout the file, Roziers is described as leading a potentially harmful cultural-propagandistic campaign in Poland stemming from his interest in cultural exchange.[64] Roziers relied heavily on Foucault for the implementation of his plans, and yet, against all reasonable expectations given these SB suspicions and the prominence of the two men, there is no further mention in his file of these cultural efforts.[65]

Roziers's file was the first indication that files can upend reasonable expectations, that grave accusations can be leveled in a marginal note and then seemingly forgotten. Roziers's material also propelled our investigation in a tangential direction. We thought that if his file is incomplete, perhaps a portion of it might be held in a different city's archive. The few informational pages in the ambassador's file recount his travels through Poland and his meetings with French consuls and cultural figures propagating French culture in other cities. We know that Foucault's work also involved such travel, so, our reasoning went, we could possibly learn more about him or the kind of work he did at this time from files including information about Roziers's work trips. So off we went to Roziers's most important Polish destination, Kraków, to search its local IPN archive. There, we got to know one of Roziers's most frequent interlocutors: "VG," French consul to Kraków in the mid-1950s.

We requested a file on the French consulate in Kraków and were joyously terrified when the archivist rolled up a cart holding seventeen volumes.[66] The file is dedicated to the consulate as a whole, but its greatest benefit to us is that it tells the kinds of stories that we know should be told about Foucault. The consulate was a hub for French lecturers, visiting embassy employees, Foucault's predecessors and successors in the role of cultural attaché: people much like Foucault, albeit not Foucault himself.

NEAR-FOUCAULTS

The consulate file supported our initial expectations regarding Foucault having a secret police file in Poland. Some doubt had been cast on this assumption upon encountering the thin Roziers file, which seemed to suggest that perhaps the Polish secret police did not concern itself as much with foreigners and diplomats as secret police did in some other Eastern Bloc nations. The consulate file confirmed that even if certain individuals might have fallen through the cracks, it was reasonable to think that not everyone did, since vast diplomat files do exist.

As our research progressed over the years, our expectation of finding Foucault's file no longer rested only on knowledge of dossiers in other countries or on a passion for Cold War spy novels; instead, it became based on the many men who resembled Foucault in biography and function, and who did not manage to escape the SB archives. In reading their dossiers, we learned what a Foucault file might have included. We read the files of these "near-Foucaults," as we call them, learning what should have been there about our subject, while at the same time starting to understand why there wasn't much.

All the men occupying Foucault's position at the Center for French Culture after he left have their own extensive SB files. The files describe their work trips, their personalities, their habits, and their wives. In fact, their wives (who often served as vice directors of the center) tend to have files richer and more detailed than those of their spouses. They were social butterflies who conversed with scholars, and introduced Poles and French citizens to one another at their well-attended parties. Hidden in boxes at the Center for French Studies at Warsaw University, we found notes scribbled by Foucault about dinner dates with invited French scholars, but Foucault was most likely not social enough to merit the kind of interest that Regina Carbonnet or Michelle Bozec did.[67] The SB's interests often didn't coincide with those of posterity, ours included.

In fact, Foucault's colleague, cultural advisor Jean Bourelly, also shines through his absence in the archives. Perhaps the lack of concrete information on Bourelly can be said to be even more striking than with Foucault, given that he was the cultural diplomat involved in crafting the agreement between the Polish and French governments that established the center and its mission in the first place. But unlike Foucault, Bourelly is not completely absent; he is mentioned repeatedly in other files.[68] A friend and collaborator known in relation to others, if not independently, Bourelly does not give us a mirror image of a potential Foucauldian file. Instead, his presence in other files supports the notion that even if there was never a Foucault file, there ought to be Foucault traces in other ones.

A book published in Polish in 2017 identifies some of these traces.[69] In *Foucault w Warszawie*, Remigiusz Ryziński has undertaken a parallel to our investigation but with other goals in mind, as he states on his opening page: "Michel Foucault is the hero of this book. But not he alone. Warsaw is also the hero. The boys with whom he preferred to spend his time are also the heroes." In line with this opening, Ryziński's focus is on the homosexual community in Warsaw in the 1950s, and he paints a picture of what Foucault's life there was possibly like based on interviews with people who knew him. Whereas our study dwells on Foucault's traces and silences, Ryziński attempts to fill the gaps with what *might have been*. The chapter "Facts and Imagination" (*Fakty i wyobrażenia*), for instance, consists of a scripted dialogue between Foucault and Jurek on an imagined walk in Warsaw.[70]

Ryziński also visited IPN, where he found mention of Foucault in a report from 1962. A certain "Waldek," upon being accused of murder, was compelled to inform on Warsaw's homosexual community, and the young lecturer Michel Foucault, with whom he had had an affair in 1958, made the list. As far as we know, no other lover of Foucault's ever mentioned him. Even upon learning the identity of Foucault's paramour "Jurek," Ryziński encountered no reference to Foucault in Jurek's files. Jurek was an informant for some time, but a note from 1978 indicates that from that point on, he ceased to cooperate. And Waldek's single entry was made three years after Foucault had left Poland. In Ryziński's findings, Foucault thus appeared in the archives as a minor recollection, not an active participant. As seen in the IPN evidence Ryziński unearthed, Foucault was an extra in a flashback to a story of murder that happened years after he had left Poland, not the lead actor in his own tale of intrigue.

In our search, we also found one trace of Foucault from his visit to Poland in 1982: his signature.[71] That year, Foucault joined a French delegation of Médecins du Monde headed by Bernard Kouchner, whose file briefly tells a story of international tensions. During the trip, the delegation were informed that the Polish state planned to give them an award for their humanitarian work. The French refused to accept the gift, as they explained in a letter.[72] Considered rude by the Poles, the letter was signed by, among others, Yves Montand, Simone Signoret, and our archival ghost, Michel Foucault. Alongside some of the names of the undersigned, including Foucault's, there are handwritten marks in ink.[73] The following page requests that Foucault and several others in the delegation be written up in a list of individuals who are unwelcome in Poland. Again, there is a handwritten mark by Foucault's name. In the margin, someone has scribbled in Polish: "Who are the foreigners? What do we know about them? Please send information!"[74] Since the requested information does not appear in the Kouchner dossier, we cannot know today what the little mark by Foucault's name meant. It might as much indicate that the SB had information on him as that they did not. We can speculate, of course, as Ryziński does in his efforts to offer a complete picture, or we can move beyond the particular question of what the SB knew, to what they were likely to know.

Bourelly was similar to Foucault in terms of his status and role in Poland, but Foucault also had something in common with a bigger fish: the consul "VG." Here was someone who, like Foucault, might have been blackmailed and forced to leave Poland in the late 1950s as a result of a sex scandal. VG is the focus of the large consular file that is our pot of gold, and while he is the best friend of the researcher, he was the greatest foe of the embassy, a constant troublemaker who was a real thorn in the ambassador's side. Then, suddenly, he left. His hasty departure paralleled Foucault's brief stay and mysterious departure from Warsaw and later resonated in center director Daniel Beauvois's sudden exit in 1972, which likewise stunned the SB.[75]

For all the details about VG in the many consular volumes, there is a remarkable lacuna on the reasons for his departure. In only one paragraph, it is stated that he was forced to leave Poland on account of having been a spy but that he was given the opportunity to exit quietly without causing any damage to his reputation.[76] The paragraph is brief and appears seemingly out of nowhere. Prior to this point, there was no sign of VG acting in concert with French intelligence. There was also little reason to believe that this man would have been captured as a spy but then be allowed to stay and gracefully host an upcoming party that evidently concerned him more than the criminal allegations. It is more likely that VG left Poland quickly and discreetly, because his numerous extramarital affairs were being used against him. Indeed, as recorded by the police, a sizable portion of VG's time in Poland was spent with his many mistresses, one of whom was an agent with whom he was caught in flagrante. Rather than VG unexpectedly turning out to be counterintelligence, it seems probable that the SB's real focus in his case—his romantic excursions—would have finally given them something to use to force him out. This use of a sex scandal to force suspicious foreigners out of Poland is documented in another file, devoted to "RD."

In 1965, RD worked as a French lecturer in Poznán. The year before, he had become a priority by accident when he was interviewed by the SB, who at that point knew almost nothing about him. In their conversation, RD confessed to having been interviewed by French police prior to his departure for Poland, making him a person of operational interest. In 1965, an agent involved in RD's case wrote: "It should be mentioned that during penetration [of RD's apartment], a fragment of D's memories/recollections was revealed about the year 1958 . . . In these materials, the subject's pederastic tendencies run like a thread, and if they were to unwind and be confirmed on Poznan soil, he needs to be compromised using that against him as university lector and potentially expelling him from Poland under this pretext."[77] In RD's case, the reference to sexually compromising material occupies merely one, albeit clearly stated, sentence; in the case of VG, compromising photographs and materials constitute the focus of seventeen volumes yet they are omitted in the mention of his departure.

Even though homosexuality was decriminalized in Poland in 1932, it was still not considered socially acceptable.[78] The secret police reportedly exploited the generally negative popular opinion of gay people by seducing and blackmailing gay men, in particular.[79] Recent research confirms this picture: the blackmailing of informers and agents through accusations of homosexuality is documented as early as 1948, when "65 percent of agents and 33 percent of informers" were recruited using compromising materials including "improper sexual orientation."[80]

We encountered another example of the SB's interest in homosexuality when we began our research into Foucault's 1982 visit to Poland. In the course of our investigation, we made the acquaintance of another near-Foucault, "The Mustache."[81] The Mustache had caught the attention of SB the year before Foucault's Médecins du Monde trip to Poland. His movements were tracked on forty-six pages with the explanation that "the subject is suspected of homosexual relations with people in the cultural sphere."⁸² It is requested that compromising photographs be taken of him, if possible. The dossier states that it has not been established that the subject is familiar with the methods of counterintelligence; rather, it appears that his purported danger resides solely in his homosexuality and in his relations with Poles, two criteria Foucault fulfilled a year later and had already fulfilled in 1958.

The search for Foucault's file brought us to his professional affiliations: the Center for French Culture; his employer and friend, Roziers; Bourelly; the consul VG; and many more diplomatic files. While we learned little about Foucault himself, this search shed light on the agency's interest in French diplomats, and led us to another one of its targets: homosexuality. We finally turned to Defert's most striking claim about the man who seduced Foucault and then turned him in. This man, whom Defert referred to as Jurek, was in charge of the "French library in Warsaw." The center that Foucault directed had a library, so we returned there once to inquire whether they had records about who was their librarian in 1958. The administrator told us that that position was occupied only by women, but she smiled and coyly informed us, "While he was not a librarian, there was a certain someone who would come around a lot . . . Foucault's 'special friend.'" She was intrigued by the rumor, and delighted that she was the one to tell us that the special friend was a prominent French translator and poet, whose name just happened to be Jurek—the same name Defert offered for Foucault's lover.⁸³

We learned that this Jurek, whom we will refer to as Jurek L., has an informer file in the IPN.⁸⁴ There is no clear evidence in the files of any involvement between Jurek L. and Foucault. The information we found speaks both for and against the possibility that the two men had a relationship. Jurek L. was a good friend of the center: over the years, he was a frequent visitor at its events, and his phone number is consistently on the books. As a homosexual man (his friends marveled at his marriage, since he was gay) who frequented the center, he may easily have inspired such gossip.⁸⁵ According to Defert's story, however, the Polish lover and agent visited Foucault in Paris with the objective of gathering information about French intellectuals, and Jurek L. did not travel to France at the time this visit supposedly took place.

Jurek L. never mentions Foucault, but he does talk at great length about other people of cultural import. Still, accounts of his reports consistently end in the SB agents' complaint that Jurek L. is not committed enough, and that he does not give them what they want.[86] He speaks freely about sensitive matters, such as rumors of the SB's involvement in the suicide/murder of Henryk Holland,[87] yet he was a constant disappointment to the SB. This disappointment stemmed not from his silence or an obvious lack of cooperation, but from his frequent and skillful misdirection. SB entered into conversations with stated goals; Jurek L. would offer something else. There is a discrepancy between what was told and what was desired. The abundance of Jurek L.'s words thereby functioned as a kind of silence.

Then came a new break in our research: the file of a subsequent center director mentioned the SB's code name for the center: Obcy, "the stranger." We ordered the Obcy dossier and waited, sure that the IPN archivist would roll up carts of seemingly endless volumes, as had been the case with the file of the Kraków consulate.[88] Instead, the file that we received is 197 pages long and it begins in 1965. IPN files are not always chronological, however, so the fact that the first page in the file dates to 1965 did not necessarily mean the Foucault period would not be in there somewhere, especially since many of the files that we examined are feats of repetition: the same language, words, and even boring documents recur over and over. Indeed, this is how the center's file begins, with repeat notices from 1965 indicating that the case is changing hands and copies of the 1957 agreement by which the center was established. But after reading more than a quarter of the file, a new note appears, and it is the key and explanation for why our Foucault project was so quickly renamed "Not Finding Foucault": "Most of the materials currently lack operational value and may be destroyed."[89]

Evidently, whatever had remained from Foucault's time in Warsaw in his role as center director was not deemed important enough to keep. The report explains this by stating what was in the original file: merely the 1957 agreement and some reports based on phone tapping. But why would the Kraków consulate's file from the same year be so rich and that for the center be so weak on content? Professor Lajarrige, a French lector followed by the SB when Foucault was in Poland, had it right, it seems, when he commented in a wiretapped conversation that the Warsaw secret police was overwhelmed: "One thing is certain: cultural work is slowly beginning to unravel and they can't keep up in Warsaw."[90] The young professor might have been referring to cultural work that was spiraling out of control, or to what this file confirms to be true: there were not enough agents in Warsaw to keep pace with this spiraling. It appears from the existing files of our near-Foucaults that there was indeed an overwhelming amount of cultural work and of foreigners in the capital, making it impossible for the SB to keep up and cover all of it.

WAS THE SB OVERWHELMED?

There was good reason for the SB agents to be overworked around the time of Foucault's visit to Poland; the year 1958 brought with it new, significant challenges beyond just the opening of the Center for French Culture at the university. First of all, the very launching of the center was perceived as a much greater undertaking than the educational endeavor it might sound like today. This exchange program between French and Polish universities opened the door for student exchanges, visiting professorships, and language instruction. Yet, the SB regarded this collaborative effort as a sign of something much more nefarious: as a component of the French embassy's cultural-propagandistic work, whereby the French were not only teaching the Poles, they were also in effect reprogramming their youth.[91] A page from November 1963 in the center's file explains that French influence in Poland had diminished, and that in order to reach Polish youth the French forces in Poland were intensifying their "cultural propaganda" efforts by infiltrating the realm of higher education.[92] Foucault's center might thus have been a much more politically sensitive matter than imagined.

Furthermore, there were other developments around this time that concerned the SB. One of Roziers's first acts upon his arrival in Poland was to decentralize the embassy's cultural work, assigning that responsibility to the French consuls. The manpower required to infiltrate French intellectual work now had to be divided across multiple centers.[93] From the SB's perspective, 1958 thus marked a turning point in the French capitalist campaign. Moreover, this expansion of French cultural work coincided with significant reductions in the SB staff due to severe layoffs in 1956.[94] The reduction in the number of agents also meant a corresponding drop in the number of secret collaborators working with said agents, which reportedly dipped by 80 percent from 1953 to 1956![95] At this time, files of cases in progress were transferred to archives, resulting in "a build-up of an enormous volume of material waiting for better days."[96]

It is worth noting in this context that alongside the excuses that files have been destroyed or gone missing, one common assumption about the

SB is that it was made up of incompetent amateurs. Indeed, anecdotal evidence from the files corroborates the SB's own statistics, which show that even senior agents were poorly educated: in 1953, only seven out of sixty-two directors and deputy directors of departments held university degrees.[97] Thus, the SB appears to have been understaffed and with its workforce largely consisting of poorly educated individuals unable to keep up with the high number of people they deemed suspicious. Thus, even if Foucault's "thick manuscripts" should have worried them, as Foucault believed, there was a high probability that the agency did not have the trained personnel to understand that threat or follow up with proper surveillance.

Yet, with his Polish experience behind him, Foucault wrote: "Do not ask who I am and do not ask me to remain the same: leave it to our bureaucrats and our police to see that our papers are in order."[98] Our findings suggest that at times the police did not see that papers were in order. It seems more likely that Foucault, and, following him, his readers, overestimated the police and its archives, regarding them from a mystifying distance. Getting closer to the SB archives, we encountered a different view of Foucault's case and the Polish secret police. This shifting perspective on Foucault's case calls into question the writing of (auto)biography, and turns our attention back to archival silences.

AN ARCHAEOLOGY OF SILENCE IN THE ARCHIVE/S

Daniel Defert's testimony about Foucault's departure from Poland echoes a familiar picture of Eastern Europe from this time.[99] We recognize the exaggerated, by now quaint, attention paid to intellectuals and their writings, especially to any contacts between foreign and local intellectuals. And as we begin to learn more about the inner workings of the secret police, we start to recognize the tendency to use homosexuality as a trap, a cover, and even a catalyst for secret police action against so-called undesirables.

The ways our expectations echo in the Foucault/Defert story is perhaps why the story sounds true and has not been challenged despite the lack of supporting documentation. In Foucauldian terms, the story met the historical conditions under which statements may qualify as being true; it fit with the mechanisms that regulate why some statements and not others "can lay claim to truth."[100] Of course, this does not make the story empirically true. It is the function of Foucault's and Defert's testimony to confer credibility on the narrative. But the archive, usually there to document, to ascertain, here remains obstinately silent, indifferent, taunting us with questions: If we use its holdings as proof, why not its silences? How long are we willing to hold on to our well-rehearsed truths against the evidence of its silences, stutters, interruptions, and redactions? The story that Defert tells makes a lot of sense and checks many boxes; it is a good story. The silences that the archive presents us with are confusing, and may never amount to much of a story at all. And yet, in his key writings from this year in Poland, Foucault repeatedly and insistently urges us to engage "in an archaeology of that silence" rather than in the "history of [the] language" of truth.[101]

As we have seen in our archival searches, there is much silence and many lacunae surrounding Foucault's 1958–59 stay in Poland, giving us plenty of material for our archaeology. In the rich, generally accepted Foucault chronology compiled by Defert, there is, for this whole period, just one striking fragment of a November 1958 letter written to an unnamed friend in France. It starts with the sentence about Poland being nowhere, and continues:

> Do you know that *Ubu Roi* is set in Poland, in other words nowhere. I am in prison: that is, on the other side, but that's worse. On the outside: impossible to come in; grating on the railings, the head hardly getting through, just enough to see the others inside, who are going around in a circle. A sign, they are already further away, one can do nothing for them, except to watch out for when they come around again and prepare a smile. But in the meantime, they've been kicked and no longer have the strength or the courage to respond. The smile isn't lost, somebody else will take it for himself and carry it away this time. Clouds continually rise from the Vistula. Nobody knows what light is anymore. They place me in a socialist palace. I work on my "Madness," which is in danger, in this outpouring of insanity [*dévidage du délire*], of becoming a little more like what it always pretended to be.[102]

We already noted that the dismissive phrase "in Poland, in other words nowhere" contains a reference to the political status of Poland in 1795, when it was a nation divided among three foreign powers, erased from the map, and silenced. I would add that in his description of contemporary Poland, Foucault characterized himself as silenced, reduced to communicating by a vague sign that failed to signify and a smile that failed to reach its victimized recipient, except by directing the violence of the guard against him.

The smile ricocheted and reached another prisoner, and some last traces of communication were preserved in this ricochet. Yet the moving picture that Foucault describes here lacks any words, and instead barely brings to awareness the muffled sounds of disciplined bodies walking under duress, or the thuds of the guards' kicks. This enforced silence makes the witness aware of his bodily position, which corresponds closely to his political position.

Having started by establishing the strong link between this shared silencing of the prisoners and of Foucault as witness, the passage ends by explicitly connecting this experience of being silenced and coming undone (*dévidage du délire*) in Poland to the writing of "History of Madness." This recalls Defert's comment about Tunisia and Poland's strong, if usually not explicitly recognized, influence on Foucault's texts.[103] Foucault was hard at work rewriting his dissertation immediately following his arrival in Poland, in October 1958. A month after his letter on Ubuism, around Christmas, he turned in the manuscript to Georges Canguilhem, and in February, he finished the "Preface." The latter is, as mentioned above, structured around the imperative of attending to "the archaeology of [the] silence" and to "all those imperfect words, of no fixed syntax, stammered, in which the exchange between madness and reason was carried out."[104] Foucault's study tracks the ways in which this cacophony was plunged into forgetting once the language of medical reason took over.[105] What is the site of this archaeology of silence, where does one find these imperfect words, the stammer of this distant suffering? The answer that Foucault provides features his first published mention of the word "archive": "the slightly dusty archives of pain."[106]

This is a surprising response for those aware of the famous Foucauldian definition of "archive" in *Archaeology of Knowledge*. In that work, Foucault begins by defining "archive" in terms of what it is not: "not the sum of all texts that a culture has kept upon its person as documents attesting to its own past, or as evidence of a continuing identity; nor do I mean the institutions, which, in a given society, make it possible to record and preserve those discourses that one wishes to remember and keep in circulation."[107] Indeed, it has been noted that Foucault's lasting, powerful mark on the word is already visible in the erasure of the French plural.[108] *Les archives* in the plural commonly signifies the literal buildings and documents housed in them; Foucault's definition shifted to the singular, *l'archive*, which he described more capaciously as the ensemble of statements that can be made at a certain time.

In terms of our project, Foucault's SB archive (*l'archive*) is not what can or cannot be found in the IPN archives but everything that the SB could have said about him (the head of the Cultural Center, the gay man pulling up in a white Jaguar, the up-and-coming philosopher writing thick manuscripts on madness and confinement, the friend of the French ambassador, and whatever other author and nonauthor functions Foucault performed in their eyes). The actual documents that we find about and pertaining to Foucault are a great place to start, but the net should be cast much wider, getting to their *dispositifs*, to the conditions of the emergence and transformation of their statements, to the limits that separate us from them, which throw some light on our continuities and discontinuities from them.

THE ARCHIVES OF PAIN

As Knut Ove Eliassen shows in his erudite "The Archives of Michel Foucault," this memorable sense of "archive" in the singular was only one, albeit the best known, of the senses in which Foucault employed the word in his works. Foucault developed this famous definition of "archive" most extensively in *Archaeology of Knowledge* and employed it "in this very restricted sense in the period between 1966 and 1970, when he more or less abruptly stops using it."[109] Eliassen shows that there are at least two other kinds of archives that appear in Foucault's writings, which work in tandem "with the concept of 'archeology' as 'the history of that which makes a certain form of thought necessary.'"[110] One sense of the word "archive" that Eliassen already discovered in 1968 and again encountered, repeatedly, in the 1990s is that of archives as "actual archival and historical institutions and the archives contained in them. In this sense, the archive is both a collection of documents and an instrument of power, discipline and knowledge."[111] The last sense of the archive that Eliassen distinguishes is the archive as Foucault's laboratory, "his preferred place of work, his refuges, spaces of experiment and experience," a privileged example of heterotopia.[112] We argue that the "dusty archives of pain," the first archives Foucault calls by that name in his writing, deserve attention as a category of their own. Long ignored in the typology of Foucauldian archives, the archives of pain are both the earliest ones cited by Foucault and the most enduring in his work. They recur throughout his writings, from the dissertation on madness, through the 1977 "Lives of Infamous Men," and continuing all the way to his 1982 work on the Bastille *lettres de cachet*, published just a few years before his death in 1984.[113] In deliberately reverting to the time before "the monologue of psychiatry" took over the archive, Foucault attempted to find in the dusty archives the old records of "a rupture in a dialogue" between "all those imperfect words, of no fixed syntax, spoken falteringly, in which the exchange between madness and reason was carried out."[114] As he wrote earlier in the "Preface," "the language of psychiatry, which is a monologue by reason *about* madness, could only have come into existence in such a silence."[115] As a result, this dusty archive of suffering comes with its own archaeology: an archaeology of silence.

This description of the stammering, syntax-deprived, and ultimately silenced subjects to whom Foucault attempted to bear witness recalls the Ubu letter. It also recalls the kind of displacement or "sliding" operation that Giorgio Agamben calls for in his critique of Foucault's notion of archive, which also founded Agamben's own famous concept of "testimony":

> In opposition to the [Foucauldian] archive, which designates the system of relations between the unsaid and the said, we give the name of testimony to the system of relations between the inside and the outside of langue, between the sayable and the unsayable in every language—that is, between a potentiality of speech and its existence, between a possibility and an impossibility of speech. To think of potentiality in act as potentiality, to think enunciation on the plane of language is to inscribe a caesura in possibility, a caesura that divides it into a possibility and an impossibility, into a potentiality and an impotentiality; and it is to situate a subject in this very caesura.[116]

In the attempt of the "Preface" to register the barely audible murmur of those outside the confines of the language of reason, Foucault himself already performed the sliding between the sayable and the unsayable that Agamben powerfully articulates in *Remnants of Auschwitz*. While *Archaeology of Knowledge* is more concerned with the relationship between the sayable and the said, in his earliest (and also latest) works on archives, "the problem is," as Foucault clarified in 1966, "not so much *langue*, as the limits of enunciability."[117]

Intriguingly, there are suggestions in both the Ubu letter and in "History of Madness" that providing testimony to others who fall beyond the limits of enunciability can render the witnessing subject speechless or overwhelm his limits. Thus, in the Ubu testimony, Foucault describes himself as silenced, confined, in effect mirroring through his own bodily position the position of the prisoners, to the point where he is barely able to communicate. The passage ends with an "outpouring of insanity" into the "History of Madness" manuscript that threatens to become "what it always pretended to be." What does this mean? It seems the manuscript unfolds itself and, touching too close to home/self, it becomes an expression of unreason rather than reason. The next entry of the chronology notes that indeed the manuscript had become "very thick." In his review of the text, Maurice Blanchot makes the connection between its bulging, unwieldy size and its "unreason," when he characterizes it as "this rich book, insistent and, through its necessary repetitions, almost unreasonable [*déraisonnable*], (and as this book is a dissertation, we note with pleasure this collision [*heurt*] of the University and of unreason [*déraison*]."[118]

There are different kinds of silences, however. The silences broken by the almost-words or no-longer-words without syntax, the silences of a redacted text, the silences of a destroyed text. Deafening silences. "Silences of intellectuals" and "silences of shame."[119] Silences that silence further and some that make music resound. The archaeology of silence was spearheaded in Foucault's search for the marginal in his "archives of pain," from "History of Madness" on to his work on the "Lives of Infamous Men" and the Bastille *lettres de cachet*. It was critiqued and pushed further in the work of subaltern studies, and it flourished in the study of colonial archives.[120] There are also the silences and gaps in the police discourse, the silence of the silencer. We hope to go beyond this dichotomy of the silenced and the silencer. This would not mean effacing the difference between different kinds of silence or abandoning discernment. On the contrary. For just as power is not limited to the institutions of state power, but, according to Foucault, flows through us, silence and stammer may not be the exclusive domain of the marginal, but could also haunt the institutions and discourses of power. Indeed, as Renisa Mawani writes in "Law's Archives," "Foucault's . . . conception of the archive as a system of enunciability combined with his later formulations on power/knowledge have remained central to mapping the accumulations, gaps, and silences of archival production" in recent archival theory, such as that of Ann Stoler.[121] Our findings in the SB archives strongly support

Stoler's thesis about colonial archives, which she often sees not as "a site of omniscience, surety and rationality," but as "condensed sites of epistemological and political anxiety," uncertainty, power in the making or in the process of disintegration.[122]

Now, just because the powers that be, in this case the SB, were uncertain, anxious, and at times incompetent, it does not mean they were not powerful, that they did not appear or act powerful. It also does not mean that they did not inflict harm, or that their uncertainty or limited data on the population made them less potent or vicious. The following erroneous argument is often made: the files were all compiled by clueless agents worried about getting a paycheck or a promotion; as such, the archives don't contain anything relevant. While this argument may be innocently advanced, it is often used politically by those intent on closing archives and suppressing judgment on the many crimes of the past. In fact, it is often at their moments of maximum anxiety and lack of actual power that the secret police presented shows of power that were extremely harmful and at the time credible. Therefore, in our project we investigated kinds of silences and what produced them. We considered silencing agents, omission as negligence and as strategy. We also attended to discourses that were just coming into stuttering or strident being at the time. We made silences resound in the midst of the varied noise and speech that surrounded them.[123] In his later work, Foucault emphasizes the importance of silence and its coterminous relationship to speech. He dwells on "the things one declines to say, or is forbidden to name, the discretion that is required between different speakers."[124] As Luise White notes in her essay on Foucault: "Silence 'functions alongside things said.' Together speech and silence form discourse; speech or silence alone do not."[125] The aim is to give these silences a shape, to start tracing them and grasping their contours and consequences.

THE ARCHIVAL NO-HIT: ON RUMOR, SILENCE, AND FICTION IN POLICE STATES

Let us now return to our archival searches—in this case, Foucault; in previous ones, Paul Celan, Roland Barthes, and Herta Müller—and see how silence and its consequences shape discourse. All these searches, like hundreds of others entered into the secret police databases over the past twenty-five years, have for years retrieved no hits. Silence. One great danger of the no-hit silence of the archives is that it silences further. First, the no-hit threatens to hit again the silenced victim. Second, it threatens to silence the researcher, who accepts the no-hit result and says, "There is nothing there," and thus moves on. After all, there are vast numbers of files to be read in the archives, files that the secret police carefully prepared and that present-day archivists make readily available. However, once you enter your search term and obtain a no-hit, stopping is not a simple matter, because the no-hit has already affected the status of the existing testimony. When they point to silences in the archive, the testimonies of the past ask us to listen to these silences, and to read the extant documents in relationship to these silences. Let us take the case of Foucault.

The archival no-hit, the stubborn absence of proof of Foucault's surveillance and framing by the secret police, offers the possibility that this was a nonevent—that it never occurred. We could discard Foucault's story as such, dismiss it as mere rumor. Yet historians, ethnographers, and literary scholars alike have taught us that rumors are rich sources that can illuminate as nothing else can past fantasies, anxieties, and subversions.[126] As Stoler subtly demonstrates, "rumors registered what people believed could have happened in the past and what could happen in the future."[127] Even if they did not recount the factual, "rumors voiced the possible."[128] They established "hierarchies of credibility." In this diagnostic relationship to the possible, rumors can be helpful as we try to trace not just the said but also the sayable. The archive is, Foucault explained, "what can be talked about" at a certain point in time, what it is possible to say, the sayable. Stoler has even argued that in repressive cultures rumors do the hard work of stretching the limits of the unspeakable toward the spoken. Paramount for regimes where so much was censored, "rumors were the medium through which the *unspeakable was spoken*, with no one party on hand to blame."[129]

Given our objective of understanding Foucault's SB Polish archive as an archive of both the said and the sayable, it seems important to consider what we can gain from considering Foucault's statement regarding the secret police as not just fact but also rumor. For one, a whole new set of questions arises, such as: if this was a rumor, then does its telling as an event by myriad sources and its persistence all these years not tell us something (about Foucault, the SB, and our own credulity)? Indeed, let us consider this statement in its various plausible relations to the possible. Why would Foucault initiate this rumor, and why would we all believe it? Depending on the story's relationship to the possible, it could be categorized as gossip, rumor, slander, fantasy, paranoia, fact, truth, fiction, or self-mythologizing. As more information is added or withdrawn, we see the original anecdote shift between such rather disparate genres before our eyes. Only when we bypass the temptation to choose one possibility, to deliver a single verdict, do we become aware of how much is at stake in contemplating this shifting "hierarchy of credibility."[130]

So, rather than sending the reader on the wild goose chase of a verdict, let us caution that we are not necessarily asking you to cast your vote for one of these alternative genres—was it slander, rumor, or self-mythologizing? There has been much important scholarship on the differences between even the more similar genres, such as gossip and rumor. We are interested less in precisely identifying one genre than in showing how the maddening back-and-forth among these genres, undecidability itself, defines the experience of living under a police state. One often did not know if and to what degree they were being followed; whether they were engaging in intimate gossip with a friend or participating in the creation of a political slander with an informer; whether they were being paranoid or careless around the secret police, which was at times ludicrously incompetent and at other times maddeningly thorough—and it was precisely because of this that one's experience as well as their statements describing that experience were potentially shifty. Trying to fix their meaning in a retrospective reading that would adjudicate—this was a true statement, this was a false statement—is sometimes possible based on the evidence. In many cases, we may now be able to tell with a fairly high degree of certainty whether or not person X was under surveillance. Sometimes, however, we run the risk of making a mistake: additional information has a way of surfacing in these archives, or a document that one thought was reliable turns out to have been a forgery (there was, after all, a special department dedicated to misinformation, and its lessons had been disseminated throughout the institution).[131] That is embarrassing enough for the researcher. Even worse is when such judgments dismiss the actual suffering of the individuals who at times may have thought, felt, and suffered under a belief in surveillance that the researcher with the advantage of hindsight knows to have been false. Yet we need to be careful to not throw the baby out with the bathwater. In other words, when we discover that there was no file, no surveillance, we should be mindful not to discard the experience of the people who lived their lives, made their small and big decisions believing themselves to be the objects of surveillance. Nor should we dismiss the vast range of techniques, manpower, and resources that the secret police used to fashion those beliefs in surveillance, even—or especially—at those times when the beliefs were false.

Harassment of homosexuals and foreigners, rumor, self-mythologizing, paranoia, carefully covered-up diplomatic scandal: all these are plausible scenarios. And as such, they make Foucault's accusation against the SB credible, just as they made it possible for the SB to get away with potentially not expending much of its scarce resources on this flamboyant French academic. They had already convinced him, and all those who had believed Foucault's story for the past decades, that it was utterly possible for him to be followed, that he was probably being followed. They had built a panopticon out of the French consul's bedroom with its surveillance camera clicking away from the closet, the French Cultural Center, the embassy, and many other of Foucault's Polish haunts. As Foucault would write later, in certain ways it matters little whether the panopticon observation tower was empty or not, whether the guard was actually watching or just giving the inmates that impression.[132] Following this logic, it matters little whether the files actually exist or not. They did their work partly through the theatricality of their mise-en-scène, a much more sophisticated one than that of Jeremy Bentham's panopticon. They broke through the fourth wall, and left their studio behind—the prisons, interrogation rooms, the literal panopticons, no matter how impressive their architectures. Instead, they opted for shooting on location. In city and countryside alike, few locations were safely cordoned off from becoming their mise-en-scène, one that included not just the space, but also its inhabitants, the lights and the power cuts, and all sorts of other "special effects" and affects—misinformation, the breaking of networks, isolation, mistrust, paranoia, and fear.

This is why the aesthetics of the secret police—often histrionic; as times went on, more drably realistic—were so important.[133] The archives held the scripts and production notes of this immense reality show mounted by the secret police, a show that reached inside apartment buildings, where people talked, ate, and loved, and fell silent as if they were listened to when they were not and vice versa. So, are we facing a nonevent? Ultimately, whether Foucault ended a stay in Poland and a relationship because of the SB really spying on him or just giving him that impression is a question of limited scope. It does, however, bring up a larger question: For those who spent lifetimes not telling their children what they believed out of fear of a bugging device, or out of suspecting a relative of turning into an informer, is it a game changer if the bugging device turns out, now, decades later, not to have been there?

In the many cases where we did not find the files, because they have perhaps been destroyed or misfiled, or because they were never created in the first place, is the damage less severe, or more so? Keep in mind that in many cases the secret police did not even bother to record the harassment. In fact, the worse the harassment was, the less likely they were to record it. There are few traces of torture in the files, even though the police were at times careless enough to incriminate themselves in their own documents. However, for the most part, the secret police files are not Amnesty International reports: their aim was not to document human rights abuses but to impress superiors. Moreover, the damage was not just individually targeted; rather, individuals were meant to serve as examples. Therefore, understanding the archives' holdings and the modus operandi of the secret police is relevant not only for the cases where harm was inflicted individually, but also for all the harm that was deliberately meant to be extrapolated by the audience of this enormous show. The files of the "near-Foucaults" are ultimately more informative than any particular Foucault file.

CONCLUSION: CAN THE ARCHIVAL SUBJECT BE SILENT?

So, to recapitulate the facts, and the silences, of the IPN archive relating directly to Foucault's honey trap: what Anna Krakus unearthed in the IPN was the note that the French Cultural Center files were expunged because they were unimportant. From Ryziński's research, we also encountered a huge blank for the 1959 honey trap and for the 1960 visit, from which we had been led by Defert's interview to expect Foucault's own report on himself, translated by Jurek. Instead, there was just an inane passport file; a name drop in an unrelated murder case in 1963; and a much later, 1978 informer file whose main holdings state that Jurek did not want to inform, a complaint we find in our own Jurek's file as well. Yet this is potentially the most important kind of information in the files: that at this time there were people who resisted informing, who kept silent. This silence may have been the most courageous gesture or act that was available to them. It is usually not recorded, and when it is, we usually pass it by, disappointed that we don't get the story. We may instead reconsider: stop and take note of this overlooked silence. It often took all the courage people had to be silent, plus a lot of chance for the police to actually record their silence.

This project was inspired by Foucault's promise, made at the time of his first Polish sojourn, to not only write the "history of [the] language" of power, but also "the archaeology of . . . silence."[134] In treading on this path, we found that silence, like power, bridges boundaries between the policed and the policing. We learned that the archives of power do not just conceal the silence of the silenced but also the silences and stutters of the police itself. While often representing itself as omniscient and coherent, the power at work in the secret police archives was revealed to have been often overwhelmed, immature, and poorly educated. In the course of our research, we learned to think beyond the dichotomy between the silence of those silenced and the silence of the silencer. We also realized the importance of going beyond the dichotomy between the language of power and the archaeology of silence and considering intermediate genres like rumor or slander, and the terrifying interpretive undecidability that defined life in police states. Amid these conditions, the refusal to inform, silence itself, as may have been the case with Foucault's lover/translator/informer, can be power. Not the power of the powerful but "power of the powerless."[135] We know that at times this silence took lives, livelihoods, sanity, cunning, and myriad other "weapons of the weak and the watched" over the course of decades.[136] The question is not just whether the archival subject can speak, but also whether the archival subject can keep silent. It is time for us to devise more ways to attend to the hard-won silence that the overflowing archives do their best to both cover up and discredit.

TWO

Intermedia

The Files, Film, and Photo Albums of a Socialist Bank Heist

When presenting versions of this chapter at conferences on the declassified archives of the former Soviet Bloc, I often take a moment to crowdsource a list of mediums that my colleagues have encountered in their archival research.[1] I use the plural "mediums," in line with the common practice in the arts and art history, rather than the clear preference for "media" in communications and the sciences. My choice of the plural, as will become clear over the course of this chapter, is also meant to signal an engagement with the term's shadowy second meaning—defined by *OED Online* as "a person claiming to be in contact with spirits of the dead and to communicate between the dead and the living." Answers to my crowdsourcing exercise have ranged from paper, parchment, handwriting, type, sketches, drawings, paintings, maps, and postcards to carbon copies and photocopies, photographs and photonegatives in various formats, video and audio tapes, cans of film ranging from 8 mm to 35 mm, textiles such as religious vestments and fabric odor samples kept in airtight jars, wood and glass icons, playing cards, fingerprints, weapons, and x-rays. Within minutes we have a good sense of the capacious understandings of what constitutes a medium in the archive. The exercise also provides ad hoc proof of the extreme hybridity of mediums that defines these collections where standard preservation requirements mandating the separation of mediums were overridden by forensic imperatives.

The creators and preservers of these archives deliberately marshalled a diversity of mediums as evidence of their incriminating narratives. It is thus no accident that the encounter with medium hybridity is a widespread challenge for contemporary researchers in the declassified archives. How do we engage with this challenge? Mostly, we don't. There are powerful, and sometimes even good, reasons why we don't. One is the digital revolution that has been contemporaneous with, and really inseparable from, the archival revolution: this bewildering array of mediums is remediated into a single medium through digitization. Another reason is disciplinary specialization: most scholars have been trained to work in one medium—most often text, maybe still or moving image, less often sound, or textiles—and are understandably wary of taking on material that exceeds their expertise. Yet I will argue that since the carefully choreographed medium hybridity was foundational to the ways in which these archives made and preserved meaning, it is important to embrace, rather than bypass, our encounter with the many mediums of the archives. Indeed, engaging in this intermedial encounter allows us to better understand these archives; furthermore, we can tap the violently suppressed potential of this hybridity not just to bolster but sometimes to nuance or even undermine their master narratives.

I chose the secret police investigation of a 1959 heist of the Romanian National Bank as this chapter's case study due to the remarkable diversity of mediums it employed. The part of the case that has received the most attention so far is the reenactment film, *Reenactment* (*Reconstituirea*, 1969), which the secret police produced together with the national documentary film studio, Sahia. The reenactment film infamously cast the arrested suspects in the main roles, with supporting roles filled by secret police agents, and compelled them all to reenact in front of the camera the preparations for the bank heist, the event itself, the arrests, and parts of interrogations. I have devoted a separate article to a close reading of the film alongside an examination of its place within Soviet Bloc documentary traditions, researching its precursors, its place within the under-studied genre of cinematic collaborations between cinema and the secret police, and its rich cinematic afterlife.[2] By contrast, this chapter attempts an intermedia analysis of the case, paying particular attention to the interplay among mediums that makes this case study a model of archival medium hybridity. Indeed, the twenty-seven-volume file dedicated to the case contains hundreds of pages of handwriting and type, as well as two volumes of production stills from the shooting of the reenactment—one of original photographs, and one of their carefully captioned photocopies—together with confiscated personal photographs, police sketches, ID pictures (fig. 2), mugshots (fig. 3), oversized drawings and sketches, maps and surveillance visual aids, confiscated book pages (fig. 4), and an envelope of scalloped-edge family pictures. An order "to attach material evidence to the penal investigation file" gives us a sense of even more "corpora delicti and documents," "some as originals and some as photocopies," that were part of the file during the investigation itself, including "14 pistols and one automatic gun . . . over 1,000 pieces of ammunition and 'white weapons,' over 1,200,000 lei [Romanian currency], 7,300 dollars, the uniform of a militia officer, counter-revolutionary leaflets," and more.[3]

I use this case, then, to devise interpretation strategies that pay attention to the collusion and tension among the mediums in the case—the way they cover up for each other, fill in each other's blanks, and engage in repetitions with or without significant differences. I focus on the thickenings of the representational planes where mediums overlap, thickenings that sometimes come together as evidence yet at other times merely smack of artifice. For example, the body of the chapter mines the declassified files for traces of the movie's production and reception, and allows us to see the texts and moving images not just as finished products but as overlapping processes. The analysis of the case study ends with photo albums of production stills, a peculiarly intermedial genre that is predicated on the interaction between still images taken during the filming process, which in turn depend on text captions to produce their narratives. The chapter concludes with a theoretical meditation on the most forgotten archival medium. I am withholding my proposal for what this medium may be until the end of the chapter as an invitation for the reader to consider their own answer to this question. My concluding meditation builds on contemporary scholarly and artistic attempts to address the challenges and potentials of intermedia hybridity in the archives.

Before we delve into the particulars of this case, I would like to clarify the stakes of this chapter's focus on intermedia by tracing the shifting place

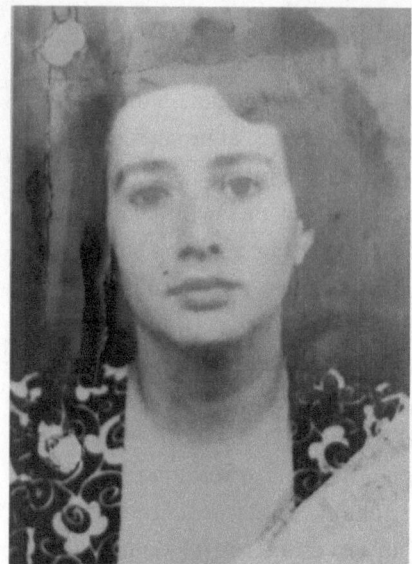 

FIGURE 2. Identity cards of bank heist suspects Monica and Igor Sevianu. P 181, 22:3, ACNSAS.

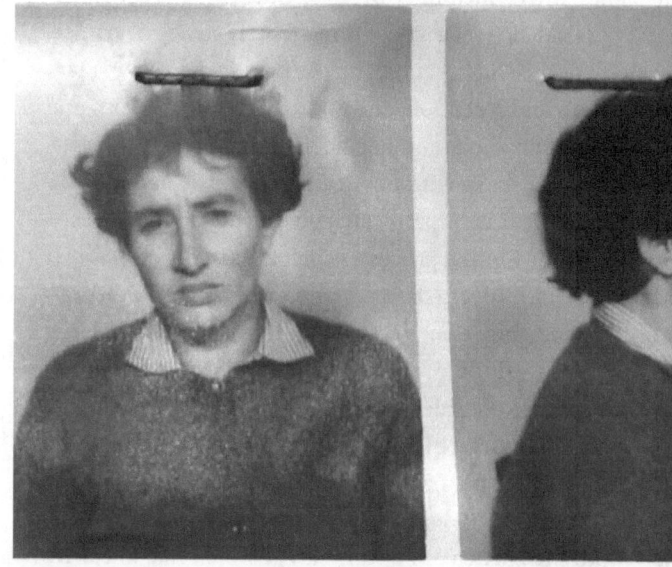

FIGURE 3. Mug shots of Monica Sevianu from prison files. P 181, 24:94, ACNSAS.

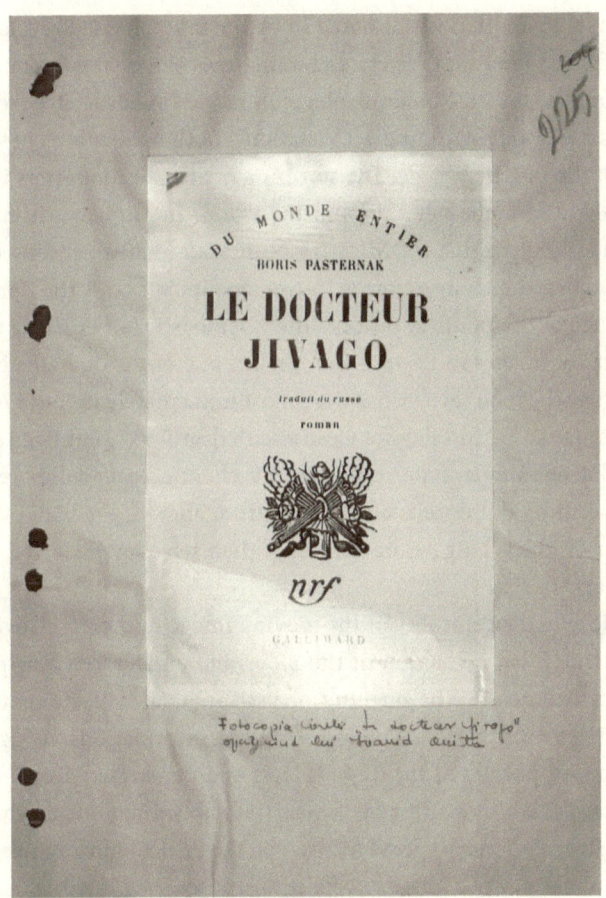

FIGURE 4. Photocopy of front page of French edition of the banned *Doctor Zhivago*, confiscated during house searches and glued onto file page. P 181, 11:224, ACNSAS.

of medium in the changing scholarly reception of the archival revolution as well as the overlap of the archival and digital revolutions.

REMEDIATING THE ARCHIVAL REVOLUTION

The archival revolution was ushered in by the first televised revolutions in the world: the sometimes velvety and sometimes bloody revolutions of 1989 in Eastern Europe. The Romanian Revolution was broadcast live around the world, and was fought around a TV station—both momentous firsts in the history of the moving image. The storming of Stasi headquarters in Berlin was filmed, and made news around the world. In Hungary, film footage shot clandestinely inside the Ministry of Interior archives incensed public opinion about the destruction of secret documents and the continuing surveillance of the political process after October 1989.[4] Furthermore, the circulation of images in Eastern Europe was one of the domains in which the effects of the 1989 revolutions were most immediately visible. For example, in Romania, within days of Ceausescu's death, we went from just two hours a day of a single, state-controlled TV channel to a media overload of satellites dishing out dozens of channels from abroad. We had TV ads for consumer products long before the things themselves even started arriving on the market.

Yet, despite the centrality of the moving image to the post-Soviet transition, the archival revolution of the 1990s and early 2000s was predominantly text-centered. The opening of vast archival collections that had been amassed over the Soviet period caused an informational deluge whose ripples shaped politics at the highest level and penetrated deeply into the private lives of ordinary citizens. Understandably, then, most scholarship in the postrevolutionary period focused on the critical information emerging from these newly accessible collections. It took well over a decade for questions of rhetoric and interpretation to surface and come to the fore. Thus, participants in "Engaging Documents," a 2014 roundtable on archival methods at the national conference of the Association of Slavic and East European and Eurasian Studies (ASEEES), concluded that "over the last decade, anthropologists and historians have begun to look at documents rather than through them; they have attended to marginalia, minor orthographic mistakes, mistranslations, and a document's circulation in order to provide a richer understanding of the powers that have structured archives and thereby influenced scholarly interpretations."⁵ Yet scholarship remained chiefly preoccupied with textual sources. Images remained mostly ignored or heuristically used as illustrations rather than analyzed in themselves or in relation to other mediums of the archives.

Slow to emerge, a preoccupation with visual aspects of the declassified archives is now noticeable both in scholarship and in artists' engagement with the archives. We are becoming more aware of the treasure trove of long-overlooked and sometimes downright disposed-of images. The bibliography on the visual aspects of secret police archives remains limited, but it is growing.⁶ While my article on the cinematic aspects of *Reenactment* attempted to contribute to a scholarship that is mindful of the specificity of the visual medium—in particular, film—I think it is now time to remediate the archival revolution by focusing on relationships among different visual mediums, such as still and moving images, and also on their interaction with the myriad other mediums in the declassified archives.

We are likely becoming more aware of the materiality and medium richness of archives as these qualities recede into the past, superseded by digital remediation. This sharpening of our perception and insight is symptomatic. We often pay attention to concepts when what they refer to is no longer present, or at least when part of what they refer to is about to undergo dramatic change or disappear. Hannah Arendt wrote that we attempt to define authority when it is on the wane, when the question is not "what *is* authority?" but "what *was* authority?"⁷ Similarly, are we so preoccupied with medium, materiality, and intermedia hybridity today precisely because what we should ask is not what intermedia hybridity is but what it *was*, as intermedia is being swallowed by remediation? Or, as computer scientist Wolfgang Coy puts it, if "all written, optical, and electric media . . . will merge into one universal digital medium," then is "the concept of intermediality still tenable in the sense of an interaction between two technologically and materially different media?" ⁸ In their 2013 book, *Heterogeneous Objects: Intermedia and Photography after Modernism*, Pirenne and Streitberger assert that "most of the new voices within intermediality studies provide a positive answer": intermedia is still a viable concept.⁹ However, it is also apparent that intermediality will not emerge unchanged from its passage to, or through, the digital. For studies of intermediality, the advent and diffusion of digital technology signified a crisis as much as a reorientation:

> even though all media depend on one and the same universal code in the realm of the digital, they still may preserve their specific qualities and functions (the photographic, filmic, painterly, etc.) according to their use and appearance (Paech and Schroter, 2008: 11). From this point of view, media are not defined on the basis of their technological or material characteristics, but as 'multimedial communication devices (Rajewsky, 2002: 7) *that constantly shift, change, and reorganize themselves according to institutional social, and economic contexts for which they are produced, and in which they operate. Transformation is at the very heart of intermediality— not only on an aesthetic or technological level in artworks* (Spielmann, 2001: 61)*—but also in terms of 'dynamic intermedial networks' that should be studied to reflect their 'social and historical function' as processes* (Muller, 2010: 242).[10]

Whether or not we agree with every theorist's claim in this quote, it seems apparent that intermedia and the archive have much in common with Arendt's authority, including this: archives and their material mediums as we know them are partially disappearing, while their definitions, uses, and functions are being fundamentally displaced and altered. What *is* an archive is bound to elicit very different answers from what *was* an archive, particularly when we turn to the question of medium.

Archives, as some of us remember them, were a predominantly textual—but also visual, tactile, olfactory, and physical—experience. Some of the "allure" or "taste of the archive," to quote Arlette Farge's classic work, came from touching the myriad textures of paper or parchment, the occasional film, glass plate, or cloth, or from inhaling the ink, as well as the archival dust, which, as Carolyn Steedman reminds us in *Dust: The Archive and Cultural History*, is partly made of bits of other people's bodies, dead cells exfoliating and caught up in the manuscript they were once hunched over.[11] Many of us still experience archives this way, but there is also the unmistakable fact of their migration, their remediation to the digital medium.

In the midst of these dramatic shifts in the literal as well as discursive space that archives occupy in our culture, my call to remediate the archival revolution aims to bring attention to medium and to remediation as a process where revolution is inflected by disappearance, transformation, and uncharted potential. How can we think of the medium in the archive at a time when medium is, as Rosalind Krauss reminds us in "Art in the Post-Medium Condition," uncertain of survival? What does it mean to attend to the question of medium and remediation in the archive? In their influential book *Re-mediation: Understanding New Media*, Jay David Bolter and Richard Grusin define remediation as "the representation of one medium into another," and distinguish between different types of remediations.[12] They argue that what is "new about new media is the way they remediate older media," describing remediation as a process that has been under way for centuries (for example, early film remediated theater, literature, and various public entertainments). Archives are largely absent in Bolter and Grusin's *Remediation*, yet archival remediation is in full swing.

The very meaning of "archive" is being altered not just by the overlapping processes of digitization and declassification but also by the cross-pollination of scholarly, artistic, and curatorial practices loosely referred to as "the archival turn."[13] Engrossed in (typically textual) documents, scholars used to pay little mind to the archive itself. In recent decades, however, a diverse scholarly community has turned to archival texts, images, sounds, and silences. We have become more mindful of the archive itself, and more aware of our place within it. We don't just study in the archives; we turn the spotlight on their practices, assumptions, lacunae, and potentialities. This is the archival turn: the archive turned from taken-for-granted repository location of valuable contents into something new (and here the debates thrive)—a space, an exclusion, an experience—to be investigated, with growing awareness of the investigation itself. Attention has turned to what was long left out of official archives: "counter-archives, black boxes, the erased, the forgotten."[14] As a result, archives have acquired new epithets: spectral, invisible, diasporic, queer, decolonized, erased, redacted, and fabulated. Scholarship cannot take full credit for these new directions—indeed, many of these new understandings of archival pitfalls and potentials can be seen as the rich outgrowth of the "archival impulse" that Hal Foster identified and welcomed in contemporary art of the 1990s.[15] In his view, the archival impulse was also a productive turn away from a Foucauldian conception of the archive as a totality to be excavated.[16] Instead, contemporary art uses archives as construction sites and even creates new kinds of archives. Indeed, in recent decades much of the most innovative thinking about archives has originated in archival art and curatorial practices. Thus, at the end of this chapter I turn to contemporary artists who engage the same declassified archives for inspiration on attending to the intermedia aspects of the archives.

THE BANK HEIST CASE

On July 28, 1959, the Romanian National Bank was robbed in broad daylight by masked individuals carrying guns. At such a time and place, the bank heist must have seemed like something out of the movies. Even though Stalin had been dead for six years, de-Stalinization had not yet reached Romania. The secret police were busier than ever destroying the last remains of political opposition and pursuing crimes whose names were still neologisms, such as "undermining the social and economic order." "A smile, or even intonation," as a judge explained, had become crimes punishable by law.[17] An old-fashioned crime like a bank heist was completely out of place in this newly policed socialist society. The arrest of the suspects brought on a new shock. Even though, according to the police, they had used "the methods of American gangsters," the suspects were all Romanian citizens of Jewish descent. Furthermore, it turned out the five men and one woman had been communist cadres, even, as the secret police wrote in disbelief, "members of the repressive organs," some of whom had recently lost their positions due to a new wave of anti-Semitism. The guns they used had been stolen from the Ministry of Interior by one of the defendants, a former policeman who used his uniform as a disguise during the robbery. Within just a few months of the bank heist, the suspects were caught, judged, and sentenced. All sentences were speedily carried out: the men were shot and the sole woman defendant, Monica Sevianu, was sent to a women's prison—but not before all six prisoners were made to participate in a feature-length film reenacting their crime.

The Surveillance and Capture of the Suspects: The Film vs. the Files

The film, *Reenactment* (*Reconstituirea*, 1960), opens with a collection of old history books that slowly recede into the background.[18] These written records are in short order replaced by a close-up of a film camera, as the booming voice-over states that "this unprecedented objective record of history" gives us "live images that are identical to reality." After a triumphant cinematic review of the new socialist reality, we are abruptly taken to a trial.

Through point-of-view shots, the camera places the audience in tantalizing identification with a military judge, who starts leafing through the secret police file of the case. The file is presented in teasing close-up, yet the words on the page remain illegible. Instead, through a cinematic trick, we are presented with the title and credits of the film, superimposed over the cover of the file.

The perspective of the film and that of the secret police are explicitly linked as we are informed that the film was created by the documentary studio Sahia with the collaboration of the Ministry of Interior. This link becomes an identification in the next shot: as the hand of the judge thumbs through the files, the voice-over identifies with this hand matter-of-factly by telling the story of "these files that *we* are thumbing through" (emphasis mine). The cinematic trick that superimposes the credits of the film onto the binders of the secret police files seems to proclaim a relationship of seamless equivalence; it suggests that the film and files are interchangeable, with the credits framed between two shots of the files. The presence of the files recalls and questions the film's first pompous declaration, that today's camera replaces the written historical records of the past. Giving the lie to that declaration, the film does not replace written records fully but instead exchanges history books for secret police files. Indeed, the superimposition suggests that the film could be an adaptation of the secret police files. But how and why is a secret police file adapted or remediated into the medium of film?

The film's opening strongly affirms its authority as rooted in the collusion of the new documentary film image with the files that scripted it. My analysis instead plays these words and images against themselves and each other to uncover that collusion. I was fortunate enough to thumb through the files not only through cinematic identification with the military judge, but also on my own.[19] A close analysis of these files challenges any glib identification with the film and instead throws light on the fascinating, if entangled, relationships among the mediums they contain. Volume 18 contains a plethora of written documents pertaining to the movie, such as versions of the script and shooting directions.[20] These documents throw some light on the meaning of the "collaboration" between the filmmaking studio and the Ministry of Interior. It appears that the film originated in a "plan of action" drawn up by the Ministry.[21] The document starts by asking for one director and two cameramen, and then provides a rough draft of the script. A second plan of action revises the initial script, which had asked for the participation of the actual agents and the witnesses connected to the case, and adds the participation of the prisoners together with the genre of reenactment.[22] The first three scripts, which reveal a process of careful revision, give no credit to any author, while the fourth credits the Ministry of Interior.[23] The name of the film director does not appear in these documents; instead, each bears the Ministry of Interior's seal of approval. The last such note laconically states: "The recording of the film can begin."[24] Thus the Ministry of the Interior had the first and last word on the script.

The chronological beginnings of the case file already bring together an assortment of documents. A leaflet inviting the population to civil disobedience is used by the police to identify the bank heist as the beginning of a larger subversive movement.[25] Hand-drawn composite portraits put together descriptions of witnesses.[26] They show a vague likeness to their models, and a striking likeness to the mug shots. Despite the vagueness of these portraits, a witness's testimony did identify Igor Sevianu, Monica Sevianu's husband. Once they identified the suspect, the task of the police changed to characterization through surveillance. Igor Sevianu's *dosar de cadre*, the file kept on him at his former workplace, provides a schematic biography.[27] His first characterization by the secret police draws on this biography but complements it with information from "local sources," that is, neighbors. Synthesizing this information, the report concludes that "Sevianu has a standoffish attitude and is arrogant toward the proletariat, since he does not have friends in the neighborhood ... In her neighborhood [Monica Sevianu] is characterized as a reticent and arrogant person ... They are secretive people; this is apparent when neighbors ask their children for information."[28] Clearly hindered by the Sevianus' reticence, some of these neighbors/informers still managed to draw a rather intimate picture of the couple. We even find out that they ate mostly uncooked food, since Monica did not like to cook. Even though an early plan of the film devoted significant attention to the police's recruitment of an informer, and to his work thereafter, this sensitive topic was dropped in the final script.[29] The local informants and their intimate portrait of the Sevianus are absent from the film, which instead emphasizes the large informational network officially available to the police, including criminal and driving records. We are shown the agents after long hours of archival work being rewarded by the identification of the suspects.

In the case file, however, the intrusion of the police into the Sevianus' private lives is made graphically obvious in two sketches of their apartment.

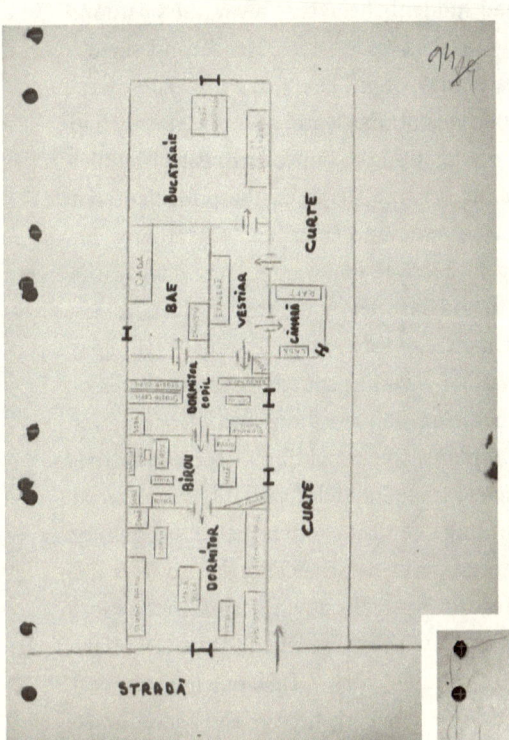

FIGURES 5A-B. Surveillance sketches of the suspects' apartment. P 181, 22:94, 98, ACNSAS.

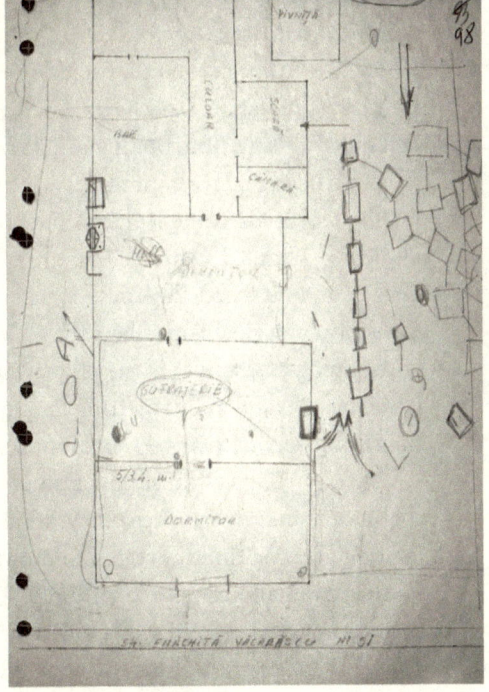

In the first image, as if the roof had suddenly been torn away, the positions of each chair and table are clearly marked and visible. The second sketch, more amateurish and approximate, may have been a draft, or the secret police may have relied once more on neighbors. Secret agents certainly had ample opportunity to check the information during covert visits. The files show that the moment the Sevianus became suspects, the police entered their house as well as their vacation suite and installed wiretapping devices.[30] The resulting wiretapping transcripts make up a large part of the files. Hidden from the Sevianus but laid bare before the reader, the wiretapping device defines the unique character of these texts. The reader plunges straight into the everyday intimacy of a young couple in the summer of 1959—their money worries, their bedroom conversations and silences, their political frustrations and vacation plans, their scolding of their children, and simply unqualifiable trivia. Every once in a while, an intriguing word appears—revolver, gun, money, hiding—but most often the sound quality is so poor that the transcriber cannot make out the context, and thus the significance, of those words. The recording breaks down or ends in the most awkward places: "Mr.: 'My child got sick with scarlet fever. (At this moment the gentleman asks the children to be quiet.) Mrs.: "Take out the revolver! (?) Mr. '. . . it was not found, right?' The tape ends here."[31] The surveillance transcripts reveal not just the presence and working of the device, but also, and mostly, its malfunctioning and breakdowns, often in the midst of the most intriguing conversations.[32] Static breaks down the transcript into unintelligible shreds. Sentences fade and break down as the Sevianus move out of the bug's limited radius.[33] Sometimes the couple switches to foreign languages, and this bares the limits of the writer, a provincial agent who needs the help of polyglot transcribers from the capital.[34] The defining mark of the wiretapping transcripts is the ellipsis, which stands for missing text, followed by question marks alerting the supervising agent to the transcriber's uncertainty about their version of the text.

The surveillance transcripts also contain alternative stories that resist the master narrative. Often, they are not even buried very deep; on the contrary, they at times threaten to drown out the police narrative. It takes all the power and complicity of writer and reader, that is, transcriber and investigator, to streamline this unruly material into an incriminating narrative. The film prunes this material even more, adapting it so that it can be shown to a general audience. In the film, there is no mention of wiretapping. This investigation method was at the same time too intrusive and too clumsy to be paraded before viewers. Instead, surveillance is represented by a policeman who smiles mischievously at the audience from under his street cleaner disguise. While collecting information, this jovial, clever fellow is also socially useful: he sweeps away the dirt from in front of the Sevianus' house together with the unpalatable image of wiretapping. Not only do the transcripts show too much of the investigation, they also show too much of the defendants. We get to know Monica Sevianu's dry, brilliant wit, her peculiar career plans involving the cultivation of mushrooms in her basement; Igor Sevianu's dreams of living a long, quiet life. The film, like the prosecutor's report, muffles the all-too-intimate and fuzzy picture of the transcripts behind the black-and-white mug shots of terrorists.

Interrogation Transcripts vs. Cellmate Informer Reports
On the day of the arrest, the file splits into two distinct accounts. The first of these is formed by interrogation records.[35] According to these records, the interrogations took place almost every day for about two weeks and then continued less intensely up to the trial. Each of the five suspects was usually interrogated independently, although a few "confrontations" were staged to bring together two or more of the accused. Interrogations routinely lasted for six hours, although some went as long as eleven. The records present a suspiciously neat narrative. Beginning with the first interrogation, the suspects told the story of their crimes, starting with failed attempts at robbing various state institutions and leading, in an evenly paced and strictly chronological order, to the bank heist, and up to the arrest. The detailed story took about two weeks of daily interrogations to unfold. According to the police records, each interrogation started with the invitation that the accused tell the story of their crimes; more often than not, the accused proceeded to describe their deeds in meticulous detail over the course of five to eight typed pages, often without any interruptions from the investigator. Their accounts are surprisingly similar, as individual differences in expression are muffled under the strong rhetoric of the police. For example, the accused refer to themselves as "terrorist group," "inveterate enemies of the regime," and to each other as "criminal elements," while designating the bank heist as "the criminal action targeting public property."[36] Their confessions regarding the bank heist are virtually interchangeable. However, when it comes to extraneous charges, such as plans for writing a book about

the heist or for assassinating Central Committee members who took a hard line against the Jewish population, there is a range of responses—some of the suspects implicating other acquaintances and some strongly denying the accusations, despite the duress they endured.[37] Partly for personal reasons that will become clear later in this chapter, and partly in line with this book's attempt to shed light on women's less studied presence in these hostile archives, I chose to focus on the interrogation and detention records of Monica Sevianu.

No film like *Rashomon* could be based on these strangely univocal interrogation records. However, a parallel account did run alongside them. Also started on the day of the arrest, a separate, voluminous file consists of daily informer's reports written by cellmates of the accused.[38] These cellmate reports were crucial for the investigation. After undergoing torture, Sevianu returned to her cell swearing that no matter how many times they tortured her, she would not divulge any secrets, out of loyalty to her friends.[39] Then she went on to divulge these very secrets to the cellmate, who immediately reported them to the investigator. The investigator then presented Sevianu with these revelations, pretending that they had been extracted from the other accused, who had also been mined for information by their cellmates. Seeing that their friends were collaborating with the police was extremely demoralizing for the accused, and convinced them that all their efforts to withstand torture were in vain.[40]

These informer reports were crucial in obtaining confessions. At the same time, they offhandedly exposed what lay behind the tidy narrative of the interrogations. Thus we learn that on 23 September,

> as a consequence of the second physical correction applied to her, Monica Sevianu returned to her cell with the definite intention of committing suicide as soon as possible . . . She told me among other things that they will not get anything more from her beyond what she already declared, no matter how many corrections will be applied to her. [She was] very tired and disconcerted, desiring death as a liberation.[41]

The interrogation file from 23 September is as deceivingly bland as any other.[42] According to this record, the investigator did nothing but open the discussion at eight in the morning with his usual, "Talk about your criminal activity," while she responded by speaking uninterrupted until two in the afternoon, for what amounts to five typed pages. From the cellmate reports, we learn that her abuse continued, so that on 21 October 1959, she is "spiritually broken" (*demontată sufletește*), "in a very bad mental and physical state. She refuses to eat, has insomnia, and is extremely intimidated by the atmosphere maintained by her interrogator."[43] The cellmate reports were instrumental in producing the confessions recorded in the interrogation files, but they also present us with alternative views of the interrogation, such as these proofs of the matter-of-course use of torture during interrogations, rare evidence filed within the secret police archives themselves.

Monica Sevianu's cellmate was an educated woman with good writing skills and a penchant for psychological analysis. The reports provide a detailed daily description of Sevianu's intellectual and emotional struggles. Unsure of the police's interests, the cellmate repeatedly asked them for concrete questions. However, in the absence of precise instructions, her reports cover what appears to be the entirety of her conversations with Sevianu, thus providing an extremely rich record of the latter's experiences. Prison memoirs of this era often bemoan the distance between the moment of writing and the moment of experiencing. Since "of course we had no pen and pencil in [Romanian communist] prisons," writers often feel that the immediacy of the experience is irretrievably lost.[44] The cellmate depositions provide the closest contemporary account of these extreme experiences.[45] While these reports are certainly not transparent accounts of the prisoners' experiences, they are probably the most revealing and gripping contents of the secret police files. Like the wiretapping transcripts, they plunge the reader into the often unguarded intimacy of the prisoner. Unlike the wiretapping transcripts, the cellmate accounts are not cluttered with trivia and fragments of conversations to be mined by the reader for a story. Instead, they present a discerning, in-depth description, based on well-plotted stories. And, unlike the interrogation reports, they provide a highly individualized picture of the prisoners, a detailed narrative of their shifting reactions, emotions, anxieties, and hopes.[46] It is here that we learn of Sevianu's passionate love for her husband, or of her plans to become a writer. Sevianu also had a tendency to mix fact and fiction for dramatic effect, thus claiming that she was the brain not only of the bank heist but also of a Jewish organization that spread throughout the country and aimed to undermine the government and "to steal even more money in order to feed all the starving Jews."[47] The informer reports transmit not only hard facts but also fantasies, aspirations, and self-justifications—contributing to a complex portrait of the subject.

Endings: The Files vs. the Film, Revisited

The last document of the investigation file was titled "Conclusions for the Prosecution."[48] Written by the chief investigator as a summary of the investigation, the "Conclusions" replaced the dozens of voices and hypotheses of the investigation files with a single authoritative story. The intended reader was the state prosecutor, whose stamp of approval dominates the first page of the "Conclusions."[49] The trial prosecutor's speech was not only, as expected, based on the investigator's work.[50] It virtually reiterated the "Conclusions," while adding the final blow: the request for the death sentence. Its close reading against the final script of the film reveals that it is this prosecutor's speech that the script of *Reenactment* faithfully mirrors.

Just like the film, the prosecutor's speech starts seemingly malapropos to a contemporary audience, but in a standard way for the time: by eulogizing the construction of socialism in Romania.[51] Against this bright background, the prosecutor introduces the despicable deeds of unidentified "isolated elements" that are attempting to undermine the new socialist order. The prosecutor then briefly introduces the "attack on the national bank" as one such crime against the people. The film follows this scenario by presenting a short reenactment of the crime that leaves out the identity of the perpetrators. These threatening, elusive criminals are then identified one by one, thanks to the work of the secret police: just as the film shows the identification of each criminal in turn, the prosecutor's narrative devotes a paragraph to each defendant.[52] Monica Sevianu's description singles her out from the others by presenting her as sexually promiscuous ("an adventuress and a woman of loose morals" [*o aventurieră și o destrăbălată*]); unrelated to any of the evidence, the accusation instead fits into a larger pattern of the secret police's treatment of women that we have already seen in Nina Cassian's file and which we will examine in more depth in the files of Herta Müller.[53] Once these quick and damning identifications are performed, both the film and the speech proceed to reconstruct the bank heist. And both the prosecutor and *Reenactment* end with a one-by-one presentation of the accused and their crimes before the court.[54]

Once the defendants enter the courtroom, the film no longer just reconstructs the events narrated in the file: it actually records them. For the first time in the movie, the prosecutor's speech is not a reconstructed scene but footage of the actual trial.[55] The hitherto disembodied, mysteriously authoritative voice-over is now revealed to be a mouthpiece for the prosecutor. As the latter is seen speaking, the voice-over quotes the prosecutor's presentation of the defendants, while shots of the reenactment are edited to match his descriptions. Thus *Reenactment* is revealed to be an illustration of the prosecutor's speech. After the montage of reenactments, the film cuts back to the prosecutor, a clear reminder of whose perspective we are following. Seamlessly, the voice-over melts into the prosecutor's voice as he blasts out the request for the death sentence. As he reads off the defendants' names, the camera obediently illustrates each with a close-up of a face. The prosecutor takes control not only of the prisoners' lives but also of the film.

The strong structural and literal parallels between the film and the prosecutor's speech reach a climax in the identification between voice-over and prosecutor. This moment recalls Alexander Medvedkin's dream about the camera's revolutionary role as a prosecutor.[56] But this is a revolution from above: the state's repressive arm, The Ministry of Interior, appropriates cinema for its own purposes, and cinema has little choice but to obediently play that role. If the film has superseded history books, it submissively bases its script on secret police files. Its adaptation of the files is, however, highly selective. The film follows one narrative in particular—the prosecutor's speech—and leaves out the bulk of the investigation files. By so doing, the film takes a convoluted story that is full of gaps and grounded in unclear motivations and replaces it with a reductive, black-and-white story where each detail serves as incriminating evidence. As a result, the defendants are stripped of any voice and ultimately become interchangeable as subhuman criminal elements. The files also reveal, often unwittingly, dirty investigation practices such as wiretapping and torture. The film, by contrast, not only sweeps away such unpalatable material but also unremittingly glamorizes the process of investigation.

The "cooperation" of the film studio with the Ministry of Interior was little more than servile complicity, as the film obediently ventriloquizes the prosecutor's voice. Helpless before the police, the film puts on a full show of power. It is one thing to catch and prosecute suspects, but it is quite another to have them put on a self-incriminating show in front of movie cameras. The film mustered all of its visual devices to capture the already arrested, helpless suspects and to coax and threaten the audience into accepting its interpretation of the events.

HISTORIES AND ETHICS OF RECEPTION

And yet, *Reenactment* was never released for public viewing. After several showings in front of a hand-picked audience of journalists and party members, the film was shelved and did not resurface until after the 1989 revolution, when Monica Sevianu's granddaughter, filmmaker Irene Lusztig, battled the reluctant Romanian Film Archives to unearth it.[57] There is no explanation for this perplexing decision to bury the film either in the twenty-seven volumes of files connected to the case or anywhere else in the Securitate archives I've searched.[58] Instead, in my most serendipitous archival find, I came across a possible reason for this decision in the Open Society Archives in Hungary. A short secret report prepared by an unnamed source for Radio Free Europe suggests that the reason was the carefully monitored audience reaction.[59] Knowing smiles were registered at the exits of the screening, and the emaciation of the protagonists was repeatedly noted.[60] Even this hand-picked audience misbehaved and misinterpreted. The secret police did not take any chances with the general audience; instead, they promptly censored themselves.

This record of the wry smiles of the hand-picked audience, buried in a forgotten archive file, suggests that the encounter of words, images, minds, and bodies, even if emaciated or saddled in a cinema seat, can collude to seal off what actually happened but can also exceed that carefully choreographed suture: that encounter can put a dent here or there, or maybe, who knows, even split the suture open for the length of a smile, or make it close into itself, like the film rolls of *Reenactment*, sulkily coiled in the canisters in which they had been shelved for half a century. Furthermore, this act of self-censorship boomeranged. As I have argued at greater length elsewhere, instead of being neutralized, this censored film became the repressed origin against which a new tradition of self-reflexive Romanian cinema was born and belatedly flourished. Even beside the three films made in direct response to the secret police movie, *Reenactment* cast long formative shadows over the development of Romanian cinema, from Lucian Pintilie's legendary *Reenactment* (1968) to Corneliu Porumboiu's *Police, Adjective* (2009).[61]

Yet I am afraid I cannot end on this happy note of audience resistance. At first sight, those smiles may seem to signify the audience's transformation from "ignoramuses invited to see people suffering," as Jacques Rancière describes the Platonic view of the spectator, into "emancipated" spectators who resist the places assigned to them and instead question the old dichotomy between active and passive viewing by engaging in viewing as an action.[62] Such an emancipated spectator "observes, selects, compares, and interprets. She links what she sees to a host of other things that she has seen on other stages, in other places. She participates in the performance by refashioning it in her own way—by drawing back, for example . . . They are thus both distant spectators and active interpreters of the spectacle offered to them."[63] It is true that the smiles of *Reenactment*'s audience suggest a certain distance from the spectacle and a refusal of the place assigned to the hand-picked spectator. They may even represent a certain critical distance toward the visual pedagogy that the secret police tried to inculcate by modeling the ways we look at others, through the eyes of the military judge, the prosecutor, or the documentary camera, that strip masks and identify enemies under the semblance of ordinary citizens.[64] Those smiles may even have been responsible for the film's censorship. Yet, I do not think they qualify as a sign of emancipated spectatorship. The smiles did take note of the accused in ways that the secret police did not intend, but the audience reaction to the emaciation and to the death sentences that end the movie is, to say the least, strange. The Radio Free Europe source explains that "the audience left the cinema looking at each other smilingly, because they knew the reality of the facts, which were different from those exposed in the film."[65]

I doubt it. In a manner quite common at the time, the audience indeed left thinking the facts were different from those presented in the film, and thought they knew the facts, yet they did not actually know them. Even the best informed members of the public, such as the Radio Free Europe sources, were in fact wildly misinformed, giving incomplete, fantastic, and contradictory reports. One report dated August 1959, written by an escaped political prisoner based on conversations with a secret police driver, could only muster a couple of sentences on such a top-interest story; what is more, even that very limited and tentative information turns out to have been wrong. The report states that the secret police believed there were three male bank robbers (rather than five), one of whom might have been a woman in disguise.[66] A longer report on the bank heist, dated January 1960, adds more fantasy than fact. It notes that "three men and one woman got out of an official car carrying film cameras."[67] Pretending to be making a film about the national bank, they asked "the bank workers to take certain positions, which the latter obediently did," while "the robbers left with the stolen money and the cameras."[68] One possible explanation for this fantastic story is that the informant took the filmed reenactment for the actual bank heist, or that somehow the reenactment and the original event got mixed up and blurred. The reenactment, this time the actual performance rather than the ensuing film, misfired once again when it was used by yet another Radio Free Europe source as proof that the suspects, apprehended while emerging from the police car for on-location filming, appeared "terrified and bent over, as a result of the beatings they had received."[69]

While seeing the emaciation, the smiling audience looked through these bodies. The Romanian phrase used in the report for "emaciated" is "foarte slăbiți" (very thin/weak); a more fitting synonym would have been "strǎvezii," which literally means "see-through." The smiling members of the audience saw through the protagonists, rather than seeing them. The audience's belief that they knew "the reality of the facts" only preserved and furthered the ignorance, as did the blanket superior smile that some put on in response to the representation of that reality in the movie. While the smiling audience did not fall into the trap of believing everything that was placed before their eyes, they did fall into the trap of distancing themselves from, and smiling at, everything they saw, including the emaciation. As a result, they could smile at the emaciated bodies as a giveaway of the secret police film rather than empathize with the people whose bodies they in fact saw through. Stuck in their defensive suspicion—it's all a show—they seemed unable to ever suspend their disbelief. Emancipated spectators, as Rancière reminds us, indeed suspend their disbelief, dissociate, and create a distance between their own interpretation of the spectacle and the lesson that the spectacle may want to teach. But they also preserve the ability to associate, to bridge that distance, to empathize. Emancipated spectatorship is "exercised by an unpredictable interplay of associations and dissociations."[70] Instead, in regard to the emaciation, the knowing smiles testify to a rigid dissociation that blunts both perception and judgment into one indiscriminate reaction.

I am critical of this indiscriminate reaction because it is not a thing of the past, when audiences were drastically limited in their spectating attitudes by censorship and surveillance. Instead, this generalized, smug suspicion is one of the two default contemporary reactions to the holdings of the secret police archives. This position may be preferable to the other default position—the belief in the unquestionable authority of the archives, which are often still taken at face value and given the power to alter lives and political careers without sufficient scrutiny. However, such generalized suspicion is also dangerous. The assumption that "these are all lies" too easily leads to the question, So why bother to read? and to the conclusion that it would be better to close the archives once and for all. This assumption also overlooks too much—sometimes the precious little—in these archives that calls for our discernment. In order both to see and to responsibly respond to what is loudly trumpeted and what is barely a trace of an absence—like the emaciation—we must go beyond such binary reactions. As reenactment scholar Katie King urges us, we can resist the use of reenactments as repetitions that desensitize us further to mediated experience by blunting our sensorium and instead turn them into participatory experiments in "learning" and "re-learning to be affected."[71]

The contemporary reactions to the movie, including the two documentary films made about it—*Reconstruction* and *The Great Communist Bank Robbery*—present a catalogue of motivations for the crime and for the defendants' participation in the movie.[72] In Monica Sevianu's case, contemporaries point to love for her husband, domestic abuse, desperation at anti-Semitic measures, political protest and hopes of drawing international attention, and youthful adventurism. The cellmate informer reports also give us some precious clues about these motivations. "After the reenactment of the attack, once returned to her cell, Monica Sevianu described in great detail and with the emphasis of a satisfied heroine the unfolding of the whole action. Her mood is exceptional and the thought of suicide completely deserted her ... The fact that she could see Igor and that she talked to him seems to have reawakened her power to fight."[73] We can also speculate about the temptation of walking out of a prison cell and back through the streets of one's city, or returning to one's house, or smoking a cigarette—all things that the prisoners did during the shooting of the movie. Monica Sevianu seems to have also been animated by "the firm conviction that the trial would be public, and that it would include the movie which will be shown to foreign journalists."[74] She further hoped that the movie would be shown at the United Nations, where it "would attract attention to the Jewish problem" in Romania and "lead to its urgent solution."[75] Yet I still do not think I can see the protagonists well enough through these compromised representations to confidently identify their motivations or paint their portraits. Instead, the more I worked on this case, the more I became convinced of the necessity of a basic first step in the interpretation of these materials: working against the carefully staged, long-lasting temptation to see *through* the subjects of these representations. This work requires undoing the multiple, overlapping illusions at play here—the transparency of the emaciated protagonists, the loudly trumpeted transparency of the secret police film, and the audience's deluded self-assurance that "they understand the reality of the facts."

Turning our attention to the friction points between mediums is one way of undoing these illusions. Reading the film against its evolving scripts and the other files connected to the case made it possible to identify the mysterious source of its authoritative voice-over in the prosecutor's indictment. The juxtaposition also allowed glimpses of other discarded, suppressed, or marginalized stories in early scripts, surveillance transcripts, and cellmate informer reports, stories that were trimmed in the final script of the movie. Most significantly, reading the cellmate informer reports against other case materials offered rare proof of the routine use of torture in interrogations; it also provided proof of torture's strategic cover-ups in interrogation records as well as in visual representations of the case. Knowledge of such cover-up strategies could raise red flags during our reading of other interrogation records in the usual absence of clearly documented torture. Furthermore, tracking the reactions to the bank heist case in Radio Free Europe archives exposed the film's lasting power over its protagonists and over the audience.

THE PHOTO ALBUMS

Among the twenty-seven volumes of the bank heist files, two immediately stand out as intermedia artifacts par excellence. Volume 14 calls our attention from the sea of gray binders with its burgundy cover. This is a commercial photo album turned file. Most glossy photo pages reproduce two production stills of the movie, with captions (some pages contain just one photograph). The original production stills and captions are saved, this time inside a volume whose folders look as gray as all of the others—volume 27, the very last volume of the file. No reason is given for this exact replication, for this repetition that poses the original a few volumes after its copy. I studied the photo albums in the archives at the same time as all the other twenty-five volumes, but it took an inordinate amount of time to receive digital copies, as if these most choreographed, hand-picked images of the film, made for public viewing were more sensitive to declassify than all the written texts— including the cellmate informer revelations of torture, the interrogation records, and the movie's anti-Semitic scripts. Maybe the present-day holders of the former Securitate archives intuitively know something about Walter Benjamin's concept of photography's optical unconscious, the idea that the photograph often captures more than the photographer intended.[76]

If the film was so tightly controlled and shaped by the secret police, its production stills would likely only be more so. After all, carefully selected and annotated production stills, arranged into a linear narrative in an album, or even two, would only further freeze the narrative that I tried to pry open by juxtaposing various versions of archival materials—script drafts, interrogation files and cellmate reports, or file marginalia. The production stills do offer the iconic moments of the film, from the perspective of the secret police, what they wanted to remember, what they felt was important to remember. For example, one of the main visual narratives of film, its quest for visual identification and obsession with masks and unmasking, is clearly represented there in the photos.

An examination of the first pages of volume 27 gives us a good sense of its aesthetics. The first page shows the suspects in medium shot with their backs to the camera, thus challenging identification, while the next page masterfully introduces the idea of masking. Captioned "Ioanid with false mustache together with Monica Sevianu at their surveillance post," the photo shows the two suspects ostensibly looking at each other. Besides the false mustache, which the caption makes sure the viewer does not miss, there are also Ioanid's sunglasses, another disguise, peeking out of his chest pocket. Monica Sevianu's face is not masked, but is turned in a three-quarter pose, so we cannot see it too well. Instead, the viewer's eye is captured by an uncanny mask in a shop window. Adding to the estranging effect of the mask is the position of the two protagonists. While they are ostensibly turned toward each other in studied, stiff, three-quarter poses, their gazes don't in fact intersect— the trajectories of their gazes do not lead to each other or to a common point in their midst but past each other. This is again explained by the caption—they are there "on surveillance" and thus are looking not at each other but at the surrounding environment. The composition reinforces the caption's message, as all lines move the vision centrifugally, creating a real tension with the ostensible orientation of the

FIGURE 6. Back shots of the suspects. P 181, vol. 27, f. 3:1, ACNSAS.

PAUL IOANID cu mustață falsă împreună cu
MONICA SEVIANU la postul lor de supraveghere.

FIGURE 7. "... at their surveillance post." P 181, vol. 27, f. 3:1, ACNSAS.

suspects' bodies. Thus the mask and the crutch in the shop window point to the left, while the angle of the street sign points to the right. In the middle, the striking black-and-white metal gridwork of the locked door behind the characters further thematizes the crisscrossing of their lines of vision. The secret police hired competent photographers, just as they hired competent filmmakers who caught on to the visual drama of the case in terms that the secret police favored—such as masking and unmasking, acting, identification, and surveillance.

But the photo album also contains this page, which rewards close observation: These two badly framed photographs are so satisfying because their poorly cropped margins reveal a secret that the film and the production stills worked hard to hide, after that initial show of self-reflexivity when the movie opens on a movie camera, which then disappears, leaving us with images of "live reality." The photos take apart the fantasy of the unmediated and uncoerced film, unwittingly revealing both the film camera and the guard as the (usually metaphorical but here very literal) pair they formed. In a world where the official image and text were so airbrushed, the challenge and the potential of the archive is that it sometimes contains, if not the truth, then at least some revealing words and images that were preserved in the archive by mistake or oversight. Additionally, the archive also at times preserves words and images that had been tried out, used, and discarded in the creation of the airbrushed record.

The archive sometimes holds such revealing artifacts, but what it holds more often are masses of artifacts in various mediums that can be played alongside and against each other as the context for a particular artifact in need of being estranged. The archive also can hold the various series out of which a "best shot" was selected. These series can suggest different narratives than that of the selected shot or of a whole movie like *Reenactment*. For example, the two almost identical photographs on the page shown above tell a whole story through their minor differences: while in the first photograph the suspects look at the camera, in the second they look away. In contrast to either of the two pictures taken separately, their sequence shows how the gazes were choreographed, with the visual address to the camera/spectator being edited out from the movie. The archive sometimes stammers through its repetitions, and while I share the natural impulse to get through with the reading of these overflowing files, attending to the archive's stammers can open up alternatives to its authoritative narratives.

FIGURE 8. Sequence of two photographs of suspects looking at the camera peeking out from behind a tree, while another man, likely a secret police guard, watches from behind. P 181, vol. 14, f. 11:1, ACNSAS.

Similar to the strategies of reading across textual and cinematic mediums that I have proposed—such as paying attention to repetitions and variations of the movie script drafts and the final cut—analysis of the production stills suggests kindred strategies, such as attending to archival stammers, tracking the cuttings of the airbrushed record, and looking in the out-of-focus margins rather than in the focused center.

ARTISTIC MODELS OF ENGAGEMENT WITH THE SECRET POLICE ARCHIVES

I might have easily missed the poorly cropped margins in the kind of perusing that files measured in kilometers numb you to performing had I not spent the previous day at the Bucharest National Museum for Contemporary Art. On show was a retrospective of subReal, the Romanian art group formed of Iosif Király and Călin Dan that since the 1990s had engaged in a series of artistic endeavors, such as the Art History Project, meant to "exploit the oppressive fascination of data and to play with the magic of authority surrounding the Archives."[77] The root of their projects was also a discarded archive: 600 kg of photographs and negatives constituting the archive of the magazine *Arta*. According to the artists, the images were saved from being insipid reproductions by their "generously wrong" framing. The photographed art turned out to be just a centered detail, while around it emerged people, gestures, and objects meant to have been edited out of the final image. "Cropping was the standard procedure for cleaning the surrounding mess in the pre-printing phase." The artists then decided that "their part"—or, less modestly, their art—was "to do a *counter-cropping* and *edit the negatives like movies*, by cutting the predictable parts and enlarging the "messy" details."[78]

Counter-cropping and enlargement of messy details are exactly the mental strategies that we need to perform in processing the two *Reenactment* production stills, if we are to reveal their secrets: the uncropped camera in the margin of the image and the minute face of the background figure (behind the left shoulder of the shorter suspect, in the lower photograph on the page) inadvertently caught on camera. Another strategy gleaned from artists' engagement with the visual materials from the Securitate archives in another exhibit, *Second Life in Communism* (*Platforma, MNAC ANEXA May 2012*), is recontextualizing, by bringing in other images, either new,

FIGURE 9. SubReal, *Serving Art 1*. Black-and-white print of a negative from *Arta* magazine archive. Reprinted by permission of Iosif Király.

FIGURE 10. SubReal, *Five Suitcases*. Reprinted by permission of Iosif Király.

FIGURE 11. SubReal, *Serving Art 2*. Photo installation detail, Romanian Pavilion, 48th Venice Biennale, 1999. Reprinted by permission of Iosif Király.

like Google views and maps, or period images and objects, like surveillance manual maps, frames, and postcards. Related strategies involve abstracting, marking, and indexing the image, as well as reframing or retouching it.

In *Parallel Archives*, Bogdan Bordeianu, Simona Dumitriu, and Iosif Király juxtapose a found archive of postcards from the 1970s and 1980s with Securitate surveillance pictures from that same period. To me, the addition of the postcard archive seemed unnecessary: postcards, intercepted by mail censors before reaching their destination, actually abound in Securitate archives, their blue skies periodically interrupting the gray of the files. Indeed, the secret police archives already contain many parallel archives within their holdings: family photos, letters, literary manuscripts, subversive writings. They even contain the estranging juxtapositions, the collage effect of the colorful postcards alongside black-and-white photos. It's just that most of the time we don't pay attention to these juxtapositions, and to the many different archives embedded in the secret police archive. The overarching structure of the archive, hand in hand with rigid disciplinary training, does its best to muffle archival hybridity. Projects like *Parallel Archives* or *Art History Archive* retrain our vision and attention so that we can let ourselves see not just new juxtapositions but also what was always already there, which sometimes means letting ourselves be distracted from reading to watch in other ways. This does not always come easily, especially if reading is what one has been trained to do and what one meant to do in the archive in the first place; or when the cases are so convoluted that one struggles to follow and decipher the plot—who betrayed whom and for what reason. However, reading for plot is problematic here, as it often requires participation in the writer's logic, and thus a complicity in the way things

FIGURE 12. Iosif Király, *Open Skies. Revisiting Public Space*. Digital montage. Reprinted by permission of Iosif Király.

end up, which is too often dismally. So this is where I found artistic meditations and practices around archives—like subReal's practice of looking at a still image cinematically, through counter-cropping and enlarging the detail, truly inspirational, while remaining committed to close-reading a file that I had been commanded in the opening of *Reenactment* to watch like an illegible image.

Contemporary art theory and practice allow us a glimpse into what we can gain when we move past *reading* the various mediums of the archives and try instead to attend to their particular visual and/or hybrid nature. Is "attending"—a word that emphasizes the act of attention to the demands of the archive, maybe even as an act of care—a better word for what we do in the archives than "reading"? I think sometimes it is; but sometimes these hostile archives also fully deserve the practice of "messing with archives" developed by Terri Francis. A film scholar and the former director of the Black Film Center/Archive at Indiana University, Francis takes advantage of the unprecedented freedom to manipulate previously untouchable, now digitized, archival material to weave together different stories, and to ponder different subject positions. Rather than advocating one approach over another, I pointed to a range of such possible approaches to visual and intermedia archival material, not because everything goes, but because the hybridity of the archives requires a carefully calibrated hybridity of research methods.[79]

The most moving artistic engagement with the bank heist story manages both to powerfully attend to its archive and to mess with it. *Reconstruction* (2001) is a documentary movie by Irene Lusztig, a filmmaker whose career has been marked by a productive fascination with archives. Lusztig's engagement with this particular archive is also deeply personal, as she is Monica Sevianu's granddaughter. Her *Reconstruction* reappropriates much of the footage from the secret police *Reenactment* and artfully juxtaposes it with materials from the secret police file and family archives, as well as interviews with contemporary witnesses. These range from family members and friends to old neighbors, Sevianu's prison cellmates, and even one member of *Reenactment*'s 1959 film crew.[80] Lusztig's original goal was to make her own cinematic reconstruction of the bank heist, investigating contemporary traces of the controversial events with a focus on the enigmatic figure of her grandmother.

This contemporary investigation unearths no definitive truths but rather a variety of memories, reactions, and interpretations of the events. This dissonant, often jarring, range of memories and interpretations is also visible at the conclusion of another documentary film about the bank heist, Alexander Solomon's *The Great Romanian Bank Robbery*, which ends with the documentary's talking heads watching and debating the documentary they had been part of. Yet Lusztig goes far beyond making space for a diversity of participant and spectatorial positions. While in Solomon's film each participant holds on to their partial, often self-interested, version of the story, the rare achievement of Lusztig's cinematic experiment is that she makes space for her participants, for her audience, and, amazingly, for herself to shift positions, to evolve, to learn—about the story and about themselves. This involves letting go of both the official audience reaction as scripted by the secret police film and the presumption that "the audience knew the reality of the facts, which were different than the ones being presented." Indeed, Lusztig's *Reconstruction* showcases and performs a whole range of shifting interpretive positions, thus inviting its own spectators to engage with the film beyond the rigid binary of audience compliance or dissent.

Lusztig employs a nuanced arsenal of self-reflexive, experimental personal documentary strategies to quote, appropriate, unsettle, and at times crack open the original secret police *Reenactment*. To me the most salient and inspirational model of engagement with hostile archives is her remediation of the scene of her grandmother's arrest. Lusztig's movie replays at four key moments the secret police sequence of her grandmother climbing the stairs to her apartment door, where four agents arrest her and then escort her down the stairs. Lusztig repeatedly remediates this original scene by slowing it down and modifying the soundtrack, with the result that the four repeated scenes differ notably through changes in the tempo of the slowdown and audio-visual juxtapositions.

The arrest scene is introduced at the beginning of Lusztig's film, illustrating an interview with Miki Lusztig, Monica Sevianu's daughter and the filmmaker's mother. She comments, as the secret police sequence plays, that she remembers little of her mother, and that if in fact there is a part of her that remembers, she is not in touch with it. The original image of Sevianu's climbing and descending the stairs is slightly slowed down, while Miki Lusztig's voice and an accentuation of Sevianu's footsteps replace the original suspenseful music. We catch a fleeting glimpse of the movie's heroine as she climbs the stairs, and hope for a different angle during the descent,

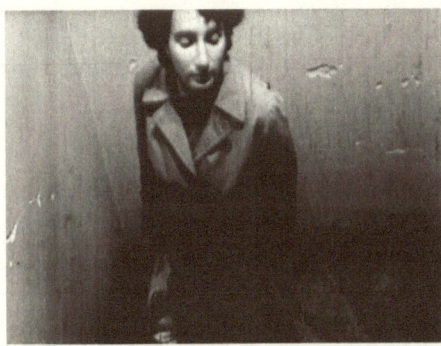 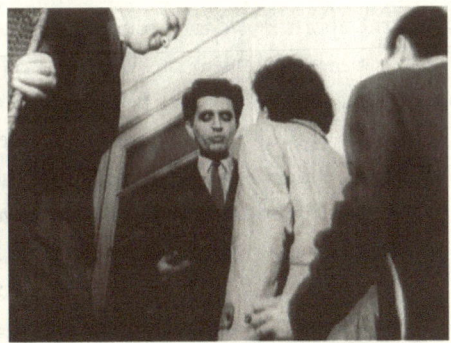

FIGURES 13A-B. Arrest scene. Image from *Reconstruction* (2001), directed by Irene Lusztig.

but her figure is eclipsed by two agents who interpose themselves between her and the camera, so that the scene intrigues more than it satisfies our curiosity. The second time the arrest sequence appears, it plays at the original speed accompanied by the original music, superimposed with a critique of Monica Sevianu delivered by her sister, who notes Sevianu's desire to be original and her disdain of petty bourgeois life. Not much insight is gained into her character, other than her isolation from even her closest family and their agreement with the state's harsh judgment of her crime.

It takes more than half of the movie for the third remediation to literally open up the original secret police sequence, allowing us an unforgettable view into the extradiegetic space of the scene that remains behind the closed apartment door. This time, the arrest sequence is more radically slowed down, as Miki Lusztig tells the story of the arrest from her perspective as a fourteen-year-old. We learn that about an hour before Monica Sevianu walked home and to her arrest, her daughter Miki had returned from school. When Miki rang the bell, the door was unbolted by men pointing guns at her and threatening to shoot if she and her little brother did not stop crying. After an hour's wait, Monica Sevianu was heard climbing the stairs. She was promptly arrested, her hands tied (a detail omitted in *Reenactment*), and carried off. While her mother would reenact her last walk home in front of secret police cameras, Miki's walk home that day was the last of her childhood, not only because she was adopted by her aunt and moved to a different home, but also because "that was the end of a sort of childhood." Coming more than halfway through the movie, her interview dramatically opens the very background against which the arrest sequence was filmed—

the apartment door—offering us a new view of Sevianu, as "a wonderful mother—as long as she was there." We now see her disappearance from the perspective of her terrified children, and we begin to contemplate the consequences of her absence, an absence that still resonates in their own and their children's lives, all the way to the present, more than sixty years later.

During this replaying of the slowed-down scene, Miki affirms that she remembers vividly "every detail of the day of the arrest—colors, images, smells, noises," in sharp contrast to her first interview in which she affirmed the absence of memories of her mother. She, and the audience through her, have traveled a long distance. We are more than halfway through the film, a film whose making had already brought her back to Romania and to her childhood home after more than thirty years abroad. It appears unlikely that she would have confronted her recurring nightmare of looking for her childhood home had her daughter not decided to move to Romania and make a movie about her maternal grandmother. Miki Lusztig's trip, like her interviews, seems at best ambivalently rooted in the desire to revisit the past; instead, they wholeheartedly engage with and support her daughter's quest—no matter the literal and emotional distances.

Lusztig, however, does not end her remediations of the arrest scene with this powerful revelation. In the last reworking of Monica's ascent of the stairs, Lusztig zooms in on the image of her grandmother's face. While at first the zooming indeed allows a closer view of her face, it slowly disintegrates the original image, until only grains of black and white remain, Sevianu's eye a patch of darkness against the lighter background of her face.

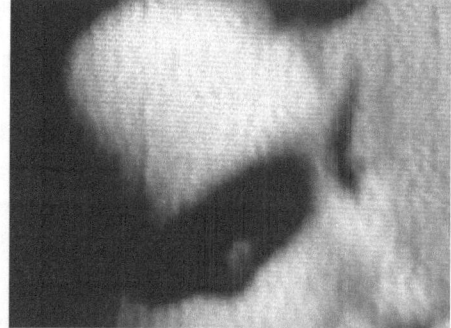

FIGURES 14A-B. Remediated arrest scene. Image from *Reconstruction* (2001), directed by Irene Lusztig.

Lusztig reaches here a different ending of her engagement with the secret police image of her grandmother. At the end of all the slowing down, replaying, and zooming in, the image does not allow any ultimate insight into Sevianu but instead is made to reveal its own materiality as a medium, a piece of celluloid whose repeated digital remediations reveal it to be anything but what the secret police *Reenactment* claimed documentary film to be, "transparent and identical to reality."

If the film remains haunted by the grandmother's absence, it is brought to life by the mother's powerful presence before her daughter's camera. The movie progresses because of Miki Lusztig's ability to move from her initial reluctance "to remember her mother or to connect to the part of herself that remembers her mother" towards her final interview, when she confesses having reached a new attitude toward her mother in the process of helping her daughter with the making of the film. Even a brief analysis of the arrest sequence remediations reveals how this intergenerational collaboration manages to open up not just fissures but whole new dimensions outside of the secret police narrative. Together, mother and daughter manage to remediate the hostile images of Monica Sevianu by reminding themselves and each other, in the sense both of bringing back an array of memories and of retraining their own—and, in the process, our—ways of remembering, watching, listening, and asking questions.

Lusztig's artistic remediation of the secret police film transforms the scene of her grandmother's double capture—by the secret police and by the camera—into an act of searching for her grandmother and an act of mutual care between herself and her mother. I am grateful to *Reconstruction* for all these layers that it added to the secret police film sequence. The remediation of the arrest scene made it impossible for me to watch even the original secret police film as a proof that this woman "did not deserve the title of human being," and opened up ways to seeing her other-wise. I am grateful also for my difficulty in keeping the mothers, grandmother, and daughters straight while writing these paragraphs. This difficulty is rooted in Lusztig's artistic and ethical tapping of cinema's potential to disturb temporal continuity. In the process, a granddaughter deprived of her grandmother's presence becomes the caretaker of her grandmother's image, while giving her own aging mother, who was deprived of Sevianu's motherly presence as a child, the cinematic gift of following in her mother's footsteps as Sevianu climbs the stairs not for the last time, but again, and again, and again. Every time Lusztig's film plays, the reenacted secret police film sequence that was meant to freeze a punishing version of the past is replayed and repurposed in an unfolding present.

I am particularly grateful that I saw *Reconstruction* just as I was starting my own work in the secret police archives. Lusztig shared with me copies of the bank heist case files that she had obtained as a family member before researchers were allowed into the Romanian secret police archives. I was fortunate to watch the 2001 premiere of her film with a deep awareness of both Lusztig's and her mother's bodily presences close to me in the movie theater. That awareness of the real resonances of these documents in the fabric of their very being has served as a precious antidote against the ways these hostile archives frame our reading experience. That awareness was a great responsibility and a gift that has kept on giving over the subsequent decades of tackling hostile archives that radically disembody and dehumanize their subjects in part by desensitizing the reader.

The artists surveyed here model a variety of ways of engaging with and remediating secret police archives. Their experiments in remediation affect not just the secret police materials themselves but also our modes of seeing, listening, remembering, questioning, and carrying on the conversation. We learn to attend to backgrounds and margins over the foreground, to the seams and tension points where mediums come together, to the bodies on the screen and in the archive, cinema, and our own homes. As such, these artistic engagements with the Securitate archives help us move closer to Jacques Rancière's ideal of emancipated spectatorship as "exercised by an unpredictable interplay of associations and dissociations."[81] Ranging widely between critical disbelief and empathy, such emancipated spectatorship is particularly necessary when propaganda is ventriloquized through an emaciated body.

THE MOST OVERLOOKED ARCHIVAL MEDIUM

The crowdsourcing exercise described at the beginnning of this chapter never fails to produce dozens of archival mediums, but my audiences always forget to mention one: ourselves. Yet we may soon be the last analog medium left in the archive, and the one on which the whole question of intermedia hybridity hangs. For if our encounter with the past *can* be mediated through paper and textile and painting and photographs, it *is* and always *will be* mediated through our sensorium. In attending to the intermedia challenges of the archives, we unlock our potential as sophisticated mediums deeply immersed in the processes of archival mediation and remediation.

At the present moment, calling ourselves sophisticated archival mediums may be wishful thinking. In fact, if we were to take the time to scrutinize our performance as mediums and remediators, we may find that often, especially during long archival research hours, we work as remediation filters or, to put it more plainly, as remediation censors. We filter out the input of mixed media and intermedia material, letting in mostly written messages, parts of which we scribble down. Furthermore, this rather censorious remediation goes on not only in regard to external stimuli such as the research material directly in front of us, which may contain information of a visual, haptic, or olfactory nature; we also filter out a wide variety of internal stimuli—memories and affects triggered by the research material, such as bodily discomfort or hunger, which we may guiltily compare and contrast with the experiences of the files' subjects.

Reading has long reduced the intermedia potential of the archive to the hegemonic dominance of one medium. Historically, that dominant medium has been text, with the digital currently breathing down its neck. Yet the archive fulfills its intermedia potential only when we carefully attend to it. Furthermore, attending to the intermedia potential of the archive has transformational potential not just for the archives but also for us. As we deliberately turn on more parts of our sensorium to attend to the archive—its visual and auditory layers, its taste, its traces of differently mediated humanity—we enrich that sensorium. Like literature, the archive has the potential to expand our sensorium, to train or numb our attention, to quicken our pulse, to plunge us into dilations and compressions of time from document to document, page to page. Unlike literature, however, the archive does a significant part of this work through the shift in its material supports—crinkly paper fragments, oversized maps, traces of ink, and photographs. Different temporalities and provenances are materially marked. Their differences are usually first signaled through a change in material form rather than content. The medium hybridity of the archive reaches out to our brains through the many different parts of our sensorium. This is in line with research on cognition and reading, which shows that the average person's brain is multisensory and that the way we make sense is by integrating the senses continually, whether we are aware of it or not.[82] Thinking of the archival encounter as an intermedia encounter opens the field for a hermeneutics that does justice "to the whole of the work in our [variously mediated] relations to it."[83]

Extending Bolter and Grusin's insight that a new medium is that which remediates older media, we can conceive of ourselves as new archival mediums in the process of remediating the many older mediums we encounter in the archive.[84] In *Performing Manuscripts*, Elizabeth Eva Leach explains how a book, depending on its reader, can go beyond its status as a visual object and become a sonic one—"at least in interaction with the memory of a reader with suitable knowledge."[85] In *The Ancient Phonograph*, Shane Butler sees readers as "media players" whose minds "play back" both the human voices and the nonlinguistic sounds encoded in ancient manuscripts.[86]

Going back in time, the idea of the human body as a medium is as old as performance, and forms the basis of performance studies. So it is not surprising that it took a performance studies scholar to go beyond thinking of the body as a medium of performance to the body as an archival medium, even to the point of equivalence between body and archive. André Lepecki concludes his theoretical introduction of "The Body as Archive" thus: "In dance reenactments there will be no distinction left between archive and body. The body is archive and archive a body."[87] Shannon Jackson, another performer and performance studies scholar, brought the benefits of this attention to the body into discussions of archival work. In her preface to her work in the archives of the Chicago Hull-House Settlement, Jackson affirms her "animating belief that the skills of the performer—her navigation of sightlines, props, and blocking—can be expanded to understand the intimate mediation of visuality, material culture, and embodiment" that she finds in archival work.[88] In their "Turning Archival," Daniel Marshall and Zeb Tortorici informatively outline the significant contributions of queer as well as critical disability or crip studies to reshaping our understanding of archival labor through notions of embodiment and questions of access.[89] In the context of secret police archives, James Kapaló has convincingly argued that "in order for the texts and images in the archives to speak fully of the complexity of lived realities, we need to take special care, and intentional methodological steps, so as not to disembody the characters and past lives we encounter in the archives."[90] Kapaló cites David Morgan's call for foregrounding "images, emotions, sensations, spaces, food, dress or the material practices of putting the body to work."[91] He adds: "Each of these traces of course potentially could be fabricated or distorted, but through their totality, multi-vocality and complexity (Verdery 2014, 42), and their materiality, they carry the potential to reveal much more than they distort if we approach them as records of performed, embodied action."[92] This call to attend to the embodied experiences recorded in the archive clearly differs from Lepecki's conception of the body as archive or from Jackson's attention to the embodied aspects of archival work. It is important to attend to the differences as well as the reinforcing effects and potential of this attention to embodiment on all sides of the archival encounter. So let us follow Jackson in considering the embodiment of the archival reader, which will eventually lead us back to the embodiment of the archived subjects.

Jackson starts her archival investigation the way we all begin work in the archive, with the physical act of sitting, except that she actually writes about it. She writes about sitting at length, for the whole long first paragraph of her tour-de-force introduction, entitled "Theorizing":

> Daily I sit before a microfiche machine perched on cement-colored formica in a fluorescent-lit room, looking at reels of copied archives in the Special Collections at the University of Illinois Library... The only break from the glare of the screen is the wall of corkboard behind it, which, before I know it, appears to expand, move forward, and close in on me. I shift in my chair; my body feels slightly stiff.[93]

These minute observations on the bodily experience of archival work occupy the entire first page, followed by just two taut lines: "Sitting, writes Elaine Scarry, is controlled discomfort. Thinking, I write, involves an awful lot of sitting."[94] Next, Jackson weaves a beautiful meditation on an archived letter about a woman's swollen feet, which recalls the researcher's own numbed legs, and Walter Benjamin's privileging of such moments when the "historian finds her view to the past interrupted by the sensuous self-recognition of the present."[95] Jackson concludes: "Callused fingers, numb limbs, and swollen feet are all quite literal reminders of the bodily basis of research... For me, the sentient recall of Benjamin's 'dialectical image' seems a prerequisite to writing a history of performance; at the same time, its shock to historical continuum helps me understand the performance of history." As such "imagery moves from the archive to less benign historical resemblances," Jackson hopes to dramatize the social stakes "of not attending to the safety of the dead." In so doing, she answers Benjamin's call for "the historian who will have the gift of fanning the spark of hope in the past," the one who is aware "that even the dead will not be safe from the enemy if he wins."[96] This erasure of the dead—and even of their memory—that Benjamin and then Agamben wrote about in relationship to the Nazis can be the literal destruction of the record. However, more often, and more insidiously, it is performed in the creation of archives, such as the secret police archives, which desensitize readers to the destruction they record.

The stakes of conceiving of the researcher as embodied medium are suddenly very high, and especially so in hostile archives that contain toxic materials as well as criminal silences whose power can be easily manipulated but also positively activated by contemporary readings. Here I borrow the concept of activation of the archive from the performance theorist Diana Taylor. Her landmark book, *The Archive and the Repertoire*, reveals ways in which dominant archives can be subversively activated through embodied practices of reception and protest. She gives the example of photographs of disappeared persons being taken from a police archive and movingly recontextualized as part of an art exhibit by the sons and daughters of those killed.[97] Another example is the use of photographs of disappeared sons and daughters during protests by the Madres de Plaza de Mayo movement in Argentina:

> When the madres took to the streets to make the disappearances visible they activated the photographs, performed them. By wearing the small photo IDs around their necks, the madres turned their bodies into archives, preserving and displaying the images that had been targeted for erasure. Instead of the body in the archive associated with surveillance and police strategies, they staged the archive in/on the body, affirming that embodied performance could make visible that which had been purged from the archive.[98]

With characteristic economy of means, Irene Lusztig performs a similarly powerful embodied counteractivation of archival images and silences. She first reproduces *Reenactment*'s climactic scene of Igor Sevianu's identification by a witness who pulls out his photograph from a table covered with photographs of suspects. Then she reenacts it, with a significant difference, by pulling one photograph from a collection of her grandmother's family photos, some of which had been appropriated by the police.

FIGURE 15A. Identification scene of Igor Sevianu. Screenshot from *Reenactment* (1959).

FIGURE 15B. Irene Lusztig. Image from *Reconstruction* (2001), directed by Irene Lusztig.

Lusztig ends the scene by holding a photograph of her grandmother, which stands out through her direct inquisitive look at the camera and through the fold that conspicuously splits the photo into unequal halves. The fold is the material trace left by the way this image had been handled; it identifies this as the beloved image of her mother that Miki Lusztig had carried in her wallet for years. This new act of selecting, holding, carrying, and caring for the image is framed in direct contrast to the police's use of the image for identifying and capturing its subject.

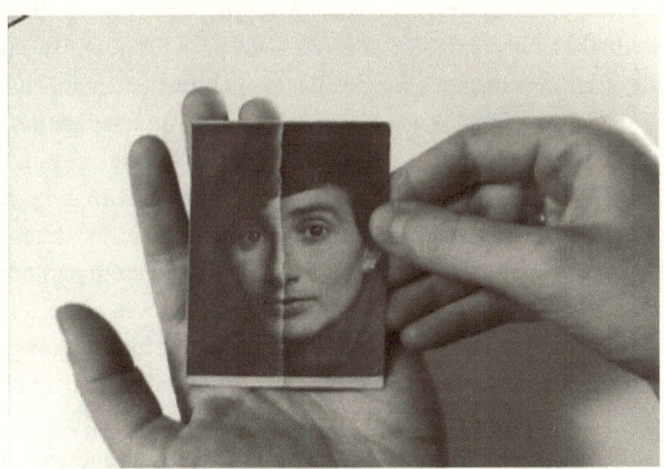

FIGURE 16. Irene Lusztig holding her grandmother's photograph. Image from *Reconstruction* (2001), directed by Irene Lusztig.

Lusztig thus reinserts the image of her grandmother, which the police had both literally and figuratively captured, into a different chain of images and image practices, which the designer of this book's cover has now evocatively added to. In Lusztig's *Reconstruction*, we are shown photographs of Monica Sevianu holding her daughter, and in time, for brief precious moments, her granddaughter, the present-day filmmaker. As a result of these remediations, by the time we see Monica Sevianu's image cradled in her granddaughter's hand, we experience it as a rare illustration of Benjamin's "dialectical image" that "gives a shock to historical continuum," by offering us "a view to the past interrupted by the sensuous self-recognition of the present."[99]

CONCLUSION

This chapter built on scholarly and artistic attempts to "re-mind" ourselves of our own potential as embodied mediums in the archival encounter and to develop new modes of attending to and messing with the archives.[100] Paying attention to the intermedia character of these archives is one way of recuperating archival hybridity. This is important so that we don't further disembody subjects such as Monica and Igor Sevianu, who were rendered "see-through" by a combination of strategies that ranged from hunger and beatings to wiretapping, interrogations, recording, filming, and archiving. This resistance to disembodying the archival subjects is predicated on our own embodied archival presence. Once we assume our position as embodied mediums in the archival encounter, we radically open the intermedia potential of any such encounter. Most case files do not bring together such a wide array of mediums as that mustered by the bank heist investigation. Even when all we have is a bare-bones archival text, the archival encounter has the potential of an intermedia encounter between at least two differentially mediated subjects—the archived subject and the present-day interpreter. Usually, there is a crowd—even in personal files there are traces of many different archived and archiving subjects. Thankfully, even if the act of archival reading can seem in itself a lonely enterprise, the interpretive work of scholars, artists, and survivors provides inspiration and moving reminders of the potentials of remediating the archival encounter, starting with our own reading positions. This inspiration is precious because to truly remediate the archival revolution, we must remediate our own reading practices.

THREE

Fictions

Literary Guides to Reading in the Secret Police Archives

In researching the secret police files of Herta Müller and other German-language writers from Romania, I was struck by the extensive presence of *fiction* within the files. Partly because the investigators could not read the incriminated books in the original but had phrases or even whole stories translated from German into Romanian and then inserted within longer investigation records, these files teem with fiction. Once attentive to its presence, I discovered a genuine fiction fixation on the part of the police. Besides the infamous fictions spun by disinformation departments, we also find literary fictions within investigation files, as well as in secret libraries where confiscated manuscripts and published novels were kept.[1] This chapter explores the phenomenon of fiction in the archives and, more precisely, the fiction nested inside the document. It considers the disinformation campaign that created a fictional informer doppelgänger for Herta Müller and focuses at length on the presence of her literary fiction inside her secret police files. My wording intentionally recalls Natalie Zemon Davis's classic work, *Fiction in the Archives*. My first book, *Police Aesthetics*, was already indebted to Davis's seminal insight—that archival documents can be valuable beyond their truth-value (or lack thereof) when read *like* fiction, with attention paid to their narrative and rhetorical devices. This chapter reverses the terms of Davis's argument and inquires into the archival drive to incorporate actual fiction within the document—and further to *read actual fiction like a document*. Close-reading Müller's fictional short stories against their immediate context—the file they were incorporated in—I find that these arrested fictions have much to teach us about reading in the archives. Reversing the direction of the inquiry, I also attempt to understand what is to be learned about literature when reading it in this strange, and estranging, context of the files.

Like many of the heterogeneous holdings of the archives, literary fictions were confiscated, copied, if necessary translated, excerpted, and then incorporated as incriminating evidence. Close-reading the literary fiction within the file questions its forceful incorporation and the original hierarchy that places fiction as the document's appendage within the file. Furthermore, rather than just extracting the nuggets of fiction from the archive, I wonder if we can rethink the archive through the prism of the fictions it contains. To do so, we need to become attentive to the ways fictions of all kinds haunt the archive, sometimes participating in its master narrative and sometimes unsettling it. This chapter attempts to move in this direction through a focus on Müller's secret police archives alongside her autobiographical writings.[2]

The Romanian Securitate opened Müller's personal investigation file (Dosar de Urmărire informativă, or DUI) in 1983 under the code name "Cristina." The file contains almost six hundred folios divided among three volumes.[3] Opening the file, we find that the piece of paper that bears the mark "page one" was, not uncommonly, written long after the file had been started. If one is intent on finding beginnings, the chronological beginning could seem like a more straightforward place to start than "page one." Most file pages are carefully dated, so one can with relative ease find the page that bears the earliest date in the file, even if it was not bound as the first page. Upon closer inspection, however, one often discovers that the chronological origin of the file is a copy, rather than an original. The page that bears that first date is often copied from a different file—someone else's file, where the protagonist of our file might have appeared as a more or less fleeting presence. Or the beginning could be a copy from an original still in the "problem file," such as the file on the German minority in Romania, where our protagonist appeared episodically as part of a much larger group. A file starts many times, as if one were reading the unfinished manuscript of a novel where the author has still not chosen one beginning out of the few drafted versions. However, unlike the case of a manuscript, a file's various beginnings often have different authors. The first pages of "Cristina's" file introduce us to a variety of writers—investigators, archivists, informers, sometimes even the subject herself.

The reader may reject all these tangled, incomplete, competing beginnings, as Müller herself does, and instead posit a missing beginning. And yet, to make some sense of the file, the reader usually chooses one of the available beginnings, however imperfect, over others. Whether conscious or not, this heuristic choice makes it possible to get past the first few confusing pages, and keep reading. The choice of a beginning also reveals a lot about the reader, their view of the files, and their interpretative strategies. William Totok— an Aktionsgruppe Banat member whom the Securitate followed at this time, and a writer who has been singularly dedicated to studying and exposing the declassified files—settles on one beginning for Müller's file. It is a particularly vitriolic early informer's report on her prose that concludes with the sentence: "Criticism, and more criticism, such destructive criticism, that you ask yourself, what's the use of these texts?!"[4] Totok's decision has its advantages. As in any good drama, the story starts with an intrigue, woven by a person who in this case even hides under a false name. Had this person not been, suggests Totok, had this Iago, codenamed "Voicu," not woken the investigator's interest in Müller, maybe this DUI would not have been opened. Totok's reading crosses over the confusing false or partial starts of the file and replaces them with a particular narrative. His interpretation assigns the responsibility for the opening of the file to one person. In his story certain individuals—the informers—have decisive agency, and writing plays the role of corpus delicti.

When faced with the many superimposed and disparate beginnings of Müller's file, my first thought was—what a huge gap between the *fabula* and the *siuzhet*. In their attempt to theorize narrative, Russian formalists came up with a now classic distinction between the chronological unfolding of the story, the *fabula*, and the way a narrative organizes that story—the *siuzhet*.[5] While one might be tempted to think of the *fabula* as the bare-bones origin of the narrative, the *fabula* is actually often an afterthought, an after-effect of the story, an exercise that literary critics devise to better foil the complexity of the narrative. What exists on the page is the *siuzhet*. The *fabula* is an extrapolation, something a particular kind of reader might construe while, or mostly after, reading. This peculiar kind of reader, with time on their hands to reconstruct chronological timelines out of jumbled narratives, could be a formalist critic. This reader could also be an investigator reconstructing the events as they happened, with the particular attention to temporality paid by someone interested in alibis and unaccounted-for time. It is not coincidental that in explaining the *fabula*, critics often link it to policing. Thus, David Bordwell explains: "The *fabula* embodies the action as a chronological, cause-and-effect chain of events . . . as in most detective tales, there is an overt process of *fabula* construction, since the investigation of a crime involves establishing certain connections within events . . . That is, the story of the investigation is a search for the concealed story of a crime. By the end of the typical detective tale, all story events can be fitted into a single pattern of time, space, and causality."[6] Jacques Derrida, in attempting to define the word that Roland Barthes had influentially used to translate *fabula* into French, *récit*, linked "the origin of the origin" of *récit* to policing:[7]

> I suggest, for example, that we replace what might be called the *question of narrative [la question du récit]* ("What is a narrative?") with the *demand for narrative*. When I say *demand* I mean something closer to the English "demand" than to a mere request: inquisitional insistence, an order, a petition. To know (before we know) what narrative is, the narrativity of narrative, we should perhaps first recount, return to the scene of one origin or narrative, to the *narrative* of one origin . . . to the scene that mobilizes various . . . "subjects," some of which demand the narrative of the other, seek to extort it from him, like a secretless secret, something that they call the truth of what has taken place: "Tell us exactly what happened." The narrative must have begun with this demand. In this sense any organized narrative is a police affair *[affaire de police]*, even before constituting itself in a genre (detective novel).[8]

In our case, the story becomes even more complicated when the file, "the story of the investigation," is not just "a search for the concealed story of a crime," but the story of a life, a biography. And then, mirroring the demand for the origin of the story made by the police file, its erstwhile subject, Müller, newly empowered, turns the question around, questioning the file and its creators in view of finding its beginning. There are of course differences between fictional narratives, detective stories or not, and investigative file narratives. In the case of the files, some events did at least sometimes happen first, before they were represented. Yet at other times, representations and even willful misrepresentations of events can be used to instigate events to happen, as in the case of a made-up denunciation used to prompt a very real house search, an interrogation, maybe an arrest.

In the case of Herta Müller's file, the gap between the *fabula* and the *siuzhet* is by far the greatest in the file's beginning, when documents are arranged wildly out of chronological order. Once the investigation got under way, the *siuzhet* seems to track the *fabula* quite closely, if at times more avidly and at other times more lazily: sometimes reports crowd next to each other on my makeshift timeline, and sometimes the gaps between one report and the next spread wide. But nowhere is the chronology so garbled as in the beginning. So why were some documents filed before others, despite the fact that they were created after them? If at some points in reading the file one suspects oneself of overinterpretation, much like coming up with an elaborate theory of why names starting with A are usually filed before those starting with B, this obvious manipulation of chronology in the beginning of the file is enough of an intentional act by the creators and archivists of the file to reward interpretation. In fact, contrasting the actual chronological unfolding of the events with their distinctly nonchronological arrangement in the file's beginning could be one way of getting at the logic that organizes the files, at their temporality, at the way files construct narratives, and finally at their poetics. If it appears too difficult to find the original order of events at this early stage, we could start more modestly by reordering the documents chronologically. What we notice then is that there are three reports written before the file was opened. So it was after the file was opened, and a plan of action was drawn up, that these three earlier informer reports were attached to it. These three informer reports that antedate the file are placed between "The Proposal to Open the File" and the "Plan of Measures" to be taken in the file. The first document after this plan of measures looks like another informer report, from an informer codenamed "Petra." It appears to be the first informer report written especially for Müller's file. If I had to choose a beginning for Müller's file from the declassified material, this would be it.

THE FICTIONAL BEGINNING: "ON THIS DAY"

This document pulled me out of the light-headed monotony of deciphering page after page of various handwritings and gave me goosebumps. It is filed at page 9, and I reached it around the point in the archive day when the adrenaline rush of opening a new file was starting to be replaced with the tedium of reading the same tired accusations over and over again. My mind quickly registered it as an informer report. I scanned the heading that identified it as such: "Nr. I.A/AI/28.615 1005. Herta Müller . . . Source: "PETRA" Received: Cpt. Adamescu. Date: 22.03. 1983." However, I did not immediately try to carefully decipher all the acronyms, or to hypothesize about the informer's code name.[9] This is a time-consuming exercise that I usually leave until after I have read the contents of the informer report, which gives much more information about the informer (usually one can infer relation to subject, occupation, gender, education) than the code name used in the heading. The code name often gives just one clue—gender—and even that can be a red herring. (In this file, the gender of informers matches their code names: Petra and loquacious Eva are identified as women; Totok's villain, Voicu, as a man).

So I start reading:

> On This Day
> On this day—it was a school day, because Inge was coming back from school and was soaping her hands covered in chalk—on this day, when the chalk, red as blood, green as grass, blue as ink, white as snow, was not coming off her hands, when the foam was making itself into warts on her fingers, and she was washing without touching the skin—on this day when . . .[10]

What I had expected to be yet another informer report turned out to be, in the course of a few lines, literature. When exactly does the turn happen? When do the words on the page start to bristle under my readerly expectations, pushing out of that category I had summarily boxed them into, "yet another informer's report," and spelling out "literature"? There's that first stutter, the first words repeating the title. "On this day. On this day—it was a school day . . ." This looks like someone's school composition, you might think, one of those primary school compositions with titles like "My Family," "Our Town," or "My Summer Vacation" that Müller and other writers of her generation parodied in their short stories. But my readerly expectations of an informer's report won over these first words. I read over the possibility that this might be a school exercise like the ones I was busily writing myself in 1983, my first year in school, no less a literary parody of such exercises. For the whole first line, I thought I was reading an informer's report: "On this day—it was a school day, because Inge . . ." Müller was a schoolteacher during much of the time of her DUI, and there is no shortage of school-related informer reports in her file: the informer running into her on the way to school, the informer running into another teacher on the way back from school, where she had seen Müller who told her that . . . That original stutter and the dash for punctuation hiccupped the reading of that first line as an informer report, maybe even began to spell the word "literature" in my mind, but it was really Inge's hands, bursting out on the page full of chalk, that produced that shock of recognition—not only literature, but *Müller's* literature. The extreme close-up, and the detail of the hands. Not that a police report would not be interested in details, in close-ups, and particularly in the close-ups of hands. It often happens that the first direct trace of the subject in the file is precisely the trace of a hand, of a hand covered in ink rather than chalk, and whose imprint—the fingerprint—is preserved on the page. But while the fingerprints are absent from this file, the entrance of Müller's own words in her file has the mark of her writing hand all over it. The text exhibits the general marks of her style, repeatedly described by the better readers among the informers—the remarkable use of detail, the estrangement effect, the metamorphosis of the everyday into the grotesque.[11] Furthermore, these first lines also project a particular image—the chalk covering the subject before she fully emerges in words, and a particular stylistic device—the stutter.

In Müller's debut volume, *Nadirs* (*Niederungen*), published in 1982, a year before the opening of her DUI, the protagonist, Inge, tells some stories about Wendel, her childhood neighbor and friend, with whom Inge played "husband and wife." He stutters. Bully "schoolchildren write on him with chalk, and he must walk through the streets with his back full of chalk marks and his face spattered with ink, and he can't go home until he cries."[12] For Müller, chalk is not something you write with, but something that is written on a child when he "hasn't learned to speak yet," and while he learns how to speak and to read and write. Like Wendel, Inge is written on, dirtied by writing, before she enters the text, much less starts speaking. No wonder that in this first paragraph we find that she has trouble speaking, that she can't articulate that "something that she has always wanted."

Unlike Wendel, "who speaks fluently when he is alone and talking to himself," the adult Inge stutters even when she talks silently to herself. And so does the narrator. Maybe the informer is even right when she enlightens the investigator at the end of her translation that "Inge [is] probably the author herself."[3] For the whole text self-consciously stutters. It stutters its way out of a neatly written informer report and into literature.

Not only does the text starts with a stutter, "On this day. On this day...," but the insipid title is repeated six times in the first paragraph. The sentence seems unable to get past its commonplace beginning. The action is delayed and delayed, for half a page, and the temporal marker "on this day," threatens to take over, or maybe even take apart, the whole first paragraph. Once we get to the end of the paragraph, we see that it might be unfair to blame the complement, it could well be that the writer cannot get to the action—to the verbs—because of the verbs themselves. Indeed, verbs prove to have uncommon difficulty naming the action. It is not for lack of trying, three tenses of the verb "to do" crowd the last lines of the paragraph, and then that other most basic of verbs, "to be," is also summoned. But they do a rather lame job of naming the action, giving the vaguest of descriptions—"On that day Inge was doing something..." Okay, the impatient reader might say, but doing what? The verbs, dragging on, protract the telling one more time—"something that she always wanted to do," maybe we are getting closer, "but she had not done before..." All right, that gives some information, but what we really want to know after a whole paragraph is *what* she was doing, so we read on: "because she did not know what that was." Having been set up to hope for a principal clause that would finally describe what it was that Inge was doing, the reader, after trudging through all the subordinate clauses, is stuck with a last clause that turns out to be just another subordinate clause to the mildly relevant penultimate subordinate clause. This turns us back to what has now been revealed to be, really *faute de mieux*, the principal sentence of this whole paragraph, the one that kept about as far as a verb can keep from describing an action: "she was doing something."[14]

By the time we make our way through the first paragraph, we realize that this text is more interested in delaying the action that it narrates than in telling it. Its defining move is to turn back on itself, to the very points that might seem least promising in advancing the telling of events, to the fillers. The text resists narrative, the events, and instead turns us back on fillers, and on the subject. At some point, one might suspect that there is a link between these fillers and the subject. The fillers retard action, and contribute some (scant) information about the subject. But as indulgent as one may be, one sees that just as might be expected of fillers, the information they give is rather vague. It is also not clear whom it concerns: is it the narrator, who stutters, over and over—"on that day"—and turns back in her tracks to tell us it was a school day? Is Inge telling her own story? Why then the use of the third person? Free indirect style usually weaves in and out of narrative, with the narrator making use of the ability both to enter the character's mind and to exit it, making statements of their own, establishing a certain distance from the subject. Here, the free indirect style takes over the whole story, with little to differentiate the narrator and her subject other than the use of the third person. The reader even starts to suspect that Inge is the kind of person who talks about herself in the third person, as children do—indeed, the way most of us started talking about ourselves. Maybe it is not only the primitive metaphors and grammatical analyses that take over this school-like composition, but also the use of the third person, which inflects the very way Inge refers to herself.

More than anything, however, the repeated fillers tell us that the speaker, whoever she is, has some gaps to fill. That she would rather throw word fillers over those gaps than go on to the end of the story, when the gap finally gets named, opening wide and staring at her:

> She took the bottles from the pantry and put them in the bookshelf. The grammatical gender of bottle is feminine. She took the books from the furniture and put them in the pantry. The grammatical gender of book is neuter. She took her handbag and put it in the fridge. The grammatical gender of handbag is feminine. She put her shoes on the table. The grammatical gender of shoe is masculine [...]
>
> Inge opened the door to her house ... She sat down on the floor and was looking fixedly at nothing (*in gol*). The grammatical gender of nothingness (*golul*) is neuter, said Inge to herself.
>
> When her friend came that evening—at that time he was still coming—he stopped ~~he sat unmoving~~ in the open door.
>
> She is crazy, he said, aloud. He did not say, she became crazy. Inge was looking straight at his lips as he was saying it. [...]
>
> Inge stood in front of him and put her hands under the dishes.
>
> The grammatical gender of friend is masculine, she said, through the now empty (*goala*) door.[15]

The repeated fillers also suggest that when she can no longer turn back to the past, or turn around the furniture in the house, when she finally has to face the gap, this mysterious subject, barely divided between someone telling and someone being told about, will turn to language: "The grammatical gender of nothingness is masculine, she said."[16]

The narrator has her ways of dealing with this nothingness—she registers it, and then seems to move away from its signified—from the image itself and from its emotional weight—toward the signifier, the word itself and its grammatical gender. It is hard to blame her, the signified is always hard to think of, and thinking of the signified of "nothingness" takes the problem to yet another level of difficulty. The more we stare with Inge at this nothingness, at the way it is spoken or framed—by the doorway, by fillers, by the impoverished language turning back on itself—we discover traces of the subject. What is she like? She is strangely turned to language, constantly losing track of the signified because of the signifier. In this particular text, it is unclear whether this turn to language happens to her, whether it is a compulsion, something that she cannot help. It could be that the primitive grammar Inge teaches her students—"the grammatical gender of flower is feminine"—has taken possession of her brain the way a cheesy tune does (propaganda tunes, more appropriate in this context, do the same). Read in the larger context of Müller's work, this turn to language could also be a personal game, maybe even therapy, a way of keeping the world at a distance, of taking one's mind off something even while having to hear it or see it.

We here come across one of the strongest hallmarks of Müller's writing: the fascination with the moment when language turns figurative, or rather when it turns away from the places it is supposed to be taken and is instead dislodged, sometimes even wildly chased through the present for impressions or through the past for associations. In much of Müller's writing this turn toward the figurative aspect of language is something willed, something she works hard at, often with the more or less overt aim of keeping the narrative from going on. It is not only in "On This Day" that this turn to language tries to keep things from going to their proper places, which are deadening. The narrator of *The Land of Green Plums* (*Herztier*) thinks of it as a ruse and therapy, one of the tricks that she devises so as not to go mad in the midst of the harassment she experiences from the Securitate.[17] In time, Müller's female narrators devise quite a few such tricks: one whistles a tune in her head while in the interrogation room, an association that takes her away from the present to the past or to somewhere else. Another superstitiously eats a nut before facing an interrogation. But more often than not, the narrators turn, obsessively, to language. In *The Land of Green Plums*, the obsession with finding a trick to keep the narrator from going mad opens and frames the book: by the end, we learn that it is the book itself that could be that trick. In *The Appointment* (*Heute wär ich mir lieber nicht begegnet*), a few years later, a trick is still needed.[18] As a trick, this turn to language can be therapeutic, but it is no definitive solution. Furthermore, the language trick can look pretty close to the madness that it is trying to trick—"she is mad, he said, not she turned (became) mad." So as far as retardation devices go, "On that Day" then prefigures an important hallmark of Müller's mature work, not only by turning back on itself but also by turning figurative: "red as blood," "green as grass," "blue as ink," "white as snow." These most primitive of figures tell us that the chalk has left marks not just on Inge's hands, but also on her (or on the narrator's?) mind as well. The text harkens back to the first introductions to figurative language, those first times one learned that "red like blood" was a simile. These "introductory" similes are, however, already dead similes, mere clichés, used to death by others before you, and somehow stuck to your brain against your will. It is often late in Müller's texts: by the time they come to her characters, words have been used to death: people have already been written on, like Wendel and Inge, in ways that stop their own words in their mouths before they even know what those words were.

WHEN OTHERS WRITE YOUR AUTOBIOGRAPHY: "OUR TOWN," PARAPHRASED

Besides being written on, people are also written about, as another text published by Müller at the same time as "On That Day," and incriminatingly featured in her file, "Unsere Stadt" ("Our Town"), notes.[19] A German-speaking informer paraphrases the story for the Securitate thus: "The autobiographies and biographies of these people have been written by others, usually the past is more important than the present—the future is just a threat."[20] I had not read "Our Town" before reading Müller's file. So her words first reached me, translated and paraphrased, from inside her file.[21] They produced a real shock of recognition. In my first book, I argued that the Soviet-era secret police structured the personal files as biographies, which attempted to cover the whole life of the suspect, as distinguished from standard Western police files, which focus on the resolution of one crime and are structured more like detective stories.[22] I then argued that these powerful biographies had an impact on how people conceived of and wrote about their lives, whether in autobiographies or in novels. I hoped I had shown this through analyses of the narratives of the files and of various works of literature, so with time I became slightly weary of the question, "Did the authors explicitly state that they viewed the files as biography?" I responded that I knew of no such explicit statements, which would in any case have been imprudent at the time. Thus, I experienced a shock of recognition when I saw my view of the files explicitly expressed in the files themselves, in their paraphrase of Müller's story. One may argue that Müller's original paragraph still retains some ambiguity about who these "others" who write people's biographies and autobiographies are (although, read in the context of her work's unyielding preoccupation with the Romanian secret police, that ambiguity is slight).[23] However, the appropriation of her words inside the very file that strives not only to record but also to influence her biography—thus doubly "writing" it—made these two phrases from "My Town" (cited at the start of the paragraph) a close fit with my view of the personal file as biography. My shock of recognition was in fact so strong that for the first few times I read this file paraphrase of "My Town," I missed what I now think is the deeper point that Müller makes here—not only were the biographies, like hers, written by others, but so were autobiographies. How could this be possible? Doesn't the very definition and etymology of auto-bio-graphy, "self-life-writing," rebel against Müller's verdict?

Before we get to this paradoxical proposition, let us backtrack to its simpler companion: ". . . the biographies of these people were written by others." Müller's file provides ample proof for her statement. Before "On This Day" Müller's DUI provides a list, covering eight double-sided pages, of other texts about her, written by others, whether informers or agents. Against my desire to establish her short story as the beginning of her file, to have her enter the file in her own words, her statement, just like the archival pagination, reminds me that "the biography" written by others came first. Just as Totok wanted the file to begin with the informer, I catch myself still wanting the file to start, for once, with the subject's own words, which in this case are strikingly crafted, to boot. Müller's "On This Day" comes as close as any file beginning that I have ever read to fulfilling this desire—it is the first document, after the plan of action. The text itself, first published in 1983, was probably conceived and written before the file was initiated in March 1983. Yet, it is fitting that its prose reminds us that the subject's own words, even spoken to herself, even describing herself, have already been used by others, used to death, turned to clichés. "On This Day" also fittingly reminds us that the subject has been literally written on, with school chalk that won't come off and instead bleeds through her hands deep into her psyche, filling her mind with deadening clichés.

THE TRADUCED FICTION READS BACK

Furthermore, the text of "On This Day" that we read in Müller's file is not quite, and not fully, made up of her own words. To begin with, some words have been cut from the story. In two places, the translator professionally marks these cuts with bracketed ellipses. Toward the end of the story, when Inge's friend comes to visit, Müller had written: "And his face was standing around his mouth, which was in the middle." The translator cut this phrase, maybe to get around a challenge—as the translation given here proves, the sentence can sound awkward in translation. However, at the end of the second paragraph of the story, there is a more significant cut: "She cut the flowers above the rim of the flowerpot and she threw them in the toilet bowl and flushed the toilet. The flower is feminine. She bit off a clump of earth from the flowerpot. The earth is feminine. She painted some green eye shadow over her lips. She painted some blue eye shadow over her cheeks."[24] This cut scene explains why the boyfriend says aloud, upon arriving at the scene, "She is mad," and why Inge only takes issue with the tense of his verb: "He didn't say she turned mad."[25] The translator left out the most disturbing part of the story. She may have done that to protect Müller. In her "interpretation" of the text that follows her translation, the translator seems intent on doing that when she writes: "In the opinion of the source this prose underlines human loneliness and the impossibility to communicate, a general theme taken up by the majority of contemporary writers, not only German writers . . . Inge (probably the author herself) tries to change her own way of life, but without much success, because at the end she is still left alone." From the receiving investigator's note, we find out this is the first attempt to use Petra for "the translation and the interpretation of a literary work." His superior advises caution: "It's no good at this early stage of our activity to draw her attention to our objectives."[26]

Whether or not we may discern in this case some good will on the part of the translator, we should bear in mind that Müller's words had been cut up and translated before being added to the file. In the context of the file, even an otherwise benign translation often comes closest to the etymology that links it to traducing, to betrayal, a link that Barbara Johnson finds particularly telling in the following translation of the first sentence of Kafka's *The Trial*: "Someone must have traduced Joseph K, for without having done anything wrong he was arrested one fine morning."[27] Since neither Captain Adamescu nor Müller's main investigator, Pădurariu, read any German, the file could not have been put together without the work of translators: after Petra's initial attempts, most translations of Müller's literary texts were done by Hildegard Schleich, code-named "Eva." Valentina Glajar notes that "although translation played a significant and complex role in allowing the Securitate to effectively surveil the German Romanian communities, scholars have paid little attention to it."[28] Glajar dedicates an informative subchapter to Eva, whose vast output (in three years she provided 150 reports) consisted mainly of literary translations: "she was professionally apt and knowledgeable, with a degree in Germanistik . . . At the German theater, her first job after graduation, Schleich was a literary reviewer, an ideological censor of sorts."[29] Eva's job for the Securitate was to "comb . . . writers' texts for subversive allusions, translate selective 'hostile' segments," identify the hidden meanings of "interpretative literature," and offer some commentary as to their incriminating potential.[30] When Eva tries to exculpate Müller—as when she concluded her report by explaining that "this pessimism, this despair in Müller's prose must be explained through the writer's present day situation at the time; she is without employment"—her handler, Adamescu, dismisses the excuse by noting that "Müller had the same style even when she was in the workplace."[31] In time, Eva learns from her contacts with her handlers that they are less interested in her excuses or literary analysis than in her ability to find and translate incriminating passages. Eva learns that her handlers "rarely, if ever, read these texts for their aesthetic value but instead read them for their evidentiary potential," and that the translations they expect are a particular type of incriminating forensic translation, which Glajar calls "manipulative and conspiratorial forensic translation."[32]

A prime example of this kind of translation is provided by the other main translator working on Müller's case, Sgt. Mariana Gheorghe, who, as the transcriber of the bugging recordings taken in Müller's apartment, engaged in both interlingual (German to Romanian) and intermedial (sound to text) translation. A full-time employee of the Securitate, Gheorghe did not have the same level of German language skills as Eva.[33] Besides her better awareness of Securitate concerns, the language challenges may have been part of the reason she consistently skipped over Müller's conversations on literary or cultural themes, dismissing them in a phrase: "Then literary problems are being discussed."[34] Instead, Gheorghe zeroes in on Müller's conversations about her contacts abroad and emigration plans. While Eva, the qualified translator with native German and a degree in Germanistik, is reeducated through her work for the Securitate in the practices of incriminating forensic translation, Gheorghe's hundreds of hours of listening to Müller's conversations leave no discernible mark on her interest in literary matters or in her reductive translation practices. In fact, the Securitate never expected just accurate forensic or literary translation from the translators whose services it used, as shown by the fact that even informers whose main activity was translation, like Eva, could not simply work as consultants but rather had to go through the whole vetting and recruitment process and become informers.

In the translator-informer's rendering, Müller's words from "On That Day" have been transcribed by the translator in blue ink, and then placed in quotation marks in the black ink of the investigator.[35] The investigator, Captain Adamescu, whom Müller and her circle exposed for engaging in torture, in a group letter to the Writers' Union, also took the time to underline the title with a cutesy wavelike line, making the text look even more like an elementary school exercise.[36] Müller was certainly aware of the translations, paraphrasing, and appropriations that her texts were subjected to. She likely had to withstand having the cut-up, traduced sentences thrown into her face during interrogation sessions. In *The Appointment*, the protagonist faces writing that she actually produced as well as the writing that informers framed her with. One can imagine the estrangement effect produced by this reading of your own curiously translated words during an interrogation. No wonder that when she enters this text, "On This Day," as well as her file, and her story of her encounters with the Securitate (*The Appointment*), Müller is set on the paradoxical task of writing as well as taking the text apart, frustrating its progress.

Serendipitously placed as Müller's first text in her own file, "On This Day" gives us a few precious clues as to how to read the files. This short text points us back to the phrase that we could have hastily missed in the attempt to read these files measured in kilometers: it points us back to the filler. It pushes the filler into our face until we have no choice but to contemplate it, and realize that if there is a filler, it is because there is also something to be filled, a gap that had been filled by the worn-out phrase. Sometimes that phrase is just a cliché, but sometimes a closer look at these worn-out phrases reveals the subject's sense that before she got to use language for self-description, language had already been used, by others, to write her biography. Thus, upon starting to write about her protagonist—or maybe, as the translator guesses, about herself—the writer has recourse to words that have already been marked by other compromising uses. We start to understand how even autobiography would come, in these conditions, to seem (pre-)written by others. Inge, like Müller, had been written before she appeared on the page by the tired expressions of others, expressions like "red as blood" which often hide some otherwise untold violence. Müller's short story is also good preparation for the reading of the files because it keeps turning us away from the verb to its subject, reminding us that she is its subject in the sense that actions are done to her. Reinstating the subject's primacy over the verb requires resistance over more than hurried reading habits. Joseph Brodsky wrote that "a writer's biography is in his twists of language."[37] In Müller's case, when inimical biographies and autobiographies antedate one's own autobiography and attempt to mold it and ultimately silence it, the writing of the self takes the thorough, often violent, twisting and turning of the dead figures and deadening language that had already written her.

MÜLLER'S MISSING RECORDS AND HER LITERARY GENEALOGIES

Looking for the beginning of the file, then, we find an early story by Müller: a story about a turn to language. About language as what one turns to when faced with a gap, between oneself and the closest objects and people, when one has been already written on, dirtied by others' writing, whether bully chalk marks or police (auto)biography. This could, of course, be coincidence. The informer could have chosen a different story to incriminate

Müller. But language and the beginnings of literature come up over and over again when we look for the beginning of the file. The informer reports that chronologically open the file are exclusively about Müller's "interpretive literature," unlike many others later on, when we hear about her extravagant clothes or refusal to teach kindergarten children patriotic songs.[38] On the first page of the file we find that the reason for the proposed opening of the file is "her writing, which sneaks interpretive and tendentious ideas," rather than the myriad other reasons a file could have been opened on her: contact with foreigners; close personal and professional relationships to people long before endowed with DUIs, like her partner Richard Wagner; or one of the coarse jokes that she remembers using as survival weapons during those years.[39]

Most strikingly, there are Müller's own accounts of the missing beginning of her file that, seemingly malapropos, always lead her into the story of her beginning as a writer. In *Cristina, or the Double*, a short book dedicated to the experience of retrieving and reading her file, she affirms that the Securitate had cooked the books and gutted her file of all substance. Then right away, Müller begins to restore what she thinks is missing from the file in chronological order: "The three years at the tractor factory Tehnometal where I was a translator are missing."[40] As Glajar notes, it is likely that at first the Securitate was interested in recruiting Müller as a translator.[41] Müller then relates the story of her work routine being interrupted by a Securitate attempt to recruit her as an informer and the harassment that follows her refusal, harassment that starts with the threat, "We will drown you in the river," and culminates in her being fired from her job. Between these two events, a few weeks, which seem endless to her, pass. Müller recounts that it was during these weeks that she truly started writing literature. She tells the story of being gradually displaced from her office: First, "one morning when I turned up for work, my dictionaries were lying on the floor outside the office door. My place had been taken by an engineer, and I was no longer allowed in the office ... Now I had no table, no chair. For two days, I defiantly sat my eight hours with the dictionaries on the concrete staircase that joined the ground and the first floors, trying to translate so that no one could say that I wasn't working."[42] Her best friend, Jenny, courageously clears a corner of her desk for her, but just a few days later Jenny is asked to turn her out on the grounds that Müller is a Securitate informer, slander that the Securitate themselves spread. "I took my dictionaries and sat down on the stairs again . . . At the beginning of these turbulent times my father died. I no longer had a grip on things, I had to reassure myself that I really existed in the world. I began to write down the story of my life—these writings formed the basis of the short stories in *Nadirs*."[43]

In *Cristina*, the search for filling in the gaps of the file, and in particular for filling in its missing beginning, leads to the story of Müller's beginning of writing literature. The link is paratactically made, and the story of her literature's beginnings is only sketched out in *Cristina*, anchored through a few powerful images: against the background of the loss of her father, what stands out is the demand to become an informer and her refusal, then the literal displacement from her workplace. Most oppressive is her replacement in the eyes of her colleagues by an informer doppelgänger that she describes as filling her insides and suffocating her, to the point of leading to a feeling of loss of self and reality.[44] In this account of her writing's beginning, Müller makes it clear that she did not first or primarily put pen to paper with the intention to create literature. Rather, she did so to document a threatened self, an imploding, far from self-evident self. That writing happens to turn to and into literature in the short stories of *Nadirs*.

The link paratactically made in *Cristina* was taken up and fully developed in Müller's Nobel lecture, her carefully crafted self-genealogy as a writer, a genealogy that builds up to a full-blown ars poetica.[45] Had one not read *Cristina*, or much of Müller's own writing, as many of the listeners had not at the time of her Nobel lecture, they would have been struck by her lecture's beginning. Müller opens on an everyday scene centered upon a seemingly insignificant detail from her childhood: the question posed by Müller's mother, as her young daughter took leave of her at the gate each morning, whether her girl had a handkerchief. Even more unexpected is the next story on this first page of the Nobel lecture, a story coming in immediate succession and taking up a full third of the lecture, the story of Müller's attempted recruitment by the Securitate, her subsequent harassment, the loss of her job, and the beginning of her writing. We recognize the story from *Cristina*, but this time Müller conjures up the full power of her artistry to fill in the characteristic details, and to significantly expand two episodes.

The first episode concerns the actual recruitment attempt:

> Three times in one week a visitor showed up at my office early in the morning: an enormous, thick-boned man with sparkling blue eyes—a colossus from the Securitate.
>
> The first time he sat there, cursed me, and left.
>
> The second time he took off his windbreaker, hung it on the key to the cabinet, and sat down. That morning I had brought some tulips from home and arranged them in a vase ... Then he said maliciously that he knew me better than I knew tulips. After that he draped his windbreaker over his arm and left.
>
> The third time he sat down but I stayed standing, because he had set his briefcase on my chair. I didn't dare move it on the floor. He called me stupid, said I was a shirker and a slut, as corrupted as a stray bitch. He shoved the tulips close to the edge of the desk, then put an empty sheet of paper and a pen in the middle of the desktop. He yelled at me: *Write*. Without sitting down, I wrote what he dictated—my name, date of birth and address. Next, that I would tell no one, no matter how close a friend or relative, that I ... and then came the terrible word: *colaborez—I am collaborating*. At that point I stopped writing. I put down the pen and went to the window and looked out onto the dusty street, unpaved and full of potholes, and at all the humpbacked houses. On top of everything else this street was called Strada Gloriei—Glory Street. On Glory Street a cat was sitting in a bare mulberry tree. It was the factory cat with the torn ear. ... I said: N-am caracterul—I don't have the character for this. I said it to the street outside. The word CHARACTER made the Securitate man hysterical. He tore up the sheet of paper and threw the pieces on the floor. Then he probably realized that he would have to show his boss that he had tried to recruit me, because he bent over, picked up the scraps and tossed them in his briefcase ... With his briefcase under his arm he said quietly: *You'll be sorry, we'll drown you in the river*. I said to myself: If I sign that, I won't be able to live with myself anymore, and I'll have to do it on my own. By then the office door was already open and he was gone. And outside on the Strada Gloriei the factory cat jumped from the tree on the roof of the building. One branch was bouncing like a trampoline.[46]

In this dramatized tableau, Müller initially refrains from letting her protagonists speak directly, paraphrasing their speech instead. That paraphrase ends abruptly and emphatically as the Securitate man yells out the command: "*Write.*" Müller italicizes the word, emphasizing that the core of the scene resides in this command to write. While other writers' ars poetica may speak about the muse or inner necessity as dictating them to write, in Müller's genealogy of herself as a writer, the injunction "write" is yelled by a Securitate agent. He asks her to write, not literature, of course, but about herself (and not about others, as one would have expected from an informer request). He asks her to write about her life, by taking his dictation of her "fundamental data"—her name, birthplace, and address. And she does. In her Nobel genealogy of herself as a writer, Herta Müller starts writing, about herself, while standing and following the Securitate man's dictation. It is only when the terrible word, "colaborez"—"I am collaborating"—comes, that she stops writing. The consequence of her refusal to write is that she gets displaced, threatened, terrified to the point of losing her grip on herself, and finally that she starts writing about herself, the stories that will become her first book.

Much of Müller's literature describes the abuse she suffered in the repressive society of Ceaușescu's dictatorship, with the Securitate epitomizing that abuse. There is abuse of endless kinds, from verbal abuse like the words shouted to her by Stana, to death threats, to beatings, to searching her house in her absence. And yet, in her Nobel lecture, Müller tells the story of this abuse as a command to write. In doing so, she reminds us that the Securitate was not just the most repressive arm of the state, in charge of shadowing and threatening and beating up and sometimes killing people for various reasons, the most common one in her circle being "interpretive writing." It was also the institution that most extensively wrote about those subjects, in files covering many kilometers, and which also demanded that people write about themselves and others according to the Securitate's rules, taking down, literally or not, its dictation. Common association, as manifest in the less sanitized words for informing, such as squealing and blabbering, links informing to an oral activity. If anything, one expects writing to come in subsequently, as a supplement to the oral report, as a record of it. And since Müller refused to collaborate, one could reasonably expect that she never got to the point of a written record being made of her words. And yet, while the central presence of writing in this episode might appear surprising, it corresponds to the actual position of writing in this police state, a position regulated by internal Securitate guidelines concerning their informers' network. Informer reports had to be recorded in writing. When the informer, maybe out of squeamishness or lack of education, did not write the report themselves, the agent wrote it in their place. And just like Müller, all informer "candidates" had to fill out a written informer agreement.[47] That form was the basis, the matrix, for more writing. A major difference between an acceptance and a refusal was in the kind of writing it set into motion. If the candidate agreed to become an informer, they would write "the informer agreement and an autobiography" before proceeding to write about others.[48] In case the candidate refused to write "the recruitment contract and the autobiography," regulations mandated that "we give up, but we write a biography," a biography of which they would be the object, rather than the subject.[49]

In choosing to interrupt the Securitate man's dictation, in choosing thus not to write about herself and about others following his order, "Write!" Herta Müller took the risk of being written about. We now know that there was a particular genre of writing that her refusal triggered—a biography. It was, of course, hardly coincidental that, as Katerina Clark has shown, biography was also the master narrative of socialist realism—indeed "the iconic artifact" of the "Soviet *Kunststadt.*"[50] While Müller could not have read either Clark or the relevant Securitate regulations, she did live in acute awareness of the Securitate and their writing practices, to the point of presciently describing their writing as "biographies and autobiographies" written by others.[51] She knew that, at the time of her first encounters with the Securitate agent who was in charge of her case, he already had the beginning of her biography, written down in her own hand, torn to shreds, then salvaged and stuffed in his briefcase. And it was more than reasonable for her to expect that even the first time the Securitate man entered her office, his briefcase, belonging as it did to the agent in charge of her case, would contain materials relating to her. She might not have known that according to Securitate regulations, these papers were supposed to be quite extensive. Before attempting to recruit a potential informer, Securitate agents were instructed to collect thorough data on the candidate: "The data collection will be done patiently, without leaving any question unresolved, following all leads and going all the way to surveillance . . . It will be insisted upon that we know in detail the past of the person in question, the actual way of life, the hopes for the immediate and long-term future, weaknesses and qualities, troubles and intimate difficulties."[52] Once this thorough verification was completed, a separate document entitled "characterization (referring to temperament and character)" was added to the file. Only then was the Securitate supposed to attempt to recruit the potential informer. Again, Müller could not have known all this. But the fear that this briefcase and its owner instilled in her, the fear that prevented her from touching the collection of papers that literally takes her place at the writing desk, so terrified to move it that she started taking the Securitate agent's dictation while standing, suggests that she knew more than enough about the power of Securitate biographies and characterizations. Following the death threat launched by Stana upon leaving, the file that started by temporarily displacing her from her writing desk threatened to permanently replace her.

At first sight little more than a minor prop, the briefcase is the elephant in the room. In more than one way, this briefcase is the missing beginning of Müller's file that we have been searching for all along. First, as far as probabilities go, the briefcase was initially at least as likely to contain papers about Müller as it was to contain the agent's lunch; this probability becomes a certainty by the end of the meeting, when Müller sees the shreds of her writing about herself disappearing into the briefcase. But even more than the particular pieces of paper, the brief-case, (*Aktentasche*, literally "file bag," in German) represents the personal file as a collection of documents whose existence and importance is paraded in front of the suspect just as she is denied the right to actually read its contents.[53] The briefcase stands in for the mixture of exhibitionism and secrecy that defined the files from their beginnings, when they were paraded in show trials and newsreels in a way that emphasized their authority while making sure they remained tantalizingly illegible to the public. To a certain extent, the briefcase works best as the beginning of the file when it is in fact empty of the feared documents. It works best if, upon opening, one discovered that the slight bulge that one's imagination had filled in with compromising papers was in fact produced by the oversized lunch Stana's wife had prepared for him that day. But no papers. Parading a thick file to intimidate the suspect at the beginning of an interrogation is an investigator's old trick. The paraded file can be empty or belong to someone else: its raison d'être is to intimidate the interogatee so that they would start talking and writing, and thus getting the actual production of their file into motion. The briefcase here is meant to work the same way. It could well be empty, but it advertises the existence of its written contents just as it hides them from view, creating enough panic in Müller that she starts composing file material herself. The file can start: name, birthdate, place of birth . . .

In other words, the beginning of the file was rooted in a whole network of writing practices and regulations that included a penchant for biography over records of particular crimes, as well as an elaborate show of secrecy. That show of secrecy featured briefcases, file covers, and pseudonyms, paraded in private interrogation sessions and show trials, in newsreels and print, and in the never-ending rumors painstakingly crafted in misinformation departments. The briefcase, then, could, following contemporary secret police regulations, contain papers that would describe Müller's life and character in overflowing detail. The briefcase could also be empty of any documents, that emptiness framed in such intimidating secrecy so as to prompt the proliferation of the hitherto missing documents. Indeed, the briefcase stands for the file precisely in this ambivalence between the potential excess of documentation of its subject, on the one side, and its essential, often secrecy-enshrouded, lacunae, on the other.

This still leaves open the question of why the contents of the briefcase are missing in the present configuration of Müller's file. It is possible that Stana was a follower of regulations and did his homework carefully, compiling masses of information on Müller and stowing it in his briefcase, or it could have been that Müller was one informer too many that he was to recruit that spring, and he decided to cover up his lack of documentation of her through his intimidating drama in three acts. Similarly, it could be that this recruitment attempt, torn papers and all, was itself dismissed together with Müller's dismissal from the factory, or it could have been carefully filed, but then legally or illegally purged. Or maybe the contents of the briefcase are still filed or misfiled somewhere else, not in the more easily retrievable personal files but in a larger, harder-to-guess-at problem file, such as "Provincial Tractor Factories." (For the record, I did consult the problem file of Tehnometal Timisoara, but Müller's name does not figure in it.)[54] Choosing one hypothesis over another at this point would be unjustified since so little of the archives has been read. We need to continue sifting and reading through the archives to narrow down the answers to these particular questions, but in the meantime, I think we can retain from the briefcase episode the combination of exhibitionism and secrecy, as well as the ambivalence of excessively detailed biography and fundamental lacunae or even erasure of the subject. This combination defined the writing of the secret police not only in secret police regulations but also in the terrified experience of perceptive subjects like Müller.

Müller's refusal to *write* puts her at risk of being written on as well as at the risk of being disappeared. Here is how Müller expanded this story for her Nobel Prize lecture:

> The next day the tug of war began. They wanted me out of the factory...
>
> One morning I came to work and found my thick dictionaries lying on the floor of the hall outside my office. I opened the door; an engineer was sitting at my desk. He said: *People are supposed to knock before they enter a room. This is my place, you have no business here.* I couldn't go home; any unexcused absence would have given them a pretext to fire me. I no longer had an office, so now I really had to make sure I came to work; under no circumstances could I fail to be there.
>
> ...
>
> Since now I really had to make sure I came to work, but no longer had an office, and since my friend could no longer let me into hers, I stood in the stairwell, unable to decide what to do. I climbed up and down the stairs a few times and suddenly I was again my mother's child, because I HAD A HANDKERCHIEF. I placed it on one of the stairs between the second and third floors, carefully smoothed it out and sat down. I rested my thick dictionaries on my knee and translated the descriptions of hydraulic machines. I was a staircase wit and my office was a handkerchief... A few never-ending weeks, until I was dismissed.
>
> During the time that I was a staircase wit, I looked up the word STAIR in the dictionary: the first step is the STARTING STEP or CURTAIL STEP that can also be a BULLNOSE. HAND is the direction a stair takes at the first riser. The edge of a tread that projects past the face of the riser is called the NOSING. I already knew a number of beautiful words having to do with lubricated hydraulic machine parts: DOVETAIL, GOOSENECK, ACORN NUTS and EYEBOLTS. Now I was equally amazed at the poetic names of the stair parts, the beauty of the technical language. NOSING and HAND—so the stair has a body. Whether working with wood or stone, cement or iron: why do humans insist on imposing their face on even the most unwieldy things in the world, why do they name dead matter after their own flesh, personifying it as parts of the body? Is this hidden tenderness necessary to make the harsh work bearable for the technicians? Does every job in every field follow the same principle as my mother's question about the handkerchief?[55]

For the reader of "On This Day," there is a strange déjà vu quality to this story. Just like "On This Day," this story starts with displacement—except that here, rather than the subject doing the displacing of her possessions, it is the subject herself who gets displaced. In the face of this displacement, she, just like Inge, moves about, then sits down, and turns to language. Sitting on the stairs, she soon finds a better way to erect a boundary between herself and the inhospitable world than her storied handkerchief, on which she pathetically sits. She turns her attention from her uncomfortable position to the word "stair," and looks it up in the dictionary. What she finds in that definition of the word "stair," just like those in the technical dictionaries that support her livelihood as a translator, is the figurative pull of everyday language. To her surprise (for she seems unaware of what she is looking for), this figurative language actually figures the contours of a human body and face, an embodied humanity that is so blatantly missing from her world. It is partly that emptiness—the emptiness of a doorframe through which a human figure (whether the friend in "On This Day" or the "Securitate man" here) has left, doubled by the emptiness of the record documenting those experiences—that prompts her to turn to the written language of dictionaries, and then to writing literature.

During family reunions in my own, rather ordinary Romanian family, as seemingly malapropos as during a Nobel Prize lecture, people whom I have known my whole life have started telling previously untold stories of recruitment attempts, of "visits" and "appointments" with the Securitate. I doubt that one could find many of the records of those encounters that deeply marked so many lives, that were stifled in terrified silence for years and whose telling, often awkward, strangely timed, too casual or too formulaic, still bears the marks of that silence. This pervasiveness of the informer recruitment story does not mean to trivialize Müller's own story. On the contrary, I think it is Müller's great achievement to give language to what went unrecorded because it was considered, from the point of view of the institution and the people that served it, a matter of course. Müller's literature draws attention to the unrecorded, to that silence of silencers rather than the silence of "nothing happened." Her literature also shows how the unrecorded was for its subject sometimes lethal, often life-threatening, and usually life-changing. Müller emphasizes that she gave these experiences language and not a voice, for these were things that she herself could never tell, which is why she turned to writing. With its mix of recordkeeping and carefully rendered details, this at first sight surprising story of the failed recruitment attempt is important enough to take up the first third of her Nobel Prize lecture because it is the story of her beginning as a writer. It is this unlikely scene of physical displacement and compulsory writing of the self that she would fashion into the origin of her turn to language, to figurative language, and to literature. No less significantly, however, Müller tells here the story of what happens to be missing from the official record, from her file, and points to what will always be missing from such files. Her story turns to a language that can record traces and shreds of this traumatic beginning, turning away from it as it bears witness to it. It is in this process that she even manages to turn that event into something else—into literature.

Müller herself has been and continues to be deeply preoccupied with the question of whether literature, and her own literature in particular, can be called testimony and whether it can bear witness. She confessed that "as I write them [her books], I do not think of myself as bearing witness. This is because of how I learned to write: not from speaking, but from silence and concealment."[56] But it could be, as writers on testimony as different as Shoshana Felman, Dori Laub, Giorgio Agamben, and Cathy Caruth remind us, that it is precisely its origin in silence that best qualifies her literature as testimony.[57] Müller's literature bears the traces of that long stare into the nothingness, into the gap, an experience that repeatedly predates her turn to language in her accounts of her beginnings as a writer. And it is a mark of her literature that, while originating in that gap, it does not rush to fill it. Indeed, her literature bears witness to multiple silences—to the lacunae of the official document, as to the ensuing stutter of the subject whose (auto)biography had been written through those fundamentally incomplete documents.

Users of invisible ink, also called "security ink," sometimes worry that "regular ink may 'run' when it crosses a line of invisible ink, thus betraying the presence of invisible ink."[58] In the process of writing her literature, Müller's ink has proven particularly runny, betraying and exposing a particular "security ink," the Securitate writings, shaped as they are by their defining lacunae. As the revisited self-genealogies of her writing attest, Müller conceives of her literature, and particularly of her autobiographical work, as a palimpsest: the runs into "security ink" do not just mark the surface of her literature, they are also reminders that the Securitate writing and its silences preceded her literature, which was born in response to them, as a surviving tactic. At the same time, Müller's literature bears witness to what is missing in the files, its verbose lacunae. It is a fact that deserves to be highlighted, because it runs contrary to two common misconceptions, which hold that if a personal file has been found, then the documents in that file serve not only to show the Securitate's actions toward the subject, but also to weaken the possibility that other significant actions were taken but not recorded. Müller's files, like most others I have read, undermine both of these common, if dangerous, misconceptions. While readers might bring a certain suspicion or reticence toward the actual documents in the files, understanding that they may be fabricated or censored, they often do not interrogate the large if invisible swatches of silence within a file's folders. The motto used as justification for so many unjust accusations—there is no smoke without fire, that is, there must have been a crime if the police suspected that there was one—should of course be reconsidered, but so should its reverse—there is no fire without smoke, or, put otherwise, any fire will create smoke. Many secret police fires, like the small cigarette fires burned into suspects' skin during some interrogations, left no obvious marks in the files. And yet, at a time when the bodies that bore those scars continue to disappear, the files are one of the few places where we can look for these elusive marks. Invaluable testimony, Müller's literature can also act as an alternative guide to these archives it still inhabits, a guide singularly able to expose their fundamental lacunae. In the next chapter, I focus on the foundational lacuna that Müller herself identified in her file—its purportedly missing beginning.

FOUR

Silences (Take Two)
Gendered Archival Lacunae

[My] file is a botched job of the SRI on behalf of the old Securitate. They had ten years to work on it. You cannot call this just pruning [*frisieren*], the file has been gutted/emptied of all substance [*entkernt*].
—HERTA MÜLLER, *Cristina und ihre Attrappe*[1]

There are also lacunae [*lipsuri*] in the documentation through preliminary acts of the activity of the elements under surveillance, documentation that is usually done only on the occasion of the closing and finalizing of the action. In this way we are losing sight of many significant aspects of the activity of the elements under surveillance.
—D 013381, German Nationalists[2]

Most archives incite a fascination with a return to origins, beginnings, and sources.
—PAULA AMAD, *Counter-Archive*[3]

The grammatical gender of nothingness [*golul*] is neuter.
—HERTA MÜLLER, "On This Day"[4]

To substantiate the accusation that her file had been gutted by the SRI (the heirs of the Romanian Securitate), Herta Müller first noted the absence of the file's beginning, her harassment during and after university. "After I studied I worked three years in a tractor factory. Those three years do not appear with a single word in my file."⁵ To set the record straight, Müller documents the Securitate's longstanding interest in her. She writes that by the time her file was started, in 1983, she had already been shadowed, harassed, pressured to become an informer, and, upon her refusal, threatened with death: "We'll drown you in the river."⁶ In the second epigraph to this chapter, taken from volume 13 of a 40-volume file usually buried inside the 24 kilometers of declassified Securitate files, its agents also express concern over what *is lacking* from these overflowing archives: it is again the proper beginning of files, whose lacunae the Securitate blame not on malicious purging but on a Stakhanovite interest in endings.⁷ This chapter sets out to investigate Müller's accusation and search for the allegedly missing beginning of her file, focusing on and beyond the obvious source, her personal file, into related problem files pertaining to the German community in Romania.⁸ Furthermore, I examine the varied, yet persistent preoccupations with and fantasies about such missing beginnings. In the process, I hope to throw light not only on the question of Herta Müller's file, but also on the challenge of archival silences—in Soviet-era documents and beyond.⁹

Revisiting the main challenge of chapter 1, this chapter continues to focus on the gendered dimension of secret police archival lacunae—but shifts from an investigation of the treatment of homosexuality to the treatment of women. We are only starting to understand the gendered dimensions of the creation, preservation, declassification, and reception of secret police archives. For example, Joshua Sanborn's research into the cybernetic turn in the Soviet secret police documents the low status of "'nerd work' in an institution that prided itself on its combative manliness . . . It was also suspect as a feminine enterprise, not only because it involved working with keyboards and typing, but also because a 'high percentage' of the workers were women."¹⁰ This perception of gendered work appears to have extended to other secret police tasks, such as forensic translation and recordkeeping. On the other hand, at least in the East German context, where we have statistical data, just before the fall of the Berlin Wall, "the only thing typical of a spy was a gender: about 85 to 90 percent of them have been identified as men."¹¹ Sarah Blaylock notes that "though a substantial academic study of gendered aspects of Stasi observation has yet to be conducted, anecdotal evidence resoundingly reveals a bias against women artists."¹² Blaylock further finds a gendered dimension to the artists' engagement with the archives after 1989: "all Stasi-inspired artwork[s] to date have been made by women. The interest they paid to their files stands in inverse proportion to the actual attention the Ministry for State Security paid to female artists... The omission reflects a systemic problem, namely an underestimation of women's contribution in areas outside of home."[13] The secret police's treatment of Herta Müller shows that women were surveilled differently than the majority of the subjects of personal files, who were male. In this chapter, I argue that not only were secret police documents gendered: so were their lacunae and blind spots.[14]

My search for the allegedly missing beginning of this file is not rooted in any myth of origins. I have long taken to heart the persuasive warnings against such myths, warnings influentially articulated by Jacques Derrida, and recently more specifically tailored for the Soviet context.[15] Indeed, the deconstruction of mythical origins clears room for what I hope will be a very different search into beginnings. I start out with deliberately modest expectations: I aim to see if we can find any shreds of that allegedly missing beginning. If other shreds will, as I expect, be "found missing," I am interested in determining how they have gone missing, while remaining open to the idea that they may never have been there. Was the beginning accidentally lost or was it purged, and if so, was this a routine purge, the fate that befalls about 96 percent of state-produced documents in archives worldwide, or was it a malicious act?[16] Is the beginning of Müller's file buried somewhere else? The previous chapter broached such (and other) questions, following clues that indicate that this file may have originated in an informer's report, in a typewritten copy of an informer's report, or in a mediocre translation of a short literary work. Yet before any of these documents, what meets us in the archive are the file's covers.

COVERS

Herta Müller's file, like many others, has two covers.[17] The first, typed, clean, with the letterhead of the CNSAS, the archive currently holding them, reads: "FILE concerning."[18] The two lines generously provided for the name of the suspect are left blank: Müller's name does not appear at all on the first cover. Instead, what follows is a barcode and, in clear typed letters, the file's CNSAS number: I 233477, Vol. 1. The second cover is, as it often happens,

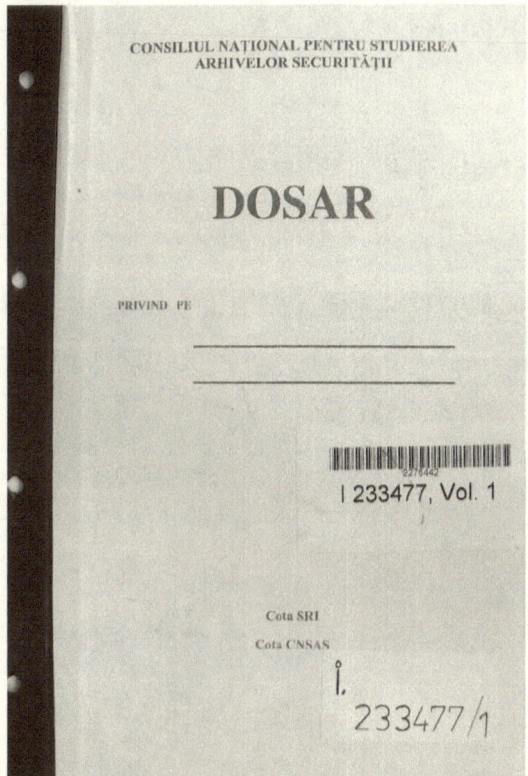

FIGURE 17. File Cover I, I 233477, vol. 1, ACNSAS.

more exciting, a Babel of names, numbers, and handwritings compared to the sparseness of the new cover. Deceptively flattened together on the two-dimensional page, the different handwritings, fonts, and stamps belong to hands and times so different as to produce sheer confusion: so is this file "Nr. 4615," "I 233477," or "200857"? [19] The present-day archivist whom I consulted reshuffled these dates and numbers, splattered in no particular order on the cover, into a chronology. He explained that the file carried each of those numbers at different times: it was baptized *Dosar de urmărire informativă 4615* (Informative Trailing File 4615, most often referred to as DUI 4615), when it was opened in 1983, and continued under this number throughout the eight years when it was an active file. It then took on the archive number 200857, when it was processed and filed in the Securitate Archives. And it was born again (or buried again, depending on your view of archives) as I 233477 when it was taken in custody by the archivist of the

FIGURE 18. File Cover II, I 233477, vol. 1, ACNSAS.

Council for the Study of the Securitate Archives, in 1993. Other times and hands, less readily identifiable or less easily fitted into a chronology, have left their marks on the cover as well. For example, the parenthesis following the "Strictly Secret" stamp, "(after being filled out)," was written at the time when this cover was not secret yet, when it was stamped in some paper factory or archive basement, in expectation of its secret contents. That short period of expectation, together with the period since it was transferred to the CNSAS—"16.08.1993," announces another handwritten note bulging out of a more recent stamp—is a rather lopsided frame around what the cover announces as ten years of strict secrecy, from the date the file was opened, "8.03.1983," to the date it was transferred to CNSAS, "16.08.1993." The last line but one of the cover promises closure with the words: "File closed on the following date." However, that promise remains unfulfilled, as no date, nothing at all, in fact, follows. The cause of this omission could be, as Herta Müller has suggested, that she was still followed by Securitate's successor, the SRI, so that her file was not closed yet at the date when it was forwarded to the CNSAS. However, the blank next to the closing date of the file is a common, if chilling, ellipsis. Files that contain explicit documents titled "Final Decision to Close the DUI," or even files whose subjects are long dead, also linger in the archives with the closing date blank. The blank could be simple negligence. Or maybe the blank is a sign that the archivist's work is never done, a file is never fully closed, as relevant information can always surface and be added at a later date. As we will see at length in this chapter, secret police file blanks can provide ample room for interpretation.

What we have then for a start are two covers, two frames for this story. And to make matters even more complicated, there are also three titles, if numbers are to be taken for the file's titles, and a few blanks. Such as the blank that should have been filled with Herta Müller's name on the first page. On the second page, the name "Herta Müller" is again absent. Instead, what we read is "Informative Trailing File Nr. 4615 concerning 'CRISTINA' (code name)." This was the original title of the file at the time it was "an active file," during the surveillance of Müller. The title gives concrete information about the kind of file we are about to open, an informative trailing file, or DUI (Dosar de Urmărire Informativă)—the most detailed kind of personal file kept by the Securitate, more thorough than the "checkup" and "verification files" that sometimes preceded DUIs as well as informer files.[20] The Securitate used code names for its informers as for the file's subject, or in its lingo "objective." For ten years the file cover kept the secret of that code name, but for us, the mystery is solved right away, as below the code name another handwriting hase scribbled obliquely in now faded pencil, "Karl, Herta, 1953." "The unexplained use of this last name [briefly borne by Müller during her first marriage but no longer in use by 1983, as she had reclaimed her maiden name] is a possible reason why the file took so long to retrieve, despite Müller's insistent requests," the CNSAS spokesperson, Ancuța Median, conjectures as we go through the file together.

To recapitulate, then: on the second cover of Herta Müller's file, there are three file numbers, a code name, and the declassification of that codename. Various handwritings. Two different archival stamps. One barcode. For the record, there are also seven punched holes, but even my drive to close-read file covers has a limit. I'll leave the holes, together with their overly symbolic number, as they are. Instead, we will discuss at length more metaphorical holes in the files, its gaps. The graphic confusion of this cover gives us a first sense of the entangled temporalities of the file. Even with the expert help of archivists trained to construct something of a timeline out of these words and numbers, some questions, such as the missing end date for the file, remain. But one thing appears quite unequivocal, blue ink on beige: the opening date of the file, "8.III. 1983." That is, 8 March, International Women's Day. In Romania, people take this celebration very seriously. The Timiș Securitate was likely sharing in the national bustle of people arranging flowers, cards, presents, and parties for that evening's celebration. It was probably amid these festive preparations that a few agents also worked on opening a DUI file on Herta Müller.

FIRST PAGES

However, once one turns the two covers and opens the file, one realizes that this file, like most others, began before its official beginning on 8 March 1983. Files usually start *in medias res*. The first document in Müller's file, "Report with proposals to open an informative trailing file concerning Karl Herta from Timișoara," was created later than the second document in this file; indeed, almost two years later.[21] It also was created at least three informer reports later, as documented by the file itself, which includes those earlier informer reports. Once we read the informer reports carefully, we realize that there also were previous informer reports that for unstated reasons were not added to the file. In what is filed as his very first report in Müller's file, a report dated 16.III.1982, a year before the official opening of the DUI, a particularly conscientious informer, "Voicu," makes references to earlier reports he had written on Müller's prose "Meine Familie."[22] The marginalia of the investigator confirm that the information was provided in an anterior report by this informer—but that report or those reports were not added to this file, and no information is given as to their whereabouts.[23]

Only five pages into the file, we already have ample evidence that the Securitate was collecting information on Müller years before her DUI file was officially opened. And there is also repeated evidence that documents pertaining to her case, such as informer reports giving information on her work, are missing from the present file. Müller's file does not keep records of these omissions—unlike other files, which sometimes note that such-and-such pages had been destroyed as part of routine archival maintenance of the file, or whose repeatedly crossed-out page numbers testify to repeated purges. In Müller's file, the difference between the two archivists' paginations is very slight, just one page, which has thus been declared officially lost. But while Müller's DUI does not conscientiously reference the missing pages, it also does not attempt to cover up at least some of the omissions, keeping instead incidental references to them. I believe this is because this DUI file never makes the claim that the Securitate surveillance of Müller started with its opening in 1983.

Müller draws this conclusion from her own reading of her file in *Cristina or the Double*. In this book, which, as the title suggests, takes on not only what is but especially what is not in the file, she uses the contradiction between the opening date of the file and the existence of previous informer reports on her as evidence that after the revolution the SRI "have removed the central things . . . as everything through which the Securitate people would implicate themselves."[24] As we saw in the opening of this chapter, the first of the central things that Müller believes is not in her file because it has been removed from it is the file's actual beginning. I doubt that the Securitate would take issue with her claim that she was "in their attention" long before the start of the DUI. Glajar finds twenty mentions of Herta Müller that predate the opening of her own file, in the personal files of some of her acquaintances.[25] Indeed, "information pertaining to Müller is also recorded in Totok's, Lippet's, Helmuth Frauendorfer's, and Csejka's files, as well as in that of ERIKA, a West German diplomat, and in various Securitate reports in several NFG [German Nationalists] volumes."[26] In fact, besides the reference to previous informer reports absent from the DUI, there are repeated notes even in Müller's own file that document their longstanding interest in her. Thus, in a commentary at the end of an informer report dated 26.III.1981, the supervising investigator notes that "Herta Müller is 'in our attention' relating problem 1909."[27] What this rather cryptic note means is that at this time Müller was not the subject of a DUI file, but was rather followed by the Securitate in a "problem file" a different type of file that was not organized individually but followed multiple people connected to a "problem." In her case, this problem file turns out to be "German Nationalists," which, despite its damning name, monitored the ethnic German minority as a whole. The Securitate branch of each county where the German minority was concentrated produced such a file, with the most important findings being forwarded to the center, the Bucharest Securitate, which compiled a country-wide file out of this correspondence.

IS THE BEGINNING ELSEWHERE? THE NATIONAL PROBLEM FILE ON GERMAN NATIONALISTS

In its present iteration in the CNSAS archive, this centralized file, D 013381, covers the years 1971–89 and contains 46 volumes, each 200–400 pages long.[28] The main topic of the file is the mass emigration of the German minority from Romania, the central drama of this historic minority that, after living in Transylvania for almost a thousand years, disappeared in a true exodus to Germany in the years preceding and immediately following the 1989 revolution. The file also documents Securitate interest in what they perceived as the other major problems related to this minority: Nazi nostalgia, West Germany's influence on the community, "writers of interpretative literature" and other intellectuals prone to dissent. The file overflows with many different types of documents, some familiar from the study of personal files, such as informer reports, or reports on the warning of particular suspects, some less so: periodic (usually yearly) syntheses sent by the local branches of the Securitate to the center, reporting the number of subjects followed in the problem file and in individual DUIs, the number of informers aimed to be added each year, and the actual rate at each informers were added. The largest volume, vol. 15, bursts at the seams with fascinating computer-generated statistics on the immigration phenomenon, with each person who had ever filed an immigration application carefully described and then entered into a variety of tables aimed at breaking down the numbers by age, gender, and socioeconomic characteristics.

As part of that bothersome group of German "writers of interpretative literature," Herta Müller, I was certain, would be featured in this file, if not by name, then through this or that particular digit added to an aggregate number. The detailed statistics on the year 1985 forwarded by the Timiş Securitate tell us that 4,800 ethnic Germans were in the Securitate database of this "problem," of whom 281 were under "priority surveillance" through D 013381, while another 49 had DUIs. Müller, who was by then endowed with a DUI, is represented somewhere in that group of 49, huddled together with all the other most dangerous "elements" in her county.[29]

But the actual browsing of the 10,000-plus pages of the German Nationalists file revealed that Müller—like most other members of her minority followed by the Securitate at this time—did not only appear as a number forwarded to the center. Instead, she appeared, repeatedly, by name. In the above-mentioned 1985 report, we find out that "Herta Müller and Richard Wagner through direct contact have been maintained under the influence of our organs and determined to abstain from publishing hostile writings. The information obtained [through bugging and informers] attests that elements like Totok William, Wagner Richard, Müller Herta, . . . all worked through DUIs, continue to situate themselves on hostile positions."[30] The report then summarizes Müller's "suspect contacts" with the West German embassy as well as her intention, uncovered through bugging, to not return from her projected visit to West Germany, an intention the Securitate agents congratulated themselves on having thwarted.[31] However, if this information can easily be gleaned from her DUI, the reading of D 013381 is especially valuable for earlier mentions of Müller, mentions that go back before the opening of her DUI. Thus, the yearly 1981 report for Timiș signals "the more and more frequent preoccupation of certain individuals, especially intellectuals, to compose writings with a tendentious character."[32] A few writers connected to the literary circle Aktionsgruppe Banat are mentioned, the very first one, out of alphabetical order, being: "Herta Müller, with literary preoccupations, known as having relations to hostile elements from this milieu, has written a so-called village chronicle which through irony and satire attempts to represent in a deforming manner realities from the villages inhabited by Swabians."[33] Detailed paraphrases of the most subversive passages of her short story follow, so that, just as in the 1985 report, a significant paragraph from this ten-page annual county-wide report is dedicated to Müller. The report mentions that in 1981 the Timiș Securitate followed 20 Germans through DUIs while another 186 were singled out and "worked" in the problem file.[34] The report attests then that by 1981, Müller, not yet endowed with a DUI, was among the most keenly followed of the 186 ethnic Germans in Timiș featured in the problem file. Whether it adds such new information to what we can glean from the DUI or just summarizes in a few sentences tens of DUI pages, the problem file is valuable as it offers a different perspective on the subject, giving us a sense of her case's importance within the larger county and further national context.

Like the DUI, the problem file also attests that, while the particular intimidation or "positive influence" techniques might have been left to the imagination of some provincial underling, the overall plan of action that concerned her, including the use of intimidation/positive influence direct contact sessions, the bugging of her apartment, or the withholding of her right to travel abroad, was drawn by high-ranking officers and approved by the Securitate leadership in both Timişoara and Bucharest.[35] Furthermore, if the record of particular direct contacts or informer recruitment attempts was not considered important enough to be added to the correspondence to the center, such contacts and informer recruitment attempts, whether successful or not, were closely monitored and entered into year-end statistics. Thus, in 1981, the year when Müller did not yet have a DUI but was among those 186 ethnic Germans "worked with priority," Securitatea Timiş reported "19 warnings, 117 attention-calling sessions (*atenționări*), 215 positive influence sessions, 193 information sessions with higher-ups [of the kind that led to Müller's firing from her job in 1979], 34 confiscation of hostile materials . . . one judicial sentence through the Militia, 787 individual counter-information sessions."[36]

What these statistics prove again and again is that these records were not meant to document the response of the subject to the Securitate's action. In the few cases where we have actual reports of warning sessions, for instance, the reports are so formulaic in describing the "objective's" response—"after being confronted with the facts the objective confessed to having been guilty, regretted their behavior, and promised not to engage in similar activities in the future"—that these people of various age, gender, and education become virtually indistinguishable.[37] So that even if one of these reports had been about Herta Müller, or even if the discovery of the now missing county problem file would unearth her warning session reports, we would not be much the wiser. The withholding of particular information, the "I don't remember" that could have mustered the subject's entire courage and moral fiber, the many shades of difference between the diffident and the servile are washed out in the standard warning reports and disappear completely in that characteristic genre of the correspondence between the provinces and the center—the statistic.[38] The mention of statistics reminds us once again that the files are not there to document the subjects, who are just "objectives," but rather to evidence the efforts of the Securitate agents themselves, to prove their hard work, measured by the number of files opened and closed every year, by the number of warning sessions and informer recruitments—to prove, as one report concludes, that "work has been done, that beautiful problems exist."[39] These documents give the picture of the Securitate in a file frenzy, excited to "finish old DUIs and finalize them [sic] and at the same time to open new files, to work new elements—especially intellectuals—since it was estimated that there are interesting cases to be actively taken up."[40]

The reason why we need to be constantly reminded of this is because it is counterintuitive. As opposed to what one might expect from an information-gathering agency, the Securitate did not use its files to research and record its subjects' actual opinions, responses, or reactions; instead, it focused most of its energy into a self-propagating, self-justificatory project of recording itself and its own "hard work." For this reason, often the most interesting part of the file is not the description of the subject, which tends to be formulaic, erasing individuals to match them to particular criminal profiles, such as "writer of interpretative literature," but rather the dialogue between the reporting and the supervising agent, the peculiar paratext formed by the underlining, marginalia, and endnotes added by the supervising agent, who usually comments more on the work of the reporting agent rather than on the subject of the file. Thus, at the end of "Nota de analiza 7.09.1983," from Müller's DUI, the supervising agent starts by commenting: "To date, informative trailing has unfolded in a dissatisfying way." Added to this comment, in yet another handwriting, supposedly that of a higher-up, is an even harsher commentary: "Atrocious."[41] Similarly, the parts of the regional file that are deemed worthy of being transmitted to the center, and even more those documents that are specially created for the center—most often the statistics—give interesting information not about the problem they ostensibly describe, that is, German nationalist fascists, but rather about the constant effort of each Securitate agent to justify their achievements and about the center's preoccupation to monitor potential failure. Thus, it is telling that these statistics, which erase the name of the file subjects, showcase the names of the responsible officers, which become the organizing principle of many a table. Thus, a 1978 table from Securitate Sibiu notes the names of each officer in charge of ethnic Germans and then notes the number of planned informer recruitments by month, offering the superior a good comparative view of the ambitions and productivity of each officer.[42] The table is followed by a commentary noting to what extent the plan has been achieved.[43] The formulation is the same as those used in almost any sector of the planned economy, whether the production of eggs, tractors, or high-school graduates. The only difference is that while most plans of the period were declared realized by more than 100 percent, the Sibiu Securitate abashedly declares its low achievement rate—only 40 percent and 75 percent of the proposed recruitments had actually been successful.[44]

Similarly, the Securitate Timiș self-critically reported to the center: "It is a negative [fact] that the 1977 recruitment plan has not been fulfilled."[45] This phrase comes from an annual report that is crucial for our search for earlier traces of Müller in Securitate documents. Written in February 1978, the document is a long review of 1977 and a plan of action for the following year. Thus, the report stretches over the key period whose absence from her file Müller denounces, the years she worked at the Tehnometal Factory, where she was hired in 1977 and then fired, due to her refusal to become an informer, in 1979. At first sight, the report is a disappointment for our search, for the name of Herta Müller does not explicitly appear. Indeed, rich in numbers, this long annual report mentions strikingly few names. It starts with the names of the three main investigators working on the case, but then mentions no suspect or informer proper names. However, among the few explicitly named targets is the Adam Müller-Guttenbrunn Literaturkreis, the small literary circle that Herta Müller was part of, as well as the German literature department of the Timișoara University from which she had graduated in 1976.[46] The only objective named, by code name rather than real name, is "Titan" alias Gerhard Ortinau, a member of Müller's group of friends whose autobiographical novel the Securitate prided itself on confiscating.[47] So while the report does not mention Müller or her friends by proper name, it refers to their group as prime targets of its attention. The report would be invaluable even just as a general picture of the Securitate's assessment of the ethnic German "problem" at what it perceived was a critical moment. But the document actually turns out to be much more deeply connected to Müller's biography. For just like her life in 1978, the report is situated at the fulcrum point between the recent past "subversive activities" of the group of young people she associated with, and the Securitate's tandem responses to those actions: continued harassment and renewed effort in the recruitment of informers. So while this report does not show the particular harassments that Müller suffered, or the particular ways she was pressured to become an informer, it does reveal the drive behind particular Securitate actions. The document clearly shows that Müller's experiences were neither exceptions nor abuses of the system; rather, such experiences were carefully designed as part of a constantly updated plan of action.

In this singularly self-critical annual report, the Timiş Securitate is concerned most of all by the shortcomings of its informer network, which it finds lacking despite its attempts to bolster this network particularly among intellectuals.[48] The report also complains about informers "who provide materials of small importance or without any value, skirt the fulfillment of their tasks, do not attend their meetings regularly, etc."[49] Given how controversial the issue of informer participation remains, this is one intriguing use of "etc." The first part of the sentence already conveys a certain lack of enthusiasm and passive-aggressive resistance among existing informers. What else was the Securitate alluding to? It is hard to tell, for the short qualitative description of the problem is soon covered under a barrage of numbers. The report notes that at the time 46 informers were working on the problem, out of whom 11 had been recruited in 1977.[50] The report sets the Timiş Securitate the goal of correcting these "shortcomings" starting with the current year, 1978, when it proposes to recruit 20 informers, thus almost doubling the number of new informers recruited the previous year.[51] The strengthening of the informer network through the recruitment of intellectuals and people who would be able to penetrate deeply "in the intimacy of the elements under surveillance" is declared necessary because of the importance and seriousness of the problem.[52] While the Securitate notes that through its geographical position and ethnic mix Timişoara has always presented a difficult situation, it assesses that this situation has been worsened by the recent involvement of "young people" in subversive activities. Thus, the Timiş Securitate declared itself deeply concerned about "young people's tendency to constitute groups that denigrate the social realities of our country, the policies of our country and state" and about "the preoccupation of certain people to produce hostile writings to be disseminated in the context of groups and literary circles, and to be published in our country or abroad."[53] The report enumerates the 1977 Securitate actions against these people: "15 warnings, the breaking of 5 groups made up of 52 elements, 58 people have been made attentive, while the leadership of the factories, institutions, and of the party has been kept updated."[54] A few pages away, another partly overlapping statistic concludes: "A large number of people have been made attentive, we have acted on many in view of their positive influencing through the [informer] network and through other factors."⁵⁵

Maybe one or two or all of Müller's encounters with the police are sealed up inside one of those numbers—15, or 58, or maybe the investigator-turned-amateur-statistician got tired of counting the reports of her and others' intimidation sessions and just wrote "a large number." Maybe such reports exist in the county or city problem file on which the national D 013381 problem file draws; after all, every such session was supposed to be recorded. The 1978 report even chides the lack of documentation, so maybe by 1979, the Securitate had shaped up, keeping such early records, maybe even those concerning aborted informer recruitment sessions. However, based on the formulaic warning session reports that we do have in D 013381, I doubt that we would be much the wiser as to Müller's experience. Fortunately, we have a whole book of Müller's, *The Appointment*, dedicated to giving words to the inconspicuous gray space right before one of these digits: a whole novel dedicated to the nerve-wracking bus trip to the Securitate headquarters for an appointment scheduled on a "Thursday, at 10 sharp."⁵⁶ It was likely the informer recruitment goals set in the same report that led to Müller's being pressured into becoming a collaborator. Müller complains that her refusal, a turning point in her life that came close to costing her not just her livelihood but also her sanity, is only documented in her DUI by a marginal note by Lieutenant Colonel Pădurariu, who confirmed her account of the failed recruitment attempt. That account, which includes the name of the Securitate recruiting agent, Müller's refusal, and the ensuing Securitate threat, was given by Müller to a friend who was actually an informer, code-named "Andreia." So the account of the recruitment attempt made its way into Müller's DUI via "Andreia's" informer report. Müller's main investigator, Lieutenant Colonel Pădurariu, scribbled at the end of the report, "The things noted here are real, so it means that our source has started to enjoy the confidence of the objective. We should continue to use the source to get to know the activity of the objective."⁵⁷ Pădurariu almost accidentally confirmed Müller's version of the recruitment; he scribbled his note for the benefit of another colleague working on the case, the officer to whom "Andreia" was reporting. He would have probably written the very same note had Müller shared her love life with "Andreia." The only reason he commented on Müller's account was because it signaled something about the informer's privileged relationship to Müller, not because he believed the account of Müller's refusal or of the Securitate threat against her were in themselves worthy of being noted. Indeed, in the 1978 report such refusals are crammed inside the unsatisfactory statistics on new recruitment attempts, or possibly inside that intriguing "etc." that described the Securitate's frustration with its informer network.

Having looked into the national problem file for the real beginning of the Securitate's interest in Müller, what we find are indeed some earlier documents featuring her, but no real origin, and certainly not the particular records documenting what Müller has described as her first encounters with the secret police. This could be because such documents existed in the problem file and were purged, but I think, based on the nature of the documents included in the national problem file, that it is rather unlikely that they existed in the first place. While it is true that there are a few more detailed personalized reports about other members of Müller's group of writers—the confiscation of a manuscript from William Totok is featured on a few pages,[58] Richard Wagner's text *Der Junge Berner* is reproduced over twenty-three file pages,[59] and the most pernicious informer from within the group, Franz Thomas Schleich, code-named "Voicu," stands accused by a personal record that summarizes his informer contribution in a few pages[60]—Müller gets more personal attention than most of the other ethnic Germans in the national problem file. The kinds of documents that we had been looking for—reports on the attempt to recruit her as an informer or reports on the warning sessions she underwent at the Securitate headquarters—are missing almost entirely from the problem file. The four individual warning session reports from Timiș that we get in this file are the exception rather than the rule, since in the same file we are told that many more warning sessions had been conducted that year. This is not because the Securitate considered the warning session to be unworthy of being documented; indeed, they carefully counted them and distinguished between warning, positive influence, and "attention-calling" sessions. However, the processing of the individual DUI and provincial problem file data into a national file shows the gradual if continuous erasure of particular subjects of the file into aggregate data. To a certain extent this is to be expected. But this movement from the individual or provincial file to the national file is more than just the adoption of a wider lens; rather, it is the expression of a larger trend visible in the creation of all files, from the most elementary effort at data collection by trailing to the synthesis of a file covering hundreds of individuals into a couple of pages. This trend is rooted in the counterintuitive lack of interest and utter disregard for the ostensible subject of the file and the self-absorbed interest in the Securitate agents' own actions. It results in the creation of reports that were faithful to a particular script rather than to the events, reports that were likely to conform to one's supervising agent's expectations rather than to add new information about the suspect.

WOMEN AS BLIND SPOTS

As could be expected, this narcissistic tendency of the files sometimes boomeranged against the Securitate. The most glaring example offered by D 013381 is the case of László Tőkés, the evangelical pastor whose revolt against the authorities incited the first protests in Timişoara, protests that eventually spread across the country and led to the demise of the Ceauşescu regime in 1989. Tőkés appears in the German Nationalists problem file, even though he was followed as a "Hungarian Nationalist." At some point, the ethnic minorities problem file seemed to mix minorities. The main document that concerns Tőkés is the decision to close his DUI, on the ground that he was seen as having stopped his subversive activity.[61] At the time when the Securitate was adding hundreds of DUIs on people whose crime was often at most the writing of "interpretative literature" destined to the drawer, at the time when Securitate agents were paid to transcribe and translate foreign correspondence including inane birth announcements, they also made the decision to close down the DUI on Tőkés, who can be convincingly singled out as the one individual most influential in the toppling of the communist regime in Romania.[62] If one reads carefully the report of his warning session, one can see his unusual character pecking out of the formulaic narrative—made to confess that his writings were interpretive and subversive, he admits not that they were so but that "they could be interpreted as such by certain people," a small departure from the usual scenario.[63] What is more surprising is that when the Securitate pressured him into becoming an informer, Tőkés signed an informer agreement and then proceeded to tell his acquaintances that he had been interrogated and made to sign an informer's agreement, but that he would never inform for the Securitate. The hurried agent, probably eager to tick off another closed file before the year-end statistic, brushes these differences under the carpet of the standard narrative—objective was contacted, intimidated, he admitted his guilt, promised to no longer engage in subversive activities—and proceeds to close Tőkés's DUI.

Besides the lack of attention to the actual subjects as opposed to the overwrought attention to creating criminal profiles, what also sometimes boomeranged against the Securitate were their own prejudices. I think part of the reason why Herta Müller may be featured less in the national file and may have had a DUI opened later than the other members of her group was that she was a woman. The Securitate was a sexist institution, and in Müller's case this was manifested early in the way they treated her: although they had information suggesting that she was the most talented writer of her group, they ironized her "oeuvre" and constantly abused her, as they did many women suspects, with gender-specific accusations.[64] In Müller's case, she remembers being accused of sleeping with eight Arab students, and when she protested that she knew none of them, the investigator commented wryly that he could produce any number of Arab students that "knew" her well.[65] But this sexism also boomeranged. The overeager identification drive of the secret police sometimes went dormant when it came to women, whose identities are erased under the names of their relationships to the men in the group.[66] Thus, in the first informer reports that identify the members of Müller's group of writers for the police, the two women in the group do not appear by name but rather as "Wagner's wife" and "Ortinau's wife."[67] The only known mention of Müller in a Securitate document from 1976 notes that "a girl" presented her poems at a literary meeting. Only when pressed for details does the informer give her name, Herta Müller-Karl, adding that the consensus was that her poems were weak.[68] This is particularly relevant in a place where being named in a file meant being added to the general Securitate database, and often having a personal record being drawn up, and from there being entered into the system. At least for a while, sexism helped "Wagner's wife" and "Ortinau's wife" escape this kind of undesired attention.

It was really only when Müller's work became of interest to a West German publisher that the local Securitate realized their oversight, both in the delay of opening a personal file on her, unlike on her closest male associates, and in the incomplete and at times contradictory information her early file contained. As Glajar puts it, on 3 November 1983, "lightning struck at the Timis Securitate," when the Bucharest Securitate announced that the West

Berlin publisher Rotbuch had contacted Kriterion, the Bucharest publisher of Müller's debut volume *Niederungen*, about its intention to republish it.[69] The "poor quality of Müller's surveillance" became evident to the main investigator of the case, Pădurariu, and to his superiors, who deemed it "atrocious" (*sub orice critică*).[70] Despite this rude awakening, the quality of surveillance was not immediately improved: the Securitate seems to have inexplicably missed the 1984 visit of the Rotbuch editor Gabriele Dietze to a Romanian mountain resort, where she and Müller worked on an uncensored version of *Niederungen* that Rotbuch then published.[71] The surveillance only got significantly better when the Securitate installed bugging devices in the apartment Müller shared with her husband, Richard Wagner. (The operation was itself clumsy, as the first microphone, installed from the apartment below, pierced the floor under a bookcase).[72] Even though most likely triggered by worries about Müller's new popularity in West Germany, the request for approval of this surveillance technology installation was strangely filed in Wagner's personal file, and not in Müller's.[73] She only appears in the report as one of his connections, among other people in his entourage. Thus it is not only for almost ten years (1974–83), when the Securitate was aware of Müller without endowing her with a personal file, that we find key information about her in the files of her male connections or in the problem file of the German community. Even once she was surveilled through her own personal file, some key documents were preserved not in her file but in her husband's. Partially traceable to the dismissive attitude of the secret police to their women targets, these gendered omissions augment the challenge of reading the secret police archives.

FOUNDATIONAL LACUNAE

My investigation found shards of the beginning Müller believes to have been purged from her file. I found some of the beginning to have been recorded elsewhere, in other personal and problem files, especially in D 01338, the voluminous national problem file on the German minority in Romania.[74] Despite these shards of beginnings, a comprehensive record of the beginning conjured by Herta Müller is still missing. Yet even unmet, Müller's expectations of her file attune us to the many lacunae in these files—their verbose silences. In Müller's case, the silences do not prove the absence of police activity. Indeed, Müller had been interpellated in a way that was to change her life forever; she had talked back, and they did hear her words (through informers, bugging, and even directly). Despite the file's silences, we know that they did their best (or worst) to silence her. Instead, I believe that the beginnings of her contacts with the secret police are still partially shrouded in silence in these secret police archives because their kilometers of files cover a very thin layer of secret police activity: the worst was often unwritten. There was silence because many things went without saying and without writing. When Herta Müller became the subject of her own DUI file in 1983, in some ways the worst was over for her. She had already been pressured into becoming an informer; she had declined. She had been harassed, fired from her job, and threatened to be disappeared. Based on my readings in the Securitate archives, I think records of these events are absent from the files not necessarily because anyone took the care to erase them carefully (which they may have done); instead, I think they are fundamentally missing because from the secret police's perspective they did not need to be in any file, no paper needed to be "wasted" on them. Pădurariu's surviving confirmation of Müller's missed beginning—the recruitment attempt—which we can still read in his offhand comment to an informer report, suggests that neither he, the main investigator on her case, nor the Securitate or the SRI archivists, thought this was something to be hidden or purged. However, it also so far appears that they did not think that their failed informer recruitment was something worth documenting in detail. A few words, such as "apply pressure so that she stops her tendentious writing," could have been considered enough to cover the harrowing episodes that Müller justly recalls in characteristic detail. In fact, "The Plan of Action" that may have been responsible for her harassment would not even necessarily have needed to mention her name. All that was needed were vague, chillingly inclusive recommendations in the group file: "apply pressure so that the group of young 'so-called writers' stop their subversive activity; work to disintegrate the group, isolate and intimidate its members, recruit new informers from their midst." Müller became the subject of a personal trailing file when she became more visible, through the publication of her work and its recognition abroad. So it is likely that the harsher measures taken against her, such as physical harassment, happened unrecorded before her DUI was opened; instead, the DUI documents some of the more subtle and more exhaustive surveillance and psychological pressure she experienced as she gained visibility abroad, even after she was finally allowed to emigrate to Germany.

In investigating Müller's charge that the Securitate and its heirs purged her file of compromising documents, we find them guilty of much more than the eventual purge: the long and complicated process by which these files were initiated, composed, then summarized, synthesized, forwarded to the center, and finally archived is shot through with questionable silences. This goes far beyond the particular purging of certain compromising documents from a particular file, like Müller's. Such purging may or may not have happened in this case: documents keep emerging from the archives as we read them. We may yet find more records of Müller's direct encounters with the secret police, or maybe even a record of her informer recruitment attempt, or even a whole verification file leading to that attempt. But even if all of these documents surface, they will not feature the number of hard-boiled eggs (eight) she was force-fed after being pulled from the street into a Securitate basement.[75] They will also likely not feature the threat that she be drowned in the river, and certainly not the wording of her diffident answers or the patterns of her resulting insomnia.[76] Such "details" are the stuff of testimony, and the files are not testimony: they are the writing over of testimony, its verbose silencing. At the risk of being controversial, I propose that the post-factum destruction of particular documents is the least of all these acts of omission: it at least contains a certain acknowledgment about there having been something wrong, or at least unseemly, about the original document, a self-critical move that is quite rare on the part of the secret police. Instead, the fundamental lacunae, the systematic silencing through omissions, euphemisms, and standardized narratives, testify to a much deeper disregard for the subject, in fact a mere objective. This disregard was doubled by the narcissistic interest in the Securitate itself, the true subject of its own writings.

FIVE

Data

The Iron Curtain's Origins and Translations

During the first years of the Eastern Bloc archival revolution the main challenge was access to missing or classified documents; nowadays we are often challenged by the overwhelming quantity of documents. In other words, while *archival access* continues to be an issue in some contexts, most prominently in Russia, recent years have seen an exponential growth in the issue of *archival excess*. Besides declassification, other factors that significantly broadened archival access included freedom of movement, international partnerships with and among Eastern European and Russian archives, and translation projects. None could compete, however, with the impact of the digital revolution, which fatefully intersected with the archival revolution from their common beginnings in the 1990s to the present. This last chapter turns our attention to the roles of digitization and digital research methods in the archival revolution. I focus on the double-edged sword of digital access, which can both magnify the challenge of archival excess and at times help tackle it. Archival excess is a reading challenge that researchers in many archives can easily identify with; it is all the more severe in the Eastern European archival revolution because of the unsurpassed reliance on propaganda, writing, and recordkeeping by the region's graphomaniac police states.

While previous chapters focused mainly on declassified materials, this chapter acknowledges that part of the challenge of reading the archival revolution has to do with the radically expanded and modified type of access to a wealth of materials that were not strictly secret but rather inaccessible or resistant to digital research methods. This challenge is both augmented and potentially alleviated by digitization. For instance, over the last three decades, the vast archives of all Russian and Soviet press from the 1917 Revolution to the present have been made accessible through the EastView databases. These ever growing collections include thousands of central and local publications and databases in Russian as well in the many other languages of the Eastern Bloc. The search engines allow us to track individual and combined words and phrases in the full body of millions of texts. But how do we read in these enormous digital archives? What is the use of our existent archival methodologies, such as close reading against or along the "archival grain," in these new digital collections?

This chapter attempts to gauge the challenge and mine the potential of these new digital archives through an archaeology of what was arguably the strongest, and strangest, political metaphor of the twentieth century—the Iron Curtain. EastView allows us to view every single mention of the phrase in the Soviet press since its 1946 coinage by Winston Churchill to the present day. The graphs that I created based on these data points allow us an unprecedented view of the origin and development of this concept, which we see morphing from a literal term for a theatrical prop to a chameleonic political metaphor. Its translations and recontextualizations range from the earlier meaning of a curtain of secrecy raised by the Soviets to its opposite, a smoke screen created by the West to hide its belligerence. This chapter tracks the term to the present day, through its fateful transformations during the war in Ukraine that was ongoing at the time of writing. Rather than seeing digital research as a panacea to the challenge of archival excess, the chapter combines data analysis with close readings of this rhetorical war of words and translations, demonstrating the necessity of drawing on diverse existent methodologies and developing new ones.

Unlike the previous chapters, this last chapter is based on materials that have not been declassified but have been made incomparably more accessible through digitization. This is partly an acknowledgment that declassification does not exhaust the challenges of reading the archival revolution. It is also a heuristic move, as we do not have systematic, large-scale digitization of formerly secret materials. Declassified materials are often either cherry-picked or more or less arbitrarily picked for digitization. There are many reasons for this unsystematic approach, the most understandable being rooted in demands of protecting the privacy of individuals who were featured in these materials against their will. At the other end of the spectrum we have the systematic criminal as well as accidental destruction of many of these documents, so that any remaining collection is partial and skewed by its amputations.

This may be surprising, because Soviet and Eastern European secret police were pioneers in using computers and computerized data.[1] However, at this time, declassified secret police materials are not digitized on a scale that is representative. While the secret police used computer files and searching aids to organize and access their collections, their heirs made a real effort to keep these from declassification. For instance, the leaders of Romania's declassification campaign attested to being shown computerized finding aids during a visit to the headquarters of the Romanian Securitate, yet these were never turned over to the new Council for the Study of the Securitate Archives, so that the vast declassified collections long remained unsearchable and thus largely opaque and inaccessible. In my own research for chapter 4, I also found proof of Securitate's large-scale data-collecting projects in the oversized computer-generated printouts of data pertaining to ethnic Germans applying to leave Romania in the 1980s. These documents were filed among the thousands of pages of the German Nationalists File, but none of the computer files they were based on had been transferred to the CNSAS. We can only hope that this lingering lack of digitization of declassified materials will be partially rectified with time, and I hope that this chapter's work on digital research methods will then be helpful or updated. In the meantime, this is a preliminary effort to understand, if not secret documents, then the icon of secrecy, as well as the challenges and potential of digitization and digital research methods, and their crucial role in the archival revolution.

The Iron Curtain turned into the powerful metaphor we all recognize during Winston Churchill's "Sinews of Peace" speech of 5 March 1946, which was followed by an explosion of translations in myriad languages on both sides of the Iron Curtain that he had just named. Widely known as Churchill's "Iron Curtain" speech, "The Sinews of Peace" was considered by many, including Churchill himself, the most important speech of his life; it was also considered by many, including Joseph Stalin, the beginning of the Cold War.² To most of us, the Iron Curtain is one of those curious combinations of words, an abstract figure, a metaphor without a material referent. Yet, iron curtains existed long before Churchill made his famous speech. Iron curtains first existed, as material objects, in theaters. These curtains, made of strong screens of metal, originally iron, were introduced after disastrous theater fires in the nineteenth century, to separate the audience from the flammable objects and special effects used on stage. The term had been used metaphorically a handful of times before Churchill, as scholars have informed us after arduous research.³ In 1915, pacifist Vernon Lee first referred to an Iron Curtain lowered between the British and the Germans by the Great War, despite the deeper aesthetic connections of appreciating Bach during Christmas service.⁴ In 1918 Vasilii Rozanov described postrevolutionary Russia through an Iron Curtain fable:

> With a clang, a creak, a screech, an Iron Curtain descends on Russian History.
> 'The show is over.'
> The public gets up.
> 'Now it is time to put on coats and go home.'
> They looked around.
> But there were neither coats, nor homes anymore.⁵

Not amused, Soviet critics found great satisfaction in pointing out that Goebbels spoke of an Iron Curtain separating the Soviets from the rest of Europe before Churchill.⁶ However, for most of Churchill's audience in Fulton, as well as for the much larger audience who read his immediately widely translated speech, the term "Iron Curtain" was strongly associated with the material curtains long mandatory in theaters.

Churchill's metaphorical usage of the term "Iron Curtain" was striking—so much so that it raised unexpected translation quandaries. In this chapter I start by following the ways in which Churchill mobilized what to us are largely buried theatrical connotations of the term to create a new postwar *theatrum mundi*. I then focus on the peculiar translation choices regarding the term "Iron Curtain" made in the Soviet press following

Churchill's speech and the ways those choices rearranged the design of his *theatrum mundi*. I then move to Romania, the country that topped Churchill's infamous percentage list of Eastern European nations ceded to Soviet influence. I follow the textual as well as visual quotations and translations of the term from English, French, and Russian, to show the perception of the actual moment of the Iron Curtain's descent not just from the West and the East, but also from right underneath. The second part of the chapter tracks the Iron Curtain's long afterlife in the Soviet press, through its much featured and satirized presence in the 1950s, to a long period of tense suppression during the Brezhnev era, unprecedented popularity as a return of the repressed during Perestroika and the 1990s, to its renewed censorship and recasting as "Iron Curtain 2.0" during the war in Ukraine.

CHURCHILL'S "IRON CURTAIN" AS THE AXIS OF A NEW POSTWAR *THEATRUM MUNDI*

Let us begin with Churchill's quote that instantly propelled the Iron Curtain to international fame:

> From Stettin in the Baltic to Trieste in the Adriatic an iron curtain has descended across the continent. Behind that line lie all the capitals of the ancient states of Central and Eastern Europe. Warsaw, Berlin, Prague, Vienna, Budapest, Belgrade, Bucharest and Sofia; all these famous cities and the populations around them lie in what I must call the Soviet sphere, and all are subject, in one form or another, not only to Soviet influence but to a very high and in some cases increasing measure of control from Moscow.[7]

Churchill traveled all the way to Fulton, Missouri, deep into the heart of the American Midwest to give his momentous speech, in order to place himself in the position of distant nonparticipant observer announcing to the whole world that the Soviets were gradually dropping an Iron Curtain over Eastern Europe. By some accounts, he hoped to stop this surreptitious action from the wings by turning all gazes toward the stage. He intended to shine the lights, albeit momentarily, on all those capitals that, however "ancient" they might be, Westerners found hard to pronounce and easy to mix up. By other accounts, Churchill found a good excuse to tell his Western audience, after the brief attention-getting number featuring the capital names-dropping, that the Iron Curtain was lowered, the show was over, and it was time to go home. There was not much to see and thus worry or feel responsible for—just in time, as the Soviets and their local allies were preparing to rig elections and murder political oppositions. As historian Larry Wolff put it, "throughout the Cold War the Iron Curtain would be envisioned as a barrier of quarantine, separating the light of Christian civilization from whatever lurked in the shadows, and such a conception was all the more justification for not looking too closely at the lands behind."[8] Despite significant differences, however, in both accounts the West was placed in the position of spectator, Eastern Europeans were the victims, and the Soviets were the sinister operators of the Iron Curtain. Churchill set up this *theatrum mundi* around his key topos, the Iron Curtain; the theatricality of his rhetoric appears much more muffled to us than to his audiences, for whom the Iron Curtain was not yet primarily a metaphor but was still very much associated with the theatrical firewall. Churchill bolstered his creation of this *theatrum mundi* throughout his speech. Thus, in preparation for the Iron Curtain paragraph, he warned: "a *shadow has fallen on the scenes* lately *lighted* by the Allied victory," so that "as I stand here on this quiet afternoon I shudder *to visualize* what is actually happening to millions now . . ."[9]

While carefully positioning himself in the quiet American Midwest at the time of the speech, Churchill was in fact, as Larry Wolff aptly puts it, "a far from entirely innocent observer of what befell the Eastern states of Europe," for he had been "eager to play a part in drawing the line and hanging the curtain."[10] Indeed, at the actual time of the drawing of the Iron Curtain, in October 1944, Churchill had been on the other side of the stage, in Moscow, where at a late-night meeting with Stalin in the Kremlin Churchill proposed the infamous portioning of Eastern Europe according to percentages:

> While this was being translated, I wrote on a half-piece of paper:
>
> | | | |
> |---|---|---|
> | Rumania: | Russia 90% | -The others 10% |
> | Greece: | Great Britain 90% | -Russia 10% |
> | Yugoslavia: | 50:50% | |
> | Hungary: | 50:50% | |
> | Bulgaria: | Russia 75% | -The others 25%[11] |
>
> After this there was a long silence. The penciled paper was in the center of the table. At length, I said: "Might it not be thought rather cynical if it

seemed we had disposed of these issues, so fateful to millions of people, in such an off-hand manner? Let us burn the paper." "No, you keep it," said Stalin.[12]

Published in 1959, this passage of Churchill's memoirs allows his reader a glimpse behind the scenes, where the two masterminds are shown in the act of pulling the strings, with Churchill performing a sleight of hand that he worried might seem so offhand to the larger audience as to warrant a burning of "the half-paper" then and there. It bears recalling that it was precisely because of incendiary gestures on stage that iron curtains were designed in the first place. While the Fulton speech depicted the Iron Curtain as being placed by the Soviets for the purposes of hiding their doings in Eastern Europe, Churchill's memoirs show him in fact masterminding the show, performing incendiary tricks, and pulling down the curtain himself. He shows himself doing it all with the classic purposes of shielding the audience from the fire and from the unwanted spectacle of the destruction of those caught behind the Iron Curtain, but also of hiding negligent stage tricks. The ending of the scene suggests that Churchill's regard for his demos was just strong enough to inspire the idea of burning the paper, hiding the deal, and lowering the Iron Curtain. Stalin appears, in this case, to be above this concern with secrecy, security, and appearances, three terms closely folded in Churchill's Iron Curtain.

THE IRON CURTAIN AND THE SMOKE SCREEN: SOVIET TRANSLATIONS

One of the first discoveries in searching for the translation of the Iron Curtain speech in Soviet newspapers is that there was a drawn-out hesitation concerning the official translation of the term. The common translation of the term, *zheleznyi zanaves*, appears only in one article (printed twice) in Russian-language newspapers in the three months following Churchill's Fulton speech.[13] It is not that the speech was not commented on. After a week of panicked silence and search for an official reaction, many full articles were dedicated to it in the main newspapers, *Pravda* and *Izvestiia*.[14] First, on 11 March *Pravda* gave a translation of relevant parts of Churchill's speech, including the Iron Curtain citation, where the term is translated as *zavesa*, not *zanaves*.[15]

This is a most peculiar choice, then as now. In Russian, there are two terms that usually translate the English "curtain": regular theatrical curtains as well as theatrical fire curtains are and were then translated as *zanaves*, while *zanaveski* refers to domestic curtains. *Zavesa* is "obs[olete for] curtain," and used "fig[uratively for] veil or screen."[16] *Zavesa* was already obsolete for "curtain" in 1935, as the *Tolkovyi slovar'* informs us.[17] The general preference for *zheleznyi zanaves* over *zheleznaia zavesa* as a translation for "Iron Curtain" is evident by running a search for each term in the Russian media—the first search yields more than 18,000 results, while the latter gives a total of 38.[18] Of these 38, 13 appear in 1946, while the other 25 are dispersed over a century! Even more striking, for the first three months after Churchill's speech, that balance of power between the two translations was reversed, with the one twice-printed article containing *zanaves* and eight articles containing *zavesa*. As the months and then years went on, the standard translation, *zheleznyi zanaves*, already in use by 1930 in the Soviet Union to refer to the Iron Curtain as a metaphorical, political twist on the theatrical prop, won out.

So what happened in those three months of translation anomaly? If we investigate the two appearances of the standard translation of *zanaves* in the first three months after Fulton, we find that they appear in the same article by Tarle published by *Izvestiia* and reprinted by the trade newspaper *Gudok*, right next to the atypical *zavesa*.[19] In that article, the two translations are not interchangeable versions of each other but are rather used in contrast to refer to two very different things. In the 12 March issue of *Izvestiia*, Tarle polemicized in detail with the term "Iron Curtain," initiating a move that would become a standard Soviet response. While deriding the accusation of the fencing of Eastern Europe by a Soviet "Iron Curtain" (*zavesa*) as ridiculous, Tarle traded defense for attack as he accused England of having recourse to its "own Iron Curtain" (*zanaves*) in Germany and Indonesia, "an Iron Curtain [again *zanaves*] that is dropped so quickly in front of the curious that it may well hit them on the head."[20] The difference in the use of the two terms gives us a clue to the translation enigma.[21] Tarle, like all other writers who chose to translate the term "Iron Curtain" in the first three months after Churchill's speech, refused the high drama of Churchill's theatrical term. However, rather than burying the term's theatrical connotations, Tarle knowingly reassigned them to the British-made Iron Curtain, thus reversing the direction of the spectator's gaze from east to west.

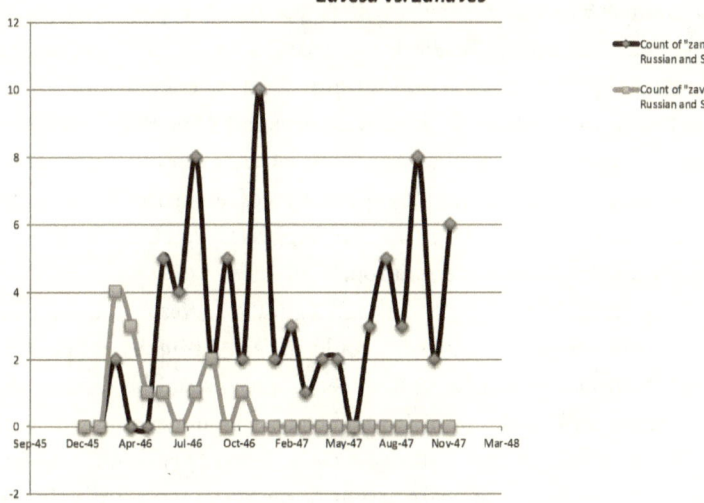

FIGURE 19. The opposing trends of the two Russian translations for "Iron Curtain."

The graph shown here suggests that this moment of translation tension may go well beyond Tarle's strategically placed *Izvestiia* article, and as such it asks for further investigation. Why, despite all linguistic common sense, was the theatrical Iron Curtain (*zanaves*) briefly replaced by the domestic curtain (*zavesa*) in the Soviet translations from the first three months that followed Churchill's speech in March 1946? We can rule out ignorance. The term and the link between the fireproof iron curtain in theaters and the political metaphor is documented already in 1930, when a striking front-page article in *Literaturnaia gazeta* was titled "Zheleznyi zanaves."[22] The author's purpose was to announce that an Iron Curtain was being created to separate Russia from the West. Delving into a drawn-out parallel between the theatrical iron curtain and the metaphorical Iron Curtain, he then explained that from the point of view of the bourgeoisie, in Russia the fire of communism had been burning for the past decade; thus the bourgeoisie and its reactionary press had decided to put up an Iron Curtain toward Russia. In this account, the Iron Curtain was created by the West. However, writing from Paris in the last days of 1929, the author also warned that "reckless and unwise people have tried to push the levers and to lower the Iron Curtain" on the Soviet side as well, for example by attacking Soviet writers who travel abroad. The 1930 article presented what already by 1887 the journal *British Architect* had argued was the best design for theatrical iron curtains: "two screens of wrought-iron plate" (in this case one Western-, one Soviet-wrought).[23] The *British Architect* recommended that "6 inches of air space" be left between the two screens. In the 1930 article, there was not yet any mention of "air space" between the Western and the Eastern screens of the double-paneled Iron Curtain; by 1946 that space would be called Eastern Europe.

So, if the term, in both its literal and figurative, Western and Soviet versions, existed already in 1930, why would *zheleznyi zanaves* not be used in the first translations of Churchill's speech and instead be replaced by *zavesa*? A closer look at *zavesa* in Soviet dictionaries and encyclopedias of the time might contain a clue. In the 1932 *Great Soviet Encyclopedia*, *zavesa* has a short entry, where it appears first as "a theatrical term," referring to the "different pieces of canvas serving as part of the decorative design of the stage." As such, it appears as a synonym for *zanaves*, and also for theatrical "wings."[24] The second entry for *zavesa* is about five times longer, and it refers to the military terms "cavalry screens" (*kavaleriiskie zavesy*), the foremost part of the cavalry (riding in front even of the avant-garde), with a mission of reconnaissance and protection. In the next edition of *The Great Soviet Encyclopedia*, from 1952, the theatrical sense of the word disappeared, and the cavalry *zavesa* moved into first position with added detail.[25] Furthermore, the second and the third meaning build on the military sense, adding two adjectives. "Artillery curtain fire" (*ognevaia artilereiiskaia zavesa*) refers to rapid, continuous artillery fire on a designated line. The third entry sends us to *dymovaia zavesa*—"smoke curtain," or more idiomatically in English, "smoke screen." Russian already had then a word for "curtain/screen," which was routinely paired up with adjectives referring to fire. A search reveals that "smoke screen" (*dymovaia zavesa*) was about ten times more popular as an expression in the Russian press between 1900 and 1947 than *zheleznyi zanaves*.[26] However, *zavesa*, and the idiom it readily conjures to mind, *dymovaia zavesa*, referred not to the curtain that protected the audience in the theater from stage fires but to the curtain/screen of smoke that "one intentionally created" in order "to hide" or "mask" one's actions or "secret intentions" from the enemy.[27] It may be that, rather than a clumsy translation, the translation preferred by the main Soviet newspapers in the first three months after the Fulton speech was rhetorically strategic. Attached to a complex rhetorical edifice, the translation may have tried to shift the public perception of the divide between Eastern Europe and Russia from an Iron Curtain to a smoke screen.

The main Soviet response to Churchill's speech, Stalin's interview published on the first page of *Pravda* of 12 March 1946, worked in the same direction. Much like contemporary Soviet and East European citizens, we can look for clues as to how the wind was blowing by reading it closely.[28] First, although Stalin quoted Churchill word for word in his enumeration of the capitals of Eastern Europe fallen behind the Iron Curtain, he cut the quote so as not to include the phrase "Iron Curtain." Instead, his interview translated the phrases "Soviet sphere" and "Soviet influence." The most successful coinage of Churchill's speech, his theatrical metaphor, was excised from Stalin's rendering of the quote, and did not appear at all in the long interview. And yet Stalin made ample use of theatrical metaphors: in fact, the speech was replete with them, used to maximum effect. But all the theatrical metaphors were carefully used to refer to Churchill and his camp, and never to the Soviets and to Eastern Europe. Thus, Churchill's "tragedy," explains Stalin, "is that, as an inveterate Tory, [having just lost elections], he does not understand a simple and evident [*ochevidnoi*] truth," that the world was turning toward communism. Wanting to conceal his political loss, Churchill "sounds the alarm," placing himself in a "*comical* position with his cries about totalitarianism, tyranny, and policing." Because of these inappropriate responses, Churchill's personal tragedy of being on the losing side of world history turned into an "absurd" tragicomedy, and in the last paragraph of the interview, Stalin portrayed him as a ridiculous "Don Quixote."[29]

According to Stalin, Churchill's "ridiculous poses" "masked" not only tragedy but something more dangerous. While appealing to England's treaty with the USSR, Churchill, Stalin explains, did not understand that his actions made that treaty "an empty little piece of paper" behind which Churchill would have liked to "hide and *mask* his anti-Soviet stance." Repeating again the mention of the "empty little piece of paper" (*pustuiu bumazhku*), Stalin also reminded Churchill and his audience that the decision regarding borders, such as the borders of Poland, was made by Stalin "not alone but together with the British." Stalin mentioned the conference in Berlin, but the mention of "the little piece of paper" and the reminder that the borders of Eastern European countries and thus the Iron Curtain was not just the USSR's doing could well have been meant as veiled allusions to the October 1944 meeting in the Kremlin.

Leaving out Churchill's catchiest and long-enduring phrase, the Iron Curtain, Stalin instead craftily used fire imagery to allude to it and undermine it. Stalin argued that, while "sounding the alarm," Churchill's speech in fact hid his real intentions, imperialist war-mongering. Stalin started out the article by announcing that Churchill had placed himself, through this speech, "in the position of a war instigator." In Russian, the first meaning of the term "instigator" (*podzhigatel'*) is "arsonist." A *Pravda* caricature that later picked up on Stalin's term shows Churchill leading a detachment of pretend firefighters who at a closer look turn out to be arsonists.[30] Under the title "The War Instigators'/Arsonists' Brigade," the caricature was paired up with a humorous poem:

> Wanting to start yet again a fire
> That still creeps in the ashes
> Mister Churchill makes a speech
> About world peace.
> So that no one from the sides
> Would know
> Where the smoke comes from
> All the instigators of the war
> Scream—"War, war!"
> ...
> The garish brigade carries
> Fire hydrants ... no, in fact they are flamethrowers!

The fire as well as the smoke comes from the flamethrowers of the instigators' brigade. The epicenter of the fire is Churchill and his mouth, whose speech, just like his proverbial pipe, produces a smoke screen behind which, Stalin and the caricature imply, hide his real intentions—his belligerent imperialism, as well as his being on the losing side of history.

Responding to Churchill's most successful flight of rhetoric with his own rhetorical tour de force, Stalin's interview and the verbal as well as visual rhetoric to which it gave rise in the Soviet press categorically rejected not just Churchill's Iron Curtain, but the whole *theatrum mundi* that Churchill had built around his powerful metaphor. It is not that Stalin rejected

FIGURE 20. Churchill leading "The War Instigators Brigade." *Pravda*, 7 November 1946. EastView Databases.

the idea of *theatrum mundi* itself; on the contrary, his interview propagated it. However, Stalin reversed the architecture of the theater, the direction of the gaze, the distribution of the roles. Instead of having the West, and Churchill himself, watching from the distance of a quiet Midwestern town as the Soviets lowered the Iron Curtain over Eastern Europe, Stalin cast a very different scene, one in which Churchill was shown to have been at the heart of the East European problem, deciding the borders together with the Soviets. Showing himself in his defining gesture of unmasking, Stalin claimed to see through Churchill's smoke screen of inflammatory rhetoric and to reveal Churchill "fixing the cards." Stalin is here generating his "fund of power" by a dialectic of "concealment and revelation," a move that according to Michael Taussig defines secrecy.[31] Katherine Verdery has further argued that "in socialism this dialectic took on a characteristic form . . . in practices of unmasking and denunciation," which, as Sheila Fitzpatrick has shown, culminated in Stalinism.[32]

To sum up: once launched on the international stage by Churchill, the

Iron Curtain metaphor underwent a brief period of unidiomatic translation in the Soviet Union. By using *zavesa* instead of *zanaves*, the central press may have intended to displace the metaphor by calling to mind the idiomatic *dymovaia zavesa*, "smoke screen," and switching the area of reference from the theater to the military. Untenable in the long run, this curious translation of the Iron Curtain as *zavesa* gave place after three months to other undermining techniques already sketched out in Stalin's interview and in the other attendant responses in the Soviet press. To start with, there was straight-out censorship, modeled in the first week of tense silence following Fulton and in the erasure of the term in Stalin's interview about the speech. Yet in the same interview, Stalin also modeled the art of rhetorical undermining of the term: turning the accusation of theatricality against the West, reversing the direction of the spectator's gaze so that it was the West that was revealed putting up an unsavory show behind the infamous curtain. Once the Iron Curtain received the adjectives "British," "imperialist," and "capitalist," it could be easily displaced into a very different *theatrum mundi*, where it shielded Western wrongdoings in Latin America or Indonesia. While continuing with a close analysis of the peripetias of the term over the next seventy years would exceed the limits of a chapter, the next part of this chapter traces a suggestive roadmap, taking us through key shifts in the Russian uses of the term "Iron Curtain" up to the present moment. Before we leave the postbellum period, however, I think it is useful to consider how the Iron Curtain looked not just from the perspectives of the big powers, but also from the perspective of the small nations that found themselves caught up in its folds.

THE IRON CURTAIN AND THE SPHERE OF INFLUENCE: ROMANIAN TRANSLATIONS AND ILLUSTRATIONS

The Romanian press immediately perceived the importance of Churchill's speech. The Communist Party newspaper *Scânteia* noted that both Churchill's speech and Stalin's interview were "amply commented on" in five leading publications.[33] However, Churchill's Iron Curtain did not travel well to Romania, either. Of the more than twenty articles that I found covering the speech in the mainstream press in March, only one contains the phrase. The two times "Iron Curtain" appears in the article it is translated by the awkward *perdeaua de fier*. In Romanian there are two different words for "curtain": *cortina* (theatrical curtain) and *perdea* (window curtain). The difference between the two is much more marked than in Russian, as the words do not share a root or any resemblance. *Cortina* is of Italian extraction, while *perdea*, of Turkish extraction, was used for "window curtain" and was considered anachronistic for "theatrical curtain" already by 1927.³⁴ The one notable use of *perdeaua de fier* belongs to Nicolae Iorga, Romania's best known historian at the time, who met the news of the Soviet Union's occupation of then Romanian Bessarabia by writing: "From now the Iron Curtain [*perdeaua de fier*] will descend over the whole life, even over domestic life, to its most intimate."³⁵ Iorga's choice seems justified given his strong emphasis on the domestic domain.

This was not the case for the translator of Churchill's phrase. In choosing to translate "Iron Curtain" by the anachronistic *perdeaua de fier*, the writer turned away from the strong theatrical metaphor, refusing to place himself and his country on the stage. Although he did use theatrical vocabulary, he used it, just like his Soviet counterparts, to describe Churchill:

> Mr. Churchill—although constantly *playing at being "particular"*—has however searched to synthesize as faithfully as possible the thoughts and plans of the reactionaries of all countries . . . His highness has not forgotten Romania. Bucharest finds itself . . . in his opinion . . . beyond the "Iron Curtain" [*perdeaua de fier*] . . . Mr. Churchill puts on trial the freedoms in East and Central Europe, aiming in this direction *the tip of his spade* . . . Mr. Churchill will not be able to make anyone forget that we beyond the "Iron Curtain" *eat Soviet bread* and that we gained our independence and liberty aided by the Soviet Union.³⁶

In the course of this translation commentary, the Iron Curtain has gained quotation marks, which will become one canonical way of its representation in the Soviet Union and Eastern Europe. The quotation marks indicate the phrase as the speech of another, as the so-called Iron Curtain, weakening it, and making it part of a false discourse.

Indeed, the whole phrase, like the larger discourse initiated by Stalin's interview and developed in the translations and commentaries in the Romanian press, either rejects or reverses the positions of the watcher and watched, audience and spectacle, life and fiction, all dichotomies that the Iron Curtain had set up. Thus, in the paragraph quoted above, it is Churchill who "plays at being 'particular'" being faithful to a fictive ideology, striking an overly theatrical pose as he aims "the tip of his spade" to Eastern Europe. On the contrary, the people of Eastern Europe are not playing at anything, they prove their reality by going through the age-old reality check applied to anyone from ghosts to extraterrestrials—they eat bread, with a twist, Soviet bread, and engage in political action, gain their freedom and independence, with quite the twist, independence with the aid of the Soviet Union. The title of another article even more clearly reverses the direction of the gaze, setting Churchill's speech as a curtain of words: "Behind Churchill's speech hides reactionary politics."[37] Continuing with this logic of unmasking, where the hidden is to be found not on the eastern but on the western side of the "Iron Curtain," another early report on the speech announces that "in reality the call of Mr. Churchill is a call to war and international conflict tending to divide the world in two . . . a Western and a Russian bloc."[38] The real divide is then not the Soviet-operated Iron Curtain, but Churchill's speech itself, which, following Stalin's lead, the article frames as a smoke screen hiding the West's expansionist tendencies.

In the more than twenty articles that followed Churchill's Iron Curtain speech in March, as well as through the following year, as they continued commenting on the speech and on the peace conference in Paris where the borders of postbellum Europe were being drawn, the Romanian press avoided the phrase "Iron Curtain," using instead *sferă, bloc,* and even *lagăr* (camp).[39] Of all these, "sphere" was the favorite. This is most likely because "sphere" was the synonym Churchill used, almost in the same breath, in his Fulton speech. While in the West "sphere" was eclipsed by the success of his metaphorical coinage of the Iron Curtain, in Romania the reverse was true. Part of the reason seems linked with the caricaturists' irresistible soft spot for the parallelism between Churchill's outward appearance, particularly his iconic belly and round head, and his use of the word "sphere." For the next year, the Romanian communist press had a ball representing the deepening divide between the East and the West and what they saw as the West's threatening expansionist tendencies, through the use of caricature. In its 11 October issue *Contemporanul* edits a selection of cartoons from the international press to express its disappointment about the Paris Peace Conference, then in its closing days.[40]

A large man wearing a suit sprawls over the globe, laughing satisfied. The only writing that is visible is "Adriatique," the one end of the Iron Curtain named in Churchill's speech, typed as a north–south divide along the

FIGURE 21. Collection of international cartoons titled "The Peace Seen by the Foreign Press." *Contemporanul*, 11 October 1946.

Iron Curtain. As almost half of his body crosses over the line, the man says: "Let everyone keep his positions." The adjacent cartoon has a small Churchill figure, with a head looking like a globe divided with longitude lines and a spherical belly divided in half, eyeing a pathetically strutting peace dove, who, offended, rebels: "I am not what you think!" While, at first, we are made to think of peace as a sex worker who has been bought or sold at the conference, we see the bird strutting in the direction of the next cartoon, where it is cooped up in a cage.

The cage and Churchill reappear together, in a centrally placed and locally produced anonymous cartoon of 4 January 1947.[41] Here Churchill gestures to a little boy and a girl, inviting them to enter a cage set up with a jug and two cups. The top hat, tuxedo, and white gloves, as well as the exaggerated gestures and the cage, all suggest a circus impresario. The caption, "Come, little ones, let us federalize you," makes the immediate link with the weighty title of the article "The Wings of the Plans of Federalizing Europe (From Kant and Rousseau to Winston Churchill)."[42] The article is indeed substantive. Briefly mentioning Kant, Rousseau, and Schiller, it spends ample time providing background on current American literature on federalizing Europe, also discussing French contributions such as the then recent full volume, *L'avenir de l'Europe Centrale*. Churchill gets a subheading as leading proponent of federalism. Equal space is dedicated to Lenin, who, the article argues, had shown, *avant la lettre*, how federalist ideas mask capitalist and imperialist expansionism. The article ends with the longest subheading,

FIGURE 22. Caricature of Churchill in the Romanian press captioned "Come, little ones, let us federalize you!" *Contemporanul*, 4 January 1947.

titled "Against and . . . for Small States." Together with the caricature, the subheading led me to think that the article was going to end by militating for the rights of small states against the machinations of large imperialist powers. However, the article shows that this would be unrealizable as it was in contradiction with "present social life and with the fight that is carried on for the undoing of a just and democratic peace." Instead, the article ends with the expected call to collaboration between all countries.

However, the concern and disappointment of one of "the little ones" is at times visible even in the pages of the socialist-friendly newspapers, as a striking caricature captioned, "We are the defenders of the small countries," shows with surprising openness.[43] The caricature depicts two monsters sitting with their five mouths wide open. It does not take much perspicacity to make out Stalin's features behind the two-mouthed monster, whereas the three-mouthed monster is harder to identify, being potentially a composite portrait of Western leaders. The monsters' enormous spherical bellies are full of gold coins and resemble both piggy banks and geographic globes, with the contours of countries traced by the amalgamations of coins. The caricature was published on the first page of the influential cultural weekly *Contemporanul*, accompanying a lead article titled "The Peace Conference at Work . . ." While the article focused on the conflicts *between* small countries—the problems of the Hungarian minority in Czechoslovakia and the territorial disputes between Greece and Bulgaria—the one actual map illustrating it shows the link between the small nations and big nations and their problems: the disputed border between Greece and Bulgaria was, of course, a portion of the descending Iron Curtain, marked with a thick black line on the map. Romania is barely mentioned in the Paris Peace Conference review itself. However, the article shares the first page with just one other lead article titled "The Crisis of Romanian Culture," whose illustration parallels and contrasts the monster duo with a duo of brooding men that could be sketches after Rodin's *Thinker*.[44] The caricature and its juxtaposition with the more somber illustration of Romania's crisis expresses the magazine's anxiety toward Romania's situation as a small nation in the aftermath of the Paris Peace Conference in graphically arresting, if unimpeachable, clarity.

So why does the Iron Curtain get lost in Romanian translation, replaced by "sphere of influence"? It seems the Romanian press at the time imagined its world as a sphere whose longitudinal lines were coming more and more to resemble a cage's grid. The cage, the globe, Churchill's and Stalin's heads and bellies all roll into each other in what appears to be dangerously engulfing circularity. The line, if it appears at all, is somewhere else, farther away, at the border of "Greece with all its splendors" and Bulgaria, still on the top of the agenda at the Paris conference. Romania's "deep crisis" had to do with its position so deep inside the belly of the beast that it was no longer talked about by the great powers. This was a secret that could not be said out loud or even written about in the more and more censored Romanian press. As a result, the Romanian press at the time engaged with abandon in ambiguous translations, quotations, and juxtapositions of texts and images from the international press, divesting itself of responsibility for the obscured message. In so doing, it precariously brought together on the pages of a small country's press worlds that were dramatically drifting apart at that very moment, leaving Romania not on the dramatically lit stage of history but rather deep within the belly of the beast.

Spectacle, theatricality, and secrecy were not absent from the Romanian press coverage of the Iron Curtain speech in 1946. But if the world was still seen as a stage at times, this was not Churchill's theater design. Churchill, and the West, were not seen watching innocently from afar as the Iron Curtain fell on Eastern Europe. Rather, through more or less faithful or tendentious translations from the English-, French-, and Russian-language press, and through commentaries, juxtapositions, cutting and pasting, and the addition of quotation marks, the Romanian press painted a very different view. In this picture, Churchill, and the West, appeared as the dubious ringmasters of this show, which resembled an open-air circus more than a dignified theater with safety features like iron curtains. They were more likely to use incendiary language or put up smoke screens than to need protection from fires, of which there seemed to be no trace of in Romania. In this vision, the Romanian press, like the Soviets, turned the accusation of theatricality toward Churchill and the West, and saw theatricality and spectacle as a cover for real secret intentions. Rather than a dispassionate observer, Churchill appeared as a histrionic ringmaster, gesturing dramatically, dissembling and misleading the world toward war for imperialist profit. The Romanian press's twist and difference from the Soviet position was that at times Stalin did not look that different from Churchill. From the perspective of "the little ones," the big powers with their enormous bellies and many mouths ready to swallow small countries lose their distinctions. Rather than the two-dimensional map with its linear Iron Curtain line, the globe may have been the favorite geographic representation at the time in the Romanian press because its longitudinal and latitudinal lines were so easily graphically matched over the gridlock of a cage. That view persisted. In a brief review of the uses of the term in the contemporary Romanian press, Rodica Zafiu notes that "the Romanian *cortina de fier* (Iron Curtain) is perceived, not just like a barrier, but as a kind of *cort* (tent), (a word which is etymologically related), as a form of cover and pressure."[45]

Rhetoric and translation played a key role in the shaping of the postbellum world. An archaeology of its main partition, the Iron Curtain, shows the foundational interpenetration of secrecy with theatricality. Theatricality defined the Iron Curtain from the start, so that once the curtain was hung, the world was staged as a *theatrum mundi*. But that is about where the consensus ended, and the fierce battles over who were the actors, the audience, the ringmasters, and the Iron Curtain operators truly began. There were also disputes about what kind of show—tragedy, comedy, circus, or absurd tragicomedy—the world was in for. The first part of this chapter investigated how the views differed depending on one's position in this *theatrum mundi*, looking closely at the role played by rhetoric and translation in securing those seats. We will now move on to track the development of the Iron Curtain metaphor in the Russian-language press through the Soviet period and up to the present. The last section will focus on the redefinition of the term during the 2022 Russian invasion of Ukraine, focusing on Russian-language press from Russia, Ukraine, and elsewhere, alongside some preliminary research in the Ukrainian-language press.

THE IRON CURTAIN: OVERALL PATTERNS OF USE AND ABUSE IN THE RUSSIAN-LANGUAGE PRESS

How does the Iron Curtain fare after the explosion of reactions that followed its propulsion onto the international stage in 1946? Curious to see whether there is a discernible pattern in the density of its uses, or whether it follows more or less random ups and downs through the decades, I decided to record its yearly counts in Russian-language newspapers from 1900 to the present day, and then create a graph to visually represent the information. The EastView Humanities and Social Sciences Database allows us access to an unprecedented wealth of newspapers and journals in Russian. Both centrally and locally distributed press, including Russian-language newspapers from the Soviet republics, such as Ukraine or Georgia, is available for word searches that cover not just the titles but the entire text. Thus, I could both see the overall number of articles featuring the term "Iron Curtain" for each year, as well as access the context of that mention, adding various degrees of context—the passage in which it appeared, the article, with its illustrations, the newspaper page, and the whole issue, which allows both distance reading as well as close and contextual reading. I then considered this information against existing histories and timelines of the Iron Curtain.[46]

The graphs show extremely clear trends, rather than scattered data. After being mostly absent from public discourse, use of the term exploded in the press following Churchill's speech, then significantly lost currency for about three decades, to rise to unprecedented use during Perestroika and continue as a strong presence until about 2015, when its uses started vertiginously falling. To better understand these trends, I first reviewed the

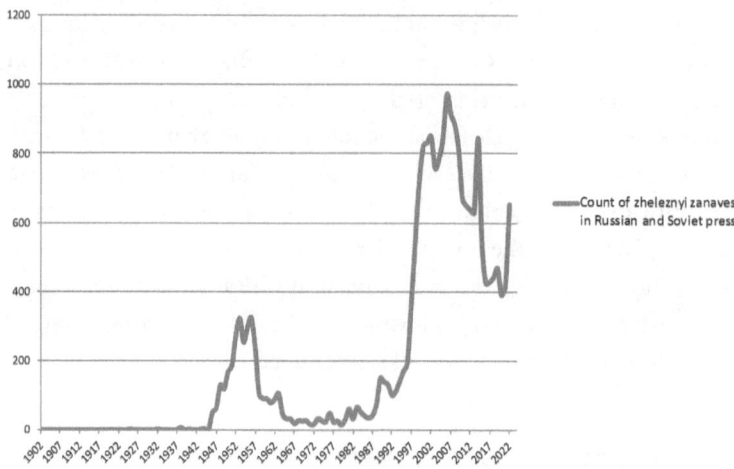

Data Source: *East View Universal Services*, including *Russian Central Newspapers (udb-com+)* and *Digital Archives*

FIGURE 23. Count of *zheleznyi zanaves* (Iron Curtain) in Russian and Soviet press, 1902 to 2022.

passages featuring the phrase "Iron Curtain." For the most influential, representative, or striking uses, I then engaged in close readings of the passage in the context of its article. While this last step potentially introduces the biases of my judgment in the selection of the paragraphs for close readings, I hope that the use of different zoom lenses to approach the data will give a more layered view of the uses and abuses of the Iron Curtain over time.

The term enjoyed popularity for more than a decade after the Fulton speech. Besides direction-setting articles in *Pravda* and *Izvestiia*, often reproduced by newspapers such as *Pravda Ukrainy* and *Gudok*, these years show a significant number of mentions in the leading Soviet humor magazine *Krokodil*, which had a ball making fun of the term as an "old fairy tale," "fantasy," and "invention." Another popular trope was the surprise of Western visitors at the absence of an Iron Curtain in Russia.[47] Following in Pravda's steps *Krokodil* also produced many caricatures to illustrate its derision of the phrase. The December 1955 cover of the magazine, showing a Western theater group bowing to their Soviet audience after performing *Hamlet*, carries the caption: "Hamlet: I don't see any Iron Curtain, just the velvet one . . ."[48] It was also the norm for the term to appear in quo-

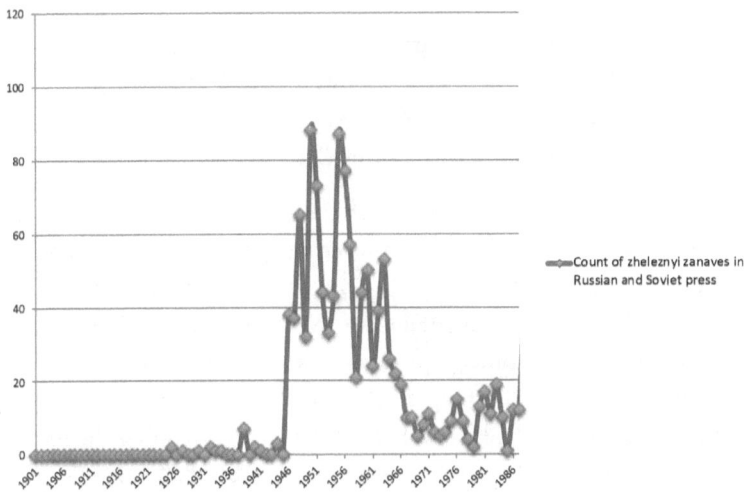

Data Source: *East View Universal Services*, including *Russian Central Newspapers (udb-com+)* and *Digital Archives*

FIGURE 24. Count of *zheleznyi zanaves* (Iron Curtain) in Russian and Soviet press, 1900 to 1986.

tation marks or preceded by the qualifier *tak nazyvaemyi*, "so-called Iron Curtain." The same year, *Pravda Ukrainy* published an article by the well-known Indian writer Prahlad Keshav Atre, who attempted to clear up the misunderstanding: "In India there are still people who believe that in the Soviet Union there is an Iron Curtain and a police regime."[49] Based on his travels in the USSR, he concluded: "There is no Iron Curtain! The only Iron Curtain I have seen is the fire curtain in the Tashkent Opera House."[50]

In 1956 the term starts a vertiginous fall in usage. It also loses its humorous appeal. While in the decade after the Fulton speech the Iron Curtain appeared in thirty-three *Krokodil* articles, from 1958 to 1967 the phrase does not appear at all![51] These were, however, some of the tensest years of the Cold War, spanning the division of Germany, the building of the Berlin Wall, and the Cuban Missile Crisis.[52] The official position, as taken by Khrushchev, was that "there is no Iron Curtain in the Soviet Union."[53] In a testy conversation with an American journalist, who reminds Khrushchev of the invasion of Hungary in 1956 and of his saying that we should not look over a neighbor's fence, the journalist asks why Russia built the fence in the first place:

Khrushchev: 'Which fence?'

Correspondent: 'The Iron Curtain.'

Khrushchev: Young man, have you been to the Soviet Union? You have not, and you are talking... Travel to the Soviet Union, we will give you a visa, and you will see that there is no Iron Curtain.[54]

Other than dismissing the Soviet Iron Curtain as a myth of Western propaganda, the Soviet press at times used the term to go on the counterattack, by speaking of Western "Iron Curtains"—whether created to hide the achievements of the USSR or as a colonial tactic. In these cases, the Iron Curtain sometimes loses its customary quotation marks: "For decades, Africa has been hidden from us by the impenetrable Iron Curtain of colonialism. Now this curtain has fallen... the world of socialism is extending the hand of friendship to Africa."[55] A *Pravda* article published in April 1962 in celebration of the Soviet space program states: "Some five years ago the countries of socialism were surrounded by an 'Iron Curtain' forged by the reactionary forces of the capitalist powers. But as soon as the first Soviet satellite went up into space and flew over the Iron Curtain, it [the Iron Curtain] began to collapse," as everyone saw the Soviet achievements hidden by Western propaganda.[56]

The term's uses remain at a steady low practically amounting to disappearance on the official horizon during the Brezhnev era (1964–82). In the rare cases when it does appear, it is treated as the "favorite theme of anti-Soviet propaganda" and is attributed in quotation marks to paranoid Western speakers:[57] "We were not surprised by the combination of the words 'iron' and 'curtain,' this is quite in the style of *The Times*, which willingly extracts such 'curiosities' from archival dust."[58] In the first part of this chapter I argued that Stalin's unusual translation of Churchill's Iron Curtain, as *zheleznaia zavesa* rather than *zanaves*, insinuated that this curtain was more of a smoke screen (*dymovaia zavesa*) used by the West to hide its own bellicose intentions. Thirty years after Stalin's *Pravda* article, in August 1976, the point is directly made on the first page of *Pravda* in a summary of an article by the Senegalese journalist Ali Ndai in the Dakar newspaper *Soleil*:

> The inventions of the supporters of the Cold War about the existence of some kind of "Iron Curtain" [*zheleznyi zanaves*], allegedly erected by the USSR, emphasizes the author of the article in the newspaper *Soleil*, are com-

pletely refuted by the entire Soviet reality. This mythical "curtain" [*mificheskii zanaves*] is nothing more than a smoke screen [*dymovaia zavesa*] for those who still stubbornly oppose contacts with the Land of the Soviets.[59]

Instead, the explosion of interest and of publishing venues brought on by Perestroika raised the popularity of the term sharply. The repressed term came back with a vengeance, mainly to refer to the past when it was not spoken about. Publications that had long denied the existence of the Iron Curtain except in the paranoid imagination of the West now spoke of the Cold War–era Iron Curtain as a given fact of those times, taken down during the Perestroika: "The Iron Curtain is almost destroyed, and the fragments of the former metal structures only disfigure the political landscape, causing ironic sympathetic sighs for the visiting foreign tourist."[60] The Soviet Iron Curtain was largely acknowledged in Russia retroactively. Yet, given the explosion in the use of the term, and the fact that journalists did not miss a beat in adopting a term that had been supposedly long relegated to archival dust, it is likely that the term never actually lost its use/currency, despite losing its visibility in the Soviet press. For instance, under the title "Collaboration: Monument for Washington," a May 1988 article in *Nedelia* reports on the creation of a monumental sculpture about the victorious destruction of the Iron Curtain and the end of the Cold War.[61] The journalist visits the studio of the best known sculptor of the Perestroika period, Zurab Tsereteli, "the favored sculptor of Moscow during Iurii Luzhkov's term as mayor, a magnet for controversy," whose monumental sculptures filled Moscow despite repeated intelligentsia protests.[62] Tsereteli describes his plan for a 30-meter-high sculpture he had been invited to create for a development near Washington, DC. The model shows "the Iron Curtain broken in two."[63] Through its opening a man emerges, "a man who brings the world the light of goodness and reason." At his feet are "the ruins of a cold war."[64] The thorny question of who created the Iron Curtain, the Soviet Union or the West, is suspended in the interest of the new collaborative enterprise. It turns out that the Iron Curtain could now not only be talked about, but also graphically and monumentally represented, as broken and relegated to a past that had either mocked or denied its existence.

In 1994 Odesa-born director Savva Kulish released a film titled *Iron Curtain*, which presented the Stalinist years from the autobiographically based perspective of a young boy. The movie was well received, and in 1995 Kulish was awarded the title of People's Artist of Russia. The Iron Curtain not only gave the film its title but also dominated its striking poster, where a dome-like Iron Curtain does not divide East and West as much as it threatens to envelop the two protagonists, together with the moon and the clouds. In 1998, Kulish gave a glowing review of his experience presenting this film at the first US-based Russian Film Festival in Washington, DC. He noted that "despite the bad press they have in Russia," American viewers appeared highly interested and sympathetic. Further, he recalled "an elderly American lady" who came up to him after the movie to say: "We also had an Iron Curtain, and for us it was no less terrible than for you."[65] Such critical views toward the role of one's own country in the erection of the Iron Curtain were a novelty of the Perestroika period and then became even more prevalent

FIGURE 25. Film poster, *The Iron Curtain* (1998), directed by Savva Kulish.

in the 1990s. However, they often came with real limitations, such as an exclusive focus on Stalinism, and the perspective of being an internal victim of the Soviet Iron Curtain without much regard to one's participation in its creation of the Iron Curtain or in its victimization of smaller countries.

After the unprecedented explosion of uses during the Perestroika period and the 1990s, a vertiginous downward trend in the Russian use of the phrase "Iron Curtain" continued through the Putin years, with three spikes around 2006, 2014, and 2022.[66] In the following section, I attempt a preliminary discussion of this last spike, as it is inextricably related to an issue of urgent contemporary interest, the war in Ukraine.

THE IRON CURTAIN AND THE INVASION OF UKRAINE

The invasion of Ukraine adds a new chapter in the history of the Iron Curtain. On the first day of the full-scale invasion, 24 February 2022, the Ukrainian president, Volodymyr Zelensky, released a video address on his Facebook page warning that the Russian attack was creating a new Iron Curtain: "What we heard today is not just rocket explosions, battles and roar of aircraft. This is the sound of a new Iron Curtain that has descended and closes Russia from the civilized world. Our national task is to make sure that this curtain does not fall on our land but on Russia's homes."[67] The statement was then carried by all international news outlets, often without the last impolitic few words. The Iron Curtain metaphor was thrust again into the spotlight of history's stage. Zelensky deployed it as a main prop of his powerful rhetoric, which in a few words expressed his worldview: it was the Soviet Union that violently dropped the Iron Curtain on Ukraine. Rather than a tired metaphor, the Iron Curtain became weighted with the real noise and destruction of bombs and artillery fire. After 24 February, usage of the phrase exploded in the Russian-language press, while its meanings were hotly contested and in dramatic flux. The last six days of February registered more hits than the first twenty-four days, and the phrase made a record 115 hits in March, more than four times the number of January uses. While definite conclusions are difficult to reach at this stage, given press censorship and publishing lags, the first twelve months after the invasion offer us a fascinating window into the struggle over the new meanings of the metaphor. More unstable at first, these meanings then start to congeal into harder shapes.

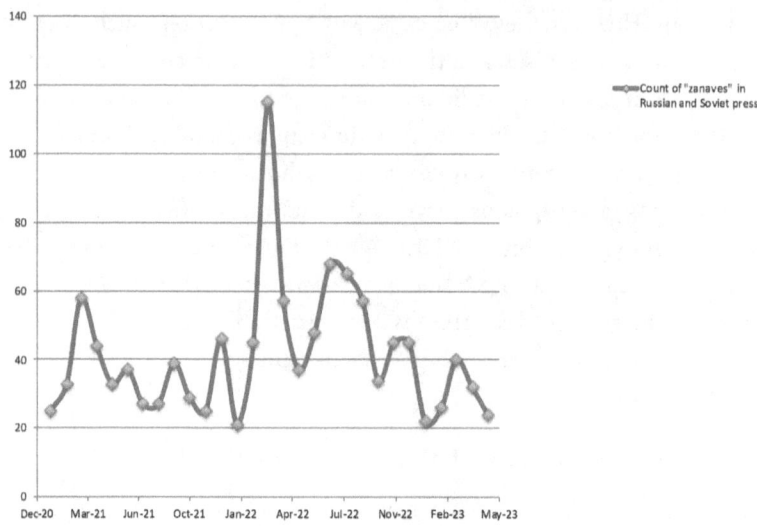

FIGURE 26. The spike in mentions of "Iron Curtain" (*zheleznyi zanaves*) after the Russian invasion of Ukraine on 22 February 2022.

Critics of the invasion writing in Russian (from Russia, Ukraine, or internationally), follow Zelensky's lead in warning against the creation of a New Iron Curtain of Russia's making, through violent war as well as through censorship. The closing down of Instagram and placement of limits on social media was announced as an instance of the falling of the Iron Curtain.[68] The metaphor also routinely pops up in descriptions of travel and banking restrictions, as well as supply chain crises, especially in critical domains such as medicine.[69] On 6 May Zelensky returned to the metaphor, again assigning the agency for the creation of the New Iron Curtain to Russia, linking it to the Soviet-made Iron Curtain and emphasizing its nefarious consequences for the population: "Now Russia makes for itself an Iron Curtain—the same way as the Soviet Union did before, and we don't need to interfere—it will be taken down by a different generation of Russians, who will receive the consequences of this curtain."[70] He then moved on to envision a long-term end to the Iron Curtain: "When all this is free, and when their brains are free, and when the whole world is free from their threats, then we ourselves will stand on a chair with you to remove this Iron Curtain."⁷¹

While here I track primarily Russian-language uses of the phrase "Iron Curtain" in 2022, including publications based in Ukraine and abroad, it is important to at least get a sense of the uses of the phrase in the Ukrainian-language press. Because I don't read Ukrainian easily, I am grateful for research assistance from Oksana Popova, librarian at the Odesa State Library, who fled to Germany during the war. Based on our collaborative work, it appears that the Ukrainian press had denounced the New Iron Curtain erected by Russia well before the full-scale invasion started. Thus, already in June 2021, Oleksandr Levchenko, Ukrainian ambassador to Croatia, warned that the situation between Russia and the West is close to "an Iron Curtain."⁷² After February 2022, President Zelensky's words about the Iron Curtain were often echoed in the Ukrainian press, with further clarifications. Thus, on the 25 May, Ukrainian deputy prime minister Iryna Vereshchuk declared: "The Iron Curtain, which descends on the territory of the Russian Federation, will pass on the eastern border of Ukraine, and not on the western one."⁷³ On 4 June 2022, journalist Olha Kurnosova detailed the many ways in which Russia is closing itself with a New Iron Curtain—by restricting travel and study abroad, but above all, by blocking information. In her opinion "this is the main component of the 'Iron Curtain,' which is going down from now on. Because we live in the information age, and trying to tear people off from information is the most important thing that is happening."⁷⁴ A caricature illustrating her article not only clearly assigns agency for the dropping of the Iron Curtain to Vladimir Putin but also suggests that he, or at least his Pinocchio nose, may well get caught in its closing.

The question of a digital Iron Curtain also deeply preoccupies Russian opposition politicians and journalists, who, however, tend to see the Iron Curtain being created on both sides. Thus, a June 2022 Deutsche Welle roundtable entitled "Both Russia and the West Are Building a Digital Iron Curtain" (*tsifrovoi zheleznyi zanaves*) brought together Maria Makeeva, editor and presenter of the OstWest TV channel in Berlin, and Leonid Volkov, former head of Alexei Navalny's headquarters.⁷⁵ According to Makeeva, the wave of Western companies, such as Facebook and Google, leaving since February 2022 "only helped to build a new Iron Curtain."⁷⁶ Volkov detailed how "the emerging 'digital curtain'" not only poses economic threats,

FIGURE 27. "Putin lowers the 'Iron Curtain.'" Caricature: uainfo.org, published in *Dim*, 4 June 2022. https://kanaldom.tv/uk/serjozni-protesty-u-rosiyi-najimovirnishi-u-veresni-kurnosova/.

but also prevents independent media and opposition politicians from "delivering a message" to their audience. He concluded that "the fight against the emergence of a new Iron Curtain will require efforts from both sides."[77]

Tracking the Iron Curtain through the prowar press after 24 February 2022 presents a strongly divergent view. After a while, one discerns a strong narrative, most prominently expressed by Foreign Minister Sergei Lavrov and President Vladimir Putin, and then echoed in the prowar press. Already on 2 March Lavrov set the tone by "refusing to worry about the Iron Curtain."[78] In an interview with Al-Jazeera immediately publicized by Interfax, Lavrov reminded his audience that the Iron Curtain was introduced by Winston Churchill, and that for the British it triggers "nostalgic feelings":

> Everyone understands that building an Iron Curtain is the lot of those who think in the old categories: the categories of colonialism, neo-colonialism. But if the West has decided so, then, I assure you, we will find an opportunity to continue to live, develop, and we won't even worry too much about what our Western partners did, once again proving their absolute unreliability and complete inability to negotiate.[79]

In June, Vladimir Putin reiterated and further developed Lavrov's position. Putin concurred that it is the West that is trying to create an Iron Curtain against Russia through its sanctions. Russia, however, cannot be fenced in.⁸⁰ There is a new global order, which makes the Cold War–era Iron Curtain obsolete, as Russia is strongly connected to most of the world—China, India, and Latin America.⁸¹ Putin allows that Russians will experience some short-term nuisances, because the West has some technological advantages, but he then emphasizes that Russia has always been known to prevail against difficulties, and in the long run, Russia will come out of this conflict stronger, more independent, while the West has already started to hurt from its own sanctions, plunging itself into inflation and an economic crisis.⁸² This position was briefly reiterated at the end of June by Lavrov, who declared that because of American and European attitudes, "the Iron Curtain between Russia and the West is almost already descending."⁸³ Minimizing the impact of the Iron Curtain on Russia, he dismissively advised his Western colleagues to be more careful, so that they "shouldn't pinch anything."⁸⁴

It is instructive to follow the new adventures of the Iron Curtain in the prowar press because we can see this narrative taking shape over the first few months after the full-scale invasion. However, we can also see an unexpected number of partly divergent positions, which I believe betray the anxiety and uncertainty around the shifting course of events, which, despite Putin's assurances, has not always gone "according to plan." One of the main differences concerns Putin's position about the Cold War–era Iron Curtain, which, he squarely admitted, was created by the Soviet Union: "We will not have a closed economy. The closed economy was in Soviet times, when we massacred ourselves, created an Iron Curtain with our own hands. And now we are not going to do this, we will not step on the same rake. Our economy will be open. Whoever does not want to [cooperate] will rob himself."⁸⁵ Not only do his words go against the long-lived official Soviet position, they go against a strong trend in the prowar, especially communist press, which sees the current Western-created Iron Curtain as just another iteration of the "many Iron Curtains that the West has repeatedly lowered on Russia."⁸⁶ In an extensive review of the history of the Iron Curtain, the newspaper *Trud* places the origin of the Iron Curtain in Clemenceau's advice that Western Europe build "an Iron Curtain" against Bolshevik Russia.⁸⁷ In fact, Clemenceau had used a different phrase, *cordon sanitaire*, a phrase coined by Maréchal Foch in 1919 during the Versailles peace talks.⁸⁸ Foch presented Bolshevik Russia as an epidemic against which one should deploy a sanitary barrier, which he imagined would be made by the newly reconfigured states of Eastern Europe, in particular Romania and Poland.[89] The article flattens and rewrites this sanitary barrier as an original Iron Curtain, and follows its transformations through Churchill's speech, and then the conflicts leading to the construction of the Berlin Wall and the Cuban Missile Crisis, concluding that "the West has many times, with and without reason, erected Iron Curtains against Russia."[90] Russians are seen at the receiving end of these Western initiatives, with the exception of some Stalinist measures, such as the death sentence applied en masse to those who failed to return to the motherland.[91] One of the most instructive articles dedicated to the Iron Curtain occupied the first three pages of the newspaper *Sovershchenno sekretno* (*Strictly Secret*), on 15 March 2022.[92] The article brands the New Iron Curtain as the "Iron Curtain 2.0." "This (financial sanctions) is far from all that the West has done against our country . . . But it is already clear that we are talking about a full-fledged 'Iron Curtain.' Although not very tight."[93] It is here that the discourse turns dismissive, much like the Soviet era as well as Putin's sarcasm: it brands the Iron Curtain 2.0 a "leaky curtain," which "obviously differs from the previous one, built during the first cold war," because this is a globalized world in which the West plays a limited role compared to emerging markets in Africa, China, India, etc.[94]

Yet despite the prolonged attention to the differences between the current Iron Curtain and the Soviet one, the article's illustration, which takes the full first page of the journal, shows a long wall enclosing not just Russia, but all of Eastern Europe and the Baltics.[95] This may well be an oversight of the graphic designer, stuck with the image of the old Iron Curtain, when asked to illustrate an article about the "Iron Curtain 2.0." Yet, as an Eastern European, rather than getting a kick out of catching an oversight on the first page of *Sovershchenno sekretno*, I registered the dark contours of the wall as ominous.

Despite the starkly divided differences of anti- and pro-war Russian press, there are some shared assumptions. One is that a New Iron Curtain is descending—whether of Western or Russian design, whether catastrophic for Russia or merely a short-term nuisance. What they also share is a striking absence, or at least a strong underrepresentation, of Ukraine, Eastern Europe, and the Baltics from their accounts of the Iron Curtain. Reading these debates, it is easy to forget that the metaphor has long covered up the fact that this is not a theater curtain that divides two superpowers, but rather a living and dying reality for the people caught underneath. This is why Zelensky's words on the day of the invasion were so powerful—because they graphically focused on the bombs and terror that make up the very thick fabric of the Iron Curtain for those caught under it. Rather than a vertical curtain or definite boundary, Zelensky showed that the Iron Curtain can envelop cities, countries, to the point of making the sky invisible or blanketed in threats. Rather than a vertical sheet of metal, the Iron Curtain has acted more like a heat dome, covering whole countries. The Iron Curtain has always been a loaded, dangerous metaphor, seen differently from different sides. However, maybe its most pernicious feature is the implication that it is a flat boundary between two superpower camps with a negligible third dimension—width. Zelensky's words, as well as the initial reactions of the Romanian press to Churchill's Iron Curtain—are a powerful reminder that it is precisely in this neglected dimension, largely invisible in Russian discussions of the Iron Curtain, that the suffering of entire peoples takes place.

Historian Anne Applebaum subtitled her book *The Iron Curtain*: "The Crushing of Eastern Europe."[96] This chapter has shown the persistent blindness of the Russian and Western press perspectives on the Iron Curtain to this very reality of the Iron Curtain as the crushing of Eastern Europe. This reality, however, is visible in Eastern European views from right under the Iron Curtain, as documented by research in the Romanian and Ukrainian press. From a methodological point of view, this chapter has shown that digitization and digital archival methods can reveal long-term trends that would remain illegible at close range; it has also shown that digitization often reinforces the long-entrenched perspectives of major power centers. In the case of Russia and Eastern Europe, Russian-language press archives have been digitized and made available to researchers in Russia and abroad at a rate that far exceeds those of any other Eastern European language. Market demands and constraints have reinforced the historic marginalization of the Eastern European points of view. So, while exhaustive Russian-language press archives from the entire Soviet and post-Soviet period are easily searchable on EastView from the comfort of my own New York City library, it took on-the-ground research in nondigitized libraries to unearth the reaction to the Iron Curtain in the postbellum press of my own country, Romania, a country that topped the infamous list that placed Eastern European countries behind the Iron Curtain. It was even more challenging to find information on the Ukrainian positions in the recent surge in the use of the phrase "Iron Curtain" that followed the invasion of Ukraine. Oksana Popova, the Ukrainian librarian whom I consulted for help in this matter, had to leave her workplace at the Odesa National Library and fled to Germany. While she still had her expertise as a trained librarian bilingual in Russian and Ukrainian, she no longer had access to the resources of the print or digital resources of her old library. Instead, she gleaned and shared with me partial views of the Ukrainian-language reaction to the New Iron Curtain in open-source digital materials, from online newspapers to social media feeds created by people, like herself, pushed to cross the previously impenetrable borders of the Cold War–era Iron Curtain to save themselves from being crushed under the New Iron Curtain their president warned Russia was intent on dropping, one bomb at a time, over their country.

This study also warns against digitization and digital research's potential to unwittingly reinforce past censorship. Because of the censorship quickly imposed by Soviet rule in Romania, a digital phrase search for "Iron Curtain" would not be likely to access any nonconformist attitudes. What digital research would mostly pick up would be the support for the Soviet regime and a mockery of Churchill's stance that parroted the Soviet press. But since any different points of view were either unprintable or brought severe repercussions to writers and publications alike, such attitudes—which I show ranged from anxiety to desperation to black humor targeted at both superpower blocs—are not legible through digitization or word searches. Instead, they found expression in the peripheral and in-between spaces that censors, as well as the digital search engines, were and are more likely to miss. In the Romanian press, cartoons provided such refuge, often in the invisible yet highly suggestive space between words and images. Indeed, taken separately, the words and the images are often unimpeachable; it is in the space of their tense juxtaposition, whether inside one cartoon, in a multi-cartoon collage, or in the more ample space of an article which the cartoon accompanies, that we can start to discern the less controlled, more varied, complex, and fascinating contemporary perspectives from right under the descending Iron Curtain. Medium-focused disciplinary divides reinforce our blind spots, making it easy to miss these precious refuges for polyphony, because these refuges are often found in the spaces between mediums. Yet reading in these hostile and censored archives makes it imperative that we move beyond the comfort zone of "reading" our chosen medium and attend to the polyphony of the archive whenever it may have taken refuge—which is sometimes in the engine-unsearchable space in-between words, mediums, and even languages.

POSTSCRIPT

Toward a Polyphonic Reading Practice, II

POLYPHONY: ORIGINS, REVISIONS, AND NEW DIRECTIONS

While this book aimed to map and tackle the wide range of challenges posed by Soviet-era declassified archives, it has also identified common threads running through all these challenges, chiefly the hybridity of archival collections. In my attempt to do justice to the hybridity of the declassified archives, I started out by building on a variety of reading methodologies and gradually worked toward what I came to call a polyphonic reading practice. The term "polyphonic" harks back to the ancient Greek *polyphonia*, literally "many sounds/voices." It was influentially adopted from music theory into literary studies by Mikhail Bakhtin, in a book, *Problems of Dostoevsky's Oeuvre*, first published in 1929, the year he was also arrested and sentenced to imprisonment in the infamous Solovki camp.[1] After his sentence was commuted (on a plea of ill health) to exile in Kazakhstan, Bakhtin spent the next decades of Stalinism revising the book and its central concept—polyphony. The much expanded second edition of the book was only published in 1963.[2] As a literary term, Bakhtin's "polyphony" described a rare form of dialogue, first achieved in Dostoevsky's novels, where characters' voices are given free play, without subordination to the authorial voice. The characters of a polyphonic text interact in their constitutive "otherness," "unfinalizability," or openness as human beings, rather than as objects of a "monological"/"authoritarian" authorial discourse.[3] Bakhtin made the ethical, political, and theological roots and implications of this literary theory as "explicit" as he could at that moment in history.[4] This does not mean, however, that the literary term was just a screen for a subversive political message that could not be plainly articulated. At the time of the extreme Stalinist experiment in imposing the monologic discourse of an authoritarian state, literary polyphony was a space where different relationships among human beings were at least imaginable. Bakhtin's dogged dedication, over the long Stalinist decades, to teaching others how to discern polyphony, the otherness of others' voices, in literature, proves that literary polyphony was a precious, vital resource to be cultivated at high risk. So while Bakhtinian polyphony is traditionally seen as mainly describing an authorial creative stance, Bakhtin also sketched, I believe, its potential and urgency as a reading practice.

My book attempts to develop this undercover potential of polyphonic reading. I strive for a polyphonic reading practice that is aware of the limitations of its "proper" textual domain. To do so I mine and expand Bakhtin's understanding of polyphony's defining pull toward other mediums, originally music, and in our case, visual media. Further, I build on Bakhtin's deeply embodied understanding of polyphony, as seen in his emphasis on the voice, and further on the vulnerable body, which is polyphony's prime medium.[5] This is a reading practice rooted in an urgent need to go beyond itself and attend to what has been left out. This can include the voices of others (in all their otherness) and what Foucault pointed to as "all those imperfect words, of no fixed syntax, stammered," "the words without language...the dull sound from beneath history."[6] This repressed "background noise" requires, as Foucault argued, not just a history of "the monologue" of power, but also "an archeology of silence."[7] For while polyphony is for Bakhtin mainly about the interplay of independent "voice-ideas," the term's etymology reaches past the voice to a multiplicity of sounds, which can be echoes, half-words, stammers, and even what is often passed over as "noise." Following Jacques Rancière, I use "noise" here to describe sounds of those who "have no part" in political discourse, those who "have to prove that they are indeed speaking beings, participating in a shared world and not furious or suffering animals."[8] Similar to literature's potential for Rancière, I believe that polyphonic reading of nonliterary texts also has the potential to make "visible what was invisible, mak[ing] audible as speaking beings those who were previously heard only as noisy animals," thus participating in the "redistribution of the perceptible" that links politics and literature.[9]

POLYPHONY AND THE EMBODIED ARCHIVAL ENCOUNTER

In this book we have seen some of the many types of silences in the archives—the different silences of the never-written or the redacted, the silent spaces that echo back our assumptions and expectations, the silences of refusal, resistance, complicity, and fear. And then there are the times when the word "silence" has more to do with our limitations than with the actual contents of the archive. As Jane Hirshfield pithily puts it: "As silence is not silence, but a limit of hearing."[10] Working in the photographic archives of the African diaspora in Europe, Tina Campt cautions against our tendency to categorize as silent that which we are unable, unwilling, untrained, or too hurried to hear. She draws a memorable distinction between "silent" and "quiet" archives: "contrary to what might seem common sense, quiet must not be conflated with silence. Quiet registers sonically, as a level of intensity that requires focused attention."[11] Using a scientific understanding of sound based on frequency, Campt calls our attention to what lies below "audible frequency," defined as "the periodic vibration whose frequency is audible to the average human."[12] These lower-than-audible frequencies are "generally felt rather than heard." Audiologists refer to them as infrasound. For Campt it is crucial that "while the ear is the primary organ for perceiving audible frequencies, at lower frequencies, infrasound is often only felt in the form of vibrations through contact with parts of the body."[13] Campt uses an understanding of sound as "an inherently embodied process that registers at multiple levels of the human sensorium . . . sound need not be heard to be perceived. Sound can be listened to, and, in equally powerful ways, sound can be felt; it both touches and moves people."[14] In order to make out these lower frequencies of the objects of her archival encounters—such as identity photographs meant to control the movement, freedom, and identities of the African diaspora in Europe—Campt develops a practice of "listening to images":

Analogously, quiet photography names a heuristic for attending to the lower range of intensities generated by images assumed to be mute. Redirecting Ariella Azoulay's evocative proposal to "watch" rather than simply "look at" images is a conscious decision to challenge the equation of vision with knowledge by engaging photography through a sensory register that is critical to Black Atlantic cultural foundations: sound.[15]

Campt's imbricated archival theory and practice is painstakingly developed throughout her archival encounters and powerfully performed in *Listening to Images*. While the complexity of Campt's book much exceeds my brief gloss, I would like to return to the subtitle of her introduction: "Listening to Images—an Exercise in Counterintuition." This counterintuitive approach is rooted in a deliberate mismatching of senses and mediums in the archive or, more precisely, in stretching our sensorium to attend to the objects of the archival encounter beyond the usual pairings: vision with images and text, the ear with voices and other sounds, and touch . . . overlooked. Campt's counterintuitive approach means listening to images and also registering their haptic and affective impact.

Campt introduces polyphony as the hoped-for outcome of this embodied archival encounter: "the polyphony made audible when listening to these images," "a polyphony of quietly audible questions that reverberates in these lower frequencies."[16] This polyphony is made available by "attending to their lower frequencies in a way that means being attuned to the connections between what we see and how it resonates."[17] Not only does Campt use the same strange term, polyphony, as Bakhtin, but Bakhtin's polyphony has also often been described as "deeply counterintuitive."[18] The "foundational counterintuition" that they share is the apparent mismatching between mediums and the parts of the sensorium usually allocated to them, so that Campt listens to images, while Bakhtin listens to the polyphony of the novel's printed text through reading, which he defines as "mute perception."[19] The ability to perceive the polyphony of an image or a text is dependent on the openness to displacing the privileged sense organ, the eye, from its exclusive dominance over a privileged medium—the image, in Campt's case, and print text, in Bakhtin's—and mustering all you have: the ear, touch, the very capacity to be affected. Campt writes: "Attuning oneself to such frequencies and affects is more than simply looking and more than visual scrutiny. To look or to watch is to apprehend at one sensory level. Listening requires an attunement to sonic frequencies of affect and impact. It is an ensemble of seeing, feeling, being affected, contacted, and moved beyond the distance of sight and observer."[20] The distant archival observer, another avatar of Denise Ferreira da Silva's "transparent I," has been moved, stirred, embodied.[21] Attending to the polyphony of the archives—the coexistence of voices, low frequencies, infrasounds, murmurings, and cries of pain—necessitates letting go of the pernicious dichotomy between the objectively distant observer and the affectable subject.

Attending to the archival encounter requires an openness to being what cognitive science now tells us we have been all along—embodied subjects whose perception is not cyclopic but multisensory in ways that often overlap vision, hearing, touch, affect, memory, and blind spots, to name just a few things.[22] We are subjects whose "conscious thought is the tip of an enormous iceberg. It is the rule of thumb among cognitive scientists that unconscious thought is 95 percent of all thought," and that it "shapes and structures all conscious thought."[23] In their book *Philosophy in the Flesh: The Embodied Mind and Its Challenge to Western Thought*, George Lakoff and Mark Johnson argue that philosophy has to be fundamentally rethought from the perspective of major discoveries in cognitive science, which they summarize thus:

> The mind is inherently embodied.
> Thought is mostly unconscious ...
> Reason is not disembodied ... but arises from the nature of our brains, bodies, and bodily experience ...
> Reason is not completely conscious, but mostly unconscious.
> Reason is not purely literal, but largely metaphorical and imaginative.
> Reason is not dispassionate, but emotionally engaged.[24]

Lakoff and Johnson compellingly argue that these new scientific findings about our cognition and perception require a rethinking of philosophy's main categories—including those of self and subject. The archival reader/observer has so far remained mostly untouched by such rethinking and re-embodying. So I drew on pioneering attempts to move in this direction whether they came from my immediate field or from other disciplines and contexts.[25]

I was also inspired by new work in the emerging field of neurocognitive poetics.[26] Studies in the reception of fiction have shown that we do not have separate parts of our nervous systems to respond to emotions and to other people depending on whether they are encountered in our everyday life, in nonfiction, or in fiction.[27] Kneepkens and Zwaan have shown that *fiction feelings*—the fear, disgust, or other strong emotions we experience as a consequence of events in the text-world—activate the same parts of the brain that are activated when those emotions are elicited in the real world.[28] Relatedly, the pain of others—whether encountered in a hospital, in a novel, or in a secret police medical report—is also deeply interdependent, indeed inseparable, from our own experiences of pain, which include physical trauma as well as culturally engrained ways of responding to it.[29] This does not mean that all others exist at the distance of fiction, and neither does it mean that fiction can be as affective as immediate experience. There are differential intensities, frequencies. But it does mean that, as unsettling as it is to admit, we are much closer to the archived subjects—ourselves shot through with pain, fiction, and even illegibility—than to any transparent Cyclops. We are mostly illegible to ourselves. Some 95 percent of my cognition remains largely illegible to me.[30] The 5 percent of our conscious thought does not usually perceive, much less read or understand, the remaining 95 percent of the cognitive unconscious that grounds and shapes it, but if "the cognitive unconscious were not doing this shaping, there could be no conscious thought."[31] This may be of little concern to my reader, if what we were referring to when we speak of the cognitive unconscious was my soul, or the old Freudian understanding of my repressed unconscious. But the part of myself that remains largely illegible to me is my own cognition, my own way of perceiving and making sense and interpreting the world, including what I read in these archives. An awareness of my own illegibility as a reader is humbling, and also potentially transformative of the archival encounter.

The archival encounter is not the reading of an affectable, largely illegible, past subject by a present, transparent, or objective observer; it is the encounter of a subject largely illegible to herself with traces of other people that activate conscious cognition, perception, and interpretation, as well as the other, much larger and multilayered parts of our unconscious cognition that shape the conscious cognition. An archival encounter can throw a spark, activate, and sometimes bring to consciousness a buried trace of the past, not only on the page, but also within the reader. I suspect that this is one of the reasons we keep coming back to the archives: not just for their sake, but also for ours. Challenged not only by their illegibility, but also by our own, we often stage encounters that project all that illegibility onto the archives and give us the role of transparent sense-maker. There is comfort in this position, and certain kinds of knowledge can be derived from it. I think there is also promise to be derived from attending to the ways various kinds of knowledge, meaning-making, and illegibilities come into contact in each archival encounter. This means attending to the ways that subjects on both sides of the archival encounter, including ourselves, are differentially affectable, embodied, and mediated. This recognition undermines the old authority of the distant and transparent observer/reader. It also allows for our senses of self and others to evolve—stretch out—to the point of sometimes hearing polyphony, with its multiple voices and infrasounds, not only in the archives, and not only within ourselves, but in the eventful encounter that reading can be. It may even be that we can move from hearing or listening to polyphony as something that is already there, if muffled, to stoking it, participating in it as an in-between process determined not just by the archives or by ourselves but by the open-ended event of our encounter.

POLYPHONY, COUNTERPOINT, AND HETEROGLOSSIA

Let me here return to Bakhtin, for it would be a mistake to quickly gloss his understanding of polyphony. As Bakhtin scholars warn us, his polyphony is a rich and "deeply counterintuitive" concept, which I believe holds ample, if sometimes deeply buried, potential for us.[32] Bakhtin was aware of its "strangeness," and did his best to preserve it, abstaining from driving it away by ever "explicitly defining polyphony."[33] His writing, which turns and returns to polyphony as one of its central contributions, is performatively faithful to the protean nature of the concept. As a result, the term has given rise to many interpretations and misinterpretations, and has been adapted in a wide variety of fields and disciplines, from literary studies to linguistics, rhetoric, communication theory, pedagogy, and psychology. So let me elucidate how this concept can be useful for reading declassified archives.

One way to understand polyphony is by comparison with another famous musical term more recently appropriated in literary studies—counterpoint.[34] Counterpoint is one among many types of polyphony (such as heterophony, homophony, and drone polyphony).[35] It became a key word in literary studies through Edward Said's *Culture and Imperialism*. Said chose the musical term to denote his influential practice of reading: "In practical terms, 'contrapuntal reading' as I have called it . . . must take account of both processes, that of imperialism and that of resistance to it, which can be done by extending our reading of the texts to include what was once forcibly excluded . . . In reading a text, one must open it out to both what went into it and what its author excluded.[36] *Culture and Imperialism* prodigiously performed the imbricated aesthetic and political potential of contrapuntal reading that it ambitiously laid out: "In juxtaposing experiences with each other, in letting them play off each other, it is my interpretative political aim (in the broadest sense) to make concurrent those views and experiences that are ideologically and culturally closed to each other and that attempt to distance or suppress other views and experiences."[37] Like many readers before me, I find Said's contrapuntal reading inspiring in the postcolonial context and beyond.[38] While reading in the secret police archives, I came to believe that "we must read" not just "the great canonical texts," but also these challenging files, "with an effort to draw out, extend, give emphasis and voice to what is silent and marginally present or ideologically represented . . . in such works."[39]

In his erudite monograph on Said's writings on music, *Postcolonial Polyphony*, Wouter Capitain argued that while Said's contrapuntal reading did a lot of work in advocating for a comparative method, where "each cultural artefact can only be understood in terms of its other," Said's particular choice of the term "counterpoint" also had major issues, which have been the subject of spirited scholarly debate.[40] Instead, based on a careful evaluation of Said's concept that includes a thorough review of its development as a political, ethical, musical, and literary concept in Said's published work as well as in his archives, Capitain proposes a polyphonic rather than contrapuntal approach inspired by Said's original term, counterpoint, but not hindered by its limitations:[41]

> A polyphonic perspective therefore tunes the ear not only to the possible differences between historical voices, but also—and especially—to their different patterns of interaction: as relatively equal and independent, interdependent in close harmony, in mimicry, or with one voice lingering in the background as an accompanying drone to a more prominent voice. Understood as such, polyphony is a descriptive term that encompasses multiple forms of interplay between voices, in contrast to counterpoint, which as a musical technique prescribes the relations between them.[42]

L. A. Gogotishvili argued that a similar critique of counterpoint as a limited, indeed, "monologic" (*monologichna*) type of polyphony already animated Bakhtin's understanding of polyphony.[43] Indeed, while the origins of Bakhtin's understanding of polyphony are often traced to his experiences of multilingualism and cultural exchange at the margins of Russian, and then Soviet, space in Vilnius and Odesa, it is noteworthy that Bakhtin also had discriminating views on musical polyphony and counterpoint.[44] Gogotishvili argues that Bakhtin perceived the kind of counterpoint epitomized by Bach as limited, and that his description of Dostoevsky's polyphony is more in line with the atonal polyphony of Schoenberg.[45]

A sometime teacher of music theory and history with a lifelong fascination for folklore, Bakhtin was certainly aware that folk polyphony long antedated counterpoint. Traditional Russian music is defined by polyphony (more specifically, *podgolosochnaia polifoniia*, or literally "the polyphony of under voices"). Even better known types of folk polyphony originate from the margins of the Russian empire/Soviet Union, with world-famous Georgian polyphonic styles documented as early as the eighth century.[46] Indeed, this multinational region spanning Eastern Europe and Asia is known for a richly varied polyphonic tradition, with interplays of voices wildly exceeding counterpoint's more prescriptive character. While I find Gogotishvili's argument about Bakhtin's critique of counterpoint convincing, I would not rush to limit Bakhtin's polyphony by tethering it to any one other composer, such as Schoenberg, or even to a single tradition, such as Russian *podgolosochnaia polifoniia*. Instead, I believe that the general term "polyphony" best illustrates Bakhtin's understanding of multiple, arguably unfinalizable, "forms of interplay between voices," spanning and even exceeding the range of subservience, solidarity, mimicry, or subversion. Indeed, I believe, in line with Capitan's argument, that polyphony's potential as a contemporary reading practice is rooted less in the innovation of any individual composer or writer, whether Bach, Schoenberg, or Dostoevsky, than in the unlocking of its potential through the interpreters' performance, which can often be improvisational. In many folk polyphonic traditions, as well as in the radical polyphonic experiments of free jazz, individual authorship as origination is often unknown or beside the point. Instead, a melody or fragment of melody known by different interpreters is taken as a starting point for a polyphonic performance where different voices enter a wide variety of relations that leave more or less room for improvisation.[47] As Kwami Coleman showed in the context of free jazz of the early 1960s, this kind of radical polyphonic performance satisfied a joint aesthetic and social/political goal for musicians and audiences.[48] Traditional polyphony has also been defined as a confluence between aesthetic and social practices.[49] While Bakhtin was careful not to name any particular type of musical polyphony as the source of his literary metaphor, he was highly invested in the defining intersection of the aesthetic, social, political, and ethical dimensions of the concept.

While polyphony allows for a wide variety of relations among many voices, not any interplay of many voices/sounds qualifies as polyphony for Bakhtin. It is important to distinguish polyphony from the other Bakhtinian term it is most often conflated with—"heteroglossia," whose literal meaning, "different voices," suggests a near synonym. Yet, for Bakhtin, "polyphony is not even roughly synonymous with heteroglossia."[50] Heteroglossia "describes the diversity of speech styles in a language."[51] In his influential celebration of the novel's heteroglossia, Bakhtin described its defining incorporation of different voices, as well as "various genres, both artistic (inserted short stories, lyrical poems, dramatic scenes, etc.,) and extra-artistic."[52] Of the innumerable possible examples, Bakhtin often returned to "the confession, the diary, travel notes, biography, the personal letter," shopping lists, telephone conversations," or "public rumor, gossip, [and slander]."[53] This quotation could easily, if reductively, also describe the declassified archives, which include all these extra-artistic genres, as well as whole novels *and* their nemesis as defined by Bakhtin—monological/authoritative discourse (such as the discourse of religious dogma or of an authoritarian state). Indeed, the secret archives' heterogeneity is capacious enough to contain both, heteroglossia and authoritative discourse galore. Yet while heteroglossia is an ingredient of polyphony, it does not suffice to create polyphony. What more is needed? What distinguishes polyphony from heteroglossia and gives it such an elevated value in Bakhtin's pantheon? My short answer, further developed in the paragraphs below, is a certain intersubjective relationship that is based on a radically dialogic recognition of the other as that other freely and reciprocally reveals themselves. This answer includes the canonical answer given by Bakhtin studies but does not fully coincide with it, rather extending it.

The canonical answer usually given in Bakhtin studies is that polyphony has to do with the position of the author in the text, a position that allows a variety of characters' voices to speak independently of the author's own voice, which is not framed as superior to the those of the characters.[54] An author can tap heteroglossia's potential for becoming polyphonic by allowing each of those voices free play, but most authors stifle heteroglossia, subordinating their characters' voices to their own monologic vision of the world. For Bakhtin, polyphony is a very rare feat, first accomplished by Dostoevsky.[55] The polyphonic novel's achievement is that its "heroes are . . . *not only objects of authorial discourse, but also subjects of their own directly signifying discourse* . . . The consciousness of a character is given as someone else's consciousness, another consciousness, yet at the same time it is not turned into an object, is not closed, does not become the simple object of the author's consciousness."[56] This "new artistic position of the author with regard to the hero . . . affirms the independence, internal freedom, unfinalizability, and indeterminancy of the hero. In a polyphonic discourse, for the author the hero "is not a 'he' or 'I' but a fully valued Thou."[57] For Bakhtin this Thou is fully embodied, thus his emphasis on voice, which is deliberately strange with regard to print texts.[58] This embodiment is further emphasized in Bakhtin's hybrid "voice-idea," through which Bakhtin labors to foreground the individually voiced, particularly embodied human subject rather than a disembodied "no-man's idea."[59] In choosing the metaphor of voice and polyphony, Bakhtin puts the metaphor to its constitutive work, of carrying us from one realm to another, from the merely textual to the phonic, and back again, through a subject that is emphatically embodied and vulnerable in their very subjecthood, a subject always threatened with becoming a mere character in a monologic discourse.

Polyphony allows for the coexistence of such multiple embodied subjects, as well as for their "freedom" *relative* to their author and to each other. At the same time, polyphony requires an encounter, or dialogue, between these different voice-ideas, which cannot exist as monads, but depend on each other for their very being as subjects. This relative freedom and intersubjectivity differentiates polyphonic discourse from heteroglossia. Heteroglossia has the potential to turn into polyphony, or into monologic discourse, but is neither one nor the other.

THE POLITICS AND ETHICS OF POLYPHONIC READING

There are few places where this battle between a monological, authoritative discourse intent on ruling out the vulnerably embodied polyphony of voices was more graphically carried out than in the archives under our consideration. Here, it was not just literary characters that were deprived of their freedom, subjectivity, or humanity; these were actual human beings, whose embodiment is made so salient through deprivation and duress that our mirror neurons cannot help firing our own distress, a distress only augmented by the fact that there are no living bodies to mirror anymore. Bakhtin knew this, of course. His sustained revision of polyphony in his Dostoevsky book spread over the long decades of Stalinism, while he was experiencing an extreme form of silencing of his own voice, along with those of myriad others who had contributed to the polyphonic experimentations of the 1920s. He could not write about the politics of polyphony directly, but as Morson and Emerson demonstrate, "greater explicitness would hardly been possible either in 1929 or in 1963."[60]

> A man never coincides with himself. One cannot apply to him the formula of identity A = A. In Dostoevsky's artistic thinking, the genuine life of the personality takes place at the point of non-coincidence between a man and himself, at his point of departure from the limits of all that he is as material being, *a being that can be spied on, defined, predicted apart from its own will,* "at second hand." The genuine life of the personality is made available only through a *dialogic* penetration of that personality, during which it freely and reciprocally reveals itself.
>
> *The truth about a man in the mouths of others*, not directed at him dialogically and therefore *secondhand truth, becomes a lie degrading and deadening him*, if it touches upon his "holy of holies" that is "the man in the man."[61]

This is the ultimate stake of polyphony in Bakhtin, the shoring up of "the genuine life of the personality" against being "at second hand," "that can be spied on, defined, predicated apart from its own will." As the pathos and urgency of Bakhtin's call intimates, the stakes are even higher when we speak of the battle between actual persons and the secondhand paper personas that are often all that is left of them in the archives. Few texts have degraded and deadened their subjects as much as the holdings of these archives. So it is no wonder that the attempt to hear the archival subject speak often fails, or pushes us toward ventriloquism rather than authentic recovery or reparative reading.[62] Indeed, the archives yield more easily when we read them along the grain, letting them speak for themselves and the institutions they served rather than for any of their subjects. These documents rarely preserve traces of the voice of "the man in the man"; most often they hide/obscure that voice, speaking mostly of themselves. They often remind me of the famous description of the archived subjects in Foucault's *Lives of Infamous Men*:

> What shall be read here are not a collection of portraits: they are snares, weapons, cries, gestures, attitudes, ruses, intrigues for which the words have been instruments. Real lives have been "played out" in these few sentences; I don't mean by that expression that they have been represented there, but that, in fact, their liberty, their misfortune, often their death, in any case their destinies have been, at least partly, therein decided. These discourses have really affected lives; these existences have effectively been risked and lost in these words.[63]

For their subjects, the files often acted more like paper cloaks of Nessus, covers that not only hid but often deformed or killed the person inside them.

So how can we even speak of polyphony in the context of these archives? Despite their abundant heteroglossia, brimming in the diversity of their holdings, polyphony seems to be glaringly missing, the potential that was forever lost when the authoritative discourse of the secret police reduced their heteroglossia. Yet I argue that while these archives' potential for polyphony is fragile, it is only doomed if *we* map the author onto the secret police and the characters onto the victims, informers, and so on. These archives fall woefully short of polyphony in the strict sense of "a theory of creative process" based on a free and equal relationship between author and character. In this scenario, at the time of their creation, authoritative monologic discourse corraled all the heteroglossia of these archives. This one-to-one mapping of Bakhtin's terms onto these archives risks reducing the suppleness and generative force of his thinking as well as the messy reality of the archives themselves. First, giving the secret police authorship over archives teeming with personal confessions, literary manuscripts, letters, and more is highly problematic. This is a complicit, rather than critical or reparative, reading. It is also plain wrong. The secret police may well have wanted to pass as a unified, monologic, authoritative author of the archives, but in practice we have seen it as shifty, cacophonous, uncertain, and divided. When we look at the actual textual practices of these archives, we discover that the power to quell the strong heteroglossia of the archives and to thwart its potential for polyphony resided largely in reading practices.

As surprising as it may seem, in these archives polyphony was mainly endangered by acts and practices of reading, even more than by those of writing. In the clear hierarchy instituted by the archives, reading was both a sign and a practice of power—the realm of the supervising agents and archivists. Writing, on the other hand, was often coerced and as such a sign and practice of subordination—the realm of confessing subjects, censored writers, informers, translators, and lower ranking agents preparing dossiers to be read by their supervisors. The order that Herta Müller received from the secret police agent was "Write!" At the other end of the spectrum looms the image of Stalin as ultimate reader, both as chief censor and as the reader who crosses out or checks names on infamous arrest and execution rosters.[64] This authoritative reading is the dominant reading model offered by the archives, one that violently stamped out their potential for polyphony. And lest the learned ring of ancient Greek muffle the real tragedy of polyphony's extinction, let us recall that the term stands for the awesome yet fragile and already impoverished register of voices and silences that teem in the archives. The history of these archives makes clear that polyphony cannot survive just as a writing practice, that it needs a reading practice to sustain it. This book is born out the urgent call for such a polyphonic reading practice to salvage these archives' potential for polyphony.

If we let go of the narrow understanding of polyphony as limited to the creative process, we can chart new possibilities for reading practices that build on its conceptual and tactical strengths. This pushes polyphony outside of its canonically understood limits, a move that I think is more Bakhtinian than any loyalty to the letter of his text. Furthermore, Bakhtin himself left strong indications that polyphony cannot be limited to the creative process, but has to be extended to the reading process. To start with, as polyphony was being violently stamped out around him, he dedicated decades of his life to teaching *how to read polyphony*, not how to write it. He taught how to recognize polyphony's workings in the novels of Dostoevsky, not to write like Dostoevsky. His struggle against monologic reading frames his whole Dostoevsky book. The revised book's first chapter is an exhaustive literature review, where, in true polyphonic manner, Bakhtin gives ample space to other Dostoevsky scholars, allowing them long quotes and entering into a spirited dialogue with readers of his book's first edition. It gives us a good sense of the times, and the stakes of Bakhtin's book, that one such reader was Anatoly Lunacharsky, the Commissar for Enlightenment, who had written a review of Bakhtin's 1929 book, a review that he titled, "About Dostoevsky's 'Multivoicedness'" (*O 'mnogogolosnosti' Dostoevskogo*).[65] Bakhtin ended that first chapter with an indictment of previous readings of Dostoevsky as incapable of recognizing polyphony: "Everyone interprets his own way Dostoevsky's ultimate word, but all equally interpret it as a *single* word, a *single* voice, a *single* accent, and therein lies their fundamental mistake."[66] The last sentence of the book frames the call to "renounce monologic habits" as its ultimate conclusion, rooted in Bakhtin's keen awareness that no matter how dialogic or polyphonic a text is, it can be, and most often is, read as a monologic text.[67] Thus the importance of his reading lessons, lest we deprive Dostoevsky's text, or any other polyphony, of its voices through our monologic reading.

More encouraging for archival reading is Bakhtin's suggestion that we can create polyphony through our reading even if it did not exist before we came to the text. Morson and Emerson argue that "even if [Bakhtin's interpretation of Dostoevsky's works] should prove mistaken, Bakhtin's polyphonic reading of them at least accomplished his most important purpose: to prove the conceivability of polyphony. However unconceivable polyphony may appear to critics . . . Bakhtin suggests, it is a genuine possibility and perhaps an accomplished fact."[68] It is, of course, much more difficult to create or even restore polyphony to a monologic text than to recognize polyphony in Dostoevsky. This is why the training in reading polyphony in Dostoevsky or elsewhere comes in handy before we approach the archives. In the worst-case scenario, these texts have already carried out their internal genocide of all other voices, so that just the monologic voice of authority can sound. Yet not even the secret police archives have managed this sinister feat.

The lives recorded here have left many kinds of traces. Sometimes these traces are just "brief, incisive, and . . . enigmatic—at the point of their instantaneous contact with power."[69] At times they are precious because "the brief and strident words which come and go between power and the most unessential of existences, are doubtless for the latter the sole monument that has ever been accorded to them."[70] But in the massive and heterogeneous archives under our consideration, we find much more. We find the stutters of the files' subjects next to the stutters of power—the worried drafts of executive orders, the irritated or confused marginalia of supervisors and archivists. We also find drafts of autobiographies, novels, artists' sketches, and letters of all sorts. They all remind us that archives can be polyphony's breeding grounds, a polyphony often muffled in the published piece. (Bakhtin wrote about this—he showed how even the polyphony of Dostoevsky's published work pales in comparison to the polyphony of his archives.) Hearing this polyphony often requires "straining [our] ears, bending down towards [their] murmuring."[71] There is certainly a lot of bodily *bending down* while reading these archives. But I also found myself, more often than I had expected, reaching as high as I could to texts that taught me how to read them, and in the process saved me (to the limited extent that I had the wisdom to let myself be saved), from facile, complicit, overly judgmental or overly relativistic readings that I feared I would produce. These are texts that have been created by myriad people whose experiences and struggles with being read, recorded, and archived far surpassed the limits of my experience, and sometimes even my imagination.

What stands in the way of polyphony in these archives is not the absence of voices of "genuine personalities" in a Bakhtinian sense. They exist alongside, and sometimes inseparable from, stammers, half-words, and silences. What stands in the way of these archives' polyphony is the absence of benevolent, genius author to guarantee that all of these voice-ideas are given free play. Here we come face to face with the limit of polyphony as a theory of the creative process: its precarious dependence on the creative powers of an author who has both the uncommon genius and ethics to allow his characters freedom. When it comes to the archives, we do not have the luxury of any such single ethical author/demiurge who would ensure polyphony. But neither do we have any all-powerful monologic monster who stamped out polyphony once and for all. What we have are traces of the many people who have contributed to the writing, reading, and preservation of the archives. We are latecomers to this archive world, but when we enter it through reading, we make our own choices of reading monologically or of striving toward polyphony.

This is the ethical call to reading others polyphonically that Bakhtin launched in the two versions of the book that bookended Stalinism. We cannot leave all the responsibility of polyphony to the past. The game goes on, for each of us, each time we read. It may be easier to consider this a foregone conclusion, something that happened long ago, so that Dostoevsky's novels are forever enthroned in their polyphony, while hostile archives are forever doomed to murderous monologic. But we are not off the hook, and every time we read anything, we can bypass and thus destroy polyphony or participate in it. And the stakes, as clarified by Bakhtin, are high: polyphony is the name for the voices of real others as well as for my own ethical position in the world. Maybe these voices, infrasounds, and silences can be read by someone else polyphonically, or maybe it's too late. But as far as my own ethical/reading position in the world, no one else can do that work for me. Yet the game goes on every time we read, whether Dostoevsky or the archives, as we wittingly or unwittingly make our choices.

While the system that supported these archives and their secondhand knowledge has suffered a spectacular collapse, the fallout from that collapse continues to shape our world. The modes of obtaining, recording, and manufacturing information and disinformation, and all the resulting secondhand knowledge on display in these archives, have many afterlives. It seems unwise to wait for a benevolent genius like Dostoevsky to save or revive polyphony for us. Even if such a polyphony hero reappeared, it's only too easy to destroy authorially created polyphony through monologic reading. That dependence on the author was Bakhtinian polyphony's weak link, both because it's easily destroyed and because it was always hard to believe in its possibility—for how, as my perceptive students always skeptically ask, can an author maintain the otherness of all *his* characters, all the "others" he allows free play in his work? So it seems urgent to uncouple polyphony's potential from its weak link, which is the authorial creative process. Instead, it seems more strategic and credible to tether polyphony to reading practice, which is by definition intersubjective and multiply disseminated through a plurality of readers. There is little chance that any one reader could restore the polyphony of these texts, or see every "man-in-the man" (not to mention any human-in-the-human, or nonhuman) in these archives.[72] But the more readers approach these archives, chances rise exponentially. The practice of *poly*phony is carried out by each reader individually and further through dialogue with others. Polyphonic reading attends to the call and response among the many kinds of *phōnḗ* (voices, sounds, murmurs) within and outside of the archives. The polyphony of the many voices in the archives depends on our reading—it can be stifled or activated by it. In turn, our own polyphony can be stifled or activated by how we, and those around us, read. When we read polyphonically, we activate our own polyphony and potential to tackle current reading challenges.

Notes

Acknowledgments

1. M. Tubiana, "Wilhelm Conrad Röntgen et la découverte des rayons X [Wilhelm Conrad Röntgen and the discovery of X-rays]," *Bulletin de l'Academie nationale de medecine* 180, no. 1 (1996): 97.

2. National Institute of Biomedical Imaging, "X-rays," (2022), https://www.nibib.nih.gov/science-education/science-topics/x-ray.

3. For a thorough treatment of the topic, see Golfo Alexopoulos, *Illness and Inhumanity in Stalin's Gulag* (New Haven: Yale University Press, 2017).

4. As we will see in more detail in The Introduction, the understanding of being affected as a capacity is theorized by Brian Massumi, based on Spinoza. Brian Massumi, *Politics of Affect* (Cambridge: Polity Press, 2015), 91–92.

5. To my radiologist friend, the x-ray appeared normal, but the quality of the image left her with a question mark about the right lung. She was impressed with the medical care the patient received (the x-ray itself, as well as an expensive funduscopic evaluation) based on the filed medical records, yet it is unclear to what extent the records can be trusted. Oana Panțel Nebunescu, July 1st 2022. Besides these lingering questions about authenticity, the x-ray also raised questions about the media, technologies, and ethics that went into the files' production, preservation, and reception, all questions addressed at length in this book.

Introduction

1. My postscript discusses the neurocognitive poetics research that underlies this view, in particular Kneepkens and Zwaan's work on "fiction feelings" and the Panskepp-Jakobson hypothesis. Eleonore Kneepkens, and Rolf A. Zwaan, "Emotions and Literary Text Comprehension," *Poetics* 23 (1995). See also Arthur Jacobs, "Neurocognitive Poetics: Methods and Models for Investigating the Neuronal and Cognitive-affective Bases of Literature Reception," *Frontiers in Human Neuroscience* 9, no. 186 (2015). For a fascinating discussion of developing a "biliterate reading brain" with expertise in both print and digital reading, and further "building [a] kind of pluripotential brain circuitry" through reading different mediums, see Maryanne Wolf, *Reader, Come Home: The Reading Brain in a Digital World* (New York: Harper, 2018), 169–71.

2. The literature on the contemporary crisis of reading is vast. An influential early contribution to this debate was Sven Birkerts, *The Gutenberg Elegies: The Fate of Reading in an Electronic Culture* (Boston: Faber & Faber, 1994). For further bibliography and a comprehensive engagement with the topic that draws on both neuroscience and literature, see Maryanne Wolf's extensive scholarship, especially Wolf, *Reader, Come Home*.

3. For a resonating critique of archival writing and reading practices, and a celebration of an alternative way of remembering (i.e., the repertoire), see Diana Taylor, *The Archive and the Repertoire: Performing Cultural Memory in the Americas* (Durham, NC: Duke University Press, 2003). The complex choices involved in reading against or along the archival grain have been most influentially explored by Saidiya Hartman and Ann Laura Stoler. Good starting points for exploring their prolific work on the topic are Saidiya Hartman, "Venus in Two Acts," *Small Axe* 12, no. 2 (2008); Ann Laura Stoler, *Along the Archival Grain: Epistemic Anxieties and Archival Common Sense* (Princeton: Princeton University Press, 2009). A landmark polemical stance on alternative modes of reading that has deeply influenced this book is that of Eve Kosofky Sedgwick, "Paranoid Reading and Reparative Reading, or, You're So Paranoid, You Probably Think This Essay Is about You," in *Touching Feeling: Affect, Pedagogy, Performativity* (Durham, NC: Duke University Press, 2003). A provocative edited volume excavates the genealogy and development of reparative and critical reading, and ponders their futures: Elizabeth Anker and Rita Felski, *Critique and Postcritique* (Durham, NC: Duke University Press, 2017), 1–30. See also Kirstin Weld, *Paper Cadavers: The Archives of Dictatorship in Guatemala* (Durham, NC: Duke University Press, 2014); Robert Reid-Pharr, *Archives of Flesh: African America, Spain, and Post-humanist Critique* (New York: New York University Press, 2016); Zeb Tortorici, *Sins against Nature: Sex and Archives in Colonial New Spain* (Durham, NC: Duke University Press, 2018). The ethics of researching in declassified Eastern European archives has preoccupied the Hidden

Archives collective, whose prolific work is repeatedly referenced in this book. See also the special issue of the Romanian journal *Martor* titled *Visual Ethics after Communism*, particularly its introduction: David Crowley, James Kapaló, and Gabriela Nicolescu, "Introduction. Visual Ethics after Communism," *Martor* 26 (2021). The thought-provoking methodology section of the magisterial *Peasants under Siege* also interrogated the limits of reading in hostile archives and argued for the need to complement it with oral history. Gail Kligman and Katherine Verdery, *Peasants under Siege: The Collectivization of Romanian Agriculture, 1949–1962* (Princeton: Princeton University Press, 2011), 464–71.

4. Hal Foster, "An Archival Impulse," *October* 1, no. 110 (2004). The terms "archival impulse" and "archival turn" are treated in more detail in chapter 2.

5. The term "quantum leap" is taken from Sheila Fitzpatrick, "Impact of the Opening of Soviet Archives on Western Scholarship on Soviet Social History," *Russian Review* 74, no. 3 (2015): 377. For thoughtful accounts of the "archival revolution," including further bibliography on the term, see Donald J. Raleigh, "Doing Soviet History: The Impact of the Archival Revolution," *Russian Review* 61, no. 1 (2002); Jan Plamper, "Archival Revolution or Illusion? Historicizing the Russian Archives and Our Work in Them," *Jahrbücher für Geschichte Osteuropas* 51, no. 1 (2003).

6. Michael David-Fox, "Into and Beyond the Stalinist Paradigm of Secret Policing," in *The Secret Police and the Soviet System: New Archival Investigations*, ed. Michael David-Fox (Pittsburgh, PA: University of Pittsburgh Press, 2023), 6.

7. David-Fox, "Into and Beyond the Stalinist Paradigm of Secret Policing," 4.

8. See, for example, Juliet Johnson, "2023 President's Address: De-centering Russia: Challenges and Opportunities," blog post, *ASEEES Blog* (2023), https://www.aseees.org/news-events/aseees-blog-feed/2023-presidents-address-de-centering-russia-challenges-and; Davis Center for Russian and Eurasian Studies, "Decolonization in Focus Seminar Series" (2023), https://daviscenter.fas.harvard.edu/insights/announcing-decolonization-focus-seminar-series.

9. Besides the rehabilitation of former political prisoners, declassified archival records also played a central role in the "screening, lustration and public identification of perpetrators." In her comparative study of the place of archival resources in transitional justice, Lavinia Stan shows that "archival records were of remarkable utility for the trials against former leaders and the truth commissions in Latin America, but the advantages—and the disadvantages—of using archival records for transitional justice purposes were particularly clearly revealed in post-communist Eastern Europe." Lavinia Stan, "Entries on Transitional Justice Debates, Controversies, and Key Questions," in *Encyclopedia of Transitional Justice*, ed. Lavinia Stan and Nadya Nedelsky (Cambridge, UK: Cambridge University Press, 2014), 112.

10. There are thousands of informer scandals across the former Soviet bloc,

some of which—such as those concerning Lech Wałęsa, István Szabó, Milan Kundera, or Julia Kristeva—made international news.

11. Some scholars warned early on that the term "archival revolution" could not be justified solely by the quantity of new sources. Stephen Kotkin, "The State—Is It Us? Memoirs, Archives, and Kremlinologists," *Russian Review* 61, no. 1 (2002); Mark von Hagen, "The Archival Gold Rush and Historical Agendas in the Post-Soviet Era," *Slavic Review* 52, no. 1 (1993). There were lively debates about whether "new perspectives derive from open archives or whether such openings only reinforce preconceived categories of analysis." David-Fox, "Into and beyond the Stalinist Paradigm of Secret Policing," 7. As David-Fox concedes, in the first decade, scholars warning that "often uninterrogated purpose and structure of the archival repositories themselves, the search for revelations their opening engenders, and the way fields use them to pour old wine into new bottles makes the knowledge they create less than revelatory" found ready ammunition for their critique. However, David-Fox continues, "with the hindsight of over three decades of Soviet history in the archival era, it has become clearer that the availability and allure of new sources have served as a potential, often even necessary impetus to widen and re-focus our vision." David-Fox, "Into and beyond the Stalinist Paradigm of Secret Policing," 7. Rather than a defeat of those initial critics, the quality of this new research and its self-reflexive interest in methodology has likely benefited from those early warnings.

12. Jane Hirshfield, *Hiddenness, Uncertainty, Surprise* (Hexham, UK: Bloodaxe Books, 2008), 53.

13. As the poet Yehuda Amichai reminds us, difficulty yields interpretations and commentary in a way that straightforwardness does not: "Interpretations grew around them, as / When the Talmud grows difficult, / It shrinks on the page, / And Rashi and the commentaries, / Close in on it from all sides." Difficulty also makes interpretation and its conclusions visible, putting them on display and thus subjecting them to critique, revision, and reinterpretation. Yehuda Amichai, *Yehuda Amichai: A Life of Poetry 1948–1994*, trans. Benjamin Harshav and Barbara Harshav (New York: Harper Collins, 1994), 38.

14. *OED Online* provides usage examples: 1796 R. Southey *Joan of Arc* vi. 50 "The sentinel . . . with uplifted lance / Challenged the darkling travellers." 1833 *Regulations Instr. Cavalry* i.i.28 "On any one approaching his post, he must challenge them by the words '*Who comes there?*'"

15. According to *OED Online*, our current word "challenge" originates from the Latin *calumnia* (a false accusation, calumny), by way of Middle English *calenge* (an accusation, claim).

16. Cristina Vatulescu, *Police Aesthetics: Literature, Film, and the Secret Police in Soviet Times* (Stanford: Stanford University Press, 2010), 5; Hannah Arendt, *The Origins of Totalitarianism* (New York: Meridian Books, 1958), 351–73.

17. See the section "Reading 'Other'-Wise" in Denise Ferreira da Silva, *Toward a Global Idea of Race* (Minneapolis: University of Minnesota Press, 2007), 30–33.

18. The term "chronotope" (*khronotop*) originates in Mikhail Bakhtin's work. See Mikhail Bakhtin, *The Dialogic Imagination*, ed. Caryl Emerson, trans. Mikhail Holquist (Austin: University of Texas Press, 1981), 425–26.

19. For a fine-grained study of the differences among three Eastern European secret services in the aftermath of World War II, see Molly Pucci, *Security Empire: The Secret Police in Communist Eastern Europe* (New Haven: Yale University Press, 2020).

20. The auditory imagination is receiving increased attention in contemporary sound studies. For an engaging study of the auditory imagination through a fascinating focus on earworms, see J. Martin Daughtry, "Listening beyond Sound and Life: Reflections on Imagined Music," in *The Oxford Handbook of the Phenomenology of Music Cultures*, ed. Friedlind Riedel, Harris M. Berger, and David Vander-Hamm (Oxford, UK: Oxford University Press, 2022). For a book-length, historically grounded analysis of the topic, see Viktoria Tkaczyk, *Thinking with Sound* (Chicago: University of Chicago Press, 2023).

21. As we will see in more detail in the postscript, Tina Campt argues for counterintuitive "listening" to archives that appear silent but in fact emit on "low frequencies." Tina Campt, *Listening to Images* (Durham, NC: Duke University Press, 2017), 23–45. J. Martin Daughtry proposes a similarly transmedial approach but coming from the opposite direction, conceptualizing sound through the originally textual metaphor of the palimpsest. J. Martin Daughtry, "Acoustic Palimpsests," in *Theorizing Sound Studies*, ed. Deborah Kapchan (Middletown, CT: Wesleyan University Press, 2017).

22. Francisco Varela, Evan Thompson, and Eleanor Rosch, *The Embodied Mind: Cognitive Science and Human Experience* (Cambridge, MA: MIT Press, 2016).

23. Silva describes the dynamic dependence between this transparent "I" ("Man, the subject, the ontological figure consolidated in post-Enlightenment thought") and the affectable "I," as the European construction of non-European minds. She defines "affectability" as "the condition of being subjected to both natural (in the scientific and lay sense) conditions and to other's power." Silva, *Toward a Global Idea of Race*, xv–xvi and 1–17.

24. Brian Massumi, *Politics of Affect* (Cambridge, UK: Polity Press, 2015), 91–92.

25. Massumi, *Politics of Affect*, 92.

26. Massumi, *Politics of Affect*, 57.

27. Massumi, *Politics of Affect*, 57–58.

28. Katie King develops Bruno Latour's invitation to learn to be affected into a whole book project: "Learning to be affected is what this book is all about." Katie King, *Networked Reenactments: Stories Transdisciplinary Knowledges Tell* (Durham,

NC: Duke University Press, 2011), 274–75; Bruno Latour, "How to Talk about the Body? The Normative Dimension of Science Studies," *Body & Society* 10, nos. 2–3 (2004).

29. See the section "Reading 'Other'-Wise" in Silva, *Toward a Global Idea of Race*, 30–33.

30. For a radical critique of listening practices as trespass, see Dylan Robinson, *Hungry Listening: Resonant Theory for Indigenous Sound Studies* (Minneapolis: University of Minnesota Press, 2020).

31. Anca Șincan, "Ethical Questions in Researching the Religious Underground in Romania's Secret Police Archives, Part I–II," blog post, *All the Russias' Blog*, Jordan Center, https://jordanrussiacenter.org/news/our-story-ethical-questions-on-researching-the-religious-underground-in-the-secret-police-archives-part-i/#.Ya UTHC1h1TY.

32. Șincan, "Ethical Questions."

33. Șincan, "Ethical Questions."

34. Șincan, "Ethical Questions."

35. Here Șincan quotes Catherine Wanner's term "hybridity of religion," a term for "instances where the political context spurs change in orthodoxies of faith and praxis." Șincan, "Ethical Questions." For further development of the term, see Catherine Wanner, "Introduction," in *State Secularism and Lived Religion in Soviet Russia and Ukraine*, ed. Catherine Wanner (New York: Oxford University Press, 2012).

36. Șincan, "Ethical Questions."

37. Their refusal to read, first expressed through this striking body language, was then discussed at length among the community and later explicitly articulated and maintained by the community leaders.

38. Kinga Povedák also thoughtfully documents the moral dilemma she faced as a researcher when the community whose files she studied expressed their preference that she refrain from publishing photographs she had discovered in the secret police archives. Povedák models a respectful, resourceful, and creative approach to the ethics of reading in the archives, by approaching the files' subjects for permission that she legally did not need, hearing their preference, and collaborating with them to find alternative ways of individually and communally processing the images through an innovative method of "photo-elicitation" and further through a moving public exhibition based in part on her archival research. Kinga Povedák, "Methodological Notes on Visual Ethics: 'Choosing Not to Reveal,'" *Martor* 26 (2021). The exhibit was held in Budapest, at Galeria Centralis, Blinken Open Society Archives, as a Hidden Galleries project. It is available online at James Kapaló, Gabriela Nicolescu, "Faith-Trust-Secrecy. Religions through the Lenses of the Secret Police" (2021).

39. Nicolae Steinhardt, in his accounts of his interrogation and prison experi-

ence, repeatedly returns to the idea of "making oneself obscure." Nicolae Steinhardt, *Jurnalul Fericirii* (Cluj: Dacia, 1997). See also the influential discussions of a kindred term, "deliberate opacity." Édouard Glissant, *Poetics of Relation* (Ann Arbor: University of Michigan Press, 1997); Paul Gilroy, *The Black Atlantic: Modernity and Double Consciousness* (Cambridge, MA: Harvard University Press, 1993), 37; Saidiya Hartman, *Scenes of Subjection: Terror, Slavery, and Self-Making in Nineteenth-Century America* (New York: Oxford University Press, 1997), 35–36. For a fascinating take on the related practice of obfuscation, in the contemporary US context, see Finn Brunton and Helen Nissenbaum, *Obfuscation: A User's Guide for Privacy and Protest* (Cambridge, MA: MIT Press, 2015). In chapter 2, I explore the intertwined master narratives of identification, visibility, and legibility. For an in-depth look at the first two (identification and visibility), see Cristina Vatulescu, "The Mug-Shot and the Close-up: Identification and Visual Pedagogy in Secret Police Film," in *The Secret Police and the Soviet System: New Archival Investigations*, ed. Michael David-Fox (Pittsburgh, PA: University of Pittsburgh Press, 2023).

40. Kligman and Verdery, *Peasants under Siege*, 450, emphasis mine.

41. Vatulescu, "The Mug-Shot and the Close-up." For example, in V. Musatova, *This Concerns Us All*, a suspect turns his back and uses his coat to hide from the camera, and a woman suspect attempts to hide her face from the camera with her headscarf. V. Musatova, *This Concerns Us All [Eto trevozhit vsekh]* (Moscow: TsKDK, 1960).

42. See, for example, the original and altered arrest photographs of Maria Tishchenko, SBU Archive, f. 6, spr. 69346, ark. 249 rev and ark. 242, discussed in Tatiana Vagramenko and Gabriela Nicolescu, "The Hand at Work or How the KGB File Leaks in the Exhibition," *Martor* 26 (2021).

43. While the word "subterfuge" has more recently acquired largely negative connotations, I use it to harken back to its powerful literal/etymological roots, *subter* (secret/underground) and *fuge* (to run, escape), which have given us its older meanings of "hiding place" and "secret refuge." *OED Online*.

44. Particularly memorable was the TV series *Memorial to Suffering [Memorialul Durerii]*, which told the story of political repression through interviews with survivors and secret police personnel; the film was shot on location at former camp and prison sites. Lucia Hossu-Longin, *Memorialul durerii* (Bucharest: Televiziunea Română, 1991).

45. Steinhardt, *Jurnalul Fericirii*.

46. Consiliul de stat al Republicii Socialiste Romania, "Decret Nr. 770 din 1 octombrie 1966 pentru reglementarea întreruperii cursului sarcinii [Decree no. 770 from 1 October 1966 regulating the interruption of the course of pregnancy]" (Bucharest: Buletinul Oficial [Official Bulletin] 60, 1966). The classic study on Ceaușescu's reproductive policies, including the abortion ban, is Gail Kligman, *The Politics*

of Duplicity: Controlling Reproduction in Ceaușescu's Romania (Berkeley: University of California Press, 1998). See also Vladimir Trebici, *Genocid si Demografie [Genocide and Demography]* (Bucharest: Humanitas, 1991); Cristian Pop-Eleches, "The Impact of an Abortion Ban on Socioeconomic Outcomes of Children: Evidence from Romania," *Journal of Political Economy* 114, no. 4 (2006); Corina Doboș, *Politica pronatalistă a regimului Ceaușescu: o perspectivă comparativă [The Pronatalist Policy of the Ceaușescu Regime: A Comparative Perspective]* (Iași: Polirom, 2010); Andreea Andrei and Alina Branda, "Abortion Policy and Social Suffering: The Objectification of Romanian Women's Bodies under Communism (1966–1989)," *Women's History Review* 24, no. 6 (2015).

47. Roxana Cazan, "Constructing Spaces of Dissent in Communist Romania: Ruined Bodies and Clandestine Spaces in Cristian Mungiu's '4 Months, 3 Weeks, and 2 Days' and Gabriela Adameșteanu's 'A Few Days in the Hospital,'" *Women's Studies Quarterly* 39 (2011).

48. This image of the *decreței* as tools of the state turned against their own parents and the population at large was taken to an extreme in the "orphan myth," examined by Peter Siani-Davis amid the many theories concerning the "terrorists," the feared group of armed Ceaușescu supporters on whom many Romanians blamed the deaths and terror during and after the 1989 revolution. It was rumored that some of the *decreței* abandoned by their parents were raised in special orphanages and turned into special forces fanatically devoted to Ceaușescu. As Siani-Davis has shown in his thoughtful research on the "terrorists," much of the killings and terror of those days was the result of actions by the secret police as well as mistakes, accidents, and their cover-ups. The orphan myth is, however, telling of the many unprocessed fears and traumas of the socialist regime, including the fraught relationships between parents and the *decreței* generation as well as the secret existence of death-orphanages whose revelation shocked Romanians as well as the world in the early 1990s. Peter Siani-Davis, *The Romanian Revolution of December 1989* (Ithaca, NY: Cornell University Press, 2007), 161.

49. Cristian Pop-Eleches, "The Impact of an Abortion Ban." The premiere of *Children of the Decree*, the first documentary film about this long-reaching pronatalist policy, took place, fittingly, in a factory, a site where women had been standardly subjected to forced gynecological exams en masse. Florin Iepan, *Children of the Decree* (Germany, Romania, 2004). At the after-viewing discussion, the then-minister of culture, Mona Muscă, asked the women in the audience how many of them had been affected by the abortion policy. Everyone raised their hands. Sandra and Simona Chitan Scarlat, "Vedetele Epocii de Aur aveau liber la avort [The Celebrities of the Golden Age Were Allowed Abortions]," *Evenimentul Zilei*, 19 May 2005.

50. The extensive reach of the pronatalist policy among the general population is also documented in the chapter dedicated to the policy in the Final Presidential

Report on the communist period's abuses, a chapter strongly based on Kligman's 1998 study. "Politica demografică a regimului Ceaușescu," in *Raport Final*, ed. Dorin Dobrincu, Vladimir Tismăneanu and Cristian Vasile (Bucharest: Humanitas, 2007).

51. As Șincan's Calendarist case study suggests, not even my lengthy enumeration (scholarly, ethical, political, aesthetic) exhausts the different qualities of these reading challenges, which for the monks were of a religious/spiritual nature.

52. Vivian Sobchack, *Carnal Thoughts: Embodiment and Moving Image Culture* (Berkeley: University of California Press, 2004), 2. As Sobchack persuasively argues, much of the extensive scholarship in the humanities that focuses on the body overlooks embodiment, thus reinforcing the objectification of the body that it openly decries. Sobchack, *Carnal Thoughts*, 1–2.

53. Sonja Luehrmann, *Religion in Secular Archives: Soviet Atheism and Historical Knowledge* (New York: Oxford University Press, 2015), 24; Katherine Verdery, *Secrets and Truths: Ethnography in the Archive of Romania's Secret Police* (Budapest: Central European University Press, 2014), 51–52.

54. The term "super-hybridity" was introduced by Jörg Heiser as a "possible catchall for the aesthetic output of our digitally sped-up moment, where artists mine the explosion of cultural contexts, available at the click of a mouse," and was debated in *Frieze*'s 2010 September issue.

55. As chapter 2 demonstrates, to complicate matters, we also come up against the powerful wave of digital remediation, which erases medium hybridity by replacing it with the digital medium; additionally, we come up against old disciplinary models of archival scholarship, which are often rooted in the separation of mediums, usually privileging the textual.

56. The beginnings of "distant reading" are usually associated with Franco Moretti, who defined it in direct opposition to close reading: "One thing is for sure: it [distant reading] cannot mean the very close reading of very few texts—secularized theology, really ('canon'!)." Franco Moretti, "The Slaughterhouse of Literature," *MLQ: Modern Language Quarterly* 61, no. 1 (2000): 208. This and related essays were later collected in *Distant Reading* (London: Verso, 2013). The last chapter argues for the potential of these reading strategies to complement each other.

57. Sedgwick, "Paranoid Reading and Reparative Reading."

58. Stoler, *Along the Archival Grain*.

59. There is a rich literature and debate on Aesopian writing and reading practices in Russia and Eastern Europe. For key arguments for reading along and between the lines in Soviet-era archives, see Jochen Hellbeck, *Revolution on My Mind: Writing a Diary under Stalin* (Cambridge, MA: Harvard University Press, 2006); Igal Halfin, "Poetics in the Archives: The Quest for 'True' Bolshevik Documents," *Jahrbücher für Geschichte Osteuropas* 51, no. 1 (2003); Halfin, *Terror in My Soul:*

Communist Autobiographies on Trial (Cambridge, MA: Harvard University Press, 2003); Svetlana Boym, "How Soviet Subjectivity Is Made," in *The Svetlana Boym Reader*, ed. Cristina Vatulescu et al. (New York: Bloomsbury, 2019).

60. Bakhtin, *The Dialogic Imagination*; Bakhtin, *Problems of Dostoevsky's Poetics*, trans. Caryl Emerson (Minneapolis: Minnesota University Press, 1984); Tina Campt, *Image Matters: Archive, Photography, and the African Diaspora in Europe* (Durham, NC: Duke University Press, 2012); Campt, *Listening to Images*.

61. As we will see in more depth in the postscript, Campt develops the concept of archival low frequency in *Listening to Images*, 23–45. My project of stretching current definitions and practices of reading is also influenced by Matthew Rubery's work in disability studies: "Efforts to cordon off reading from nonreading are doomed to fail because there is no agreement on what qualifies as reading in the first place. The more one tries to figure out where the border lies between reading and non-reading, the more edge cases will be found to stretch the term's elastic boundaries . . . *Reader's Block* moves toward an understanding of reading as a spectrum that is capacious enough to accommodate the disparate activities documented in the following chapters . . . along with any new ones that will inevitably come to the surface." Matthew Rubery, *Reader's Block: A History of Reading Differences* (Palo Alto: Stanford University Press, 2022), 4.

62. Hartman, "Venus in Two Acts," 13.

63. Hartman, "Venus in Two Acts."

64. Jules Michelet, "Préface de l'Histoire de France," in *Oeuvres complètes, Tome IV* (Paris: Flammarion, 1974 [1869]), 613–14. For a fascinating reading of Michelet's metaphor and the articulation of a new embodied position for the archival reader, see Carolyn Steedman, *Dust: The Archive and Cultural History* (New Brunswick, NJ: Rutgers University Press, 2002), 26–28.

65. Jenny Sharpe powerfully argues that "silence can also be a form of expression rather than just a puzzle of history to be solved." Jenny Sharpe, *Immaterial Archives: An African Diaspora Poetics of Loss* (Evanston, IL: Northwestern University Press, 2020), 56. In so doing, she builds on M. NourbeSe Philip's creative work of "defining silence as a black female space of expression rather than one of negation," as well as on the works of scholars like Anjali Arondekar, who caution against "the project of filling archival gaps," and Stephen Best, who "is especially critical of the recovery imperative." Sharpe, *Immaterial Archives*, 9, 20. Anjali Arondekar, *For the Record: on Sexuality and the Colonial Archive in India* (Durham, NC: Duke University Press, 2009), 6; Stephen Michael Best, *None Like Us: Blackness, Belonging, Aesthetic Life* (Durham, NC: Duke University Press, 2018), 40–41.

66. Hartman, "Venus in Two Acts," 13.

67. Stoler, *Along the Archival Grain*, 20.

68. Thomas Rid, *Active Measures: The Secret History of Disinformation and Po-*

litical Warfare (New York: Farrar, Straus & Giroux, 2020). The uncomfortable links between KGB disinformation and the literary establishment are often obscured, but at times are made saliently clear. For instance, *"Literaturnaia gazeta* is the most important cultural journal since *The Thaw*, a go-to venue for KGB disinformation." David-Fox, "Into and beyond the Stalinist Paradigm of Secret Policing," 13.

Chapter 1

This co-authored chapter revises and expands an article first published as Anna Krakus and Cristina Vatulescu, "Foucault in Poland: A Silent Archive," *Diacritics* 47, no. 2 (2019). I am grateful to my co-author, Anna Krakus, and to Johns Hopkins University Press for kind permission to publish the current version as this book chapter.

1. Daniel Defert, "Chronology," in *A Companion to Foucault*, ed. Christopher Falzon, Timothy O'Leary, and Jana Sawicki (Chichester, UK: Wiley & Sons 2003), 25, translation modified.

2. Defert, "Chronology," 25.

3. Étienne Burin des Roziers, "Une rencontre à Varsovie," *Le Débat* 41 (September–October 1986): 133–34.

4. Defert, "Chronology," 25. Thus, in his biography of Foucault, David Macey credits his information on the Polish scandal to interviews with Daniel Defert, Sygmund Bauman, Bernard Kouchner, and Jacques Lebas. David Macey, *The Lives of Michel Foucault* (London: Hutchinson, 1993), 84–87, 45–48. The account contains details that seem to fit better the few clichés Westerners hold about Poland than any veridical details. For example, Foucault's lover is said to have been *"the son of an officer murdered at Katyn*, and therefore, given the ideology of the day, suspicious ... *Agreeing to work for the police was the price he paid for his university education."* Macey, *The Lives of Michel Foucault*, 86, emphasis mine.

5. Daniel Defert, interview by Anna Krakus, 16 November and 14 December 2009, Paris.

6. Defert, interview by Krakus. At this time, Defert did not wish to share further details, explaining that he wanted to protect the identity of "Jurek." In 2017, he offered "Jurek's" photograph and last name to Remigiusz Ryziński, who describes details from "Jurek's" biography but conceals his surname when he identifies him as "Jerzy Tadeusz S." Remigiusz Ryziński, *Foucault w Warszawie* (Warsaw: Wydwnictwo Dowody Na Istnienie, 2017).

7. Laura Engelstein, "Combined Underdevelopment: Discipline and the Law in Imperial and Soviet Russia," in *Foucault and the Writing of History*, ed. Jan Goldstein (Oxford, UK: Blackwell, 1994); Jan Goldstein and Rudy Koshar, "Foucault and Social History: Comments on 'Combined Underdevelopment,'" *American Historical Review* 98, no. 2 (1993); Jonathan Arac, "Foucault and Central Europe: A Polem-

ical Speculation," *boundary 2* 21, no. 3 (1994); Viktor Zhivov, "Chto delat' s Fuko, zanimaias' russkoi istoriei?" *Novoe literaturnoe obozrenie* (2001); Jan Plamper, "Foucault's Gulag," *Kritika* 3, no. 2 (2002); Cristina Vatulescu, "A Note on Foucault," in *Police Aesthetics* (Stanford: Stanford University Press, 2010).

8. Engelstein, "Combined Underdevelopment."

9. Plamper, "Foucault's Gulag," 265–66, 73–74, 77. On Foucault's Eurocentrism, see also Edward Said, "Michel Foucault, 1926–1984," in *After Foucault: Humanistic Knowledge, Postmodern Challenges*, ed. Jonathan Arac (New Brunswick, NJ: Rutgers University Press, 1988), 9–10.

10. Engelstein, "Combined Underdevelopment."

11. Plamper, "Foucault's Gulag," 262.

12. Plamper, "Foucault's Gulag," 256–57.

13. Plamper, "Foucault's Gulag," 276, 79.

14. Plamper, "Foucault's Gulag," 272.

15. Didier Eribon, *Michel Foucault* (Cambridge, MA: Harvard University Press, 1992), 301.

16. Defert, "Chronology," 82.

17. Eribon, *Michel Foucault*, 297.

18. Hannah Arendt, *The Origins of Totalitarianism* (New York: Meridian Books, 1958), 434.

19. For more on the "spy mania," see Antoni Dudek and Andrzej Paczkowski, "Poland," in *A Handbook of the Communist Security Apparatus in East Central Europe, 1944–1989*, ed. K. Persak and L. Kaminski (Warsaw: IPN, 2005), 264–66.

20. In Poland, around the same time when Foucault opened his Center for French Culture within the university, the French Institute was closed. Foucault was not the only director, not to mention member, of a French cultural institution to have his tenure abruptly cut short. And most center directors were, as we had expected, followed by the SB, which resulted in thousands of pages of secret police files such as BU 0204/1278 (Jean Carbonnet), vols. 1–2, Warsaw; BU 0204/458 (Daniel Beauvois), Warsaw. Vice director Sylvain Bozec's actions are described at length in his wife's file: BU 0204/1930 (Michelle Bozec), Warsaw.

21. Lavinia Stan, "Poland," in *Transitional Justice in Eastern Europe and the Former Soviet Union: Reckoning with the Communist Past*, ed. Lavinia Stan (London: Routledge, 2008), 87.

22. "By 1953, some 5.2 million Poles (in a total population of 26.5 million) had secret files." Stan, "Poland," 87.

23. Michael Szporer, "The Security Forces and Polish Communism: Reclaiming History from Myth," *Journal of Cold War Studies* 9, no. 1 (2007).

24. Dudek and Paczkowski, "Poland," 246–55.

25. Stan, "Transitional Justice," 87.

26. Stan, "Transitional Justice," 88.

27. The IPN archive and its finding aids changed during the almost ten years of our search. While in the beginning it took months to receive files and paper photocopies, CD-ROM copies brought shorter wait times, and the IPN has now progressed to a current system where the researcher can create an account and upload digitized copies instantaneously.

28. A famous case, explored in depth in chapters 3 and 4, is Nobel Prize–winning writer Herta Müller's long search for her Securitate file in Romania. She recounts the story, including her disappointment with the final finding of her file, in Herta Müller, *Cristina und ihre Attrappe, oder, Was (nicht) in den Akten der Securitate steht* (Göttingen: Wallstein, 2009).

29. Anna Krakus conducted research in the archives in Poland, and Cristina Vatulescu researched the archives in France. Fonds Michel Foucault, NAF 28730, Bibliothèque Nationale de France, Archives et manuscrits. Laurence Le Bras and Ariana Sforzini gave precious help with this collection. Archives Centre Michel Foucault /IMEC, http://portail-michel-foucault.org. We are grateful to Philippe Artières for advice on this collection and to Centre des Archives Diplomatiques, Nantes. Many thanks to Renata Szulc and to Michał Rosenberg for their help navigating the Instytut pamięci narodowej (IPN) archives in Warsaw and Krakow. Audrey Kichelewski granted us access to the archives of the French Department at Warsaw University and introduced us to people familiar with Foucault's time in Warsaw. We also consulted the archives of the Polish Academy of Science (PAN), and the Police Department archives in Warsaw. In the United States, we received Foucault's file from the FBI archives through the Freedom of Information Act. All translations of archival documents are ours.

30. Michel Foucault, *The Archaeology of Knowledge*, trans. A. M. Sheridan Smith (New York: Pantheon Books, 1972), 130, original emphasis.

31. Michel Foucault, "Réponse à une question," in *Dits et écrits* (Paris: Gallimard, 1968), 682.

32. "And yet should this [description of the archive] not illuminate, if only in an oblique way, that enunciative field of which it is itself a part? The analysis of the archive, then, involves a privileged region, at once close to us, and different from our present existence, it is the border of time that surrounds our presence, which overhangs it, and which indicates its otherness; it is that which, outside ourselves, delimits us . . . its locus is the gap between our own discursive practices. In this sense, it is valid for our diagnosis. Not because it would enable us to draw up a table of our distinctive features and to sketch out, in advance, the face that we will have in the future. But it deprives us of our continuities." Foucault, *The Archaeology of Knowledge*, 131.

33. Foucault, "Preface to the 1961 Edition," in *History of Madness*, ed. Jean Khalfa

(New York: Routledge, 2006), xxviii.

34. Defert, "Chronology," 24.

35. Michel Foucault, "Un si cruel savoir," in *Dits et écrits*, ed. Michel Foucault (Paris: Gallimard, 2001 [1962]), 243.

36. Housed in the Centre des Archives Diplomatiques in Nantes, the documents relating to French–Polish cultural relations between 1951 and 1961 are located in boxes 102–6. Consulaire PARIS-DFAE, email correspondence with Anna Krakus, 16 December 2009.

37. Boxes 102–6, Consulaire PARIS-DFAE, 16 December 2009, email correspondence with Anna Krakus,.

38. Archives Centre Michel Foucault, IMEC, http://portail-michel-foucault.org.

39. Laurence Le Bras, "Michel Foucault en Pologne—Documents dans les archives BNF, Fonds M. Foucault," 17 May 2017, e-mail communication with Cristina Vatulescu.

40. Z. Rylko, "Apollinaire na Uniwersytecie Warszawskim," *Przegląd Humanistyczny* 2 (1959).

41. As recently as December 2016, an article fantasizes about the possible contents of this lecture the author believes to be lost. Jenny Laurent, "Foucault et la littérature. Une passante," *Critique* (2016): 982.

42. Michel Foucault, Conférence à Gdańsk en 1958: sur Apollinaire, manuscrit autographe, 1958, Boîte LIV: Littérature, x, Fonds Michel Foucault, NAF 28730.The manuscript is unpaginated. The section on Poland begins on the second page and ends on the third.

43. According to Foucault, Apollinaire found the new by "capturing the word in its form, in its graphic body, against itself"; moving "beyond description the word becomes the simple, primitive image." Foucault, Conférence à Gdańsk en 1958.

44. Michel Foucault, *Histoire de la folie*. Exposé de soutenance, 20 May 1961, Boîte XLI: Les soutenances de thèse 1a, Fonds Michel Foucault, NAF 28730, Bibliothèque Nationale de France, Archives et manuscrits.

45. Foucault, "The Lives of Infamous Men," in *Power, Truth, Strategy*, ed. Meaghan Morris and Paul Patton (Sydney: Feral Publications, 1979), 77.

46. Foucault, "The Lives of Infamous Men," 77.

47. Foucault, "The Lives of Infamous Men," 77–78. This sentence is missing from the 2000 translation of the text in *Power*.

48. "Michel Foucault, Texte séminal, Boîte LIV: Littérature, IX, Michel Foucault, NAF 28730, 21. According to Terry Hole, Foucault seems to have been the first writer to write about Pauliska in recent memory. Terry Hole, "Roman Noir," in *Handbook of the Gothic*, ed. Marie Mulvey-Roberts (New York: New York University Press, 2009). The timing of Foucault's discovery of Pauliska, the Polish evacuee and adventurer, may have been connected to his interest in Poland around the time

of his stay there.

49. Foucault, "Un si cruel savoir," 243.

50. The letter is cited by Defert in his chronology of Foucault's life. Defert does not provide the addressee's name or any bibliographic information. Defert, "Chronology," 24.

51. Foucault, "Un si cruel savoir," 244.

52. Michel Foucault, "Divers: Cruautés russes envers les confédérés polonais, Boîte XXXV: Autour de l' *Histoire de la folie*, Fonds Michel Foucault, NAF 28730.

53. Defert, "Tunisia and Poland."

54. Federal Bureau of Investigation, Subject: Foucault, Michel, FOI/PA 1358488-0 (FBI Freedom of Information/Privacy Acts Section).

55. Federal Bureau of Investigation, Subject: Foucault, Michel, FOI/PA 1358488-0, 6.

56. Daniel Defert, "Chronologie," in *Dits et écrits* (Paris: Gallimard, 2001), 82.

57. Central Intelligence Agency, "France: Defection of the Leftist Intellectuals" (1985 [declassified 2011]), https://www.cia.gov/library/readingroom/docs/CIA-RDP86S00588R000300380001-5.PDF; Gabriel Rockhill, "The CIA Reads French Theory: On the Intellectual Labor of Dismantling the Cultural Left," *Los Angeles Review of Books*, 28 February 2017.

58. Central Intelligence Agency, "France: Defection of the Leftist Intellectuals," 14. For a more thorough account of Foucault's support for the New Philosophers, see "In Praise of New Philosophy: Michel Foucault and Tel Quel," in Michael Scott Christofferson, *French Intellectuals against the Left: The Antitotalitarian Moment of the 1970s* (New York: Berghahn Books, 2004), 198–201.

59. In a private conversation with Anna Krakus in June 2017, Dr. Kaminski suggested that such a file is bound to show up eventually.

60. Dudek and Paczkowski, "Poland," 248–49.

61. Dudek and Paczkowski, "Poland," 248–49.

62. BU 01220/10/202 (Etienne Burin de Roziers), 202, Warsaw. In order to protect some of the subjects of files, we will refer to the files only by their record number and not by the name of the individuals they concern. Roziers's materials, however, are limited in scope and include no personal information about him.

63. BU 01220/10/202 (Etienne Burin de Roziers), 202, Warsaw, 12.

64. BU 01299/330 (French cultural-propaganda), Warsaw.

65. BU 01220/10/202, Roziers, "Une rencontre à Varsovie," 8.

66. KR 08/137 (Karmel), Krakow.

67. In fact, even Gunnar Broberg, who writes about rumors concerning Foucault's extravagant lifestyle during his time in Sweden (1955–58), also states that the busy, hard-working French lecturer was considered a "monk," who very rarely left his monastery. Gunnar Broberg, "Foucault i Uppsala," *Uppsala Newsletter for the*

History of Science 2 (1985).

68. The Kraków consulate file notes many conversations between Bourelly and a Professor Lajarrige. Lajarrige's prominence in the file is especially interesting since he resembles Foucault in various ways: they both taught French and both arrived in Poland after having taught in Scandinavian countries.

69. Ryziński, *Foucault w Warszawie*.

70. Ryziński, *Foucault w Warszawie*, 191–93.

71. BU 1368/19263 (Bernard Kouchner), Warsaw, 21.

72. BU 1368/19263 (Bernard Kouchner), Warsaw, 20–21.

73. BU 1368/19263 (Bernard Kouchner), Warsaw, 21. As anonymous press reader A cogently notes in their review, it is significant that "both Montand and Signoret acted in Costa Gavras's film *The Confession* (1970) about Artur London's arrest and imprisonment during the Slánský Trial in Czechoslovakia. London was involved in the film's production, and Chris Marker made a film about the filming [of *The Confession*]—*On vous parle de Prague* [1971]—in which we see Signoret and Montand grappling not just with London's story, but with the complexities of the French Communist Party's relationship to Eastern Europe."

74. BU 1368/19263 (Bernard Kouchner), Warsaw, 22.

75. SB agents marveled at the surprising exodus, for instance, in BU 0999/300 (Obcy), Warsaw, 124.

76. KR 08/137 (Karmel), 419.

77. BU 0999/300 (Obcy), 56.

78. Paweł Kurpios, "Poczukiwani, poczukiwane. Geje i lesbijki a rzeczywistość PRL" (University of Wrocław, 2002); Lukas Szulc, "Queer in Poland: Under Construction," in *Queer in Europe: Contemporary Case Studies*, ed. Lisa Robert and Gillett Downing (Farnham, UK: Ashgate, 2011); Tomas Basiuk, "Notes on Karol Rasziszewski's Kisieland," in *The Archive as a Project*, ed. Krzysztof Pijarski (Warsaw: Fundacja Archeologia Fotografii, 2011); Krzysztof Tomasik, *GEJEREL. Mniejszości seksualne w PRL-u* (Warsaw: Krytyka Polityczna, 2012).

79. Kurpios, "Poczukiwani, poczukiwane. Geje i lesbijki a rzeczywistość PRL"; Henryk Piecuch, *Bruderszaft ze śmiercią* (Warsaw: Agencja Wydawnicza CB, 1999); Szulc, "Queer in Poland," 162; Tomasik, *GEJEREL*, 9–10. The best known example of SB repression of LGBTQ individuals is Operation Hyacinth (1985–87). Police raided locales where gay men used to meet, and many were detained and kept for interrogation. Some had to sign papers admitting they were homosexuals. Tomasik, *GEJEREL*, 74–87.

80. Dudek and Paczkowski, "Poland," 257.

81. BU 01220/10/1706, Warsaw.

82. BU 01220/10/1706, Warsaw, 3.

83. Around the same time, we came across journalist Kamil Julian, who was also

searching for Foucault's secret lover. Kamil Julian, "In Search of Michel Foucault's Polish Lover," *DIK FAGAZINE* 8 (2011). In the piece, Julian claims to have learned the identity of Foucault's lover/informer but chooses not to reveal his name out of respect for his widow and children.

84. BU 0204/312, Warsaw.

85. BU 0204/312, Warsaw, 12.

86. BU 0204/312, Warsaw, 33.

87. BU 0204/312, Warsaw, 32.

88. KR 08/137 (Karmel).

89. "Report describing contents of the destroyed materials" and "Report stating that materials about the Center may be destroyed," BU 0999/300 (Obcy), 65–66.

90. KR 08/137 (Karmel), vol. 4, 338.

91. Even the name of one file detailing French diplomatic work reveals this suspicion: BU 01299/330 (French cultural-propaganda).

92. BU 0999/300 (Obcy), 43.

93. BU 0999/300 (Obcy), 44.

94. Dudek and Paczkowski, "Poland," 259.

95. It was not until 1966 that the agency grew significantly. Dudek and Paczkowski, "Poland," 257.

96. Dudek and Paczkowski, "Poland," 257.

97. Security functionaries were young and poorly educated: in 1945, 80 percent had completed primary education while in 1953 that number diminished to 55.3 percent. In 1953, of the 1,455 individuals in senior posts, 36 percent were younger than thirty, with 26.9 percent having received only primary education. Dudek and Paczkowski, "Poland," 241.

98. Foucault, *The Archaeology of Knowledge*, 17.

99. Defert, "Chronology," 25.

100. Knut Ove Eliassen, "The Archives of Michel Foucault," in *The Archive in Motion: New Conceptions of the Archive in Contemporary Thought and New Media Practices*, ed. Eivind Røssaak (Oslo: Novus forlag, 2010), 7.

101. Foucault, "Preface," xxviii.

102. Defert, "Chronology," 24, translation modified.

103. Defert, "Tunisia and Poland."

104. Foucault, "Preface," xxviii, translation modified.

105. Foucault, "Preface," xxviii.

106. Foucault, "Preface," xxxii.

107. Foucault, *The Archaeology of Knowledge*, 128–29.

108. Wolfgang Ernst, *Das Rumoren der Archive* (Berlin: Merve, 2002), 90. Cited in Eliassen, "The Archives of Michel Foucault," 10.

109. Eliassen, "The Archives of Michel Foucault," 4.

110. Eliassen, "The Archives of Michel Foucault," 2.

111. Eliassen, "The Archives of Michel Foucault," 5.

112. Eliassen, "The Archives of Michel Foucault," 5.

113. Michel Foucault and Arlette Farge, *Disorderly Families: Infamous Letters from the Bastille Archives* (Minneapolis: University of Minnesota Press, 2016).

114. Foucault, "Preface," xxviii.

115. I Foucault, "Preface," xxviii.

116. Giorgio Agamben, *Remnants of Auschwitz: The Witness and the Archive*, trans. Daniel Heller-Roazen (New York: Zone Books, 1999), 145.

117. January 1966 letter to an unidentified friend, cited by Defert, "Chronology," 24.

118. Maurice Blanchot, "L'oubli, la déraison," *La Nouvelle Revue Française* 1961.

119. The "silence of the intellectuals" refers to long debates that followed Max Gallo's 1983 *Le Monde* article accusing leftist intellectuals of silence. This silence was loud enough to be picked up by the CIA, which wrote an in-depth report on it in 1985, featuring Foucault, and prefaced by a quote from Alain Touraine: "Never before have I seen such silence, such emptiness. It's like a family in which someone has died." Central Intelligence Agency, "France: Defection of the Leftist Intellectuals," 8. "The silence of shame and not the silence of the intellectual" was the accusation that Jean-Paul Aron leveled against Foucault's own discretion about his AIDS diagnosis, an accusation Defert and Miller argue against. See Jim Miller, *The Passion of Michel Foucault* (New York: Simon & Schuster, 1993), 22, 25, 34, 395.

120. For a review of how subaltern and postcolonial studies have directed and shaped the archival turn, see Renisa Mawani, "Law's Archive," *Annual Review of Law and Social Science* 8 (2012). Most directly influential for this chapter have been Gayatri Spivak's attention to the constitutive silences and exclusions of the East India Company's archives, as well as her contentious answer to the question "Can the Subaltern Speak?" Gayatri Chakravorty Spivak, "The Rani of Sirmur: An Essay in Reading the Archives," *History and Theory* 24, no. 3 (1985); *A Critique of Postcolonial Reason: Toward a History of the Vanishing Present* (Cambridge, MA: Harvard University Press, 1999). As we detail in the text, we have also been deeply inspired by the work of Ann Laura Stoler and by Michel-Rolph Trouillot, *Silencing the Past: Power and the Production of History* (Boston: Beacon Press, 1995). In the Eastern European context, there have been attempts to recover the victims' voices, but perhaps earlier than in other hierarchical archives, there has also been a strong reactive turn to recovering the voices of the agents themselves. Andreas Glaeser, *Political Epistemics: The Secret Police, the Opposition, and the End of East German Socialism* (Chicago: University of Chicago Press, 2011); Florian Henckel von Donnersmarck, *The Lives of Others* (Sydney: Roadshow Entertainment 2007).

121. Mawani, "Law's Archive," 345.

122. Ann Laura Stoler, *Along the Archival Grain: Epistemic Anxieties and Archival Common Sense* (Princeton: Princeton University Press, 2009), 4, 20.

123. Michel Foucault, *The History of Sexuality*, trans. Robert Hurley, 3 vols. (Pantheon Books, 1978), 1:20–27; Luise White, "Between Gluckman and Foucault: Historicizing Rumor and Gossip," *Social Dynamics* 20, no. 1 (2008): 85.

124. Foucault, *The History of Sexuality*, 1:20–27.

125. White, "Between Gluckman and Foucault," 85.

126. For a review of rumor and gossip literature, see White, "Between Gluckman and Foucault."

127. Stoler, *Along the Archival Grain*, 231.

128. Stoler, *Along the Archival Grain*, 230.

129. Stoler, *Along the Archival Grain*, 230, emphasis mine.

130. Stoler, *Along the Archival Grain*, 231.

131. For example, "in 1999, 80 meters of 'lost' archives, including signed declarations of cooperation and payment receipts, were discovered in a cellar of the former SB headquarters in Warsaw." Stan, "Transitional Justice," 87. The most infamous recovery of documents was the seizure of Lech Walesa's alleged informer files from the closets of the widow of General Czesław Kiszczak, Poland's former interior minister. At the time of the seizure, the widow was preparing to sell the documents. In a continuation of a scandal that has spilled over decades now, Walesa has denied the accusations, claiming that the documents were forged, as was often the case with SB documents. Adam Chandler, "An Old-New Lech Walesa Scandal," *The Atlantic*, 18 February 2016.

132. Michel Foucault, *Discipline and Punish: The Birth of the Prison* (New York: Vintage Books, 1979), 195–230.

133. On the change from histrionic to realist in the aesthetics of the secret police in the Eastern Bloc, see Cristina Vatulescu, *Police Aesthetics: Literature, Film, and the Secret Police in Soviet Times* (Stanford: Stanford University Press, 2010).

134. Foucault, "Preface," xxviii.

135. Vaclav Havel coined the original Czech term, *moc bezmocných*, as the title of his famous samizdat essay in 1978. See Vaclav Havel, *The Power of the Powerless* (New York: Vintage, 2018).

136. The "weapons of the weak and the watched" is Svetlana Boym's addition, in her discussion of Gulag literature, to James Scott's "weapons of the weak." Svetlana Boym, *Another Freedom: The Alternative History of an Idea* (Chicago: University of Chicago Press, 2010), 270; James Scott, *Weapons of the Weak: Everyday Forms of Peasant Resistance* (New Haven: Yale University Press, 1987).

Chapter 2

1. I am grateful to participants in the conferences "Political Police and the Soviet System: Insights from Newly Opened KGB Archives in the Former Soviet States," Georgetown University, 17 April 2020, and "The Secret Police and Study of Religions: Archives, Communities and Contested Memories in Central and Eastern Europe," University College Cork, 19 March 2021, for answering my questions and contributing to this list as well as offering feedback. I am also grateful to those who attended my talks at Central European University (Budapest), Columbia University, Havinghurst Center, New European College (Bucharest), and Princeton University for suggestions on earlier versions of this chapter.

2. The secret police film also generated a cinematic chain reaction after 1989, with three full-length movies taking up the subject again. Cristina Vatulescu, "The Mug-Shot and the Close-up: Identification and Visual Pedagogy in Secret Police Film," in *The Secret Police and the Soviet System: New Archival Investigations*, ed. Michael David-Fox (Pittsburgh, PA: University of Pittsburgh Press, 2023).

3. Ministerul Afacerilor Interne, "Ordonanţa [Order], 15 November 1959," in P 181, Fond Penal (Bucharest: ACNSAS, 1959), 4,:1–2. Three volumes of the files (VI–IX) mainly list in excruciating detail objects seized from the defendants: "two glass bowls, one with three legs"; "two pairs of differently colored panties, previously worn." P 181 (40038), vols. 1–27, Fond Penal (Bucharest: ACNSAS, 1959), 6:145, 7:48.

4. Renata Uitz, "Communist Secret Services on the Screen: The Duna-gate Scandal in and beyond the Hungarian Media," in *Past for the Eyes: East European Representations of Communism in Cinema and Museums after 1989*, ed. Oksana Sarkisova and Peter Apor, 57–80 (Budapest: Central European University Press, 2008). Alice Lovejoy describes how the resurgence of a previously censored collection of Czechoslovak military films "was the subject of such wonder in the press in August 1990" (Alice Lovejoy, *Army Film and the Avant Garde: Cinema and Experiment in the Czechoslovak Military* [Bloomington: Indiana University Press, 2015], 203). It took until 2015 for the collection to receive a thorough, deeply illuminating treatment in an academic study. Lovejoy's *Army Film and the Avant Garde* models the productive dialogue that took place between archival textual and visual work in the analysis of the military films within the larger context of the Army studio as an institution laid bare in "its productions, schedules, and budgets." Lovejoy, *Army Film and the Avant Garde*, 15.

5. Kate Brown et al., "Engaging Documents: New Directions in Anthrohistorical Research in and on Archives," in Association for Slavic, East European, and Eurasian Studies National Convention (San Antonio, 2014).

6. Highlights include the online *Hidden Galleries Archives* created by a team of researchers, as well as the related exhibits, exhibit catalogues, and scholarly articles: "Hidden Galleries," http://hiddengalleries.eu/digitalarchive; James Kapaló and Ta-

tiana Vagramenko, eds., *Hidden Galleries: Material Religion in the Secret Police Archives in Central and Eastern Europe* (Berlin: LitVerlag 2020); Tatiana Vagramenko, "KGB 'Evangelism': Agents and Jehovah's Witnesses in Soviet Ukraine," *Kritika* 22, no. 4 (Fall 2021): 757–86; Cindrea-Nagy et al., "Hidden Galleries"; Tatiana Vagramenko and Gabriela Nicolescu, "The Hand at Work or How the KGB File Leaks in the Exhibition," *Martor* 26 (2021); Kinga Povedák, "Methodological Notes on Visual Ethics: 'Choosing Not to Reveal,'" *Martor* 26 (2021): 164–72. See also Andrea Gullotta, "Beauty in Hell: Culture in the Gulag" (Glasgow: The Hunterian, 2017); Aglaya Glebova, "A Visual History of the Gulag: Nine Theses," in *The Soviet Gulag: Evidence, Interpretation, and Comparison*, ed. Michael David-Fox (Pittsburgh, PA: University of Pittsburgh Press, 2016); Beata Bartecka, Łukasz Rusznica, and Tomasz Stempowski, *How to Look Natural in Photos* (Wroclaw: Palm* Studios, 2021); Olga Shevchenko and Oksana Sarkisova, "The Album as Performance: Notes on the Limits of the Visible," in *Russian Performances: Word, Object, Action*, ed. Julie Cassiday Julie A. Buckler, and Boris Wolfson (Madison: University of Wisconsin Press, 2018); Cristina Vatulescu, "Secret Police Shots at Policing: The Gulag and Cinema," in *Police Aesthetics: Literature, Film, and the Secret Police in Soviet Times* (Stanford: Stanford University Press, 2010).

7. Hannah Arendt, "What Is Authority?" in *Between Past and Future* (New York: Viking Press, 1961), 91.

8. Coy is quoted in Raphaël Pirenne and Alexander Streitberger, *Heterogeneous Objects: Intermedia and Photography after Modernism* (Leuven: Leuven University Press, 2013), xv.

9. Pirenne and Streitberger, *Heterogeneous Objects*, xv.

10. In this paragraph, Pirenne and Streitberger (*Heterogeneous Objects*, xv) cite the following works: Joachim Paech and Jens Schröter, *Intermedialität analog/digital: Theorien—Methoden—Analysen* (Munich: Wilhelm Fink, 2008), 11; Irina O. Rajewsky, *Intermedialität* (Tübingen: Francke, 2002), 7; Yvonne Spielmann, "Intermedia and Electronic Images," *Leonardo* 34, no. 1 (2001): 61; Jürgen E. Müller, *Media Encounters and Media Theories* (Münster: Nodus Publikationen, 2008), 242. Far from seeing a problem for intermedia with the arrival of the digital, Jack Ox and Jacques Mandelbrojt even argue that "we have reached a period in time when it is not only much easier to perform intermedia, but our tools invite us to do so, owing to the natural capabilities of our computers. Not only is it easier to connect one system to another, but we also have a surgically precise collage tool. We can cut and paste multiple layers with multimedia." Jack Ox and Jacques Mandelbrojt, "Intersenses/Intermedia: A Theoretical Perspective," *Leonardo* 34, no. 1 (2001): 47.

11. Carolyn Steedman, *Dust: The Archive and Cultural History* (New Brunswick, NJ: Rutgers University Press, 2002), 164.

12. I.e., "'transparent,' [when the digital medium wants to erase itself, as in elec-

tronic painting galleries,] 'translucent,' [where the electronic version is offered as an improvement, as in encyclopedias online, which add features like sound or linking capabilities but "still remediate the old form without challenging it," and 'aggressive remediation,' ["which can refashion the older medium or media entirely," "therefore maintaining a sense of multiplicity and hypermediacy"]—avant-garde collage and photomontage often work with aggressive remediation." Jay David Bolter and Richard Grusin, *Remediation: Understanding New Media* (Cambridge, MA: MIT Press, 2000), 45–47.

13. For a comprehensive overview of the archival turn(s), see Eric Ketelaar, "Archival Turns and Returns," in *Research in the Archival Multiverse*, ed. Anne Gilliland, Sue McKemmish, and Andrew Lau (Melbourne: Monash University Press, 2018). For a sustained meditation on the trope of the turn in the context of archives, see Daniel Marshall and Zeb Tortorici, "Introduction: (Re)Turning to the Queer Archives," in *Turning Archival: The Life of the Historical in Queer Studies*, ed. Daniel Marshall and Zeb Tortorici (Durham, NC: Duke University Press, 2022).

14. Cited from the program of a conference organized by Mariam Ghani and Chitra Ganesh, "Radical Archives," NYU, http://apa.nyu.edu/event/radical-archives/. Another conference section, on archive ethics, considered the "archive as first document of revolution and last site of resistance," and brought together the archivist of the Occupy Movement with those of the Iranian Green Movement and the Arab Image Foundation—various people assembling, gleaning, reconstructing, or imagining new archives.

15. Hal Foster, "An Archival Impulse," *October* 1, no. 110 (2004).

16. André Lepecki critiques Foster's archival impulse for a lingering nostalgic and paranoid view of the past. Instead, Lepecki argues for the superiority of the term the "will to archive" as it pertains to the contemporary choreography's preoccupation with reenactments: "I am proposing 'will to archive' as referring to a capacity to identify in a past work still non-exhausted creative fields of 'impalpable possibilities' (to use an expression from Brian Massumi . . .). These fields . . . are always present in any past work and are that which re-enactments activate." André Lepecki, "The Body As Archive: Will to Re-Enact and the Afterlives of Dances," *Dance Research Journal* 42, no. 2 (2010): 31.

17. Stelian Tănase, *Anatomia mistificării* (Bucharest: Humanitas, 2003).

18. Virgil Calotescu and Pantelie Tuțuleasa, *Reenactment (Reconstituirea)* (Bucharest: Arhiva Natională de Filme Jilava, Ministerul de Interne, Studioul Documentar Sahia, 1959).

19. P 181, 1–27.

20. P 181, vol. 18.

21. Ministerul Afacerilor Interne, "Plan de măsuri I (Plan of Action, I)," in P 181, 18:9–15.

22. "Plan de măsuri [II] privind desfășurarea filmării unor momente principale in legătura cu săvârșirea atacului banditesc asupra mașinii băncii RPR (Plan of Action, II)," in P 181, 18:127–30.

23. "Titlurile filmului (The Titles of the Film—Final Script), 03.05.1960," 81–90. This script, written on Ministry of Interior letterhead, is dated 5 March 1960, weeks after the four defendants were executed on 18 February 1960.

24. This last seal of approval concerned the film in its entirety, including its credits, the particular selection and order of the archive, and reconstructed material. "Titlurile filmului (The Titles of the Film—Final Script), 03.05.1960," 81.

25. P 181, 22:53.

26. P 181, 22:15018.

27. P 181, unpaginated.

28. P 181, 22:56.

29. Ministerul Afacerilor Interne, "Plan de măsuri I (Plan of Action, I)," 13.

30. The Bucharest apartment intrusion and wiretapping installation is documented in P 181, 22:92–93. The installation of surveillance in their Sinaia vacation retreat is recorded in P 181, 22:48.

31. P 181, 22:105.

32. "Mr. 'I am hiding this one. And this I am also hiding. And this.' Mrs.: 'The devil knows . . .' (the recording breaks down)." P 181, 22:117; P 181, 22:117, 12.

33. "Unclear and sporadic voices can be heard from a different room. (The radio has been turned off)." P 181, 22:112.

34. P 181, 22:106.

35. P 181, vols. 3–4.

36. P 181, vols. 2 and 3, passim.

37. For example, Haralambie Obedeanu's interrogation records show a consistent refusal to confess to crimes other than the bank heist—such as assassination plans or book writing—even when confronted with other suspects who confess to these crimes and implicate him. P 181, 2:244–45, 58–59, 87–300.

38. "[Untitled: Cellmate Informer Reports]," in P 181, vol. 17.

39. "[Untitled: Cellmate Informer Reports]," in P 181, 17:167.

40. "[Untitled: Cellmate Informer Reports]," in P 181, 17:163.

41. "[Untitled: Cellmate Informer Reports]," in P 181, 17:167. Printing the names of the people mentioned in the secret police files is often contentious. I chose not to print the names of the cellmate informers, who were themselves prisoners and likely collaborated with the police under pressure. Instead, I give the names of the secret police workers involved in the case.

42. Constantin Cenușe, "Proces-verbal de interrogator, 23 September 1959 (Interrogation Transcript)," in P 181, vol. 3. (Only every other page of the report is numbered.)

43. "[Untitled: Cellmate Informer Reports]," in P 181, 17:84.

44. Nicolae Steinhardt, *Jurnalul Fericirii* (Cluj: Dacia, 1997), 3.

45. Of course, these accounts are more than problematic. They tend to emphasize the information that the cellmate judged worthy of interest to the investigators. At the same time, some prisoners were more guarded than others; some were even aware of the presence of cellmate informers and thus were likely to manipulate their self-image.

46. At a time when torture was a common practice in Romanian prisons, and when world-famous cultural and political figures were routinely discarded in communal graves, Sevianu believed that she would be granted an appointment with the Minister of Interior, where she would protest her investigator's treatment and ask for pen and paper so that she could write a novel about the bank heist. "[Untitled: Cellmate Informer Reports]," in P 181, 17:140.

47. "[Untitled: Cellmate Informer Reports]," in P 181, 17:26.

48. Constantin Cenușe, "Concluzii de invinuire (Indictment Conclusions)," P 181, 5:1–10.

49. P 181, 5:1.

50. The prosecutor's speech occupies pages 91–94 of the court transcripts from 20 November 1959. "Incheere [Ending]," P 181, 5:89–96. The same document identifies the prosecutor, Captain Pompiliu Stănescu.

51. "Incheere [Ending]," P 181, 5:91.

52. "Incheere [Ending]," P 181, 5:91–92.

53. "Incheere [Ending]," P 181, 5:91.

54. "Incheere [Ending]," P 181, 5:93–94.

55. The presence of actual footage of the trial is particularly noticeable as the same courtroom scene includes the defendant's questioning by the judge, which *is* reconstructed. This incongruous mixture was no accident; on the contrary, the script instructed that certain scenes of the trial should be filmed and introduced in *Reenactment*, while the staged reading of the death sentence should be superimposed onto actual footage of the prisoners at the trial. The differences between the reconstructed scenes and the actual footage are obvious: the speakers no longer act (poorly) for the camera, the defendants wear different clothes, the lighting is darker, and there is noticeable ambient noise.

56. Alexander Medvedkin, "294 dnia na kolesakh," in *Iz istorii kino*, ed. Institut istorii iskusstv (Moscow: Iskusstvo, 1977), 37.

57. One peculiar proof of such a screening of *Reenactment* before the Central Committee for Recreational Aviation is a letter to the Securitate signed by that institution's head of cadres, Colonel Ioan Porumb, who describes how during the movie's screening the spectators recognized their former co-worker, Igor Sevianu. Porumb sends Sevianu's workplace file to the Securitate on 21 September 1960,

months after Sevianu had been executed, just in case the Securitate wishes to study Sevianu's networks. P 181, 10:22.

58. Without any explanation, a note of 17 March 1966 from the Sahia Documentary Studio informs the secret police about the erasure of "25 boxes with 15,000 meters of magnetic tape on which the voice-over and trial scenes from the movie *Reconstituirea*" were audio-recorded. The document dutifully adds that the tape will be reused, but there is no explanation or context for this decision or its timing, in 1966, six years after the closing of the case. P 181, 20:40.

59. Anonymous, "Item No. 2869/61, Filmarea furtului de la banca RPR/Movie of Bank Robbery," HU OSA 300-60-1, Radio Free Europe/Radio Liberty Research Institute: Information Resources Department: East European Archives: Romanian Unit, Subject Files, box 103, file 803: I., 1960.

60. Anonymous, "Item No. 2869/61," 3, 2.

61. I develop this argument about *Reenactment*'s long cinematic legacy in Vatulescu, "The Mug-Shot and the Close-up." The three films made in direct response to *Reenactment* are Irene Lusztig's *Reenactment* (2001), Alexandru Solomon's *The Great Communist Bank Robbery* (*Marele jaf al băncii naționale*, 2004), and Nae Caranfil's *Closer to the Moon* (*Mai aproape de lună*, 2013).

62. Jacques Rancière, *The Emancipated Spectator* (London: Verso, 2011), 3.

63. Rancière, *The Emancipated Spectator*, 13.

64. For an article-length development of my notion of the visual pedagogy of the secret police, please see Vatulescu, "The Mug-Shot and the Close-up."

65. Anonymous, "Movie of Bank Robbery," 3.

66. "Item No. 254/60. Arrests by Ambulance. Robbing of Bucharest State Bank Car," HU OSA 300-60-1, Radio Free Europe/Radio Liberty Research Institute: Information Resources Department: East European Archives: Romanian Unit, Subject Files, box 430, file 2300, 1960.

67. "Item No. 238/60. Informatiuni din R. P. Romania. Furtul de la Banca de Stat/The Robbery of the National Bank," HU OSA 300-60-1, Radio Free Europe/Radio Liberty Research Institute: Information Resources Department: East European Archives: Romanian Unit, Subject Files, box 430, file 2300, 1960, 1–2.

68. "Item No. 238/60," 2.

69. Anonymous, "Item 3103/60, Furtul de la B.R.P.R [The Robbery of B.R.P.R]," HU OSA 300-60-1, Radio Free Europe/Radio Liberty Research Institute: Information Resources Department: East European Archives: Romanian Unit, Subject Files, Box 403, file 1803, Justice and Sentences, 1960, 3.

70. Rancière, *The Emancipated Spectator*, 17.

71. "Reenactments, understood extensively and intensively, are all about this [learning to be affected]." Katie King, *Networked Reenactments: Stories Transdisciplinary Knowledges Tell* (Durham, NC: Duke University Press, 2011), 274.

72. Irene Lusztig, *Reconstruction* (Komsomol Films, 2002); Alexandru Solomon, *Marele jaf comunist (The Great Communist Bank Robbery)* (2004).

73. "[Untitled: Cellmate Informer Reports]," 140.

74. "[Untitled: Cellmate Informer Reports]," 129.

75. "[Untitled: Cellmate Informer Reports]," 129.

76. Walter Benjamin, "A Short History of Photography," *Screen* 13, no. 1 (1972): 7. Photo albums are not routine parts of investigation case files. Yet, these photo albums are not singular; indeed, they are part of a subgenre of secret police documentation. After many requests, the custodians of the CNSAS archives showed me a collection of such albums: inside all-purpose photo albums, behind glossy floral covers, the secret police showcased photographs documenting some of their most difficult cases, including the anticollectivization campaign and the defeat of the armed resistance fighters. Reenactment photographs were often created using agents, and captured suspects were often used to supplement the paucity of other visual documentation, which includes crime scene photographs and gory photographs of dead fighters.

77. subReal, Călin Dan, and Iosif Király, "5 Suitcases."

78. subReal, Călin Dan, and Iosif Király, "5 Suitcases,"emphasis mine.

79. Like Francis, many artists and researchers are starting to experiment with new approaches to archival media hybridity, approaches that take advantage of the freedoms that digital remediation gives us in manipulating archival materials. The Hidden Archives team provides ample evidence for such felicitous remediations in their exhibits, and also in their interviews, photo-elicitations, and mediations of archival materials to and for the individuals and communities featured in or affected by the archives themselves.

80. Nicolae Marinescu, the director of photography of the original *Reenactment*, was the only surviving member of the crew willing to be interviewed by Lusztig.

81. Rancière, *The Emancipated Spectator*, 17.

82. Gabrielle Starr, *Feeling Beauty: The Neuroscience of Aesthetic Experience* (Cambridg, MAe: MIT Press, 2013), 79. Literature has long been predicated on this marvelous ability of our brain. Writers from Homer on, as Elaine Scarry has beautifully shown in *Dreaming by the Book*, have been uniquely able to create vivid moving images in our brains using static written words. But it sometimes takes decades of passionate debate across fields such as neuroscience, literary theory, and visual theory—as well as all the art of a writer like Scarry—to convince us that words can trigger images in the brain or that there is a something outside of the text. Stephen M. Kosslyn, *Image and Brain: The Resolution of the Imagery Debate* (Cambridge, MA: MIT Press, 1994); Elaine Scarry, *Dreaming by the Book* (New York: Farrar, Straus & Giroux, 1999).

83. These are the last words of Dick Higgins's path-breaking intermedia manifesto. Dick Higgins, "Intermedia," *Leonardo* 34, no. 1 (2001).

84. Bolter and Grusin, *Remediation*, 45–47.

85. Elizabeth Eva Leach, "Performing Manuscripts," in *Performing Medieval Text*, ed. Ardis Butterfield, Henry Hope, and Pauline Souleau (Oxford, UK: Legenda, 2017), 17. I am grateful to Terry Cullen for this and the following references.

86. Shane Butler, *The Ancient Phonograph* (Princeton: Princeton University Press, 2015), 110.

87. Lepecki, "The Body as Archive," 31. It is in his discussion of Lepecki's work that Ketelaar anchors his view "that the archival turn has been characterized by a turn to the body." Marshall and Tortorici, "Introduction: (Re)Turning to the Queer Archives," 8.

88. Shannon Jackson, *Lines of Activity: Performance, Historiography, Hull-House Domesticity* (Ann Arbor: University of Michigan Press, 2000), v.

89. "The queer archival turn is a meaning-making maneuver that provides news ways of theorizing the idiom of the archive and new forms of embodiment in relation to it. Similarly, the field of critical disability or crip studies has also reshaped the archive through notions of embodiment, questions of access, and notions of crip time ... And as Ryan Lee Cartwright shows, crip time in the archives breaks and reassembles order in the archives in line with the embodied experience of turning to the archive ... all of this diverse embodiment reshapes the archive itself, exposing the limitations of ableist archival imaginaries." Marshall and Tortorici, "Introduction: (Re)Turning to the Queer Archives," 4. See Ryan Lee Cartwright, "Out of Sorts: A Queer Crip in the Archive," *Feminist Review* 125, no. 1 (2020); Ellen Samuels, "Six Ways of Looking at Crip Time," *Disability Studies Quarterly* 37, no. 3 (2017).

90. David Morgan, "Material Analysis in the Study of Religion," in *Materiality and Study of Religion: The Stuff of the Sacred*, ed. Tim Hutchings and Joanne McKenzie (London: Routledge, 2017), 14; James Kapaló, "Feasting and Fasting: The Evidential Character of Material Religion in Secret Police Archives," in *The Secret Police and the Religious Underground in Communist and Post-Communist Eastern Europe*, ed. James Kapaló and Kinga Povedák (London: Routledge, 2021), 256.

91. Kapaló, "Feasting and Fasting," 256.

92. Kapaló, "Feasting and Fasting," 260. It is relevant to note that Kapaló comes to the archives from the anthropological study of religion, a field where the archival sources are consulted "in the absence of ethnographic research" conducted at the time (of socialism). The ethnographer's interest and insight into their absent embodied subjects seem to have inspired Kapaló and other researchers to seek traces of the embodied materiality of the absent subjects—the material, spatial, and somatic aspects of religion—in the documents, treating them as "'surrogates' of the

performances that led to their creation." David Zeitlyn, "Anthropology in and of the Archives: Possible Futures and Contingent Pasts. Archives as Anthropological Surrogates," in *Annual Review of Anthropology* 41 (2012): 469, citing Diana Taylor, *The Archive and the Repertoire: Performing Cultural Memory in the Americas* (Durham, NC: Duke University Press, 2003), 2. This ethnographic "attentional bias" to embodied human subjects pulls the documents outside of the traditionally textual interpretative traditions within which they are usually read, and thus enriches our understanding of them and shows the value of recontextualizing them.

93. Jackson, *Lines of Activity*, 1.

94. Jackson, *Lines of Activity*, 1.

95. It is fitting that Jackson stops to meditate on the cursive handwriting in the letter. As most researchers know, cursive introduces an instability in meaning; Jackson also finds that the swirls "can be somewhat therapeutic, as if confirming a body was once there." Jackson, *Lines of Activity*, 2–3.

96. Walter Benjamin, *Illuminations*, trans. Harry Zohn (New York: Harcourt, 1968), 255. Cited in Jackson, *Lines of Activity*, 3.

97. The children of the disappeared, like the mothers of the Plaza de Mayo, take the archival photographs and doubly remobilize them: they signal both the archival use of the ID and the performative use associated with the madres. Taylor, *The Archive and the Repertoire*, 187.

98. Taylor, *The Archive and the Repertoire*, 177–78.

99. Cited in Jackson, *Lines of Activity*, 2–3.

100. My use of the term "re-mind" is inspired by Linda Hogan's essay "Reminding," in Linda Hogan, *The Radiant Lives of Animals* (Boston: Beacon Press, 2020), 5–10.

Chapter 3

1. The description of the Manuscripts Fund of the ACNSAS reads: "Alongside books whose circulation was banned . . . Securitatea also confiscated manuscripts. In some situations, they were submitted in trial proceedings as corpora delicti . . . In the CNSAS Archive, these manuscripts can be found either in investigation files in the Penal Fund or in the Manuscripts Fund." ACNSAS, "Inventarul Fondului Manuscrise," Bucharest. For a description of the related Library Fund, see ACNSAS, "Fondul Bibliotecă," Bucharest.

2. For an interesting overview of the relationship between life and literature spanning the whole of Müller's work to date, see Lyv Marven, "Life and Literature: Autobiography, Referentiality, and Intertextuality in Herta Müller's Work," in *Herta Müller*, ed. Brigid Haines and Lyn Marven (Oxford: Oxford University Press, 2013). For an English-language literature review that covers untranslated German

and Romanian scholarship on Müller, see Brigid Haines and Lyv Marven, "Introduction," in *Herta Müller*.

3. I 233477 (DUI Herta Müller), vols. 1–3, Fond Informativ, ACNSAS, Bucharest. For a summary of the contents of each volume, see Valentina Glajar, *The Secret Police Dossier of Herta Müller* (Rochester, NY: Camden House, 2023), 5–6. Glajar provides a meticulously researched and balanced account of Müller's DUI and carefully reconstructs the chronology and narrative arc sometimes obscured by the repetitions, omissions, and jargon of the filed documents.

4. William Totok, "Informatorul și laureata Premiului Nobel (The Informer and the Nobel Prize Laureate)," *dw.de* (2010), http://www.dw.de/dw/article/0,,5115182,00.html. The informer report that Totok scans in his article is I 233477, 1:15. Totok also edits the print and online version of a journal titled *Halbjahresschrift*. Online version, http://www.halbjahresschrift.homepage.t-online.de/. This journal has published many other key pages from the Securitate files of Germans from Romania as well as their recent takes on the topic.

5. Boris Tomashevsky, *Teoriia literatury: poetika* (Leningrad: Gos. izd-vo, 1925); Viktor Shklovsky, *O teorii prozy* (Moscow: Federatsiia, 1929).

6. David Bordwell, *Narration in the Fiction Film* (Madison: University of Wisconsin Press, 1985), 49.

7. Jacques Derrida, "Survivre," in *Parages* (Paris: Galilée, 1986), 131.

8. Derrida, "Survivre," 130, 50, original emphasis; English translation, with my modifications, by James Hulbert, in Jacques Derrida, "Living On," in *Deconstruction and Criticism*, ed. Alan Bloom and Paul de Man (London: Continuum, 2004), 72.

9. "On This Day (Notă sursa "Petra," 22.III.1983)," in I 233477, 9.

10. "On This Day," 9.

11. For example, an informer analyzes the estrangement effect in Müller's prose in "Notă informativă Barbu, 26.03.1981," I 233477, 1–3.

12. Herta Müller, *Nadirs*, trans. Sieglinde Lug (Lincoln: University of Nebraska Press, 1999), 70.

13. "On This Day," 9.

14. Allan Stoekl has insightfully written about poverty of means as a defining mark of Müller's writing: "Herta Müller's is a poor writing, or a writing that uses the poverty of means to escape, momentarily, a greater and much more profound poverty." Allan Stoekl, "Herta Müller: Writing and Betrayal," in *Herta Müller: Politics and Aesthetics*, ed. Bettina Brandt and Valentina Glajar (Lincoln: University of Nebraska Press, 2013), 15.

15. "On This Day," 9. The translator's original cuts are marked in her text by bracketed ellipses: [. . .]. I preserved her marking and instead used simple ellipses

for the parts of the text that I cut above. The strikethrough is original to the file translation.

16. "On This Day," 9.

17. Herta Müller, *The Land of Green Plums*, trans. Michael Hoffman (New York: Metropolitan Books, 1996).

18. *The Appointment*, ed. Philip Boehm, trans. Michael Hulse (New York: Picador, 2001).

19. "Unsere Stadt (Our Town)," in *Phlastersteine*, ed. Nikolaus Berwanger, Eduard Schneider, and Horst Samson (Timisoara: 1982).

20. I 233477, 1:22.

21. The original phrases from Müller's story are: "Ihre Lebehsläufe heißen in unserer Stadt Biografien und Autobiografien und werden nicht von ihnen gelebt und nicht von ihnen geschrieben. Und wenn sie einmal geschrieben worden sind, sind Änderungen ausgeschlossen." A more literal translation would be: "Their lives are called in our town biographies and autobiographies and they are not lived by them and they are not written by them. And once they have been written, then any changes are out of the question." Müller, "Unsere Stadt (Our Town)," 124.

22. Cristina Vatulescu, *Police Aesthetics: Literature, Film, and the Secret Police in Soviet Times* (Stanford: Stanford University Press, 2010), 27–54.

23. In a wiretapped conversation, the Securitate heard Müller declare that "I write about the area where I live; if I live here, I write about what's here; if they want me to write more about Romania, then they should keep me here." I 233477, 3:112. As Glajar argues, "This became an argument for the couple's desire to emigrate, and possibly a reason for the Securitate to allow them to do just that [since the Securitate would have been attracted by the idea of Müller training her critical eye away from Romania and onto Germany). However, much to the Securitate's annoyance, Müller continued to write about Romania and its secret police throughout her life in Germany.

24. Herta Müller, "An diesem Tag," in *Drückender Tango (Oppressive Tango)* (Bucharest: Kriterion, 1984), 63.

25. "On This Day," 9.

26. "On This Day," 9.

27. Barbara Johnson, *Mother Tongues: Sexuality, Trials, Motherhood, Translation* (Cambridge, MA: Harvard University Press, 2003), 15.

28. Glajar, *The Secret Police Dossier of Herta Müller*, 200. An exception to this oversight is the work of Laura Laza, "Die Übersetzung als Mittel der Manipulation," in *Aus den Giftschränken des Kommunismus*, ed. M. Notwotnick and F. Kührer-Wielach (Regensburg, 2018).

29. Glajar, *The Secret Police Dossier of Herta Müller*, 175.

30. Glajar, *The Secret Police Dossier of Herta Müller*, 184.

31. I 233477, 1:19.

32. Glajar, *The Secret Police Dossier of Herta Müller*, 201. Glajar bases her argument about the departures of Securitate translations from the standards of forensic translation on Ali Darwish, *Forensic Translation* (Melbourne: Writescope Publishers, 2012).

33. Glajar provides a careful assessment of Gheorghe's translation skills, a difficult task given that the original recordings have not been preserved. Glajar, *The Secret Police Dossier of Herta Müller*, 202–3.

34. I 233477, 3:16.

35. This translated text is the only one in this file that is placed in quotation marks in its entirety. Maybe the investigator thought it was too subversive to let the words go unmarked, and instead used quotation marks, which function exclusively in this file to frame, distance, mock, turn on their head words that are considered untrue or subversive but which the investigator does not replace with his own (so-called "torture," so-called "harassment" so-called "writers").

36. Richard Wagner's DUI preserves the letter signed by Helmuth Frauendorfer, Herta Müller, William Totok, Richard Wagner, and Horst Samson, a letter that denounces the investigation of Helmuth Frauendorfer by Pădurariu and Adamescu, "the latter having also beaten Frauendorfer." I 184945 (DUI Richard Wagner), Fond Informativ, ACNSAS, Bucharest, 193.

37. Joseph Brodsky, *Less Than One* (New York: Farrar Strauss Giroux, 1985), 3.

38. In her reading of the Stasi files of experimental women artists in late East Germany, Sara Blaylock also finds that "a misogynistic Stasi evaluates these women against metrics of normative female appearance." Sara Blaylock, *Parallel Public: Experimental Art in Late East Germany* (Cambridge, MA: MIT Press, 2022), 40. She notes that while "conventional wisdom holds that the Stasi policed artists because of their potential dissident and ideological production, these artists identify the secret police's preoccupation with domesticity and private lives as a sign of rebellion." "Being the Woman They Wanted Her to Be," *Third Text* 35 (2021): 229.

39. I 233477, 1:1.

40. Herta Müller, *Cristina und ihre Attrappe, oder, Was (nicht) in den Akten der Securitate steht* (Göttingen: Wallstein, 2009), 15. I am grateful to Jacobia Dahm and Kiki Pop-Eleches for assistance with the translations from German. For a detailed discussion of what Müller identified as the particular omissions in her file, see Valentina Glajar, "'Cristina' oder was in Herta Müllers Securitate Akte steht: Über Löcher und Fehlschlüsse einer Aktengeschichte" ("'Cristina' or What Is in Herta Müller's File: About Holes and Fallacies in a File Story"), *Monatshefte* 100, no. 2 (2018). As I will show in this and the following chapter, I believe that Müller's literary work contributes a much more nuanced understanding of the lacunae in secret police documents than her more rushed and polemical take in *Cristina*.

41. "Considering the Cold War atmosphere of the late 1970s, when Stana approached Müller, technical translators must have also played the role of interpreters when various Western specialists came to visit Tehnometal. Thus it comes as no surprise that the Securitate had a clear interest in recruiting these translators/interpreters." Glajar, *The Secret Police Dossier of Herta Müller*, 110.

42. Müller, *Cristina*, 17.

43. Müller, *Cristina*, 18.

44. The loss of the father, in *Cristina* as in Müller's literature at large, is traumatic not because it represents the sudden loss of the child's grounding in the world, but because it powerfully reminds her of the father's profound failure to ever have provided that grounding. The father's funeral is the subject of a full story in *Nadirs*, and it then repeatedly recurs in Müller's writing.

45. Herta Müller, "Nobel Lecture: Every Word Knows Something of a Vicious Circle," 7 December 2009, http://nobelprize.org/nobel_prizes/literature/laureates/2009/muller-lecture_en.html.

46. Müller, "Nobel Lecture."

47. Direcțiunea Regională a Securității Poporului, "Ordin Circular nr. 399 din 23 Decembrie 1948," in *"Partiturile" Securității*, 191; Departamentul Securității Statului, "Instrucțiuni N. D-00180-1987," in *"Partiturile" Securității* (2007), 646. The second document offers a model for an informer agreement in its first annex, pp. 656–57. Another informative file of instructions on informer recruitment is D 008712, vol. 1, Fond Documentar, ACNSAS, Bucharest.

48. Direcțiunea Regională a Securității Poporului, "Ordin Circular," 191. "Ordin circular" pedantically lists all required documents in a recommended table of contents of an informer's file.

49. Direcțiunea Regională a Securității Poporului, "Ordin Circular," 192.

50. Katerina Clark, *Moscow, the Fourth Rome: Stalinism, Cosmopolitanism, and the Evolution of Soviet Culture, 1931–1941* (Cambridge, MA: Harvard University Press, 2011), 14.

51. Müller, "Unsere Stadt (Our Town)," 142.

52. Direcțiunea Generală a Siguranței Statului, "Organizarea, încadrarea si funcționarea Direcțiunii Generale a Siguranței Statului (1947)," in *"Partiturile" Securității*, 168.

53. I am grateful to anonymous press reader A for bringing the German word to my attention.

54. 9724 (Problem File for Tehnometal Timisoara, 1954–1989), 1 vol., ACNSAS, Bucharest.

55. Müller, "Nobel Lecture," 4.

56. "When We Don't Speak, We Become Unbearable, and When We Do, We Make Fools of Ourselves. Can Literature Bear Witness?" in *Witness Literature*, ed.

Horace Engdahl (Singapore: World Scientific Publishing, 2002), 15. Müller wrote the essay that most directly addresses the question of the relationship of literature to witnessing in 2002. However, during her latest trip to the United States, occasioned by the translation of her *Atemschaukel* into English, she still chose to read this 2002 essay, signaling the continuing interest she takes in the question. "When We Don't Speak, We Become Unbearable, and When We Do, We Make Fools of Ourselves. Can Literature Bear Witness?" Deutsches Haus, New York University, 3 May 2012.

57. These writers present different facets of the lacuna at the heart of testimony. Thus, in a subchapter entitled "Across the Gap," in his co-authored benchmark study on testimony, Dori Laub notes: "The perspective I propose tries to highlight, however, *what was ultimately missing*, not in the courage of the witnesses nor in the depth of their emotional responses, but in the human cognitive capacity to perceive and to assimilate the totality of what was really happening at the time." Dori Laub, "An Event without a Witness: Truth, Testimony, and Survival," in *Testimony: Crises of Witnessing in Literature, Psychoanalysis, and History*, ed. Soshana Felman and Dori Laub (London: Routledge), 85, my emphasis. Often critical of Laub's and Felman's book, Giorgio Agamben however also stresses the lacuna, what is missing, in his redefinition of testimony. Giorgio Agamben, *Remnants of Auschwitz: The Witness and the Archive*, trans. Daniel Heller-Roazen (New York: Zone Books, 1999), 13, 161.

58. Wikipedia contributors, "Invisible ink," Wikipedia, http://en.wikipedia.org/w/index.php?title=Invisible_ink&oldid=505908249.

Chapter 4

1. Herta Müller, *Cristina und ihre Attrappe, oder, Was (nicht) in den Akten der Securitate steht* (Göttingen: Wallstein, 2009), 15.

2. Serviciul I/A Inspectoratul Județean Timiș al Ministerului de Interne, "Raport, 28.02.1978," in D 013381, Fond Documentar, ACNSAS, Bucharest, 13:158. All translations from Romanian are mine. I have tried to closely preserve the particularities of the files' language even at the cost of choosing clumsy English equivalents, which at times best convey the awkwardness of the original expressions.

3. Paula Amad, *Counter-Archive: Film, the Everyday, and Albert Kahn's Archives de la Planète* (New York: Columbia University Press, 2010), 1.

4. "On This Day (Notă sursa "Petra," 22.III.1983)," in I 233477, Fond Informativ, ACNSAS, Bucharest, 1:9.

5. Müller, *Cristina*, 15.

6. Müller, *Cristina*, 15; Herta Müller, "Nobel Lecture: Every Word Knows Something of a Vicious Circle," 7 December 2009, http://nobelprize.org/nobel_prizes/literature/laureates/2009/muller-lecture_en.html.

7. The declassified archives of the Securitate are now held and made available to researchers by the Council for the Study of the Securitate Archives (CNSAS). The estimated size of the archives is 24 linear kilometers. *Raport de activitate privind anul 2011* (Bucharest: CNSAS, 2012), 5.

8. Müller's file and her relationship to the Securitate has been hotly debated in the postrevolutionary Romanian press. For thorough coverage of these debates, see Valentina Glajar, "The Presence of the Unresolved Recent Past: Herta Müller and the Securitate," in *Herta Müller*, ed. Brigid Haines and Lyn Marven (Oxford, UK: Oxford University Press, 2013). For a detailed analysis of the Romanian political context of Müller's work, see Cristina Petrescu, "When Dictatorships Fail to Deprive of Dignity: Herta Müller's 'Romanian Period,'" in *Herta Müller: Poetics and Aesthetics*, ed. Bettina Brandt and Valentina Glajar (Lincoln: University of Nebraska Press, 2013).

9. See, for example, two important discussions dedicated to the opening and interpretation of the Soviet-era archives: special issue, "Archives et nouvelles sources de l'histoire soviétique, une réévaluation," *Cahiers du monde russe* 40, nos. 1–2 (1999) ; Jörg Baberowski et al., "Diskussion: Archivlandschaften—Geschichtswissenschaft in Post-Sowjetischer Zeit," *Jahrbücher für Geschichte Osteuropas* 51, no. 1 (2003). For an informative polemic on archival lacunae that has informed my writing of this article and will be more explicitly addressed in a revised version, see Andrea Graziosi, "The New Soviet Archival Sources," *Cahiers du monde russe* 40, nos. 1–2 (1999). See also Igal Halfin, "Poetics in the Archives: The Quest for 'True' Bolshevik Documents," *Jahrbücher für Geschichte Osteuropas* 51, no. 1 (2003).

10. Joshua Sanborn, "Cybernetics and Surveillance: The Secret Police Enter the Computer Age," in *The Secret Police and the Soviet System: New Archival Investigations*, ed. Michael David-Fox (Pittsburgh, PA: Pittsburgh University Press, 2023), 393.

11. Sara Blaylock, *Parallel Public: Experimental Art in Late East Germany* (Cambridge, MA: MIT Press, 2022), 36. This statistic is based on Stasi data from 1988–89, when there were 173,000 IMS (informers).

12. Blaylock, *Parallel Public*, 28.

13. Blaylock also notes the leading role of these women artists, like Cornelia Schleime, "in the first occupation of the Stasi headquarters in December 1989—an action that prevented the planned full-scale destruction of the East German state's surveillance files." Blaylock, *Parallel Public*, 43–44. For a fascinating reading of Schleime's artistic response to her Stasi file, including its gendered assumptions, see Sara Blaylock, "Being the Woman They Wanted Her to Be," *Third Text* 35 (2021).

14. For a powerful, and very different take on the ways archival silences are gendered in the African diasporic context, see "Silence: The Archive and Affective Memory," the first chapter of Jenny Sharpe's *Immaterial Archives: An African Diaspora Poetics of Loss* (Evanston, IL: Northwestern University Press, 2020), 19–56.

15. Jacques Derrida, *De la grammatologie* (Paris: Éditions de Minuit, 1967); Derrida, *Mal d'archive: une impression freudienne*, vol. 1 (Paris: Galilée, 1995); Halfin, "Poetics in the Archives," 89.

16. Graziosi cites Patricia Kennedy Grimsted's finding that "archives the world over do not preserve more than 3–4% of state-produced documents (perhaps 10% in the case of papers related to foreign affairs)." Graziosi, "The New Soviet Archival Sources," 30.

17. I 233477 (DUI Herta Müller), vols. 1–3, Fond Informativ, ACNSAS, Bucharest.

18. For CNSAS, see note 7, above.

19. In *Peasants under Siege*, Gail Kligman and Katherine Verdery note that in some of the files they consulted, "some of these reports were written on the backs of forms and reports from the prewar period—in Transylvania, as far back as Hungarian documents from before WWI, a possible sign of financial or paper shortages or distribution problems in the newly established regime." Gail Kligman and Katherine Verdery, *Peasants under Siege: The Collectivization of Romanian Agriculture, 1949–1962* (Princeton: Princeton University Press, 2011), 21. Beyond signs of shortage, this reuse signifies a utilitarian view of history, which the new regime displayed over and over again. The appropriation of paper with its writing was a sign of power as well as of shortages. It was a way of proclaiming the new communist power victorious over the past, which it did not deem worthy of preservation. And yet, that past somehow did at times get preserved against as well as through these acts of appropriation: one can imagine some present-day readers turning the page of the communist reports to read instead the different time, and the different language, of the old Hungarian verso, thus turning it once again into the face of the page.

20. Ministerul Afacerilor Interne, "Directiva asupra organizării evidenței operative de către organele Securității Statului, a elementelor dușmănoase din Republica Populară Română (Directive regulating the organization of operative database by the organs of State Security, concerning the inimical elements in the Romanian Popular Republic)," in *"Partiturile" Securității*. Two studies dedicated to the subject of informers detail the protocol of informer recruitment, both as practiced and as mandated through internal regulations in D 008712, vol. 1, Fond Documentar, ACNSAS, Bucharest. See Mihai Albu, *Informatorul: studiu asupra colaborării cu Securitatea* (Iași: Polirom, 2008); Cristina Plamadeala, "Dossierveillance in Communist Romania: Collaboration with the Securitate, 1945–1989," in *Making Surveillance States: Transnational Histories*, ed. Rob Heynen and Emily van der Meulen (Toronto: University of Toronto Press, 2019), 215–36.

21. Timiș Ministerul de Interne, Serviciul 1/A, "RAPORT cu propuneri de deschiderea dosarului de urmărire informativă privind pe numita KARL HERTA din Timișoara, 24.II.1983 (REPORT with proposals to open an informative trailing file

concerning KARL HERTA from Timișoara)," in I 233477, Fond Informativ, ACNSAS, Bucharest.

22. "Notă sursa "Voicu," 16.III.1982," in I 233477, 1:5.

23. "Notă sursa "Voicu," 16.III.1982," in I 233477, 1:5.

24. Müller, *Cristina*, 15.

25. See "Appendix I: Müller's Surveillance Timeline: 1974–1993," in Valentina Glajar, *The Secret Police Dossier of Herta Müller* (Rochester, NY: Camden House, 2023), 261–63.

26. Glajar, *The Secret Police Dossier of Herta Müller*, 10.

27. "Notă sursa "Barbu," 26.III.1981," in I 233477, 1:4.

28. D 013381, Naționaliști Germani (German Nationalists), 46 vols., Fond Documentar, ACNSAS, Bucharest.

29. Serviciul I. A. Inspectoratul Județean Timiș al Ministerului de Interne, "Raport, 16.XI.1985," in D 013381, 36:80–81.

30. D 013381, 36:93.

31. Serviciul I/A Inspectoratul Județean Timiș al Ministerului de Interne, "Raport, 16.XI.1985," in D 013381 36:93.

32. Inspectoratul Județean Timiș al Ministerului de Interne, Serviciul I/A, "Raport, 12.XII.1981," in D 013381, 15:280.

33. "Raport, 12.XII.1981," in D 013381, 15:280.

34. Among other interesting statistics, the report also mentions that in 1981 five new DUIs had been opened and twenty-two more individuals added to the number of people "worked with priority" within the German Nationalists file. "Raport, 12.XII.1981," in D 013381, 15:284. During the same year, twenty new informers were recruited to work on this problem file, and another forty-two informers previously used by the militia were connected to this problem file. The report also mentions that priority had been given to recruiting informers among intellectuals. "Raport, 12.XII.1981," in D 013381, 15:277.

35. The "intimidation/positive influence" meetings that the Securitate initiated against Müller and other young German-language writers were part of a Soviet Bloc adoption of *profilaktika* techniques in late socialism. For a fascinating study of *profilaktika*, see Edward Cohn, "Recidivism, Prophylaxis, and the KGB," in *The Secret Police and the Soviet System: New Archival Investigations*, ed. Michael David-Fox (Pittsburgh, PA: Pittsburgh University Press, 2023).

36. "Raport, 12.XII.1981," in D 013381, 15:285.

37. D 013381, 20:322. This file contains several similar reports on warning sessions, pp. 319–22.

38. Here I have in mind Nicolae Steinhardt's famous description of his first Securitate interrogation, during which he heroically maintained his refusal to testify against his friends through the repetition of the phrase "I don't remember," despite

the mounting torture that he describes in detail. Nicolae Steinhardt, *Jurnalul Fericirii* (Cluj: Dacia, 1997), 15. The Securitate record of that interrogation does not make any mention of the torture, but does almost inadvertently document Steinhardt's courageous repetition of the "I don't remember" through citing his investigator's irritation: "You keep on hiding the truth by saying, 'I don't remember.'" P 336 (Dosar nr. 118988), Fond Penal, ACNSAS, Bucharest, 298. The interrogation record of the friend who gave in to the duress and informed on Steinhardt and others in their group compresses the whole process that led her to her compliance in the empty space between the investigator's: "You do not tell the truth," and her response: "Thinking over I decided to declare the truth." P 336, 339.

39. D 013381, 5:128.
40. D 013381, 5:128.
41. I 233477, 1:13.
42. D 013381, 13:7.
43. D 013381, 13:8.
44. D 013381, 13:7.
45. Inspectoratul Județean Timiș al Ministerului de Interne, "Raport, 28.02.1978," in D 013381, 13:160.
46. "Raport, 28.02.1978," in D 013381, 13:157.
47. "Raport, 28.02.1978," in D 013381, 13:160.
48. "Raport, 28.02.1978," in D 013381, 13:160.
49. "Raport, 28.02.1978," in D 013381, 13:158.
50. "Raport, 28.02.1978," in D 013381, 13:160.
51. "Raport, 28.02.1978," in D 013381, 13:160.
52. "Raport, 28.02.1978," in D 013381, 13:158.
53. "Raport, 28.02.1978," in D 013381, 13:160.
54. "Raport, 28.02.1978," in D 013381, 13:160.
55. "Raport, 28.02.1978," in D 013381, 13:159.
56. Herta Müller, *The Appointment*, ed. Philip Boehm, trans. Michael Hulse (New York: Picador, 2001), 1.
57. I 233477, 1:183.
58. D 013381, 25:3–12.
59. D 013381, 6:350–73.
60. D 013381, 24:153–54.
61. D 013381, 5:14.
62. For an example of such personal correspondence, see D 013381, 4:128.
63. D 013381, 5:14.
64. For an overview of Müller's stories of "rampant sexual harassment and exploitation in the workplace and by the secret police," as well as for a sophisticated treatment of gender in Müller's oeuvre, see Karin Bauer, "Gender and the Sexual

Politics of Exchange in Herta Müller's Prose," in *Herta Müller*, ed. Brigid Haines and Lyv Marven (Oxford, UK: Oxford University Press, 2013).

65. Herta Müller, "Securitate in All But Name," 31 August 2009, http://www.signandsight.com/service/1910.html.

66. An infamous example of this overeager identification drive is the phrase: "make sure to identify who this Socrates is." After a tea party at the house of Lev Tolstoy's daughter, one agent reported that the guests mentioned someone by the name of Socrates. He suggested that this suspicious character be checked since he was not yet identified in police records. Vitalii Shentalinskii, *Les surprises de la Loubianka. Retour dans les archives littéraires du K.G.B.* (Paris: R. Laffont, 1996), 50.

67. D 013381, 4:288.

68. I 184945 (DUI Richard Wagner), Fond Informativ, ACNSAS, Bucharest, 60–61.

69. Glajar, *The Secret Police Dossier of Herta Müller*, 30.

70. Glajar, *The Secret Police Dossier of Herta Müller*, 29; I 233477, 1:12–13.

71. Glajar, *The Secret Police Dossier of Herta Müller*, 34–35.

72. Glajar, *The Secret Police Dossier of Herta Müller*, 196.

73. I 184945 (DUI Richard Wagner), 216–17.

74. These conclusions are based on the analysis of D 01338 as well as my research on pages that mention Müller and her group of writers from the following problem and personal files: I 184945 (DUI Richard Wagner); R 285953, Fond Retea, ACNSAS, Bucharest; D 21 Eterul (Radio Free Europe Problem File), Fond Documentar, ACNSAS, Bucharest; D120 (Cultural Situation, Minorities), Fond Documentar, ACNSAS, Bucharest; I 234089 (DUI Rolf Bossert), Fond Informativ, ACNSAS, Bucharest.

75. Müller, "Securitate in All But Name," 4, http://www.signandsight.com/service/1910.html.

76. "Securitate in All But Name," 3.

Chapter 5

An earlier and much shorter section of this chapter has been published in *Perspectives on Europe*. I am grateful to the Center for European Studies hosted at Columbia University by the European & Harriman Institutes for permission to revisit some parts of that article here. I am indebted to Ilya Kliger for thoughtful commentary on an earlier draft. Emma Hamilton, Anastassia Koustriokova, Nicoleta Marinescu, and Oksana Popova contributed excellent research assistance. It gives me great pleasure to thank Kiki Pop-Eleches for expert advice in the creation of the graphs, and my daughters, Teodora and Veronica Vatulescu-Eleches, for helping with double-blind data entry.

1. For a pioneering study, see Joshua Sanborn, "Cybernetics and Surveillance:

The Secret Police Enter the Computer Age," in *The Secret Police and the Soviet System: New Archival Investigations*, ed. Michael David-Fox (Pittsburgh, PA: Pittsburgh University Press, 2023).

2. Fraser Harbutt, *The Iron Curtain: Churchill, America, and the Origins of the Cold War* (New York: Oxford University Press, 1986), 210.

3. A readable and thoroughly researched history of the iron curtain prior to Churchill's use of the term is Patrick Wright, *Iron Curtain: From Stage to Cold War* (Oxford, UK: Oxford University Press, 2007).

4. Wright, *Iron Curtain*, 76–82.

5. Vasily Rozanov, *Apokalipsis nashevo vremeni* (Sergeev Posad, 1918).

6. D. Zaslavskii, "Fel'eton. Lobyzanie Gebbel'sa," *Pravda*, 1 August 1946, 4.

7. James Muller, *Churchill's "Iron Curtain" Speech Fifty Years Later* (Columbia: University of Missouri Press, 1999), 8–9.

8. Larry Wolff, *Inventing Eastern Europe: The Map of Civilization on the Mind of the Enlightenment* (Stanford: Stanford University Press, 1994), 2.

9. Muller, *Churchill's "Iron Curtain,"* 8, 3.

10. Wolff, *Inventing Eastern Europe*, 2.

11. Churchill's copy of the paper is kept in Britain's Public Record Office, and available for view by following this link: PREM 3/66/7 (169).

12. Winston Churchill, *Memoirs of the Second World War* (Boston: Houghton Mifflin, 1959), 885–86. >

13. E. Tarle, "Po povodu rechi Cherchillia," *Izvestiia*, 12 March 1946, 3; "Po povodu rechi Cherchillia," *Gudok*, 13 March 1946, 4.

14. Harbutt notes the week of panicked anxiety in the Soviet Union and then follows mostly the Soviet diplomatic reaction to Churchill's speech, based on English-language sources. Harbutt, *The Iron Curtain*, 197, 203, 9–41.

15. "Rech' Cherchillia v Fultone," *Pravda*, 11 March 1946, 4. This article was reproduced in *Pravda Ukrainy* the next day. "Rech' Cherchillia v Fultone (Churchill's Speech in Fulton)," *Pravda Ukrainy* (1946).

16. Marcus Wheeler et al., "zavesa," in *Oxford Russian Dictionary* (Oxford, UK: Oxford University Press, 2000).

17. G. O. Vinokur et al., "zavesa," in *Tolkovyi slovar' russkovo iazyka* (Moscow: OGIZ, 1935).

18. I ran the search using "Aggregated Sources; Digital Archives. Newspapers; Digital Archives. Journals," *East View Universal Database* (Minneapolis: East View Publications), https://dlib-eastview-com.proxy.library.nyu.edu. This covers aggregated databases (such as Russian Central Newspapers, Russian Regional Newspapers, and so on), digital archives for both newspapers and journals, for a total of 7,915 publications between 1900 and 2022. In the final version of this chapter I excluded the journal *Novoe Russkoe slovo (NRS)*, based in New York, which exhibited

a disproportionate number of mentions of the phrase "Iron Curtain" (*zheleznyi zanaves*): 3,409 for one journal vs. 18,629 for the other 7,915 publications, so a potentially misleading one-sixth of the mentions). The trends in the data remained the same without NRS, only slightly less pronounced, which I believe gives a more accurate view of trends within the Soviet Union and Russia.

19. Tarle, "Po povodu," 3.

20. Tarle, "Po povodu," 3. For similar turns from defense to attack, where the iron curtain is shown to be a screen behind which the United States hides its true relationship to the republics in Latin America, see Nabliudatel', "Na mezhdunarodnye temy," *Izvestiia*, 13 June 1946.

21. Tarle, "Po povodu," 3.

22. L. Nikulin, "Zheleznyi zanaves," *Literaturnaia gazeta*, 13 January 1930, 1.

23. William White, "Theatre Panic and Protection," *British Architect* 28 (1887): 206.

24. Otto I. Ul evich Schmidt, *Bol'shaia sovetskaia entsiklopediia*, 65 vols., vol. 25 (Moscow: Sovetskaia entsiklopediia, 1932).

25. *Bol'shaia sovetskaia entsiklopediia*, 2nd ed., vol. 16 (Moscow: Bol'shaia sovetskaia entsiklopediia, 1952). While it is difficult to pinpoint the moment of the turn from the old theatrical meaning of *zavesa* as "thick curtain" to the military and metaphorical sense of *zavesa*, we have evidence that this happens before 1946, as a dictionary entry from the *Tolkovyi slovar' russkovo iazyka* of 1935 already calls the first meaning "anachronistic." Instead, its first definition is "that which covers, hides from view." Like the 1932 *Bolshaia*, and all other Soviet-era dictionaries I consulted, this much shorter entry also mentions the military sense of "smoke screen" (*dymovaia zavesa*).

26. "Universal Database of Russian Newspapers" (Minneapolis: East View Publications, 1999).

27. Vinokur et al., "zavesa." *Slovar' russkova iazyka* from 1957 defines *dymovaia zavesa* as "the artificial creation of a band of dust, serving as a mode of masking."

28. "Interv'iu tov. I. V. Stalina s korrespondentom 'Pravdy' otnositel'no rechi g. Cherchillia," *Pravda*, 14 March 1946, 1.

29. "Interv'iu tov. I. V. Stalina," 1.

30. Kukryniksy and S. Marshak, "Komanda podzhigatelei voiny," *Pravda*, 7 November 1946, 6. The caricature by Kukryniksy shares the same title with the accompanying poem signed S. Marshak.

31. Michael Taussig, *Defacement: Public Secrecy and the Labor of the Negative* (Stanford: Stanford University Press, 1999), 50; "Transgression," in *Critical Terms for Religious Studies*, ed. Mark C. Taylor (Chicago: University of Chicago Press, 1998), 355.

32. Katherine Verdery, *Secrets and Truths: Ethnography in the Archive of Roma-*

nia's Secret Police (Budapest: Central European University Press, 2014), 133; Sheila Fitzpatrick, *Tear off the Masks! Identity and Imposture in Twentieth-Century Russia* (Princeton: Princeton University Press, 2005).

33. *Timpul, Națiunea, Scânteia, Drapelul, Semnalul*. "Presa română și declarațiile generalissimului Stalin," *Scânteia*, 27 March 1946, 1. It is significant that the pro-Western press was largely silenced by the speech, while the pro-Soviet press was railing. Thus, the party's *Scânteia* and *România Liberă* published eleven and seven articles, respectively, on the Fulton speech in March, whereas the newspaper of the democratic opposition, *Semnalul*, published two pieces.

34. Lazăr Șăineanu, *Dicționar universal al limbei române* (Craiova: Editura Scrisul Românesc, 1929); *Dicționarul limbii române literare contemporane*, vol. 3 (Bucharest: Editura Academiei, 1957).

35. N. Iorga, "Ce se duce cu noi din Basarabia," *Neamul Românesc* 147 (1940): 1. Traian Lazăr briefly notes that Iorga's use of the term precedes Churchill's and wonders whether Churchill was inspired by Iorga, seemingly unaware of previous uses of the phrase in English and other languages. Traian Lazăr, "1940. Perdeaua de fier precede cortina de fier," in *Bătălia pentru Basarabia 1941–1944*, ed. Gh. Buzatu (Bucharest: Mica Valahie), 23–24.

36. "Declarațiile generalissimului Stalin și Romania," *Scânteia*, 16 March 1946, 4, emphasis mine.

37. "Îndărătul cuvântării d-lui Churchill se ascunde reacțiunea," *Scânteia*, 14 March 1946.

38. "Cercurile anglo-americane desaprobă discursul d-lui Churchill," *Scânteia*, 9 March 1946.

39. Some examples: "dividing the world in a western and a Russian *bloc*," *Scânteia*, 9 March 1946; "the division of the world in two camps [*lagăre*]: capitalist and communist," "Marea Britanie și întreaga lume nu au nici un viitor fără o înțelegere cu Uniunea Sovietică," *Scânteia*, 10 March 1946; "Mr. Churchill speaks . . . of 'the sphere'[*sfera*] in which Warsaw . . . Bucharest, and Sofia, would find themselves," "Conștiința lumii stă de veghe," *Scânteia*, 17 March 1946.

40. "Pacea văzută de presa străină," *Contemporanul*, 11 October 1946.

41. "Poftiți, vă rog, prichindeilor, să vă federalizăm!," *Contemporanul*, 4 January 1947.

42. P. Fedoseev, "Culisele planurilor de federalizare a Europei (Dela Kant și Rousseau to Winston Churchill)," *Contemporanul*, 4 January 1947.

43. "Noi suntem apărătorii țărilor mici," *Contemporanul*, 11 October 1946.

44. Mircea Alifanil, "Illustration for 'Criza culturii Române,'" *Contemporanul*, 11 October 1946.

45. Rodica Zafiu, "Cortina de fier," *Dilema veche*, 27 February–5 March 2014. The *cortina/cort* connection was probably more visible in the transition period,

when for the first time the Iron Curtain appeared temporary, and Romanians had a sense of being able to exit from under the tent (*cort*)—rather than to penetrate beyond the *cortina*.

46. Anne Applebaum, *Iron Curtain: The Crushing of Eastern Europe* (New York: Knopf, 2013); Wright, *Iron Curtain*; Harbutt, *The Iron Curtain*. A formal timeline, following an extensive overview of the topic appeared in Oleg Nazarov, "Zheleznyi zanaves," *Istorik* 75 (2021), https://историк.рф/journal/75/zheleznyj-zanaves.html.

47. "Thousands of guests who have visited the USSR are laughing at the stupid inventions about the 'Iron Curtain.'" S. A. Shvetsov, "O delegatsiakh i institutsiakh," *Krokodil* 8 (1956), https://dlib.eastview.com/browse/book/67829.

48. I. Semenov, "Gamlet," *Krokodil* 35 (1955), https://dlib.eastview.com/browse/book/67820.

49. Prahlad Keshav Atre, "Ia liubliu Sovetskii Soiuz!" *Pravda Ukrainy* (1955), https://dlib.eastview.com/browse/doc/66169479.

50. Atre, "Ia liubliu Sovetskii Soiuz!"

51. "Aggregated Sources; Digital Archives. Newspapers; Digital Archives. Journals."

52. Nazarov, "Zheleznyi zanaves."

53. "Vstrechi i besedy N. S. Khrushcheva v Glenkove," *Pravda* 271 (1960), https://dlib.eastview.com/browse/doc/21424826.

54. "Vstrechi i besedy N. S. Khrushcheva v Glenkove," 2.

55. V. Maerskii, "Dalekaia, bliskaia," *Pravda* 232 (1960): 6. https://dlib.eastview.com/browse/doc/21425560.

56. G. Dzukov, "Politika zakrytykh dverei," *Pravda* 113 (1962): 5. https://dlib.eastview.com/browse/doc/21506344.

57. A. Rukhadze, "Gde 'zheleznyi zanaves'?" *Literaturnaia gazeta* 9 (1968), https://dlib.eastview.com/browse/doc/26705104.

58. A. Belskaia, "Kler Lius i razdiadka," *Krokodil* 32 (1975), https://dlib.eastview.com/browse/book/68395.

59. Ali Ndai, "Razvivat' sotrudnichestvo," *Pravda* 244 (1976), https://dlib.eastview.com/browse/doc/21510865.

60. Rem Petrov, "Pogranichnaia situatsiia," *Krokodil* 1 (1990), https://dlib.eastview.com/browse/book/66982. In a similar vein, an April 1991 article starts off by conjuring Peter I's idea of a "window onto Europe," and continues: "Until the System arose, which hung an iron curtain. And suddenly the iron curtain fell. Not only the window, but also the gate was wide open ... voyages, cruises ..." Aza Pavlova, "Dorogu osilit imushchii," *Krokodil* 11 (1991), https://dlib.eastview.com/browse/book/66956.

61. Lamara Galya, "Sotrudnichestvo: Monument dlia Washingtona," *Nedelia* 18 (1988), https://dlib.eastview.com/browse/doc/54126325.

62. Stephen Woodburn, "Strategic Monuments: Zurab Tsereteli's Gift Sculptures to the United States in the Eras of Détente, Perestroika, and Anti-Terrorism, 1979–2006," *Experiment* 18, no. 1 (2012).

63. Galya, "Sotrudnichestvo: Monument dlia Washingtona," 4.

64. Galya, "Sotrudnichestvo: Monument dlia Washingtona," 5. To my knowledge Tsereteli's Iron Curtain sculpture never reached the United States, but its main ideas—the curtain broken in half and the victorious hero standing on the ruins of the Cold War—echo in the two most famous sculptures Tsereteli did manage to strategically give to the United States, *To the Struggle against World Terrorism (Tear of Grief)* and *Good Defeats Evil*, now on display at the United Nations, New York City.

65. Savva Kulish, "'Zheleznyi zanaves'—vzgliad iz dvukh stolits," *Izvestiia* 122 (1998), https://dlib.eastview.com/browse/doc/3166605.

66. From my searches of the term "zheleznyi zanaves" in Russian-language press around these dates, the first spike, around 2006, seems strongly related to the aftermath of the 2004 NATO expansion, the Orange Revolution in Ukraine, and talks about potential expansion of NATO to Ukraine, as well as the 2006 Russia–Ukraine gas crisis. The 2014 spike is even more directly traceable to the annexation of Crimea and the ensuing Western sanctions.

67. NBC News, "Zelenskyy: 'New Iron Curtain' Separates Russia From 'Civilized World'" (2022).

68. "V Rossii zablokiruiut Instagram," *Zerkalo nedeli* (2022), https://dlib.eastview.com/browse/doc/74863300.

69. "Otchipentsy," *Kommersant* (2022); Maik Mirer, "Eto ne lechitsia," *Novaia gazeta. Evropa* (2022), https://dlib.eastview.com/browse/doc/77677506.

70. "Rf robyt sobi zaliznu zavisu, yak kolys radianskyi soiuz, ne treba yii zavazhaty—Zelenskyi," *Ukrinform* (2022), https://www.ukrinform.ua/rubric-ato/3476903-rf-robit-sobi-zaliznu-zavisu-ak-kolis-radanskij-souz-ne-treba-ij-zavazati-zelenskij.html.

71. "Rf robyt sobi zaliznu zavisu."

72. Oleksandr Levchenko, "Sytuatsiia u vidnosynakh Zakhodu i Rosii blyzka do 'zaliznoi zavisy,'" *Ukrinform* (2021), https://www.ukrinform.ua/rubric-world/3260595-situacia-u-vidnosinah-zahodu-i-rosii-blizka-do-zaliznoi-zavisi-posol.html.

73. Iryna Vereshchuk, "Zalizna zavisa, shcho opuskaietsia na RF, proide po skhidnomu kordonu Ukrainy (The Iron Curtain descending on the Russian Federation will pass along the eastern border of Ukraine)" (2022), https://t.me/vereshchuk_iryna/1351.

74. Olha Kurnosova, "Seriozni protesty v Rosii naiimovirnishi u veresni," *Dim* (2022), https://kanaldom.tv/uk/serjozni-protesty-u-rosiyi-najimovirnishi-u-veresni-kurnosova/.

75. Mikhail Bushchev, "Debaty na GMF: Tsifrovoi zheleznyi zanaves vozvodiat i Rossiia, i Zapad," *Deutsche Welle* (2022), https://www.dw.com/ru/mediaforum-dw-zheleznyj-zanaves-vozvodjat-s-obeih-storon/a-62206885.

76. Bushchev, "Debaty na GMF."

77. Bushchev, "Debaty na GMF."

78. "Rossiia otkazalac' perezhit' iz-za vozmozhnosti novovo zheleznogo zanavesa," *lenta.ru* (2022), https://lenta.ru/news/2022/03/02/iron_wall_2/.

79. "Lavrov zaiavil o vozmozhnostiakh Rossii pazvivat'sia i za 'zheleznym zanavesom,'" *Interfaks* (2022), https://www.interfax.ru/russia/825829.

80. This article presents Putin's position in his own words. Viktor Iur'ev and Evgenii Maslov, "My zhiviem v epokhu peremen," *Argumenty i fakty*, 15 June 2022.

81. Iur'ev and Maslov, "My zhiviem v epokhu peremen."

82. Iur'ev and Maslov, "My zhiviem v epokhu peremen."

83. "'Zheleznyi zanaves uzhe opuskaetsia': Lavrov rasskazal ob otnosheniiakh mezhdu Zapadom i RF," *Novye Izvestiia* (2022), https://dlib.eastview.com/browse/doc/78506993.

84. "'Zheleznyi zanaves uzhe opuskaetsia.'"

85. Iur'ev and Maslov, "My zhiviem v epokhu peremen."

86. G. A. Ziuganov, "Sistemnyi krizis kapitalizma, informatsionnaia voina i zadachi KPRF v bor'be za sotsializm," *Pravda*, 5 July 2022. While the Communist Party, led by G. A. Ziuganov, is nominally in the opposition to Putin's United Russia, as far as the war and anti-Western sentiment, the communists largely align with the government, at times supporting even more bellicose and extreme views. For a short but informative assessment on the relationship of United Russia and the Russian Communist Party as far as the war is concerned, see Ben Dubow, "With Enemies Like Russia's Communists, Putin Doesn't Need Friends," *Europe's Edge* (2022), https://cepa.org/russias-communists-ally-with-kremlin-over-ukraine/.

87. Marina Kriuchkova, "Za zheleznym zanavesom," *Trud* 15–16 (2022), https://dlib.eastview.com/browse/doc/74691759.

88. Paul Mantoux, *Les délibérations du Conseil des quatre*, 2 vols. (Paris: CNRS, 1955), 2:51.

89. Mantoux, *Les délibérations du Conseil des quatre*, 2:51.

90. Kriuchkova, "Za zheleznym zanavesom."

91. Kriuchkova, "Za zheleznym zanavesom."

92. Pavel Shipilin, "Zheleznyi zanaves," *Sovershenno sekretno* (2022), https://dlib.eastview.com/browse/doc/74933845.

93. Shipilin, "Zheleznyi zanaves."

94. Shipilin, "Zheleznyi zanaves."

95. Shipilin, "Zheleznyi zanaves," 1.

96. Applebaum, *Iron Curtain*.

Postscript

1. Caryl Emerson, "Editor's Preface," in *Problems of Dostoevsky's Poetics* (Minneapolis: University of Minnesota Press, 1984), xxix; Mikhail Bakhtin, *Problemy tvorchestva Dostoevskogo* (Leningrad: Priboi, 1929).

2. Mikhail Bakhtin, *Problemy poetiki Dostoevskogo* (Moscow: Sov. pisatel', 1963).

3. Mikhail Bakhtin, *Problems of Dostoevsky's Poetics*, trans. Caryl Emerson (Minneapolis: University of Minnesota Press, 1984), 7, 63.

4. This is Emerson and Morson's verdict at the end of their excellent subchapter "Ethics and Secondhand Definitions," dedicated to the imbricated relationship between the ethics, theology, and politics of polyphony in Bakhtin. Gary Saul Morson and Caryl Emerson, *Mikhail Bakhtin: Creation of a Prosaics* (Stanford: Stanford University Press, 1990), 268, 65–68.

5. For a fascinating, in-depth meditation on the relationship between Bakhtin's aesthetics and his experience of bodily pain, see Caryl Emerson, "Shklovsky's *ostranenie*, Bakhtin's *vnenakhodimost'* (How Distance Serves an Aesthetics of Arousal Differently from an Aesthetics Based on Pain)," *Poetics Today* 26, no. 4 (2005).

6. Michel Foucault, "Preface to the 1961 Edition," in *History of Madness*, ed. Jean Khalfa (New York: Routledge, 2006), xxviii, xxxi, translation modified.

7. "Préface de l'édition originale. En marge d'Histoire de la folie à l'âge classique (1961)," in Michel Foucault, *Oeuvres* (Paris: Gallimard, 2015), 662; Foucault, "Preface to the 1961 Edition," xxxii, xxviii, translation modified.

8. Jacques Rancière, *Politics of Literature*, trans. Julie Rose (Cambridge, UK: Polity, 2011), 4. In this passage, Rancière places his understanding of aesthetics and the redistribution of the sensible in Foucault's lineage. Indeed, the critique of the distinction between "the significant language" and "background noise" that is repressed, "the discourse it denounces as not being language, a gesture as not being an oeuvre, a figure as having no rightful place in history," is already formulated by Foucault in the preface to his first book, and animates it with the "need to strain our ears, and bend down towards this murmuring of the world." Foucault, "Preface to the 1961 Edition," xxxii.

9. Rancière, *Politics of Literature*, 4.

10. Jane Hirshfield, *Come, Thief* (New York: Knopf, 2011), 47.

11. Tina Campt, *Listening to Images* (Durham, NC: Duke University Press, 2017), 6.

12. Campt cites the definition of "audible frequency" (between 20 and 20,000 Hz) from Wikipedia.com; Campt, *Listening to Images*, 7. In developing her concept of archival lower frequency Campt takes inspiration from Paul Gilroy's influential discussion of "a politics which exists on a lower frequency where it is played, danced, and acted . . . because words . . . will never be enough to communicate the

unsayable claims to truth." Paul Gilroy, *The Black Atlantic: Modernity and Double Consciousness* (Cambridge, MA: Harvard University Press, 1993), 37.

13. Campt, *Listening to Images*, 7.

14. Campt, *Listening to Images*, 6.

15. Campt, *Listening to Images*, 6; Ariella Azoulay, *The Civil Contract of Photography* (Cambridge, MA: Zone Books, MIT Press, 2008), 16.

16. Campt, *Listening to Images*, 33.

17. Campt, *Listening to Images*, 33.

18. Morson and Emerson, *Mikhail Bakhtin*, 232.

19. Bakhtin prefaces his major contribution to the theory of the novel by reminding us that the novel is "the only "major [literary] genre that is younger than writing: it alone is organically receptive to new forms of mute perception, that is, to reading." Mikhail Bakhtin, *The Dialogic Imagination*, ed. Caryl Emerson, trans. Mikhail Holquist (Austin: University of Texas Press, 1981), 2.

20. Campt, *Listening to Images*, 42.

21. Denise Ferreira da Silva, *Toward a Global Idea of Race* (Minneapolis: University of Minnesota Press, 2007), xv–xvi.

22. Gabrielle Starr, *Feeling Beauty: The Neuroscience of Aesthetic Experience* (Cambridge, MA: MIT Press, 2013), 79.

23. George Lakoff and Mark Johnson, *Philosophy in the Flesh: The Embodied Mind and Its Challenge to Western Thought* (New York: Basic Books, 1999), 13. This "cognitive unconscious" of cognitive science is to be distinguished from Freud's unconscious: "[Cognitive science] has discovered, first of all, that most of our thought is unconscious, not in the Freudian sense of being repressed, but in the sense that it operates beneath the level of cognitive awareness, inaccessible to consciousness and operating too quickly to be focused on." Lakoff and Johnson, *Philosophy in the Flesh*, 10.

24. Lakoff and Johnson, *Philosophy in the Flesh*, 3–4.

25. The influential trailblazer for this direction in archive studies is Arlette Farge, *Le goût de l'archive* (Paris: Éditions du Seuil, 1989). As far as Eastern European declassified archives go, affect and embodiment have played the largest role for writers and artists facing their own files. The first influential such account was Timothy Garton Ash, *The File: A Personal History* (London: HarperCollins, 1997). Outstanding among more recent work is Katherine Verdery, *My Life as a Spy: Investigations in a Secret Police File* (Durham, NC: Duke University Press, 2018). While Herta Müller's *Cristina and Her Double*, treated in depth in my chapters 3 and 4, provides a model for a writer's encounter with her own files, the ACNSAS archive has also conducted a fascinating oral history project. Starting with 2010, ACNSAS has invited its visitors to participate in interviews about the experience of reading their own (or their family's) files. More than 300 interviews are available for study

in the archive, and partially made public through exhibitions and publications. A description of the project with selected quotations is available at ACNSAS, "Centrul de Istorie Orală—C.N.S.A.S.." While not primarily focused on archives, Emma Widdis's *Socialist Senses* provides a long-missing sustained account of embodied sensation and affect in Soviet cinema's creation of its subjects. Emma Widdis, *Socialist Senses: Film, Feeling, and the Soviet Subject, 1917–1940* (Bloomington: Indiana University Press, 2017). As evidenced in both this postscript and my introduction, I also found much inspiration in feminist, queer, postcolonial, and Black studies and their engagements with affect theory. Tina Campt, *Image Matters: Archive, Photography, and the African Diaspora in Europe* (Durham, NC: Duke University Press, 2012); Campt, *Listening to Images*; Saidiya Hartman, "Venus in Two Acts," *Small Axe* 12, no. 2 (2008); Shannon Jackson, *Lines of Activity: Performance, Historiography, Hull-House Domesticity* (Ann Arbor: University of Michigan Press, 2000); Ann Cvetkovich, *An Archive of Feelings: Trauma, Sexuality, and Lesbian Public Cultures* (Durham, NC: Duke University Press, 2003); Zeb Tortorici, *Sins against Nature: Sex and Archives in Colonial New Spain* (Durham, NC: Duke University Press, 2018); Robert F. Reid Pharr, *Archives of Flesh: African America, Spain, and Post-Humanist Critique* (New York: New York University Press, 2016); Bill Bissell and Linda Caruso Haviland, *The Sentient Archive: Bodies, Performance, and Memory* (Middletown, CT: Wesleyan University Press, 2018). This incomplete list is both a last tribute to the influence of these scholars and artists as well as an invitation to further reading as this book draws to a close.

26. For an informative introduction to the field, see Arthur Jacobs, "Neurocognitive Poetics: Methods and Models for Investigating the Neuronal and Cognitive-affective Bases of Literature Reception," *Frontiers in Human Neuroscience* 9, no. 186 (2015), 10.3389/fnhum.2015.00186; Jacobs, "Towards a Neurocognitive Poetics Model of Literary Reading," in *Towards a Cognitive Neuroscience of Natural Language Use*, ed. Roel Willems (Cambridge, UK: Cambridge University Press, 2015).

27. "The Panskepp-Jacobson hypothesis . . . states that since evolution had no time to invent a proper neuronal system for art reception, even less so for literary reading, the affective and esthetic processes we experience when reading, (cf. Jakobson's hypothesis) must be linked to the ancient emotion circuits we share with all mammals . . . Several recent neurocognitive studies on reading indeed provide support for both the *fiction feeling* and the Panskepp-Jakobson hypothesis)." Jacobs, "Neurocognitive Poetics," 3. See also Arthur Jacobs and Roel Willems, "The Fictive Brain: Neurocognitive Correlates of Engagement in Literature," *Review of General Psychology* 22, no. 2 (2018).

28. Eleonore Kneepkens, and Rolf A. Zwaan, "Emotions and Literary Text Comprehension," *Poetics* 23 (1995).

29. For the complicated relationship between personal experience and the cul-

tural attitudes to pain, see Joanna Bourke, *The Story of Pain: Fom Prayer to Painkillers* (Oxford, UK: Oxford University Press, 2014). For an affective reading of illness and pain in Stalinist archives, see Golfo Alexopoulos, *Illness and Inhumanity in Stalin's Gulag* (New Haven: Yale University Press, 2017).

30. Lakoff and Johnson, *Philosophy in the Flesh*, 13.

31. Lakoff and Johnson, *Philosophy in the Flesh*, 13.

32. Morson and Emerson, *Mikhail Bakhtin*, 232.

33. Morson and Emerson, *Mikhail Bakhtin*, 231–32.

34. I am deeply grateful to Brigid Cohen and to J. Martin Daughtry for precious advice and references on counterpoint and polyphony from a music studies perspective. This section could not have been written without their help.

35. Wouter Capitain, *Postcolonial Polyphony: Edward Said's Work in Music* (Amsterdam: University of Amsterdam, 2021), 25.

36. Edward Said, *Culture and Imperialism* (New York: Knopf, 1993), 66–67, emphasis mine.

37. Said, *Culture and Imperialism*, 33.

38. For a brilliant use of contrapuntal reading of Russian documentary, see Natalia Klimova Plagmann, "Human Documents on Screen and Stage: A Contrapuntal Reading of Post-Soviet Documentary," PhD diss., Princeton University, 2023.

39. Said, *Culture and Imperialism*, 66.

40. Capitain, *Postcolonial Polyphony*, 23. See also John MacKenzie, "Occidentalism: Counterpoint and Counter-Polemic," *Journal of Historical Geography* 19 (1993): 340. The first issue that turns Capitain away from counterpoint and toward polyphony is its Eurocentrism. Kristine Suna-Koro summarized this now common charge against Said's choice of counterpoint: "Why, on earth, use a quintessentially European musical technique that blossomed precisely during the 'golden era' of colonial modernity to develop a postcolonial hermeneutic?" Kristine Suna-Koro, *In Counterpoint: Diaspora, Postcoloniality, and Sacramental Theology* (Eugene, OR: Pickwick, 2017), 139. Counterpoint is thus not just a particularly classical European type of polyphony, but—and here comes its second key limitation for Capitain—also a subtype of polyphony that is highly structured, "privileg[ing] developmental progress and unity." At its harshest, this criticism sees counterpoint as "the combination of multiple musical voices according to a strict, uncompromising set of rules wielded by a manipulating power," which, as Irving argues, "makes counterpoint a fitting metaphor for colonialism." David Irving, *Colonial Counterpoint: Music in Early Modern Manila* (Oxford, UK: Oxford University Press, 2010), 3–5. More tempered, the criticism reads: "Even if a contrapuntal perspective acknowledges the responsibility of the interpreter to highlight different voices, as Gould does when playing Bach, it nevertheless derives from a musical aesthetic that privileges developmental progress and unity." Capitain, *Postcolonial Polyphony*, 52.

41. Capitain, *Postcolonial Polyphony*, 23. Brian Fairley has recently shown that musical polyphony did not remain untouched by "epistemologies of white European supremacy," but was instead marshalled "into teleological theories of European musical achievement." "In many different yet related formulations . . . *polyphony* found itself as a middle term of musical progress, between *monophony* (or sometimes *homophony*), understood as a primitive or preliminary stage, and *harmony* . . . Polyphony helped to define the immanent values of European music culture in opposition to that of non-Europeans. Polyphony, initially seen as a historical stage in Western music's process of self-realization, was later employed as a term of analysis for non-European, non-elite music, but only in degraded or incomplete forms." Brian Fairley, "Polyphony," in *Keywords in Antiracist Theory* (forthcoming). While emphasizing the diversity of polyphonic traditions in diverse locales and time periods beyond the European classical period, Fairley excavated "the assumptions of European cultural supremacy that underlie the term's emergence in [Western] music studies." Fairley, "Polyphony." Taking critical account of this complicated history of appropriation, Fairley, unlike Capitain, shows that polyphony was "far from a value-neutral description of musical texture." Yet in line with Capitain's assessment, Fairley believes that "polyphony can instead serve the antiracist scholar and pedagogue as an invitation to hear multiplicity without resolution, history without teleology, and difference without separation." Fairley, "Polyphony."

42. Capitain, *Postcolonial Polyphony*, 24.

43. L. A. Gogotishvili, "Sootnoshenie mezhdu polifonicheskim romanom M. Bakhtina i muzykal'noi polifoniei," *Voprosy filosofii* 3 (2019): 146.

44. "It is possible that precisely this multilingual atmosphere [of Vilnius] created the first background for the formulation of the future concept of polyphony." A. A. Sychev, "M. M. Bakhtin: zhizn' na fone epokhi," *Gumanitarii* 33 (2016): 40. Sychev also suggests that Bakhtin's voluntary and forced moves around the linguistic and cultural margins of Russian and then Soviet space ("Wilno, Odesa, Nevel, Vitebsk, Kustanai, and Saransk") strongly impacted his literary theory.

45. Bakhtin developed his critique of V. Komarovich's understanding of polyphony and counterpoint in Dostoevsky's work in his literature review. Bakhtin, *Problems of Dostoevsky's Poetics*, 20–22. Bakhtin did not clearly differentiate between different types of polyphony in his Dostoevsky study. Yet Gogotishvili argues that through Bakhtin's critiques of previous scholars who had associated Dostoevsky's novels with Bach's contrapuntal polyphony before him, "Bakhtin indirectly makes clear that Bach's polyphony is not what he wants to compare Dostoevsky's novels with, because Bach's polyphony is harmonious . . . and therefore, for Bakhtin—monological (*monologichna*)." Gogotishvili, "Sootnoshenie," 146.

46. Indeed, traditional polyphony was widely spread in Africa, Asia, and Eastern/Southern Europe long before counterpoint. The introduction of polyphony in

the Christian Church is linked to adoption of Georgian-style polyphony into Byzantine liturgical hymns. UNESCO, "Georgian Polyphonic Singing," in *Intangible Cultural Heritage* (2008). Brian Fairley sounds a welcome note of caution about the role of polyphony in global cultural politics, as represented in the UNESCO *Intangible Cultural Heritage*: "by positing polyphony as a resource with uneven global distribution—and, most importantly, by claiming that all polyphonic musics have something in common, a 'specific mode of musical thinking, expressive behavior, and sound,' . . . they recapitulate a racial logic of fascination and exclusion." Fairley, "Polyphony," 12.

47. Not only is the interaction between interpreters more important than any original authorship, but the distinction between interpreter and audience is also often erased. "From the social point of view, during the process of performance society is not usually divided into 'performers' and 'listeners,' as in polyphonic cultures all the members of the society are usually performers and listeners at the same time." Joseph Jordania, "What Is Polyphony, or How Should We Define It?" (International Research Center for Traditional Polyphony).

48. Kwami Coleman, "Free Jazz and the 'New Thing,'" *Journal of Musicology* 38 (2021). For "a perspective on jazz improvisation that has 'interactiveness' at its core, in the creation of music through improvisational interaction, [and] in the shaping of social communities and networks through music," see Ingrid Monson, *Saying Something: Jazz Improvisation and Interaction* (Chicago: University of Chicago Press, 1996). See also Fairley, "Polyphony." The heated debate about new jazz raged at the time of Bakhtin's revision and republication of his work on polyphony, in the early 1960s. On the use of Bakhtin's concepts, including polyphony and dialogism, for understanding jazz improvisation, see Dmitrii Livshits, *Fenomen improvizatsii v dzhaze [The Phenomenon of Improvisation in Jazz]* (Nizhnyi Novgorod: Nizhgorod State Conservatory, 2003); Maria Rezantseva, "Dzhaz kak nezavershaemoe iskusstvo [Jazz as the Unfinalizable Art]," *Kontekst i refleksiya: filosofiya o mire i cheloveke [Context and Reflection: Philosophy of the World and Human Being]* 8, no. 2A (2019).

49. "Both social and musical aspects of polyphony should be present in a tradition to be regarded as polyphonic." Jordania, "What Is Polyphony, or How Should We Define It?"

50. Morson and Emerson, *Mikhail Bakhtin*, 232.

51. Morson and Emerson, *Mikhail Bakhtin*, 232.

52. Bakhtin, *The Dialogic Imagination*, 320.

53. Bakhtin, *The Dialogic Imagination*, 321, 428, 338.

54. Morson and Emerson, *Mikhail Bakhtin*, 232.

55. Bakhtin, *Problems of Dostoevsky's Poetics*, 7.

56. Bakhtin, *Problems of Dostoevsky's Poetics*, 7, original emphasis.

57. Bakhtin, *Problems of Dostoevsky's Poetics*, 63.
58. Bakhtin, *The Dialogic Imagination*, 4.
59. Morson and Emerson, *Mikhail Bakhtin*, 237.
60. Morson and Emerson, *Mikhail Bakhtin*, 268.
61. Bakhtin, *Problems of Dostoevsky's Poetics*, 59, emphasis mine.
62. See, for example, the negative answer that Gayatri Spivak gives to her quest for the subaltern's voice in Gayatri Chakravorty Spivak, "The Rani of Sirmur: An Essay in Reading the Archives," *History and Theory* 24, no. 3 (1985). This recalls Foucault's verdict that "it is doubtless impossible ever to recapture them [these lives] in themselves, such as they might have been in 'a free state.'" Michel Foucault, "The Lives of Infamous Men," in *Power, Truth, Strategy*, ed. Meaghan Morris and Paul Patton (Sydney: Feral Publications, 1979), 80.
63. Foucault, "The Lives of Infamous Men," 79.
64. For a thoroughly documented study of Stalin's reading habits, see Geoffrey Roberts, *Stalin's Library: A Dictator and His Books* (New Haven: Yale University Press, 2022). For our purposes, Roberts's chapter on Stalin's marginalia is particularly relevant: "If there was anything Stalin loved as much as reading, it was editing. His red or blue pencil marks on documents were as familiar to Soviet officials as his face." Roberts, *Stalin's Library*, 190.
65. Anatoly Lunacharsky, "O 'mnogogolosnosti' Dostoevskogo" (About Dostoevsky's 'Multivoicedness')," *Novyi mir* 10 (1929).
66. Bakhtin, *Problems of Dostoevsky's Poetics*, 43.
67. Bakhtin, *Problems of Dostoevsky's Poetics*, 272.
68. Morson and Emerson, *Mikhail Bakhtin*, 240–41.
69. Foucault, "The Lives of Infamous Men," 79–80.
70. Foucault, "The Lives of Infamous Men," 80.
71. Foucault, "Preface to the 1961 Edition," xxxii.
72. As Sona Hoisington noted, "the concept of gendered person did not concern Bakhtin." Sona Hoisington, *A Plot of Her Own: The Female Protagonist in Russian Literature* (Evanston, IL: Northwestern University Press, 1995), 45. For more on this topic and/or its absence, see Caryl Emerson, "Bakhtin and Women: A Non-Topic with Immense Implications," in *Fruits of Her Plume: Essays on Contemporary Russian Women's Culture*, ed. Helena Goscilo (M. E. Sharpe, 1993); Dale Bauer and Jaret McKinstry, eds., *Feminism, Bakhtin, and the Dialogic* (Albany: SUNY Press, 1991). By "nonhuman" I gesture to the largely unacknowledged presence of the environment, including animals, plants, rivers, and air, in the secret police archives. I think this is one of the most promising directions of further study—since the secret police supervised not only the making of maps but also large-scale transformation of the environment through such massive projects as the building of dams and deforestation.

Works Cited

9724 (Problem File for Tehnometal Timisoara, 1954–89). 1 vol. Bucharest, ACNSAS.
ACNSAS. "Centrul de Istorie Orală—C.N.S.A.S." http://www.cnsas.ro/documente/Centrul%20de%20istorie%20orala%20FINAL.pdf.
———. "Fondul Bibliotecă." Bucharest.
———. "Inventarul Fondului Manuscrise." Bucharest.
Agamben, Giorgio. *Remnants of Auschwitz: The Witness and the Archive*. Translated by Daniel Heller-Roazen. New York: Zone Books, 1999.
"Aggregated Sources; Digital Archives. Newspapers; Digital Archives. Journals." In *East View Universal Database* Minneapolis: East View Publications. https://dlib-eastview-com.proxy.library.nyu.edu.
Albu, Mihai. *Informatorul: Studiu asupra colaborării cu Securitatea*. Iași: Polirom, 2008.
Alexopoulos, Golfo. *Illness and Inhumanity in Stalin's Gulag*. New Haven: Yale University Press, 2017.
Alifanil, Mircea. "Illustration for 'Criza culturii Române.'" *Contemporanul*, 11 October 1946, 1.
Amad, Paula. *Counter-Archive: Film, the Everyday, and Albert Kahn's Archives de la Planète*. New York: Columbia University Press, 2010.
Amichai, Yehuda. *Yehuda Amichai: A Life of Poetry 1948–1994*. Translated by Benjamin Harshav and Barbara Harshav. New York: Harper Collins, 1994.
Andrei, Andreea, and Alina Branda. "Abortion Policy and Social Suffering: The

Objectification of Romanian Women's Bodies under Communism (1966–1989)." *Women's History Review* 24, no. 6 (2015): 881–99.

Anker, Elizabeth, and Rita Felski. *Critique and Postcritique*. Durham, NC: Duke University Press, 2017.

Anonymous. "Item 3103/60. Furtul de la B.R.P.R [The Robbery of B.R.P.R]." 2–5: HU OSA 300-60-1, Radio Free Europe/Radio Liberty Research Institute: Information Resources Department: East European Archives: Romanian Unit, Subject Files, Box 403, file 1803. Justice and Sentences, 1960.

———. "Item No. 238/60. Informatiuni din R. P. Romania. Furtul de la Banca de Stat/The Robbery of the National Bank." 1–2: HU OSA 300-60-1, Radio Free Europe/Radio Liberty Research Institute: Information Resources Department: East European Archives: Romanian Unit, Subject Files, box 430, file 2300, 1960.

———. "Item No. 254/60. Arrests by Ambulance. Robbing of Bucharest State Bank Car." 1: HU OSA 300-60-1, Radio Free Europe/Radio Liberty Research Institute: Information Resources Department: East European Archives: Romanian Unit, Subject Files, box 430, file 2300, 1960.

———. "Item No. 2869/61, Filmarea furtului de la banca RPR/Movie of Bank Robbery." 1–3: HU OSA 300-60-1, Radio Free Europe/Radio Liberty Research Institute: Information Resources Department: East European Archives: Romanian Unit, Subject Files, box 103, file 803: I., 1960.

Applebaum, Anne. *Iron Curtain: The Crushing of Eastern Europe*. New York: Knopf, 2013.

Arac, Jonathan. "Foucault and Central Europe: A Polemical Speculation." *boundary 2* 21, no. 3 (1994): 197–210.

"Archives et nouvelles sources de l'histoire soviétique, une réévaluation." *Cahiers du monde russe* 40, nos. 1–2 (1999).

Arendt, Hannah. *The Origins of Totalitarianism*. New York: Meridian Books, 1958.

———. "What Is Authority?" In *Between Past and Future* (New York: Viking Press, 1961), 91–142.

Arondekar, Anjali. *For the Record: On Sexuality and the Colonial Archive in India*. Durham, NC: Duke University Press, 2009.

Atre, Prahlad Keshav. "Ia liubliu Sovetskii Soiuz!" *Pravda Ukrainy* (1955): 4–4. https: //dlib.eastview.com/browse/doc/66169479.

Azoulay, Ariella. *The Civil Contract of Photography*. Cambridge, MA: Zone Books, MIT Press, 2008.

Baberowski, Jörg, Jan Plamper, Laura Engelstein, Peter Holquist, and Igal Halfin. "Diskussion: Archivlandschaften—Geschichtswissenschaft in Post-Sowjetischer Zeit." *Jahrbücher für Geschichte Osteuropas* 51, no. 1 (2003).

Bakhtin, Mikhail. *The Dialogic Imagination*. Translated by Mikhail Holquist. Edited by Caryl Emerson. Austin: University of Texas Press, 1981.

———. *Problems of Dostoevsky's Poetics*. Translated by Caryl Emerson. Minneapolis: University of Minnesota Press, 1984.

———. *Problemy poetiki Dostoevskogo*. Moscow: Sov. pisatel', 1963.
———. *Problemy tvorchestva Dostoevskogo*. Leningrad: Priboi, 1929.
Bartecka, Beata, Łukasz Rusznica, and Tomasz Stempowski. *How to Look Natural in Photos*. Wroclaw: Palm* Studios, 2021.
Basiuk, Tomas. "Notes on Karol Rasziszewski's Kisieland." In *The Archive as a Project*, edited by Krzysztof Pijarski. Warsaw: Fundacja Archeologia Fotografii, 2011.
Bauer, Dale, and Jaret McKinstry, eds. *Feminism, Bakhtin, and the Dialogic*. Albany: SUNY Press, 1991.
Bauer, Karin. "Gender and the Sexual Politics of Exchange in Herta Müller's Prose." In *Herta Müller*, edited by Brigid Haines and Lyv Marven, 153–71. Oxford: Oxford University Press, 2013.
Belskaia, A. "Kler Lius i razdiadka." *Krokodil* 32 (1975). https://dlib.eastview.com/browse/book/68395.
Benjamin, Walter. *Illuminations*. Translated by Harry Zohn. New York: Harcourt, 1968.
———. "A Short History of Photography." *Screen* 13, no. 1 (1972): 5–26.
Best, Stephen Michael. *None Like Us: Blackness, Belonging, Aesthetic Life*. Durham, NC: Duke University Press, 2018.
Birkerts, Sven. *The Gutenberg Elegies: The Fate of Reading in an Electronic Culture*. Boston: Faber & Faber, 1994.
Bissell, Bill, and Linda Caruso Haviland. *The Sentient Archive: Bodies, Performance, and Memory*. Middletown, CT: Wesleyan University Press, 2018.
Blanchot, Maurice. "L'oubli, la déraison." *La Nouvelle revue française* (1961) : 49–63.
Blaylock, Sara. "Being the Woman They Wanted Her to Be." *Third Text* 35 (2021): 227–47.
———. *Parallel Public: Experimental Art in Late East Germany*. Cambridge, MA: MIT Press, 2022.
Bolter, Jay David, and Richard Grusin. *Remediation: Understanding New Media*. Cambridge, MA: MIT Press, 2000.
Bordwell, David. *Narration in the Fiction Film*. Madison: University of Wisconsin Press, 1985.
Bourke, Joanna. *The Story of Pain: From Prayer to Painkillers*. Oxford: Oxford University Press, 2014.
Boym, Svetlana. *Another Freedom: The Alternative History of an Idea*. Chicago: University of Chicago Press, 2010.
———. "How Soviet Subjectivity Is Made." In *The Svetlana Boym Reader*, edited by Cristina Vatulescu, Tamar Abramov, Nicole G. Burgoyne, Julia Chadaga, Jacob Emery, and Julia Vaingurt, 313–25. New York: Bloomsbury, 2019.
Broberg, Gunnar. "Foucault i Uppsala." *Uppsala Newsletter for the History of Science* 2 (1985).
Brodsky, Joseph. *Less Than One*. New York: Farrar Straus Giroux, 1985.
Brown, Kate, Craig Campbell, Sonja Luehrmann, Jeremy Johnson, Deborah Alison

Jones, and Kimberly Ann Powers. "Engaging Documents: New Directions in Anthro-historical Research in and on Archives." Association for Slavic, East European, and Eurasian Studies National Convention, San Antonio, 2014.

Brunton, Finn, and Helen Nissenbaum. *Obfuscation: A User's Guide for Privacy and Protest*. Cambridge, MA: MIT Press, 2015.

BU 0204/312. Instytut pamięci narodowej (IPN), Warsaw.

BU 0204/458 (Daniel Beauvois). IPN, Warsaw.

BU 0204/1278 (Jean Carbonnet). IPN, Warsaw.

BU 0204/1930 (Michelle Bozec). IPN, Warsaw.

BU 0999/300 (Obcy). IPN, Warsaw.

BU 01220/10/202 (Etienne Burin de Roziers). IPN, Warsaw.

BU 01220/10/1706. IPN, Warsaw.

BU 01299/330 (French cultural-propaganda). IPN, Warsaw.

BU 1368/19263 (Bernard Kouchner). IPN, Warsaw.

Bushchev, Mikhail. "Debaty na GMF: Tsifrovoi zheleznyi zanaves vozvodiat i Rossiia, i Zapad." *Deutsche Welle* (2022). https://www.dw.com/ru/mediaforum-dw-zheleznyj-zanaves-vozvodjat-s-obeih-storon/a-62206885.

Butler, Shane. *The Ancient Phonograph*. Princeton: Princeton University Press, 2015.

Calotescu, Virgil, and Pantelie Tuțuleasa. *Reenactment (Reconstituirea)*. Bucharest: Arhiva Națională de Filme Jilava, Ministerul de Interne, Studioul Documentar Sahia, 1959.

Campt, Tina. *Image Matters: Archive, Photography, and the African Diaspora in Europe*. Durham, NC: Duke University Press, 2012.

———. *Listening to Images*. Durham, NC: Duke University Press, 2017.

Capitain, Wouter. *Postcolonial Polyphony: Edward Said's Work in Music*. Amsterdam: University of Amsterdam, 2021.

Cartwright, Ryan Lee. "Out of Sorts: A Queer Crip in the Archive." *Feminist Review* 125, no. 1 (2020): 62–69.

Cazan, Roxana. "Constructing Spaces of Dissent in Communist Romania: Ruined Bodies and Clandestine Spaces in Cristian Mungiu's '4 Months, 3 Weeks, and 2 Days' and Gabriela Adameșteanu's 'A Few Days in the Hospital.'" *Women's Studies Quarterly* 39 (2011): 93–112.

Central Intelligence Agency. "France: Defection of the Leftist Intellectuals." 1985; declassified 2011. Published electronically 13 March 2011. https://www.cia.gov/library/readingroom/docs/CIA-RDP86S00588R000300380001-5.PDF.

Cenușe, Constantin. "Concluzii de invinuire (Indictment Conclusions)." In *P 181 (40038)*, Fond Penal, 1–10. ACNSAS, Bucharest.

———. "Procès-verbal de interrogator, 23 September 1959 (Interrogation Transcript)." In *P 181 (Dosar nr. 40038)*, Fond Penal, 38–41. ACNSAS, Bucharest.

"Cercurile anglo-americane dezaprobă discursul d-lui Churchill." *Scânteia*, 9 March 1946.

Chandler, Adam. "An Old-New Lech Walesa Scandal." *The Atlantic*, 18 February 2016.

Christofferson, Michael Scott. *French Intellectuals against the Left: The Antitotalitarian Moment of the 1970s*. New York: Berghahn Books, 2004.

Churchill, Winston. *Memoirs of the Second World War*. Boston: Houghton Mifflin, 1959.

Cindrea-Nagy, Iuliana, Ágnes Hesz, James Kapaló, Dumitru Lisnic, Kinga Povedák, Anca Șincan, and Tatiana Vagramenko. "Hidden Galleries." http://hiddengalleries.eu/digitalarchive.

Clark, Katerina. *Moscow, the Fourth Rome: Stalinism, Cosmopolitanism, and the Evolution of Soviet Culture, 1931–1941*. Cambridge, MA: Harvard University Press, 2011.

Cohn, Edward. "Recidivism, Prophylaxis, and the KGB." In *The Secret Police and the Soviet System: New Archival Investigations*, edited by Michael David-Fox, 328–48. Pittsburgh: University of Pittsburgh Press, 2023.

Coleman, Kwami. "Free Jazz and the 'New Thing.'" *Journal of Musicology* 38 (2021): 261–95.

Consiliul de stat al Republicii Socialiste Romania. "Decret Nr. 770 din 1 octombrie 1966 pentru reglementarea întreruperii cursului sarcinii [Decree no. 770 from 1 October 1966 regulating the interruption of the course of pregnancy]." Buletinul Oficial 60. Bucharest, 1966.

"Conștiința lumii stă de veghe." *Scânteia*, 17 March 1946, 1–2.

Consulaire PARIS-DFAE. Email correspondence with Anna Krakus, 16 December 2009.

Crowley, David, James Kapaló, and Gabriela Nicolescu. "Introduction. Visual Ethics after Communism." *Martor* 26 (2021): 7–22.

Cvetkovich, Ann. *An Archive of Feelings: Trauma, Sexuality, and Lesbian Public Cultures*. Durham, NC: Duke University Press, 2003.

D 120 (Cultural Situation, Minorities). Fond Documentar. ACNSAS, Bucharest,.

D 21 Eterul (Radio Free Europe Problem File). Fond Documentar. ACNSAS, Bucharest.

D 008712. Fond Documentar. Vol. 1. ACNSAS, Bucharest.

D 013381, Naționaliști Germani (German Nationalists). Fond Documentar. 46 vols. ACNSAS, Bucharest.

Darwish, Ali. *Forensic Translation*. Melbourne: Writescope Publishers, 2012.

Daughtry, J. Martin. "Acoustic Palimpsests." In *Theorizing Sound Studies*, edited by Deborah Kapchan. Middletown, CT: Wesleyan University Press, 2017.

———. "Listening beyond Sound and Life: Reflections on Imagined Music." In *The Oxford Handbook of the Phenomenology of Music Cultures*, edited by Friedlind Riedel, Harris M. Berger, and David VanderHamm. Oxford, UK: Oxford University Press, 2022.

David-Fox, Michael. "Into and beyond the Stalinist Paradigm of Secret Policing." In *The Secret Police and the Soviet System: New Archival Investigations*, edited by Michael David-Fox, 3–23. Pittsburgh, PA: University of Pittsburgh Press, 2023.

Davis Center for Russian and Eurasian Studies. "Decolonization in Focus Seminar

Series" (2023). https://daviscenter.fas.harvard.edu/insights/announcing-decolonization-focus-seminar-series.

"Declarațiile generalissimului Stalin și Romania." *Scânteia*, 16 March 1946.

Defert, Daniel. "Chronologie." In *Dits et écrits*, 13–90. Paris: Gallimard, 2001.

———. "Chronology." In *A Companion to Foucault*, edited by Christopher Falzon, Timothy O'Leary, and Jana Sawicki, 11–83. Chichester, UK: Wiley & Sons 2003.

———. "Tunisia and Poland Are Always There in Foucault's Texts." Interview with Anna Krakus, 16 November and 14 December 2009.

Departamentul Securității Statului. "Instrucțiuni N. D-00180–1987." In *"Partiturile" Securității*, 639–64. 2007.

Derrida, Jacques. *De la grammatologie*. Paris: Éditions de Minuit, 1967.

———. "Living On." In *Deconstruction and Criticism*, edited by Alan Bloom and Paul de Man, 62–142. London: Continuum, 2004.

———. *Mal d'archive. Une impression freudienne*. Vol. 1. Paris: Galilée, 1995.

———. "Survivre." In *Parages*, 117–219. Paris: Galilée, 1986.

Dicționarul limbii române literare contemporane. Vol. 3. Bucharest: Editura Academiei, 1957.

Direcțiunea Generală a Siguranței Statului. "Organizarea, încadrarea si funcționarea Direcțiunii Generale a Siguranței Statului" (1947). In *"Partiturile" Securității*, 165–80.

Direcțiunea Regională a Securității Poporului. "Ordin Circular nr. 399 din 23 Decembrie 1948." In *"Partiturile" Securității*, 181–92.

Doboș, Corina. *Politica pronatalistă a regimului Ceaușescu: o perspectivă comparativă [The Pronatalist Policy of the Ceaușescu Regime: A Comparative Perspective]*. Iași: Polirom, 2010.

Dubow, Ben. "With Enemies Like Russia's Communists, Putin Doesn't Need Friends." *Europe's Edge*, 8 February 2022. https://cepa.org/russias-communists-ally-with-kremlin-over-ukraine/.

Dudek, Antoni, and Andrzej Paczkowski. "Poland." In *A Handbook of the Communist Security Apparatus in East Central Europe, 1944–1989*, edited by K. Persak and L. Kaminski, 221–83. Warsaw: IPN, 2005.

Dzukov, G. "Politika zakrytykh dverei." *Pravda* 113 (1962): 5. https://dlib.eastview.com/browse/doc/21506344.

Eliassen, Knut Ove. "The Archives of Michel Foucault." In *The Archive in Motion: New Conceptions of the Archive in Contemporary Thought and New Media Practices*, edited by Eivind Røssaak. Oslo: Novus forlag, 2010.

Emerson, Caryl. "Bakhtin and Women: A Non-Topic with Immense Implications." In *Fruits of Her Plume: Essays on Contemporary Russian Women's Culture*, edited by Helena Goscilo. Armonk, NY: M. E. Sharpe, 1993.

———. "Editor's Preface." In *Problems of Dostoevsky's Poetics*, xxix–xliii. Minneapolis: Minnesota University Press, 1984.

———. "Shklovsky's *ostranenie*, Bakhtin's *vnenakhodimost'* (How Distance Serves an Aesthetics of Arousal Differently from an Aesthetics Based on Pain)." *Poetics Today* 26, no. 4 (1 December 2005): 637–64.

Engelstein, Laura. "Combined Underdevelopment: Discipline and the Law in Imperial and Soviet Russia." In *Foucault and the Writing of History*, edited by Jan Goldstein, 220–36. Oxford, UK: Blackwell, 1994.

Eribon, Didier. *Michel Foucault*. Cambridge, MA: Harvard University Press, 1992.

Ernst, Wolfgang. *Das Rumoren der Archive*. Berlin: Merve, 2002.

Fairley, Brian. "Polyphony." In *Keywords in Antiracist Theory*. Forthcoming.

Farge, Arlette. *Le goût de l'archive*. Paris: Éditions du Seuil, 1989.

Federal Bureau of Investigation. *Subject: Foucault, Michel. FOI/PA 1358488-0*. FBI Freedom of Information/Privacy Acts Section.

Fedoseev, P. "Culisele planurilor de federalizare a Europei (Dela Kant și Rousseau to Winston Churchill) " *Contemporanul*, 4 January 1947, 7.

Fitzpatrick, Sheila. "Impact of the Opening of Soviet Archives on Western Scholarship on Soviet Social History." *Russian Review* 74, no. 3 (2015): 377–400.

———. *Tear Off the Masks! Identity and Imposture in Twentieth-Century Russia*. Princeton: Princeton University Press, 2005.

Foster, Hal. "An Archival Impulse." *October* 1, no. 110 (October 2004): 3–22.

Foucault, Michel. *The Archaeology of Knowledge*. Translated by A. M. Sheridan Smith. New York: Pantheon Books, 1972.

———. Conférence à Gdańsk en 1958: sur Apollinaire, manuscript autographe. Fonds Michel Foucault, NAF 28730. Bibliothèque Nationale de France, Archives et manuscrits.

———. *Discipline and Punish: The Birth of the Prison*. New York: Vintage Books, 1979.

———. Divers: Cruautés russes envers les confédérés polonais. Fonds Michel Foucault, NAF 28730. Bibliothèque Nationale de France, Archives et manuscrits.

———. *Histoire de la folie*. Exposé de soutenance. Fonds Michel Foucault, NAF 28730. Bibliothèque Nationale de France, Archives et manuscrits.

———. *The History of Sexuality*. Translated by Robert Hurley. 3 vols. New York: Pantheon Books, 1978.

———. "The Lives of Infamous Men." In *Power, Truth, Strategy*, edited by Meaghan Morris and Paul Patton, 76–91. Sydney: Feral Publications, 1979.

———. "Préface de l'édition originale. En marge d' Histoire de la folie à l'âge classique (1961)." In *Œuvres*, 660–69. Bibliothèque de la Pléiade. Paris: Gallimard, 2015.

———. "Preface to the 1961 Edition." Translated by Jonathan Murphy and Jean Khalfa. In *History of Madness*, edited by Jean Khalfa, xxvii–xxxvi. New York: Routledge, 2006.

———. "Réponse à une question." In *Dits et Écrits*. Paris: Gallimard, 1968.

———. Texte séminal. Michel Foucault, NAF 28730. Bibliothèque Nationale de France, Archives et manuscrits Fonds.

———. "Un si cruel savoir." In *Dits et écrits*, edited by Michel Foucault, 243–56. Paris: Gallimard, 2001 [1962].

Foucault, Michel, and Arlette Farge. *Disorderly Families: Infamous Letters from the Bastille Archives*. Minneapolis: University of Minnesota Press, 2016.

Galya, Lamara. "Sotrudnichestvo: Monument dlia Washingtona." *Nedelia* 18 (1988): 4–5. https://dlib.eastview.com/browse/doc/54126325.

Garton Ash, Timothy. *The File: A Personal History*. London: HarperCollins, 1997.

Ghani, Mariam, and Chitra Ganesh. "Radical Archives." New York University. http://apa.nyu.edu/event/radical-archives/.

Gilroy, Paul. *The Black Atlantic: Modernity and Double Consciousness*. Cambridge, MA: Harvard University Press, 1993.

Glaeser, Andreas. *Political Epistemics : The Secret Police, the Opposition, and the End of East German Socialism*. Chicago: University of Chicago Press, 2011.

Glajar, Valentina. "'Cristina' oder was in Herta Müllers Securitate Akte steht: Über Löcher und Fehlschlüsse einer Aktengeschichte ('Cristina' or What Is in Herta Müller's File: About Holes and Fallacies in a File Story)." *Monatshefte* 100, no. 2 (2018): 189–201.

———. "The Presence of the Unresolved Recent Past: Herta Müller and the Securitate." In *Herta Müller*, edited by Brigid Haines and Lyn Marven, 49–63. Oxford, UK: Oxford University Press, 2013.

———. *The Secret Police Dossier of Herta Müller*. Rochester, NY: Camden House, 2023.

Glebova, Aglaya. "A Visual History of the Gulag: Nine Theses." In *The Soviet Gulag: Evidence, Interpretation, and Comparison*, edited by Michael David-Fox, 162–69. Pittsburgh, PA: University of Pittsburgh Press, 2016.

Glissant, Édouard. *Poetics of Relation*. Ann Arbor: University of Michigan Press, 1997.

Gogotishvili, L. A. "Sootnoshenie mezhdu polifonicheskim romanom M. Bakhtina i muzykal'noi polifoniei." *Voprosy filosofii* 3 (March 2019): 143–56.

Goldstein, Jan, and Rudy Koshar. "Foucault and Social History: Comments on 'Combined Underdevelopment.'" *American Historical Review* 98, no. 2 (1993): 354–81.

Graziosi, Andrea. "The New Soviet Archival Sources." *Cahiers du monde russe* 40, nos. 1–2 (1999): 13–63.

Gullotta, Andrea. "Beauty in Hell: Culture in the Gulag." Glasgow: The Hunterian, 2017.

Haines, Brigid, and Lyv Marven. "Introduction." In *Herta Müller*, edited by Brigid Haines and Lyv Marven, 1–15. Oxford, UK: Oxford University Press, 2013.

Halfin, Igal. "Poetics in the Archives: The Quest for "True" Bolshevik Documents." *Jahrbücher für Geschichte Osteuropas* 51, no. 1 (2003): 84–89.

———. *Terror in My Soul: Communist Autobiographies on Trial*. Cambridge, MA: Harvard University Press, 2003.

Harbutt, Fraser. *The Iron Curtain: Churchill, America, and the Origins of the Cold War*. New York: Oxford University Press, 1986.

Hartman, Saidiya. *Scenes of Subjection: Terror, Slavery, and Self-Making in Nineteenth-Century America*. New York: Oxford University Press, 1997.
———. "Venus in Two Acts." *Small Axe* 12, no. 2 (June 2008): 1–14.
Havel, Vaclav. *The Power of the Powerless*. New York: Vintage, 2018.
Hellbeck, Jochen. *Revolution on My Mind: Writing a Diary under Stalin*. Cambridge, MA: Harvard University Press, 2006.
Henckel von Donnersmarck, Florian. *The Lives of Others*. Sydney: Roadshow Entertainment, 2007.
Higgins, Dick. "Intermedia." *Leonardo* 34, no. 1 (2001): 49–54.
Hirshfield, Jane. *Come, Thief*. New York: Alfred A. Knopf, 2011.
———. *Hiddenness, Uncertainty, Surprise*. Hexham, UK: Bloodaxe Books, 2008.
Hogan, Linda. *The Radiant Lives of Animals*. Boston: Beacon Press, 2020.
Hoisington, Sona. *A Plot of Her Own: The Female Protagonist in Russian Literature*. Evanston, IL: Northwestern University Press, 1995.
Hole, Terry. "Roman Noir." In *Handbook of the Gothic*, edited by Marie Mulvey-Roberts, 207–25. New York: New York University Press, 2009.
Hossu-Longin, Lucia. *Memorialul durerii*. Bucharest: Televiziunea Română, 1991.
I 184945 (DUI Richard Wagner). Fond Informativ. ACNSAS, Bucharest.
I 233477 (DUI Herta Müller). Fond Informativ. Vols. 1–3. ACNSAS, Bucharest.
I 234089 (DUI Rolf Bossert). Fond Informativ. ACNSAS, Bucharest.
Iepan, Florin. "Children of the Decree." Documentary film. Germany, Romania, 2004.
"Incheere [Ending]." In *P 181 (40038)*, Fond Penal, 89–96. ACNSAS, Bucharest.
"Îndărătul cuvântării d-lui Churchill se ascunde reacțiunea." *Scânteia*, 14 March 1946, 4.
Inspectoratul Județean Timiș al Ministerului de Interne, Serviciul I. A. "Raport, 16.XI.1985." In *D 013381*, 79–107. ACNSAS, Bucharest.
Inspectoratul Județean Timiș al Ministerului de Interne, Serviciul I/A. "Raport, 12.XII.1981." In *D 013381*, 277–86. ACNSAS, Bucharest.
———. "Raport, 16.XI.1985." In *D 013381*, 79–107. ACNSAS, Bucharest.
———. "Raport, 28.02.1978." In *D 013381*, 157–61. ACNSAS, Bucharest.
Interne, Ministerul Afacerilor. "Ordonanța [Order], 15 November 1959." In *P 181*. Fond Penal, 1–2. ACNSAS, Bucharest.
"Interv'iu tov. I. V. Stalina s korrespondentom 'Pravdy' otnositel'no rechi g. Cherchillia." *Pravda*, 14 March 1946, 1.
Iorga, N. "Ce se duce cu noi din Basarabia." *Neamul Românesc* 147 (7 July 1940): 1.
Irving, David. *Colonial Counterpoint: Music in Early Modern Manila*. Oxford, UK: Oxford University Press, 2010.
Iur'ev, Viktor, and Evgenii Maslov. "My zhiviem v epokhu peremen." *Argumenty I fakty*, 15 June 2022, 2.
Jackson, Shannon. *Lines of Activity: Performance, Historiography, Hull-House Domesticity*. Ann Arbor: University of Michigan Press, 2000.
Jacobs, Arthur. "Neurocognitive Poetics: Methods and Models for Investigating the

Neuronal and Cognitive-affective Bases of Literature Reception." *Frontiers in Human Neuroscience* 9, no. 186 (2015).

———. "Towards a Neurocognitive Poetics Model of Literary Reading." In *Towards a Cognitive Neuroscience of Natural Language Use*, edited by Roel Willems, 135–95. Cambridge, UK: Cambridge University Press, 2015.

Jacobs, Arthur, and Roel Willems. "The Fictive Brain: Neurocognitive Correlates of Engagement in Literature." *Review of General Psychology* 22, no. 2 (2018): 147–60.

Johnson, Barbara. *Mother Tongues: Sexuality, Trials, Motherhood, Translation*. Cambridge, MA: Harvard University Press, 2003.

Johnson, Juliet. "2023 President's Address: De-centering Russia: Challenges and Opportunities." Blog post. *ASEEES Blog*, 4 December 2023. https://www.aseees.org/news-events/aseees-blog-feed/2023-presidents-address-de-centering-russia-challenges-and.

Jordania, Joseph. "What Is Polyphony, or How Should We Define It?" International Research Center for Traditional Polyphony. https://polyphony.ge/en/home-2/.

Julian, Kamil. "In Search of Michel Foucault's Polish Lover." *DIK FAGAZINE* 8 (2011): 134–43.

Kapaló, James. "Feasting and Fasting: The Evidential Character of Material religion in Secret Police Archives." In *The Secret Police and the Religious Underground in Communist and Post-Communist Eastern Europe* edited by James Kapaló and Kinga Povedák, 254–72. London: Routledge, 2021.

Kapaló, James, and Gabriela Nicolescu. "Faith-Trust-Secrecy: Religions through the Lenses of the Secret Police." 2021. https://faithtrustsecrecy.

Kapaló, James, and Tatiana Vagramenko, eds. *Hidden Galleries: Material Religion in the Secret Police Archives in Central and Eastern Europe*. Berlin: LitVerlag, 2020.

Ketelaar, Eric. "Archival Turns and Returns." In *Research in the Archival Multiverse*, edited by Anne Gilliland, Sue McKemmish, and Andrew Lau, 228–68. Melbourne: Monash University Press, 2018.

King, Katie. *Networked Reenactments: Stories Transdisciplinary Knowledges Tell*. Durham, NC: Duke University Press, 2011.

Kligman, Gail. *The Politics of Duplicity: Controlling Reproduction in Ceaușescu's Romania*. Berkeley: University of California Press, 1998.

Kligman, Gail, and Katherine Verdery. *Peasants under Siege: The Collectivization of Romanian Agriculture, 1949–1962*. Princeton: Princeton University Press, 2011.

Kneepkens, Eleonore, and Rolf A. Zwaan. "Emotions and Literary Text Comprehension." *Poetics* 23 (1995): 125–38.

Kosslyn, Stephen M. *Image and Brain: The Resolution of the Imagery Debate*. Cambridge, MA: MIT Press, 1994.

Kotkin, Stephen. "The State—Is It Us? Memoirs, Archives, and Kremlinologists." *Russian Review* 61, no. 1 (2002): 35–51.

KR 08/137 (Karmel). IPN, Krakow.

Krakus, Anna, and Cristina Vatulescu. "Foucault in Poland: A Silent Archive." *Diacritics* 47, no. 2 (2019): 72–105.

Kriuchkova, Marina. "Za zheleznym zanavesom." *Trud* 15–16 (2022): 7–7. https://dlib.eastview.com/browse/doc/74691759.

Kukryniksy and S. Marshak. "Komanda podzhigatelei voiny." *Pravda*, 7 November 1946.

Kulish, Savva. "'Zheleznyi zanaves'—vzgliad iz dvukh stolits." *Izvestiia* 122 (1998). https://dlib.eastview.com/browse/doc/3166605.

Kurnosova, Olha. "Seriozni protesty v Rosii naiimovirnishi u veresni." *Dim* (2022). https://kanaldom.tv/uk/serjozni-protesty-u-rosiyi-najimovirnishi-u-veresni-kurnosova/.

Kurpios, Paweł. "Poczukiwani, poczukiwane. Geje i lesbijki a rzeczywistość PRL." University of Wrocław, 2002.

Lakoff, George, and Mark Johnson. *Philosophy in the Flesh: The Embodied Mind and Its Challenge to Western Thought*. New York: Basic Books, 1999.

Latour, Bruno. "How to Talk about the Body? The Normative Dimension of Science Studies." *Body & Society* 10, nos. 2–3 (2004): 205–29.

Laub, Dori. "An Event without a Witness: Truth, Testimony, and Survival." In *Testimony: Crises of Witnessing in Literature, Psychoanalysis, and History*, edited by Shoshana Felman and Dori Laub, 75–92. London: Routledge, 1992.

Laurent, Jenny. "Foucault et la littérature. Une passante." *Critique* (December 2016): 982–92.

"Lavrov zaiavil o vozmozhnostiakh Rossii pazvivat'sia i za "zheleznym zanavesom." *Interfaks* (2022). https://www.interfax.ru/russia/825829.

Laza, Laura. "Die Übersetzung als Mittel der Manipulation." In *Aus den Giftschränken des Kommunismus*, edited by M. Nowotnick and F. Kührer-Wielach, 205–15. Regensburg: Friedrich Pustet Verlag, 2018.

Lazăr, Traian. "1940. Perdeaua de fier precede cortina de fier." In *Bătălia pentru Basarabia 1941–1944*, edited by Gh. Buzatu, 23–28. Bucharest: Mica Valahie.

Leach, Elizabeth Eva. "Performing Manuscripts." In *Performing Medieval Text*, edited by Ardis Butterfield, Henry Hope, and Pauline Souleau, 11–19. Oxford, UK: Legenda, 2017.

Lepecki, André. "The Body As Archive: Will to Re-Enact and the Afterlives of Dances." *Dance Research Journal* 42, no. 2 (2010): 28–48.

Levchenko, Oleksandr. "Sytuatsiia u vidnosynakh Zakhodu i Rosii blyzka do 'zaliznoi zavisy.'" *Ukrinform* (2021). https://www.ukrinform.ua/rubric-world/3260595-situacia-u-vidnosinah-zahodu-i-rosii-blizka-do-zaliznoi-zavisi-posol.html.

Livshits, Dmitrii. *Fenomen improvizatsii v dzhaze [The phenomenon of Improvisation in Jazz]*. Nizhnyi Novgorod: Nizhgorod State Conservatory, 2003.

Lovejoy, Alice. *Army Film and the Avant Garde: Cinema and Experiment in the Czechoslovak Military*. Bloomington: Indiana University Press, 2015.

Luehrmann, Sonja. *Religion in Secular Archives: Soviet Atheism and Historical Knowledge*. New York: Oxford University Press, 2015.
Lunacharsky, Anatoly. "O 'mnogogolosnosti' Dostoevskogo [About Dostoevsky's 'Multivoicedness']." *Novyi mir* 10 (1929).
Lusztig, Irene. *Reconstruction*. Documentary film. Komsomol Films, 2002.
Macey, David. *The Lives of Michel Foucault*. London: Hutchinson, 1993.
MacKenzie, John. "Occidentalism: Counterpoint and Counter-Polemic." *Journal of Historical Geography* 19 (1993): 339–44.
Maerskii, V. "Dalekaia, bliskaia." *Pravda* 232 (1960): 6–6. https://dlib.eastview.com/browse/doc/21425560.
Mantoux, Paul. *Les délibérations du Conseil des quatre*. 2 vols. Paris: CNRS, 1955.
"Marea Britanie și întreaga lume nu au nici un viitor fără o înțelegere cu Uniunea Sovietică." *Scânteia*, 10 March 1946, 8.
Marshall, Daniel, and Zeb Tortorici. "Introduction: (Re)Turning to the Queer Archives." In *Turning Archival: The Life of the Historical in Queer Studies*, edited by Daniel Marshall and Zeb Tortorici, 1–30. Durham, NC: Duke University Press, 2022.
Marven, Lyv. "Life and Literature: Autobiography, Referentiality, and Intertextuality in Herta Müller's Work." In *Herta Müller*, edited by Brigid Haines and Lyn Marven, 204–23. Oxford, UK: Oxford University Press, 2013.
Massumi, Brian. *Politics of Affect*. Cambridge, UK: Polity Press, 2015.
Mawani, Renisa. "Law's Archive." *Annual Review of Law and Social Science* 8 (2012): 337–65.
Medvedkin, Alexander. "294 dnia na kolesakh." In *Iz istorii kino*, edited by Institut istorii iskusstv, 32–56. Moscow: Iskusstvo, 1977.
Michelet, Jules. "Préface de l'Histoire de France." In *Oeuvres complètes, Tome IV*. Paris: Flammarion, 1974 [1869].
Miller, Jim. *The Passion of Michel Foucault*. New York: Simon & Schuster, 1993.
Ministerul Afacerilor Interne. "Directiva asupra organizării evidenței operative de către organele Securității Statului, a elementelor dușmănoase din Republica Populară Română (Directive regulating the organization of operative database by the organs of State Security, concerning the inimical elements in the Romanian Popular Republic)." In *"Partiturile" Securității*, 235–51.
———. "Plan de măsuri [II] privind desfășurarea filmării unor momente principale în legătura cu săvârșirea atacului banditesc asupra mașinii băncii RPR (Plan of Action, II)." In *P 181*, Fond Penal, 127–30. ACNSAS, Bucharest.
———. "Plan de măsuri I (Plan of Action, I)." In *P 181 (40038)*, Fond Penal, 9–15. ACNSAS, Bucharest.
———. "Titlurile filmului (The Titles of the Film—Final Script), 03.05.1960." In *P 181 (40038)*, 81–90. ACNSAS, Bucharest.
Ministerul de Interne, Timiș, Serviciul 1/A. "RAPORT cu propuneri de deschiderea dosarului de urmărire informativă privind pe numita KARL HERTA din Timișoara, 24.II.1983 (REPORT with proposals to open an informative trailing

file concerning KARL HERTA from Timişoara)." In *I 233477*, 1, Fond Informativ. ACNSAS, Bucharest.

Mirer, Maik. "Eto ne lechitsia." *Novaia gazeta. Evropa* (2022). https://dlib.eastview.com/browse/doc/77677506.

Monson, Ingrid. *Saying Something: Jazz Improvisation and Interaction*. Chicago: University of Chicago Press, 1996.

Moretti, Franco. *Distant Reading*. London: Verso, 2013.

———. "The Slaughterhouse of Literature." *MLQ: Modern Language Quarterly* 61, no. 1 (2000).

Morgan, David. "Material Analysis in the Study of Religion." In *Materiality and Study of Religion: The Stuff of the Sacred*, edited by Tim Hutchings and Joanne McKenzie, 14–32. London: Routledge, 2017.

Morson, Gary Saul, and Caryl Emerson. *Mikhail Bakhtin: Creation of a Prosaics*. Stanford: Stanford University Press, 1990.

Müller, Herta. *The Appointment*. Translated by Michael Hulse. Edited by Philip Boehm. New York: Picador, 2001.

———. *Cristina und ihre Attrappe, oder, Was (nicht) in den Akten der Securitate steht*. Göttingen: Wallstein, 2009.

———. "An diesem Tag." In *Drückender Tango [Oppressive Tango]*, 62–63. Bucharest: Kriterion, 1984.

———. *The Land of Green Plums*. Translated by Michael Hoffman. New York: Metropolitan Books, 1996.

———. *Nadirs*. Translated by Sieglinde Lug. Lincoln: University of Nebraska Press, 1999.

———. "Nobel Lecture: Every Word Knows Something of a Vicious Circle." 7 December 2009. http://nobelprize.org/nobel_prizes/literature/laureates/2009/muller-lecture_en.html.

———. "Securitate in All But Name." (2009): 1–11. http://www.signandsight.com/service/1910.html.

———. "Unsere Stadt (Our Town)." In *Phlastersteine*, edited by Nikolaus Berwanger, Eduard Schneider, and Horst Samson, 123–25. Timisoara, 1982.

———. "When We Don't Speak, We Become Unbearable, and When We Do, We Make Fools of Ourselves. Can Literature Bear Witness?" Translated by Philip Boehm. In *Witness Literature*, edited by Horace Engdahl, 15–32. Singapore: World Scientific Publishing, 2002.

———. "When We Don't Speak, We Become Unbearable, and When We Do, We Make Fools of Ourselves. Can Literature Bear Witness?" Lecture. Deutsches Haus, New York University, 3 May 2012.

Muller, James. *Churchill's "Iron Curtain" Speech Fifty Years Later*. Columbia: University of Missouri Press, 1999.

Müller, Jürgen E. *Media Encounters and Media Theories*. Münster: Nodus Publikationen, 2008.

Musatova, V. *This Concerns Us All (Eto trevozhit vsekh)*. Moscow: TsKDK, 1960.

Nabliudatel'. "Na mezhdunarodnye temy." *Izvestiia*, 13 June 1946.
National Institute of Biomedical Imaging. "X-rays." 2022. https://www.nibib.nih.gov/science-education/science-topics/x-ray.
Nazarov, Oleg. "Zheleznyi zanaves." *Istorik* 75 (2021). https://историк.рф/journal/75/zheleznyj-zanaves.html.
NBC News. "Zelenskyy: 'New Iron Curtain' Separates Russia from 'Civilized World.'" 24 February 2022.
Ndai, Ali. "Razvivat' sotrudnichestvo." *Pravda* 244 (1976): 1. https://dlib.eastview.com/browse/doc/21510865.
Nebunescu, Oana Panțel. 1 July 2022, personal communication with the author.
Nikulin, L. "Zheleznyi zanaves." *Literaturnaia gazeta*, 13 January 1930, 1.
"Noi suntem apărătorii țărilor mici." *Contemporanul*, 11 October 1946, 1.
"Notă sursa 'Barbu,' 26.III.1981." In *I 233477* 2–3, Fond Informativ. ACNSAS, Bucharest.
"Notă sursa 'Voicu,' 16.III.1982." In *I 233477*, Fond Informativ, 5. ACNSAS, Bucharest.
"On This Day (Notă sursa "Petra," 22.III.1983)." In *I 233477*, Fond Informativ, 9. ACNSAS, Bucharest.
"Otchipentsy." *Kommersant* (22 February 2022): 1.
Ox, Jack, and Jacques Mandelbrojt. "Intersenses/Intermedia: A Theoretical Perspective." *Leonardo* 34, no. 1 (2001): 47–48.
P 181 (40038). Fond Penal. Vols. 1–27. 1959. ACNSAS, Bucharest.
P 336 (Dosar nr. 118988). Fond Penal. ACNSAS, Bucharest.
"Pacea văzută de presa străină." *Contemporanul*, 11 October 1946, 3.
Paech, Joachim, and Jens Schröter. *Intermedialität analog/digital: Theorien—Methoden—Analysen*. Munich: Wilhelm Fink, 2008.
Pavlova, Aza. "Dorogu osilit imushchii." *Krokodil* 11 (1991): 10. https://dlib.eastview.com/browse/book/66956.
Petrescu, Cristina. "When Dictatorships Fail to Deprive of Dignity: Herta Müller's 'Romanian Period.'" In *Herta Müller: Poetics and Aesthetics*, edited by Bettina Brandt and Valentina Glajar, 57–86. Lincoln: University of Nebraska Press, 2013.
Petrov, Rem. "Pogranichnaia situatsiia." *Krokodil* 1 (1990): 4. https://dlib.eastview.com/browse/book/66982.
Pharr, Robert F. Reid. *Archives of Flesh: African America, Spain, and Post-Humanist Critique*. New York: New York University Press, 2016.
Piecuch, Henryk. *Bruderszaft ze śmiercią*. Warsaw: Agencja Wydawnicza CB, 1999.
Pirenne, Raphaël, and Alexander Streitberger. *Heterogeneous Objects: Intermedia and Photography after Modernism*. Leuven: Leuven University Press, 2013.
Plagmann, Natalia Klimova. "Human Documents on Screen and Stage: A Contrapuntal Reading of Post-Soviet Documentary." PhD diss., Princeton University, 2023.
Plamadeala, Cristina. "Dossierveillance in Communist Romania: Collaboration with the Securitate, 1945-1989." In *Making Surveillance States: Transnational*

Histories, edited by Rob Heynen and Emily van der Meulen, 215–36. Toronto: University of Toronto Press, 2019.

Plamper, Jan. "Archival Revolution or Illusion? Historicizing the Russian Archives and Our Work in Them." *Jahrbücher für Geschichte Osteuropas* 51, no. 1 (2003): 57–69.

———. "Foucault's Gulag." *Kritika* 3, no. 2 (2002): 255–80.

"Poftiți, vă rog, prichindeilor, să vă federalizăm!". *Contemporanul*, 4 January 1947, 3.

"Politica demografică a regimului Ceaușescu." In *Raport Final*, edited by Dorin Dobrincu, Vladimir Tismăneanu, and Cristian Vasile, 421–36. Bucharest: Humanitas, 2007.

Pop-Eleches, Cristian. "The Impact of an Abortion Ban on Socioeconomic Outcomes of Children: Evidence from Romania." *Journal of Political Economy* 114, no. 4 (2006): 744–73.

Povedák, Kinga. "Methodological Notes on Visual Ethics: 'Choosing Not to Reveal.'" *Martor* 26 (2021): 164–72.

"Presa română și declarațiile generalissimului Stalin." *Scânteia*, 27 March 1946.

Pucci, Molly. *Security Empire: The Secret Police in Communist Eastern Europe*. New Haven: Yale University Press, 2020.

R 285953. Fond Retea. ACNSAS, Bucharest.

Rajewsky, Irina O. *Intermedialität*. Tübingen: Francke, 2002.

Raleigh, Donald J. "Doing Soviet History: The Impact of the Archival Revolution." *Russian Review* 61, no. 1 (2002): 16–24.

Rancière, Jacques. *The Emancipated Spectator*. London: Verso, 2011.

———. *The Politics of Aesthetics: The Distribution of the Sensible*. London: Continuum, 2004.

———. *Politics of Literature*. Translated by Julie Rose. Cambridge, UK: Polity, 2011.

Raport de activitate privind anul 2011. Bucharest: CNSAS, 2012.

"Rech' Cherchillia v Fultone." *Pravda*, 11 March 1946.

"Rech' Cherchillia v Fultone [Churchill's Speech in Fulton]." *Pravda Ukrainy* (14 March 1946): 4.

Reid-Pharr, Robert. *Archives of Flesh: African America, Spain, and Post-humanist Critique*. New York: New York University Press, 2016.

Rezantseva, Maria. "Dzhaz kak nezavershaemoe iskusstvo [Jazz as the Unfinalizable Art]." *Kontekst i refleksiya: filosofiya o mire i cheloveke [Context and Reflection: Philosophy of the World and Human Being]* 8, no. 2A (2019): 248–56.

"Rf robyt sobi zaliznu zavisu, yak kolys radianskyi soiuz, ne treba yii zavazhaty—Zelenskyi." *Ukrinform*, 2022. https://www.ukrinform.ua/rubric-ato/3476903-rf-robit-sobi-zalizni-zavisu-ak-kolis-radanskij-souz-ne-treba-ij-zavazati-zelenskij.html.

Rid, Thomas. *Active Measures: The Secret History of Disinformation and Political Warfare*. New York: Farrar, Straus & Giroux, 2020.

Roberts, Geoffrey. *Stalin's Library: A Dictator and His Books*. New Haven: Yale University Press, 2022.

Robinson, Dylan. *Hungry Listening: Resonant Theory for Indigenous Sound Studies.* Minneapolis: University of Minnesota Press, 2020.
Rockhill, Gabriel. "The CIA Reads French Theory: On the Intellectual Labor of Dismantling the Cultural Left." *Los Angeles Review of Books*, 28 February 2017.
"Rossiia otkazalac' perezhit' iz-za vozmozhnosti novovo zheleznogo zanavesa." *lenta.ru,* 2022. https://lenta.ru/news/2022/03/02/iron_wall_2/.
Rozanov, Vasily. *Apokalipsis nashevo vremeni.* Sergeev Posad, 1918.
Roziers, Étienne Burin des. "Une rencontre à Varsovie." *Le Débat* 41 (September–October 1986): 133–34.
Rubery, Matthew. *Reader's Block: A History of Reading Differences.* Stanford: Stanford University Press, 2022.
Rukhadze, A. "Gde 'zheleznyi zanaves'?" *Literaturnaia gazeta* 9 (1968): 16. https://dlib.eastview.com/browse/doc/26705104.
Rylko, Z. "Apollinaire na Uniwersytecie Warszawskim." *Przegląd Humanistyczny* 2 (1959): 197–201.
Ryziński, Remigiusz. *Foucault w Warszawie.* Warsaw: Wydwnictwo Dowody Na Istnienie, 2017.
Said, Edward. *Culture and Imperialism.* New York: Knopf, 1993.
———. "Michel Foucault, 1926–1984." In *After Foucault: Humanistic Knowledge, Postmodern Challenges,* edited by Jonathan Arac, 1–11. New Brunswick, NJ: Rutgers University Press, 1988.
Șăineanu, Lazăr. *Dicționar universal al limbei române.* Craiova: Editura Scrisul Românesc, 1929.
Samuels, Ellen. "Six Ways of Looking at Crip Time." *Disability Studies Quarterly* 37, no. 3 (2017).
Sanborn, Joshua. "Cybernetics and Surveillance: The Secret Police Enter the Computer Age." In *The Secret Police and the Soviet System: New Archival Investigations,* edited by Michael David-Fox, 382–405. Pittsburgh, PA: Pittsburgh University Press, 2023.
Scarlat, Sandra, and Simona Chitan. "Vedetele Epocii de Aur aveau liber la avort [The Celebrities of the Golden Age Were Allowed Abortions]." *Evenimentul Zilei,* 19 May 2005.
Scarry, Elaine. *Dreaming by the Book.* New York: Farrar, Straus & Giroux, 1999.
Schmidt, Otto I. Ul evich. *Bol'shaia sovetskaia entsiklopediia.* 65 vols. Vol. 25. Moscow: Sovetskaia entsiklopediia, 1932.
Scott, James. *Weapons of the Weak: Everyday Forms of Peasant Resistance.* New Haven: Yale University Press, 1987.
Sedgwick, Eve Kosofky. "Paranoid Reading and Reparative Reading, or, You're So Paranoid, You Probably Think This Essay Is about You." In *Touching Feeling: Affect, Pedagogy, Performativity,* 123–52. Durham, NC: Duke University Press, 2003.
Semenov, I. "Gamlet." *Krokodil* 35 (1955). https://dlib.eastview.com/browse/book/67820.

Sharpe, Jenny. *Immaterial Archives: An African Diaspora Poetics of Loss*. Evanston, IL: Northwestern University Press, 2020.

Shentalinskii, Vitalii. *Les surprises de la Loubianka. Retour dans les archives littéraires du K.G.B.* Paris: R. Laffont, 1996.

Shevchenko, Olga, and Oksana Sarkisova. "The Album as Performance: Notes on the Limits of the Visible." In *Russian Performances: Word, Object, Action*, edited by Julie Cassiday Julie A. Buckler, and Boris Wolfson, 43–53. Madison: University of Wisconsin Press, 2018.

Shipilin, Pavel. "'Zheleznyi zanaves.'" *Sovershenno sekretno* (2022): 1–3. https://dlib.eastview.com/browse/doc/74933845.

Shklovsky, Viktor. *O teorii prozy*. Moscow: Federatsiia, 1929.

Shvetsov, S. A. "O delegatsiakh i institutsiakh." *Krokodil* 8 (1956): 10. https://dlib.eastview.com/browse/book/67829.

Siani-Davis, Peter. *The Romanian Revolution of December 1989*. Ithaca, NY: Cornell University Press, 2007.

Silva, Denise Ferreira da. *Toward a Global Idea of Race*. Minneapolis: University of Minnesota Press, 2007.

Șincan, Anca. "Ethical Questions in Researching the Religious Underground in Romania's Secret Police Archives, Part I–II." Blog post. *Jordan Center Blog*. /https://jordanrussiacenter.org/blog/our-story-ethical-questions-on-researching-the-religious-underground-in-the-secret-police-archives-part-i.

Sobchack, Vivian. *Carnal Thoughts: Embodiment and Moving Image Culture*. Berkeley: University of California Press, 2004.

Solomon, Alexandru. *Marele jaf comunist [The Great Communist Bank Robbery]*. Libra Film: Bucharest, 2004.

Spielmann, Yvonne. "Intermedia and Electronic Images." *Leonardo* 34, no. 1 (2001): 55–61.

Spivak, Gayatri Chakravorty. *A Critique of Postcolonial Reason: Toward a History of the Vanishing Present*. Cambridge, MA: Harvard University Press, 1999.

———. "The Rani of Sirmur: An Essay in Reading the Archives." *History and Theory* 24, no. 3 (1985): 247–72.

Stan, Lavinia. "Poland." In *Transitional Justice in Eastern Europe and the Former Soviet Union: Reckoning with the Communist Past*, edited by Lavinia Stan, 76–101. London: Routledge, 2008.

Stan, Lavinia, and Nadya Nedelsky. "Entries on Transitional Justice Debates, Controversies, and Key Questions." In *Encyclopedia of Transitional Justice*, edited by Lavinia Stan, and Nadya Nedelsky, 112–279 (chap. 2). Cambridge, UK: Cambridge University Press, 2014.

Starr, Gabrielle. *Feeling Beauty: The Neuroscience of Aesthetic Experience*. Cambridge, MA: MIT Press, 2013.

Steedman, Carolyn. *Dust: The Archive and Cultural History*. New Brunswick, NJ: Rutgers University Press, 2002.

Steinhardt, Nicolae. *Jurnalul Fericirii*. Cluj: Dacia, 1997.

Stoekl, Allan. "Herta Müller: Writing and Betrayal." In *Herta Müller: Politics and Aesthetics*, edited by Bettina Brandt and Valentina Glajar, 15–19. Lincoln: University of Nebraska Press, 2013.

Stoler, Ann Laura. *Along the Archival Grain: Epistemic Anxieties and Archival Common Sense*. Princeton: Princeton University Press, 2009.

subReal, Călin Dan, and Iosif Király. "5 Suitcases." http://www.plueschow.de/fellows/subreal/suitcases.html.

Suna-Koro, Kristine. *In Counterpoint: Diaspora, Postcoloniality, and Sacramental Theology*. Eugene, OR: Pickwick, 2017.

Sychev, A. A. "M. M. Bakhtin: zhizn' na fone epokhi." *Gumanitarii* 33 (2016): 38–48.

Szporer, Michael. "The Security Forces and Polish Communism: Reclaiming History from Myth." *Journal of Cold War Studies* 9, no. 1 (January 2007): 88–95.

Szulc, Lukas. "Queer in Poland: Under Construction." In *Queer in Europe: Contemporary Case Studies*, edited by Lisa Robert and Gillett Downing. Farnham, UK: Ashgate, 2011.

Tănase, Stelian. *Anatomia mistificării* Bucharest: Humanitas, 2003.

Tarle, E. "Po povodu rechi Cherchillia." *Gudok*, 13 March 1946, 4.

———. "Po povodu rechi Cherchillia." *Izvestiia*, 12 March 1946.

Taussig, Michael. *Defacement: Public Secrecy and the Labor of the Negative*. Stanford: Stanford University Press, 1999.

———. "Transgression." In *Critical Terms for Religious Studies*, edited by Mark C. Taylor, 349–64. Chicago: University of Chicago Press, 1998.

Taylor, Diana. *The Archive and the Repertoire: Performing Cultural Memory in the Americas*. Durham, NC: Duke University Press, 2003.

Tkaczyk, Viktoria. *Thinking with Sound*. Chicago: University of Chicago Press, 2023.

Tomashevsky, Boris. *Teoriia literatury: poetika*. Leningrad: Gos. izd-vo, 1925.

Tomasik, Krzysztof. *GEJEREL: Mniejszości seksualne w PRL-u*. Warsaw: Krytyka Polityczna, 2012.

Tortorici, Zeb. *Sins against Nature: Sex and Archives in Colonial New Spain*. Durham, NC: Duke University Press, 2018.

Totok, William. "Informatorul şi laureata Premiului Nobel [The Informer and the Nobel Prize Laureate]." *dw.de* (2010). http://www.dw.de/dw/article/0,,5115182,00.html.

Trebici, Vladimir. *Genocid si Demografie [Genocide and Demography]*. Bucharest: Humanitas, 1991.

Trouillot, Michel-Rolph. *Silencing the Past: Power and the Production of History*. Boston: Beacon Press, 1995.

Tubiana, M. "Wilhelm Conrad Röntgen et la découverte des rayons X [Wilhelm Conrad Röntgen and the Discovery of X-rays]." *Bulletin de l'Académie nationale de medecine* 180, no. 1 (1996): 97–108.

Uitz, Renata. "Communist Secret Services on the Screen: The Duna-gate Scandal in and beyond the Hungarian Media." In *Past for the Eyes: East European Repre-*

sentations of Communism in Cinema and Museums after 1989, edited by Oksana Sarkisova and Peter Apor. Budapest: Central European University Press, 2008.

UNESCO. "Georgian Polyphonic Singing." *Intangible Cultural Heritage* (2008). https://ich.unesco.org/en/RL/georgian-polyphonic-singing-00008.

"Universal Database of Russian Newspapers." Minneapolis: East View Publications, 1999.

"(Untitled: Cell-mate Informer Reports)." In *P 181 (40038)*, Fond Penal. ACNSAS, Bucharest.

"V Rossii zablokiruiut Instagram." *Zerkalo nedeli* (2022). https://dlib.eastview.com/browse/doc/74863300.

Vagramenko, Tatiana. "KGB 'Evangelism': Agents and Jehovah's Witnesses in Soviet Ukraine." *Kritika* 22, no. 4 (Fall 2021): 757–86.

Vagramenko, Tatiana, and Gabriela Nicolescu. "The Hand at Work or How the KGB File Leaks in the Exhibition." *Martor* 26 (2021): 24–46.

Varela, Francisco, Evan Thompson, and Eleanor Rosch. *The Embodied Mind: Cognitive Science and Human Experience*. Cambridge, MA: MIT Press, 2016.

Vatulescu, Cristina. "The Mug-Shot and the Close-up: Identification and Visual Pedagogy in Secret Police Film." In *The Secret Police and the Soviet System: New Archival Investigations*, edited by Michael David-Fox. Pittsburgh, PA: University of Pittsburgh Press, 2023.

———. "A Note on Foucault." In *Police Aesthetics*, 53–54. Stanford: Stanford University Press, 2010.

———. *Police Aesthetics: Literature, Film, and the Secret Police in Soviet Times*. Stanford: Stanford University Press, 2010.

———. "Secret Police Shots at Policing: The Gulag and Cinema." In *Police Aesthetics: Literature, Film, and the Secret Police in Soviet Times*, 123–60. Stanford: Stanford University Press, 2010.

Verdery, Katherine. *My Life As a Spy: Investigations in a Secret Police File*. Durham, NC: Duke University Press, 2018.

———. *Secrets and Truths: Ethnography in the Archive of Romania's Secret Police*. Budapest: Central European University Press, 2014.

Vereshchuk, Iryna. "Zalizna zavisa, shcho opuskaietsia na RF, proide po skhidnomu kordonu Ukrainy [The Iron Curtain Descending on the Russian Federation Will Pass along the Eastern Border of Ukraine]" (2022). https://t.me/vereshchuk_iryna/1351.

Vinokur, G. O., B. A. Larin, S. I. Ozhegov, B. V. Tomashvskii, D. H. Ushakov, and Ushakova. "zavesa." In *Tolkovyi slovar' russkovo iazyka*. Moscow: OGIZ, 1935.

von Hagen, Mark. "The Archival Gold Rush and Historical Agendas in the Post-Soviet Era." *Slavic Review* 52, no. 1 (1993): 96–100.

"Vstrechi i besedy N. S. Khrushcheva v Glenkove." *Pravda* 271 (1960): 1–2. https://dlib.eastview.com/browse/doc/21424826.

Vvedenskii, B. A. *Bol'shaia sovetskaia entsiklopediia*. 2nd ed. Vol. 16. Moscow: Bol'shaia sovetskaia entsiklopediia, 1952.

Wanner, Catherine. "Introduction." In *State Secularism and Lived Religion in Soviet Russia and Ukraine*, edited by Catherine Wanner. New York: Oxford University Press, 2012.

Weld, Kirstin. *Paper Cadavers: The Archives of Dictatorship in Guatemala*. Durham, NC: Duke University Press, 2014.

Wheeler, Marcus, Paul Falla, Boris Unbegaun, and Della Thompson. "zavesa." In *Oxford Russian Dictionary*. Oxford, UK: Oxford University Press, 2000.

White, Luise. "Between Gluckman and Foucault: Historicizing Rumor and Gossip." *Social Dynamics* 20, no. 1 (13 May 2008): 75–92.

White, William. "Theatre Panic and Protection." *British Architect* 28 (16 September 1887): 205–7.

Widdis, Emma. *Socialist Senses: Film, Feeling, and the Soviet Subject, 1917–1940*. Bloomington: Indiana University Press, 2017.

Wikipedia Contributors. "Invisible Ink." *Wikipedia*. http://en.wikipedia.org/w/index.php?title=Invisible_ink&oldid=505908249.

Wolf, Maryanne. *Reader, Come Home: The Reading Brain in a Digital World*. New York: Harper, 2018.

Wolff, Larry. *Inventing Eastern Europe: The Map of Civilization on the Mind of the Enlightenment*. Stanford: Stanford University Press, 1994.

Woodburn, Stephen. "Strategic Monuments: Zurab Tsereteli's Gift Sculptures to the United States in the Eras of Détente, Perestroika, and Anti-Terrorism, 1979–2006." *Experiment* 18, no. 1 (2012): 264–96.

Wright, Patrick. *Iron Curtain: From Stage to Cold War*. Oxford, UK: Oxford University Press, 2007.

Zafiu, Rodica. "Cortina de fier." *Dilema veche*, 27 February–5 March 2014.

Zaslavskii, D. "Fel'eton. Lobyzanie Gebbel'sa." *Pravda*, 1 August 1946.

"'Zheleznyi zanaves uzhe opuskaetsia': Lavrov rasskazal ob otnosheniiakh mezhdu Zapadom i RF." *Novye Izvestiia* (2022). https://dlib.eastview.com/browse/doc/78506993.

Zeitlyn, David. "Anthropology in and of the Archives: Possible Futures and Contingent Pasts: Archives as Anthropological Surrogates." *Annual Review of Anthropology* 41 (2012): 461–80.

Zhivov, Viktor. "Chto delat' s Fuko, zanimaias' russkoi istoriei?" *Novoe literaturnoe obozrenie* (2001).

Ziuganov, G. A. "Sistemnyi krizis kapitalizma, informatsionnaia voina i zadachi KPRF v bor'be za sotsializm." *Pravda*, 5 July 2022, 1.

Index

Page references in *italics* indicate figures.

abortion, 18. *See also* women
Adam Müller-Guttenbrunn Literaturkreis, 146, 153
affect theory, 25, 254n25
Agamben, Giorgio, 55, 132; *Remnants of Auschwitz*, 55, 104, 241n57
agents: dialogue between the reporting and supervising, 145; Romanian secret police, 7, 11, 76, 135, 140, 143–44; silencing, 57. *See also* secret police
Aktionsgruppe Banat, 109, 143
Al-Jazeera, 184
Amad, Paula: *Counter-Archive*, 134
Amichai, Yehuda, 212n13
Amnesty International, 61
Applebaum, Anne, 187
archival revolution, 1, 5, 64, 212n11; digitization and digital research methods in the, 155, 157; Eastern European, 28, 30, 155–56; remediating the, 68–72, 106. *See also* archives; declassification
archival silences, 37, 51–58, 135; of archival subjects, 61–62; in the African diasporic context, 242n14. *See also* archives; blind spots; silence
archives: Baltic, 27; Central Asian, 27; CIA, 41; colonial, 57; declassified, 2–3, 72, 190, 196, 211n9, 242n7, 254n25; digitization of, 22, 24, 71, 156–57; Eastern European, 3, 21–22, 27, 29, 36, 41; experience of, 70, 103, 106; of the Federal Bureau of Investigation (FBI), 41; Foucauldian conception of, 54, 71; hybridity of, 23–24, 65, 190; no-hit, 57–61; of pain, 54–57; photographic, 192;

281

archives *(cont.)*
  polyphony of the, 189–207; purge of state-produced documents in, 136, 141, 154; Russian/Soviet, 156. *See also* archival revolution; archival silences; Consiliul Național pentru Studierea Arhivelor Securității (CNSAS); documents; files; Institute of National Remembrance (IPN); intermediality; mediums; Open Society Archives; reading; secret police archives
archive theory, 27–28, 71–72
Arendt, Hannah, 7, 69–70; *Origins of Totalitarianism*, 35
Arta, 91, 92
Association of Slavic and East European and Eurasian Studies (ASEEES), 68
Atre, Prahlad Keshav, 177
autobiographical writing, 3, 8, 51, 108, 117–18, 121–22, 132, 146; writing of informer agreement and, 127. *See also* writing
Azoulay, Ariella, 193

Bakhtin, Mikhail, 11, 25, 31, 253n5; *The Dialogic Imagination*, 254n19; *Problems of Dostoevsky's Oeuvre*, 190–91, 193, 196, 198–206
Baltics, 186
Barthes, Roland, 36, 57, 110
Bataille, Georges, 39
Beauvois, Daniel, 46
Benjamin, Walter, 87, 103–4, 106
Bentham, Jeremy, 60
Berlin Wall, 1, 135, 186
Bibliothèque Nationale de France (BNF), 38–39
blackmailing, 9, 37, 46–47
Blanchot, Maurice, 56
Blaylock, Sarah, 135–36, 239n38, 242n13
blind spots, 19, 22; of East German secret police, 136; of Foucault, 34; of Romanian secret police, 29; women as, 150–52. *See also* archival silences; lacunae
Bolter, Jay David: *Re-mediation: Understanding New Media*, 71, 102
Bordeianu, Bogdan, 94
Bordwell, David, 110
Bourelly, Jean, 44–46, 48
Boym, Svetlana, 227n136
Bozec, Michelle, 44
Brezhnev, Leonid, 159, 178
British Architect, 164
Broberg, Gunnar, 223n67
Brodsky, Joseph, 122
Bulgaria, 173
Butler, Shane: *The Ancient Phonograph*, 102

Calendarist community, 15–16, 217n51
Campt, Tina, 11, 25, 192–93; *Listening to Images*, 193, 213n21, 218n61, 253n12
Canguilhem, Georges, 53
Capitain, Wouter: *Postcolonial Polyphony*, 197, 256n40
capitalism, 35, 43; French capitalist campaign, 50; and imperialist expansionism, 171
Caranfil, Nae, 233n61
Carbonnet, Regina, 44
Cartesian dualism, 11
Caruth, Cathy, 132
Cassian, Nina, 9, 13, 80
Cazan, Roxana, 19
Ceaușescu, Nicolae, 18–19, 68, 126, 150, 216n48
Celan, Paul, 36, 57
censorship, 83–84, 168, 188
Central Intelligence Agency (CIA), 41
Centre des Archives Diplomatiques (Nantes), 38
challenges: of archival reading, 1–31, 89; of archival silences, 135; for the Służba Bezpieczeństwa (SB), 50–51

Chicago Hull-House Settlement, 102
Children of the Decree (documentary film), 216n49
China, 185
Churchill, Winston, 1, 30, 156–75, 178, 184, 186–88
cinema: Romanian secret police, 63–106, 228n2; self-reflexive Romanian, 82, 233n61. *See also* film
Clark, Katerina, 127
Clemenceau, Georges, 185
Closer to the Moon (film), 233n61
cognitive science, 194–95
Cold War, 1, 41, 158, 160, 177–79, 185, 240n41. *See also* Iron Curtain
Coleman, Kwami, 198–99
colonialism, 178, 184, 256n40
communism: late Romanian, 19; Russian, 163, 165, 252n86. *See also* socialism
Confession, The (film), 224n73
Consiliul Național pentru Studierea Arhivelor Securității (CNSAS), 9, 138–39, 142, 157, 234n76, 236n1, 242n7. *See also* archives
Contemporanul, 170–73; caricature of Churchill in, 171–72, *172*; collection of international cartoons in, 170–71, *171*
contemporary artists, 71–72; women as, 135–36, 239n38
Council for the Study of the Securitate Archives. *See* Consiliul Național pentru Studierea Arhivelor Securității (CNSAS)
counterpoint, 196–200, 256n40; Bakhtin's critique of, 198, 257n45. *See also* polyphony
countersign, 6–7
Coy, Wolfgang, 69
Cuban Missile Crisis, 186
Czechoslovakia, 173, 224n73

Dan, Călin, 91
data: archival, 155–89; collection by the secret police of, 127, 149; computerized, 157
Daughtry, J. Martin, 213n21
David-Fox, Michael, 4, 212n11
Davis, Natalie Zemon: *Fiction in the Archives*, 107–8
deciphering, 15; monotony of, 112; reading as, 7, 94. *See also* reading
declassification, 5–6, 9, 21, 63, 69, 71, 111, 155–57. *See also* archival revolution
decreței, 18, 216n48
Defert, Daniel, 33, 35, 40, 48, 51–52, 61, 219n6
Derrida, Jacques, 110, 136
de-Stalinization, 7, 72
Deutsche Welle: "Both Russia and the West Are Building a Digital Iron Curtain" (roundtable), 183
Dietze, Gabriele, 152
digital technology, 22, 24, 64, 69–71, 156–57, 183–84
diplomatic scandals, 60, 211n10, 227n131
disinformation: campaign of, 107; by Eastern European secret police, 29. *See also* fiction
documents: assortment of, 74; destruction of, 35–36, 68; engagement with, 68–69; housing for, 53. *See also* archives; files; mediums
Dostoevsky, Fyodor, 191, 198, 200, 203–6
Dumitriu, Simona, 94

Eastern Europe, 1, 33, 160–70, 174, 186–89, 226n120; foreign and local intellectuals in, 51; revolutions in, 68; Soviet domination of, 27, 159–62, 167. *See also* Iron Curtain
East Germany, 43, 135; Stasi files of experimental women artists in late, 239n38

EastView databases, 30, 156
Eliassen, Knut Ove: "The Archives of Michel Foucault," 54
emancipated spectatorship, 83–84
embodiment, 22, 201, 217n52; of the absent subjects, 235n92; of the archival reader, 103; of the queer archival turn, 235n89
Emerson, Caryl, 201, 204
emigration, 121, 154; mass German, 142, 157. *See also* immigration
emotions, 195, 210n1
Engelstein, Laura, 33–34
ethics: archival, 37, 210n3, 230n14; of reading, 14, 201–7, 214n38; of reception, 82–86. *See also* privacy

fabula/siuzhet, 109–11
Farge, Arlette, 70
Federal Bureau of Investigation (FBI), 40–41
Felman, Shoshana, 132
Ferreira da Silva, Denise, 11, 194, 213n23
fiction: in the archives, 29; and disinformation, 107; as guide to reading the archives, 107–33; literary, 29, 107–8. *See also* disinformation
files: covers of, 129, 136–40, *137, 138*; destroyed/missing, 50, 61; first pages of, 140–42; institutional, 53; mixture of exhibitionism and secrecy of secret police, 128; national problem, 142–50, 152; personal investigation (DUI), 108–54, 237n3, 239n36, 244n34; problem, 108–9, 129, 135, 141, 244n34; provincial problem, 149; secret police, 73, 81, 107–54, 237n4; supervision of the reading of, 11; wide array of mediums in, 106. *See also* archives; documents; interrogation
filler, 114–16, 122

film, 69, 73; Czechoslovak military, 228n4; secret police, 228n2. *See also* cinema
fingerprints, 63, 113
Fitzpatrick, Sheila, 167
Foch, Maréchal, 185–86
Foster, Hal, 71
Foucault, Michel, 1, 7, 19, 27–28, 32–62, 219n4, 223n67, 226n119, 253n8; anti-Soviet stance of, 41; definition of "archive" of, 54; Works: *Archaeology of Knowledge*, 53–55; "The History of Madness" (dissertation), 32, 39, 53, 55–56; Lecture on Guillaume Apollinaire at the Gdańsk Conference (1958), 38–39, 222n43; *lettres de cachet*, 55–56; "The Lives of Infamous Men" (essay), 39, 55–56, 202
France, 35, 37, 40
Francis, Terri, 95
French Communist Party, 33, 41, 224n73
Freud, Sigmund, 195, 254n23

gender, 8, 13–14, 25; in Müller's oeuvre, 245n64; secret police and, 134–54, 242n13. *See also* sexuality; women
Glajar, Valentina, 120, 123, 141, 151, 237n3, 239n32
Goebbels, Joseph, 158
Gogotishvili, L. A., 198, 257n45
Great Communist Bank Robbery, The (documentary film), 85, 96, 233n61
Greece, 173
Grusin, Richard: *Re-mediation: Understanding New Media*, 71, 102
Gudok, 162, 176
Gulag, 34

handwriting, 22, 46, 63, 65, 112, 137. *See also* writing
Hartman, Saidiya: "Venus in Two Acts," 25–26, 210n3

Havel, Vaclav, 227n135
Heiser, Jörg, 217n54
heteroglossia, 199–200, 202–3. *See also* polyphony
Hidden Galleries Archives, 214n38, 228n6, 234n79
Hirshfield, Jane, 5, 192
Holland, Henryk, 49
homosexuals, 8, 35, 47–48; harassment of foreigners and, 60; secret police treatment of, 28, 37, 41, 51, 135. *See also* sexuality
human rights abuses, 61
Hungary, 68, 82; Cold War invasion of, 177. *See also* Open Society Archives
hybridity: archival, 23–24, 65, 106, 190, 234n79; of mediums, 100–101; of religion, 214n35; of research methods, 21–24, 190

ideology: of censorship, 120; fictive, 169
illegibility, 14–17, 195–96. *See also* reading
immigration, 142. *See also* emigration
imperialism, 166, 171–72, 174, 197
India, 185
informers, 23–24, 29, 33, 35, 45, 61, 78, 85, 122; blackmailing of, 47; cellmate, 232n45; German-speaking, 117; recruitment of, 47, 121, 123–29, 131–32, 135, 144–46, 148–50, 153; refusal to serve as, 61–62, 123–27, 130, 135, 146, 148–50, 153; reports of, 112–19, 123, 140–41, 151; victims and, 35. *See also* secret police
Institute of National Remembrance (IPN), 36–37, 41–45, 48–49, 54, 61, 221n27. *See also* archives; Poland
Institut mémoires de l'édition contemporaine (IMEC), 38
intermedia: hybridity of, 100; mixed media and, 101; performance of, 229n10

intermediality, 23, 28, 69–70, 72, 86; of archives, 106. *See also* archives; mediums
International Women's Day, 140
interrogation, 106, 116–17, 121, 150; records of, 20, 77–78, 231n37; by the Securitate, 244n38; torture and, 86, 106, 133; tricks of, 128. *See also* files; secret police
Iorga, Nicolae, 169
Iron Curtain, 1, 3–5, 30, 41, 155–89; collapse of the, 35; digital, 183–84; history of the, 185; as myth of Western propaganda, 178–79; in Russian as *zheleznyi zanaves*, 161–64, *163*, 168, *176, 177, 182*, 251n66; and the Russian invasion of Ukraine, 159, 181–89, *184*; as smoke screen, 156, 161–70, 178–79, 248n25; as sphere of Soviet influence, 159–61, 165, 168–75, 179, 181–82; theatricality of the, 174–75. *See also* Cold War; Eastern Europe; smoke screen
Iron Curtain (film), 179–80, *180*
Izvestiia, 161–63, 176

Jackson, Shannon, 102–4
Jarry, Alfred: *Ubu Roi*, 39–40, 52
Johnson, Barbara, 120
Johnson, Mark: *Philosophy in the Flesh*, 194
Julian, Kamil, 224n83
justice. *See* transitional justice

Kafka, Franz: *The Trial*, 120
Kapaló, James, 102–3, 235n92
Khrushchev, Nikita, 177–78
King, Katie, 85, 213n28
Király, Iosif, 91, 94; *Open Skies. Revisiting Public Space* (digital montage), 94
Kligman, Gail, 16; *Peasants under Siege*, 243n19

Kneepkens, Eleonore, 195, 210n1
Kouchner, Bernard, 40, 45–46
Krakus, Anna, 27–28, 33, 40, 61
Krauss, Rosalind: "Art in the Post-Medium Condition," 71
Krokodil, 176–77
Kulish, Savva, 179–80
Kurnosova, Olha, 183

lacunae, 129, 134; archival, 242n9; foundational, 152–54; fundamental, 129, 133; gendered archival, 134–54; of official documents, 132; in secret police documents, 239n40; verbose, 133. *See also* blind spots; silence
Lakoff, George: *Philosophy in the Flesh*, 194
languages: English, 159, 162, 64, 174, 241n2; French, 22, 159, 174; German, 22, 107, 120–21; Hungarian, 243n19; Italian, 169; Polish, 22; Romanian, 22, 107, 121, 168–70, 241n2; Russian, 22, 156, 159, 161–66, 168–69, 174–89; Turkish, 169; Ukrainian, 175, 183, 188. *See also* multilingualism
Latin America, 185
Laub, Dori, 132, 241n57
Lavrov, Sergei, 184–85
Leach, Elizabeth Eva: *Performing Manuscripts*, 102
Lee, Vernon, 158
Lenin, Vladimir, 171
Lepecki, André: "The Body as Archive," 102–3, 230n16, 235n87
Levchenko, Oleksandr, 183
Literaturnaia gazeta, 163, 218n68
Lovejoy, Alice, 228n4
Luerhmann, Sonja, 23, 25
Lunacharsky, Anatoly: "About Dostoevsky's 'Multivoicedness,'" 204
Lusztig, Irene, 82, 95–96, 99–100, 104–6, *105*

Lusztig, Miki, 96–100, 105
Luzhkov, Iurii, 179

Madres de Plaza de Mayo, 104, 236n97
Makeeva, Maria, 183
Mallarmé, Stéphane, 39
maps, 23, 28, 63, 65, 94, 101; secret police supervision of the making of, 259n72
Marinescu, Nicolae, 234n80
Marshall, Daniel: "Turning Archival," 102
Massumi, Brian, 12, 209n4
Mawani, Renisa, 56
Médecins du Monde, 45, 47
media, 70; independent, 184; new, 71, 229n12; visual, 191. *See also* newspapers; social media; television
mediums: archival, 63–65, 101; Bakhtin's understanding of polyphony's defining pull toward other, 191; embodied, 104; hybridity of, 64–65, 101; most forgotten archival, 65; relationships among, 73–74, 86. *See also* archives; documents; intermediality; photographs
Medvedkin, Alexander, 81
Memorial to Suffering (television series), 215n44
Michelet, Jules, 26, 218n64
Montand, Yves, 46
Moretti, Franco, 217n56
Morgan, David, 102–3
Morson, Gary Saul, 201, 204
Müller, Herta, 1, 29, 57, 80, 107–54, 203, 221n28, 236n2, 238n23, 242n8; *The Appointment*, 13, 117, 121, 148; *Cristina or the Double*, 123–24, 134, 141, 239n40, 240n44; *The Land of Green Plums*, 116–17; *Nadirs (Niederungen)*, 113–14, 124, 152, 240n44; Nobel Prize lecture, 124,

126, 130–31; "On This Day" (short story), 117, 121–22, 131, 134; "Our Town" (autobiographical writing), 117, 238n21; "When We Don't Speak, We Become Unbearable, and When We Do, We Make Fools of Ourselves. Can Literature Bear Witness?" (essay), 240n56
multilingualism, 22, 28, 198, 257n44. See also languages
music: and silence, 56; traditional Russian, 198. See also polyphony

National Documentary Film Studio (Sahia), 7, 64, 73, 81, 233n58
Navalny, Alexei, 183
Ndai, Ali, 178
Nedelia: "Collaboration: Monument for Washington," 179
neurocognitive poetics, 25, 194–95, 210n1
newspapers: online, 188; pro-Western, 249n33; Romanian, 187–88, 242n8; Russian-language, 175–81, *176*, *177*, *182*, 187, 251n66; socialist-friendly, 172; Soviet, 164–65, 175–81, *176*, *177*, 188; Ukrainian-language, 183, 187. See also media
Nicolescu, Gabriela, 16
Novoe Russkoe slovo (NRS), 247n18

Odesa, 179, 183
Open Society Archives, 82. See also Hungary
Ortinau, Gerhard, 146, 151
Oța, Bishop Evloghie, 14

Paris Peace Conference, 170, 173
Pasternak, Boris: *Doctor Zhivago*, 67
Perestroika, 3–4, 159, 175, 179–80. See also Soviet Union
phenomenology, 25

photographs: black-and-white print of a negative from *Arta* magazine archive, 92; cropping in, 91; identity, 192–93; Irene Lusztig holding her grandmother's photograph, *105*; optical unconscious of, 87; production stills from the shooting of the *Reenactment* documentary, 65, 86–91, *88*, *90*, *98*; reenactment, 234n76; of suspects in the *Reenactment* documentary, 104, *105*. See also mediums
Pintilie, Lucian, 82
Pirenne, Raphaël: *Heterogeneous Objects*, 69
Plamper, Jan: "Foucault's Gulag," 34
Poland, 27–28, 33–40, 186; borders of, 165–66; Center for French Culture in, 38, 44, 48, 50, 61, 220n20; Foucault in, 34–37, 40–53, 60–62, 219n4, 222n48, 224n68; political status (1795) of, 52. See also Institute of National Remembrance (IPN); Służba Bezpieczeństwa (SB)
Police, Adjective (film), 82
Polish Socialist Party, 40
political prisoners: escaped, 83; rehabilitation of former, 5, 211n9; Romanian, 79, 83
polyphony: literary, 191; migration from musical term to literary term of, 31; musical, 257n41; of reading, 11, 24–26, 30–31, 190–207; traditional, 199, 257n46. See also counterpoint; heteroglossia; music; reading
Popova, Oksana, 183, 188
Porumboiu, Corneliu, 82
Povedák, Kinga, 214n38
Pravda, 161, 165–66, 176, 178; Churchill leading "The War Instigators Brigade" (caricature), *167*
Pravda Ukrainy, 176–77

prison memoirs, 79
privacy: abuses of, 9, 11; protecting, 157. See also ethics
profilaktika, 244n35
propaganda: anti-Soviet, 178–79; French, 50; tunes as, 116
Putin, Vladimir, 181, 183–86

Radio Free Europe, 17, 82–84, 86
Rancière, Jacques, 82, 84, 100, 191–92, 253n8
Rashomon (film), 78
reading: Aesopian writing and practices of, 217n59; archival, 2, 101, 106; contrapuntal, 197; cultured, 2; distant, 217n56; embodied nature of the act of, 13, 106; ethics of, 14, 201–7, 214n38; as eventful encounter, 106, 192–96; illegibility and the hubris of, 14–17; monologic, 204–5; polyphonic, 11, 24–26, 30–31, 190–207; reparative, 21, 24; strategies of reading across textual and cinematic mediums, 91. See also archives; deciphering; illegibility; polyphony
Reconstruction (documentary film), 85, 95–99, *97*, *98*, 100, 104–6, *105*, 233n61
Reenactment (documentary film, 1959), 64, 69, 72–74, 80–83, 89, 95–100, 104, *105*, 232n55; cinematic legacy of, 233n61
Reenactment (film, 1968), 82
rehabilitation, 5; of former political prisoners, 5, 211n9
remediation, 100, 106; of the archival revolution, 68–72; digital, 64, 217n55, 234n79
Rimbaud, Arthur, 39
Romania, 19, 68, 159, 173, 186, 188; abortion ban in, 18–19, 216n49, 216n50; anti-Semitism in, 72, 78, 85, 87; bank heist in socialist, 63–106; communist press of, 170, 173–74; German minority in, 29, 135, 141–50, 152, 157, 244n34; Hungarian minority in, 150; power in socialist, 18–19; press of, 168; Writers' Union of, 121. See also Securitate
Romanian Film Archives, 82
Romanian National Bank, 64, 72
Romanian Revolution (1989), 17
room bugging, 42, 49, 61, 76–77, 120, 144, 152. See also secret police; wiretapping
Rotbuch, 152
Rozanov, Vasilii, 158
Roziers, Étienne Burin des, 32–33, 42–44, 48, 50
Rubery, Matthew, 218n61
rumor, 59, 60, 62, 129, 199, 216n48
Russia, 4, 27, 33–34, 40, 176, 179–89, 198. See also Soviet Union
Russian Film Festival (1998), 180
Russian formalists, 109
Ruthière: *Anarchie de Pologne*, 40
Ryziński, Remigiusz: *Foucault w Warszawie*, 45, 61

Sahia. See National Documentary Film Studio (Sahia)
Said, Edward: *Culture and Imperialism*, 196–97
Saint Cyr, Révéroni de: *Pauliska ou la perversité moderne*, 39
Sanborn, Joshua, 135
Scânteia, 168, 249n33
Scarry, Elaine, 103; *Dreaming by the Book*, 234n82
Schleich, Franz Thomas, 149
Schleich, Hildegard, 120
Schoenberg, Arnold, 198
secret police: aesthetics of the, 60; Eastern European, 35, 44, 155–57, 213n19; East German (Stasi), 1, 68,

135–36, 239n38, 242n13; film of the, 228n2; libraries of the, 107; Polish, 1, 7, 32–62; practices of the, 7, 57, 60, 202–3; Soviet-era, 118. *See also* agents; informers; interrogation; room bugging; Soviet secret police (KGB); secret police archives; Securitate; Służba Bezpieczeństwa (SB); surveillance; torture; translators; wiretapping
secret police archives: artistic models of engagement with the, 91–100; desensitization of readers of, 104; Eastern European, 4, 29, 33–34; French, 27; generalized suspicion as reaction to the holdings of the, 84–85; presence of the environment in the, 259n72; reading documents of the, 2, 20–21, 197; Polish, 4, 27, 32–37, 40–44, 50–58; power at work in, 62; remediating, 100; Romanian, 4, 14–19, 27, 36, 73, 82, 94, 100, 137–54; Soviet, 4; visual aspects of, 69. *See also* archives; secret police
Securitate, 1, 7, 72–135, 139–54, 157; Bucharest, 142, 144, 151; declassified archives of the, 242n7; physical harassment by the, 153; reports on warning sessions at the headquarters of the, 149; as repressive arm of the state, 126; as sexist institution, 151; Sibiu, 145–46; Timiș, 142–44, 146–47, 149, 151; wiretapping of conversations by the, 238n23. *See also* Romania; secret police; SRI
Sedgwick, Eve Kosofsky, 24
self: attunement of the, 193; physical displacement and compulsory writing of the, 132; and subject, 194
Sevianu, Igor, 66, 74, 76–77, 85, 104, 106, 232n57; identification scene of, *105*; sketches of the apartment of, *75*

Sevianu, Monica, 66, 72–82, 85, 87, 95–99, *98*, 106, 232n46; sketches of the apartment of, *75*
sexuality, 9; and gender, 8; of women, 13, 80, 151. *See also* gender; homosexuals
Sharpe, Jenny, 218n65
Siani-Davis, Peter, 216n48
Signoret, Simone, 45
silence: archaeology of, 37, 51–54, 191; criminal, 104; different kinds of, 56, 133, 192, 218n65; of the intellectuals, 226n119; verbose, 47, 152–54; writing from concealment and, 132, 201. *See also* archival silences; blind spots; lacunae
Şincan, Anca, 14–15, 214n35, 217n51
slander, 59, 62, 199
Służba Bezpieczeństwa (SB), 4, 32–33, 40–51, 54, 57–60, 220n20, 225n97; documents forged by the, 227n131; repression of LGBTQ individuals by the, 224n79. *See also* Poland; secret police
smoke screen, 156, 161–68; of inflammatory rhetoric, 167; public perception of the divide between Eastern Europe and Russia as, 165. *See also* Iron Curtain
Sobchack, Vivian, 22, 217n52
socialism, 52; African, 178; Romanian, 72, 80; Soviet Bloc adoption of *profilaktika* techniques in late, 244n35. *See also* communism
socialist realism, 72; biography as the master narrative of, 127
social media, 188. *See also* media
Soleil, 178
Solidarność, 35
Solomon, Alexandru, 96, 233n61
sound, 192–94; auditory imagination, 213n20

Sovershchenno sekretno, 186
Soviet Bloc documentary films, 64
Soviet secret police (KGB), 3–4; cybernetic turn in the, 135; disinformation of the, 218n68; identification drive of the, 246n66; Ukrainian branch of the, 16. *See also* secret police
Soviet Union, 136, 164–70, 177–82, 185, 198; press of the, 159, 166, 168, 175–81. *See also* Perestroika; Russia
Spinoza, Baruch, 12
Spivak, Gayatri, 226n120, 259n62
SRI, 134, 139, 141, 153. *See also* Securitate
Stalin, Joseph, 1, 30, 158–61, 165–69, 172–74, 178, 203; reading habits of, 259n64
Stalinism, 181, 190–91, 201, 206
stammer, 53, 55–56, 89, 91, 191
Stan, Lavinia, 211n9
statistics, 144, 147–50
Steedman, Carolyn: *Dust: The Archive and Cultural History*, 70
Steinhardt, Nicolae: *Happiness Journal*, 18–19, 214n39, 244n38
Stoekl, Allan, 237n14
Stoler, Ann, 24, 57–58, 210n3
Streitberger, Alexander: *Heterogeneous Objects: Intermedia and Photography after Modernism*, 69
stutter, 113–14, 132
subReal, 91, 95; *Art History Archive* (project), 91, 94; *Five Suitcases* (counter-cropped photograph), 93; *Parallel Archives* (project), 94; *Second Life in Communism* (exhibit), 91, 94; *Serving Art 1* (black-and-white print), 92; *Serving Art 2* (photo installation detail), 93
Suna-Koro, Kristine, 256n40
surveillance, 8, 13–14, 28, 33–37, 41, 59–60, 84; Eastern Bloc, 33; Polish, 51, 58, 60; Romanian, 74, 76–77, 127, 134, 136, 152, 154. *See also* secret police

Tarle, E., 162–63
Taussig, Michael, 167
Taylor, Diana: *The Archive and the Repertoire*, 104
Tehnometal Timisoara, 129
television, 18, 215n44. *See also* media
Tőkés, László, 150–51
Tortorici, Zeb: "Turning Archival," 102
torture, 9, 61, 78–79, 81, 121; in interrogations, 86, 106, 133; in Romanian prisons, 232n46. *See also* secret police
Totok, William, 109, 112, 118, 143, 149, 237n4
transitional justice, 5, 211n9, 227n131
translation: forensic, 120–21, 135, 239n32; interlingual, 121; intermedial, 121; of literary fiction, 108, 120; problems of, 22
translators, 120–21, 123, 131; in the role of interpreters, 240n41; secret police, 8, 22. *See also* secret police
Trud, 185
Tsereteli, Zurab, 179, 251n64
Tunisia, 40, 53
type, 22, 65, 78, 136, 170

Ukraine, 2, 4, 186; Russian invasion of, 175, 181–89
undecidability, 59

Vagramenko, Tatiana, 16
Verdery, Katherine, 16, 23, 167; *Peasants under Siege*, 243n19
Vereshchuk, Iryna, 183
victims, 5, 202; Eastern Europeans as, 160; and informers, 35
Volkov, Leonid, 183–84

Wagner, Richard, 123, 143, 151–52, 239n36; *Der Junge Berner*, 149
Walesa, Lech, 227n131
West Germany, 43, 142–43, 151–52, 154
White, Luise, 57

wiretapping, 10, 81, 106, 231n30, 238n23. *See also* room bugging; secret police
Wolff, Larry, 160
women, 8; as artists, 135–36; as blind spots, 150–52; secret police treatment of, 135–54, 242n13; as sexually promiscuous, 13, 80, 151. *See also* abortion; gender
writing: in cursive, 236n95; informers' reports recorded in, 126–27; literary genealogy of Müller's career in, 122–33; as sign and practice of subordination, 203. *See also* autobiographical writing; handwriting

Zafiu, Rodica, 174
Zelensky, Volodymyr, 181–89
Ziuganov, G. A., 252n86
Zwaan, Rolf A., 195, 210n1

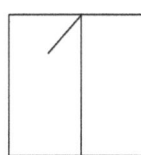

SQUARE ONE
First-Order Questions in the Humanities

Series Editor: **PAUL A. KOTTMAN**

SIMONA FORTI
Totalitarianism: A Borderline Idea in Political Philosophy

PHILIPPE HUNEMAN
Why?: The Philosophy Behind the Question

ROY BEN-SHAI
Critique of Critique

RICHARD VAN OORT
Shakespeare's Mad Men: A Crisis of Authority

DAVIDE TARIZZO
Political Grammars: The Unconscious Foundations of Modern Democracy

AMIR ESHEL
Poetic Thinking Today: An Essay

PETER MURPHY
The Long Public Life of a Short Private Poem: Reading and Remembering Thomas Wyatt

JON BASKIN
Ordinary Unhappiness: The Therapeutic Fiction of David Foster Wallace

PAULA BLANK
Shakesplish: How We Read Shakespeare's Language

PAUL A. KOTTMAN
Love as Human Freedom

ADRIANA CAVARERO
Inclinations: A Critique of Rectitude

The authorized representative in the EU for product safety and compliance is:
Mare Nostrum Group
B.V Doelen 72
4831 GR Breda
The Netherlands

www.ingramcontent.com/pod-product-compliance
Lightning Source LLC
Chambersburg PA
CBHW031758220426
43662CB00007B/456